DISCARDED

THIS KIND OF PEACE

Also by T. R. Fehrenbach

THIS KIND OF WAR
CRISIS IN CUBA
THE U. S. MARINES IN ACTION
THE BATTLE OF ANZIO

This Kind of Peace

T.R. Fehrenbach

DAVID McKAY COMPANY, INC.

NEW YORK

COLLEGE OF THE SEQUOIAS
LIBRARY

THIS KIND OF PEACE

COPYRIGHT © 1966 BY T. R. FEHRENBACH

All rights reserved, including the right to reproduce
this book, or parts thereof, in any form, except for
the inclusion of brief quotations in a review.

LIBRARY OF CONGRESS CATALOG CARD NUMBER: 66-17238

MANUFACTURED IN THE UNITED STATES OF AMERICA

FOR RICHARD CURTIS

CONTENTS

Foreword

TWENTY YEARS AFTER its inception, the idea of the United Nations is still powerful and shining. Millions of people still fervently believe in it as the last great hope of modern mankind. But too many who support the idea of a UN have failed to examine the reality of the United Nations Organization in New York.

They have always been more interested in what should be, rather than with what actually is. But history always records what happened, not what men wanted to have happen, and shows what reality is, not what people hoped it would be.

The purpose of this book is to illustrate how and why the UN came about, who made it, what it was meant to be, and, finally, what it ultimately became. Most writing about the UN has a serious flaw. It treats the UN as if it had, or could have, a life of its own, outside the world we live in. But this was never possible.

Therefore, this book is as much about the world of the United States, the USSR, and China as it is about the glass towers in New York. It is neither an attack on, nor an apology for, that world. It is an attempt to show it as it really is.

I have tried to represent the viewpoints of many powerful men, but without the official hypocrisy with which such views are usually clothed in public. This will disturb some people, and possibly invite attack. It may also make for clearer understanding of some things.

Any complete history of the UN would have to be a history of the world since 1945. I have made no such attempt. Many details, and even some world crises, have been omitted or bypassed with only a mention. I have tried to include what seems important.

Any writer who approaches current history in any manner except as an antiquarian or a mosaic-fitter, fiddling with minutiae, is bound to provoke stinging criticism. But this book, to have any meaning, has to look beyond the evidence. Also, anyone who ignores current historical fashion is in for complaint; but fashions in history are as changeable, and as germane, as fashions in ladies' hats.

I have not intended this book to trample on anyone's cherished beliefs. Nor have I tried to blaze some new trail, or propose some new solution to solve the world's great ills. But I have tried to show a certain segment of American official thinking in a way millions have never seen it, and certainly never understood it.

They may not like the vision any more than they like the reality. But it is hoped, in the words of one of the men who helped put the world together in its present uneasy form, "that what is realistic in concept, and founded in an endeavor to see both ourselves and others as we really are, cannot be illiberal."

T. R. F.

THIS KIND OF PEACE

Part I

THE FAITH

1.

Franklin D. Roosevelt and The Law of Nations

On a cold day in August, 1941, the cruiser USS *Augusta* stood off the coast of Maine. Aboard were President Roosevelt of the United States, Prime Minister Winston Churchill of Great Britain, and the British and American military and political staffs, all nervously and somewhat uncomfortably making much of their common language and common culture.

It was a weird meeting. Britain was fighting for her life against the German peril and not winning. The United States was uncomfortably but determinedly neutral against the Axis. If Franklin Roosevelt and the men around him could read the signposts of history clearly, millions of Americans still refused to travel the only road that remained open to them.

German armies were crashing toward Moscow, and Japanese fleets were stirring off the coasts of Asia. It was a bad hour for the world as Churchill, Roosevelt, and millions of Americans knew it. But as Charles A. Lindbergh, with irrefutable but short-sighted logic, had said: "Let us not delude ourselves. If we enter the quarrels of Europe during war we must stay in them in time of peace as well."

As the British, fighting for survival and with a much clearer geopolitical sense, could never understand, it was not Anglophobia, cowardice, or a refusal to defend American ideals and institutions that made American people pause. It was not even ignorance, or the feeling of being safe behind two enormous oceans. It was, as much as anything, an inverted idealism, and the haunting feeling that if America again sent its young men de-

3

mon-slaying they could no more change the nature of the world and its politics in 1941 than they had in 1918.

Nevertheless, if Franklin Roosevelt could not yet lead his people into a necessary war, he could establish firmly where America stood, and proclaim the kind of world Americans believed in. FDR could not, in August, 1941, give Churchill the ships and guns and millions of men he hoped for. He could not commit the power of the American Republic to the cause of world order. But he could and did commit the power of American principle. That commitment was the Atlantic Charter, as it was revealed in Washington on August 14, 1941:

" . . . The President of the United States and the Prime Minister, Mr. Churchill, representing His Majesty's Government in the United Kingdom, have met at sea. . . .

They have agreed on the following declaration.

First, their countries seek no aggrandizement, territorial or other.

Second, they desire to see no territorial changes that do not accord with the freely expressed wishes of the people concerned. . . .

Sixth, after the final destruction of the Nazi tyranny, they hope to see established a peace which will afford to all nations the means of dwelling in safety within their own boundaries, and which will afford assurance that all men in all lands may live out their lives in freedom from want and fear. . . .

Eighth, they believe that all the nations of the world, for realistic as well as spiritual reasons, must come to the abandonment of the use of force. . . ."

It was not a call to arms, or even an agenda for action. It was a declaration of principle, nothing more; but it was dear to Roosevelt's, and millions of other Americans', heart. Churchill, with greater powers of mind than FDR but also more pragmatic, was delighted with it. Britain was still alone in the world, but not quite so alone as she had been before. No one knew bet-

4

ter than Winston Churchill the value of a ringing phrase, and the Atlantic Charter indicated clearly that the American die was cast.

Four months later Pearl Harbor made it official.

And Churchill again came to the United States, this time to the White House. The U.S. ground forces were smaller than Bulgaria's, the Army Air Corps a gnat beside both the RAF and Luftwaffe, the battle line of the U. S. Navy already rusting on the Pacific floor—but there was no question who was and would become the dominant power in the world. The leadership of World War II passed to Washington the hour when Japanese planes flew out of the sun over Hawaii.

It was natural and significant that both Roosevelt and Churchill had not the faintest doubt in eventual victory. But it was also natural—and significant—that the United States immediately took a different attitude to war from Britain.

The British fought first for survival, then for what power they could retain. Britain had long ago given up any real hope of reforming the world; to Churchill the war was being waged to decide the question of whether Britain's own decent and pragmatic order, or Hitler's totalitarian and tyrannic order, should dominate the earth. Hitler, in slightly different terms, saw it the same way.

Looking across the cold, gray waters of the Channel in 1940, Hilter had said: "This war will destroy the old order. It will decide whether the Germans or the British are to be the master race."

But the people of the United States, for more than a century, had not been able to equate war with politics. A higher purpose always intervened. They had not died to preserve the Union, but to make men free. They had not gone to France to restore the old order, but to make the world safe for democracy. True, they had become disillusioned. But they had not abandoned their ideals.

Over Christmas, Churchill and Roosevelt worked late in the White House, drawing up a set of principles for this new war.

5

They began with the Atlantic Charter. To FDR and all the Americans present, it was important that all the allied nations agree to these provisions. As far as Churchill was concerned, he had no great faith in signatures on paper, but he thought it would do no harm.

He was aware that the American mind, whether engaged in war or in a club meeting, could not refrain from the drawing up of resolutions of principle. He was also aware that practical politicians, whether in Whitehall or the halls of Congress, paid very little attention to them unless they were backed by power.

That was going to be the American problem, not the British, because the Americans had most of the chips in this new game.

There was one immediate hitch. The small democracies of Europe, and the nondemocracies overrun by Hitler, and the Latin American states of all persuasions, were willing to sign anything the United States offered. As one statesmen said, "Sticks and stones will break our bones, but pious words will not, I believe, hurt us." But the Soviet ambassador, now allied by necessity with the West against Hitler, had an immediate, and in his eyes quite logical, objection.

It was too soon to worry about territorial aggrandizement and all that, but the Atlantic Charter's references to freedom of religion contravened not only official Soviet domestic policy but the Soviet Constitution as well, which reserved to the State the power to promote and promulgate the official Russian state religion—atheism. The Russian ambassador informed the State Department it would not be possible for the USSR to sign the Atlantic Charter.

FDR would have none of that. He called the Soviet delegate in, and from his wheel chair gave both the ambassador and Soviet domestic policy hell.

Whatever he thought of Roosevelt's arguments, the Russian finally agreed to sign. After all, the Germans were at the gates of Moscow, and Lend-Lease in this case was worth a signature. But then the Soviet mind, like the German, never placed much worth on scraps of paper, unless they were propaganda. And here began, early in the war, a series of American-British-Russian relationships that the Americans, at least, never quite understood.

The British and the Americans, Churchill and FDR, often disagreed, and quite vociferously. Churchill never failed to protest any American policy, strategy, or principle that he thought unwise or not in the British interest. But if he lost the argument—and he usually did in a game where all the chips were American—Churchill honored his commitment. Even when it was pressured out of them, the British, being gentlemen, kept their word.

The Russians were under no such compulsion. For one thing, they did not share a common morality or ethical sense with the Americans and the British. The Soviets, quite sincerely, according to their lights, considered American statements of principle like the Atlantic Charter or freedom for Poland pro-capitalist nonsense. The game of international politics wasn't played that way.

Stalin's own words, if anyone had paid any attention to them, might have been instructive: "A diplomat's words must have no relation to actions—otherwise, what kind of diplomacy is it? Words are one thing, actions another. Good words are a concealment of bad deeds. Sincere diplomacy is no more possible than dry water or iron wood!"

From here until the end of the war, on practical matters, like grand strategy, battle plans, or timed offensives, the Russians did exactly what they said they would do. On other matters, like promises to change the Soviet leopard's spots, they shrugged and signed. If the Americans actually believed in such signatures, the more fools they.

In retrospect, since the American leadership were not fools, it must always be questionable who was being the less sincere. It should be remembered that most of the promises to do right after the war were badgered out of the Soviets in hours of extremity—they were never offered freely.

When FDR and Churchill were putting the final touches on the draft of principles for World War II, the question had come up as to what the new alliance against Hitler should be called. "Allies" was dated; it belonged to the first war. Churchill had used "Associated Nations"; FDR, reading this, reached for a pen, scratched it through, and wrote in "United Nations." Churchill, who always knew a good thing when he saw it, immediately quoted a phrase from *Childe Harold* and agreed.

So, on January 1, 1942, there was signed at Washington the *Declaration by the United Nations* by twenty-six oddly assorted republics, kingdoms, dictatorships, and democracies, embodying the American concept of the postwar new order.

A declaration, however, even one signed by half of the more or less sovereign nations, by itself was no more effective than a resolution at a Rotarian fish fry. There had to be human machinery to implement it. The whole concept of American domestic government was based upon this rock of basic ideals plus practical machinery to implement them, and it was inevitable that Americans in FDR's administration would try to carry such American practices over into world affairs.

From the hour Hitler put out the lights of Europe and Japan took advantage of the darkness to try to remake the maps of Asia, the collapse of a supposed world order had haunted the statesmen and philosophers of the West. In the broadest terms, the problem seemed simple:

(1) The industrial world had passed into an enormous crisis of order in the twentieth century, in which the advanced nations struggled with each other for power, wealth, and predominance.

(2) The power struggle regularly produced wars.

(3) The wars tended to be global and total.

(4) Modern industrialism had made the world so tightly interlaced and interdependent, and modern weapons and organization were so effective, that total wars were self-defeating to both victor and vanquished. If not stopped, they could spell the end of modern urban civilization.

The problem was not to attack the concept of war, but to end

8

the crisis of order that made war inevitable. And this was not as easy as it seemed.

If the great errors of the nineteenth century had been a belief in natural order and human rationality, the enormous lesson of the twentieth was that international morality and an existing power structure were not always the same thing, and that no natural harmony of interests did or could exist.

There always had, and always would be, thrusts at whatever order existed. The problem was how to handle them. They could not be stuffed into a bottle or ignored. Like Hitler, or Harlem, the protests had a way of popping out as full-grown monsters.

The German State in 1928 was resentful and bitter, but still reasonable in its hopes and aspirations. Ten years later, Hitler, and the German people behind him, were messianic, not rational; nihilistic, not reasonable; and blinded by frustrated visions of totality. The real trouble with Munich was that it had to come at the point of a gun, and much too late.

To say, and believe, that Germans, Italians, Frenchmen, Englishmen, Americans and Chinese could or should want the same things, was itself irrational. Each people had a separate value system. They could, and must, coexist; but each people would insist in going to heaven or hell in its own handbasket, and if they had the power, would tend to trample anyone who got in their way.

The problem confronting American planners, who believed in a decent and stable and lasting world order, was that all human history—even their own history upon the North American continent—had been in some measure a power struggle. It was a problem that many of them, in fact, refused to face. The great siren song of the late nineteenth century, the "harmony of interests" between nations and classes, unconsciously adopted by Britons whose power monopoly made everyone else come into harmony with them or else, died damned hard. This was the fatal flaw, which, written into the League of Nations, killed that organization before it got off the ground.

The American subcommittee of the State Department appointed

9

to study and come up with recommendations for ending this problem of order, was well aware of the mistaken notions of the past. It was headed by Sumner Welles, a realist who had once helped a young sergeant named Batista become President of Cuba because he saw no other alternative to chaos. Welles and his men had read the Atlantic Charter and believed in the Four Freedoms, but none of them believed that the world at large lived, or ever would live, according to the precepts of Anglo-American morality.

Yet if, as Reinhold Niebuhr wrote, it was impossible to idealize the institution or institutionalize the ideal, Americans had never failed to try, from laws against liquor to laws against international aggression. The government of no other nation was so influenced by lawyers or legalistic thinking. To Americans, even those in the State Department, politics was not an art, as the British claimed, but merely a means whose end was the created law. *Consequently, no other nation tended so much to confuse the separate and distinct arenas of law, morality, and pure political action.*

The confusion worked inside America for one good reason: on most matters there was a broad base of agreement as to where morality lay. Where there was not—as with Prohibition, gambling codes, price control, and Negroes—it was another matter, and one that most Americans preferred not to face.

Thus, while the British Foreign Office told Welles that His Majesty's Government's idea for the postwar world envisioned a continuance of the wartime Grand Alliance, keeping a wary eye on the world and jolly well cutting off any new Hitler's water early, the Americans could not buy anything so untidy and practical as that.

The British argued that the most successful peace structure in human history had been the Peace of Vienna in 1815, which had had no legal or moral sanction—but which had had the power and determination of its signers to back it up. The peace had lasted for sixty-five years, and there had been no general war for ninety-nine. The League of Nations and the

Treaty of Versailles had been wrapped in all kinds of moral nonsense, and they had lasted just long enough to grow a new military generation.

The British position in World War II, which Anthony Eden put bluntly, was that the eventual victors should rule the peace. The British view was that such rule should be not legal, but political, and it should be enforced pragmatically, though based on Anglo-American concepts of morality, order, and decency.

Sumner Welles' committee agreed with the first idea. But American minds, unlike British, turned toward written, well-defined constitutions. Americans did not want an unwritten, practical world order as much as a new international constitutional law. They wanted a legal mechanism to carry international politics out.

The American view, as recommended to FDR during a series of State Department briefings in 1943, was that there should be:

(1) A new world organization, similar to the old, cold League of Nations (the idea of which died hard, too) but with the obvious faults of the League removed. There should be no nonsense about the equality of nations, or any attempt to have the weak police the strong.

(2) Methods and means within the new league to allow timely, reasonable changes in the status quo, in other words a balance between pure legitimacy and future bastardly demands for revision. No map of the world, no matter how drawn, could be expected to last.

(3) Fundamentals of a new world order written into enforceable international law, which would be binding upon all nations and peoples whether they agreed to it or not. The old League had been a voluntary organization; voluntary laws did not work.

What the State Department advisers recommended was recognizably akin to the U. S. government system. But because, in 1943, there was a deep awareness in official circles that the West had been saved more by ships and guns than its principles, there was a tacit acceptance that the prime mover in the world was na-

11

tional power. No preamble or Bill of Rights to this international constitution were envisioned.

Roosevelt accepted this concept. But he insisted on a few changes. Discussing the matter with Eden, he described a "great general assembly of all nations" which would have an advisory council of powers and an "executive council of *great* powers," which would in the future keep peace and forge international justice. Among the great powers, FDR said, would be Britain, the United States, the USSR, and China.

Eden immediately balked at the inclusion of China. He pointed out that China was not a nation in the modern sense, and its society, in the 1940's, was obviously in dissolution, as much from the impact of Western ideas as from the Japanese invasion. "China," he said, "might very well have to undergo a revolution before it emerges into the modern world."

He also stated that China's future emergence into the Pacific would probably create as many problems for the Western powers as had Japan's. This statement annoyed FDR immensely: it sounded like a belief in the balance of power, and a determination to hold the Western colonial position, both of which were vaguely immoral in Roosevelt's eyes. FDR tended to discount the several centuries of experience the British had had at *Weltpolitik*, a German term signifying the viewing of the world political scene as a whole. Also, FDR was determined to place his own geopolitical assumptions on a morally unassailable basis, and not to be bound by the British view. At Teheran in 1943 he went out of his way to try to convince Stalin that U. S. policy would *not* be influenced by British interests, with the unintended side effect that Stalin probably based his plans for the rape of Eastern Europe on this hope.

Winston Churchill was as dubious as Eden over FDR's proposed United Nations. He agreed in principle, and thought a UN might be useful. But he said the whole world could not possibly be represented in a single body. He wanted at least a European *and* an Asian organization; he considered the Western and

Oriental aspirations and outlooks too different to be included in any one working parliament. But Churchill in the end had to agree to FDR's overall view. The United States had all the nickels, and it could call the tune however Churchill glowered.

Stalin, conversely, made no objection to a world body such as FDR suggested. Possibly he saw the future organization as a potentially useful medium for the USSR, but for ends different from those FDR had in mind. It was this immediate Russian acceptance of the UN idea—with no actual details discussed—that ironically convinced Roosevelt and even some British that the USSR could be successfully and peacefully integrated into the Anglo-American world order.

Near the end of his life, Franklin Roosevelt said, "We have learned we cannot live alone, in peace; that our own well-being is dependent on the well-being of other nations, far away. We have learned that we must live as men, and not as ostriches, nor as dogs in the manger. We have learned to be citizens of the world, members of the human community."

The American people, in general, had learned no such things. They had learned that the oceans were shrinking, and that demons who had seemed far away in 1941 could be dangerous. It was not a sense of responsibility, but the shock of Pearl Harbor that brought the United States out into the world. If Americans had suddenly become the watchmen on the walls of freedom, it had been caused by necessity, never by choice. And during the war a certain dichotomy grew between FDR and the State Department on one hand, and many members of Congress and the public on the other. The rulers understood fairly well that *Weltpolitik* and world order were essentially untidy businesses; but the public and much of Congress remained idealistic and uninformed and thought once the war was over everyone could go home.

This desire to end it once and for all bothered FDR badly. He mentioned it many times, even to Stalin himself. FDR himself

13

clearly realized that there was no convenient stopping place in international politics. The U. S. was already aboard a train of events from which it could not easily step down.

Pearl Harbor had paralyzed the old isolationism, of course. The former isolationists' error was not their pessimistic view of the world scene, but their forlorn optimism that the United States could have prospered in a world dominated by Nazi hysterics and Japanese war lords. But some of the new "internationalism" that replaced isolationism was equally flawed in outlook. Pearl Harbor had not filled the American emotional vacuum toward world politics, nor had it improved the American understanding of what was required for international law and order. Millions of Americans still thought that world peace and justice were things that came about naturally, and would come about again once the Nips and Nazis were removed.

The lack of comprehension of what the pre-1914 order had been or how it came about was profound, even among educated Americans. Americans had been beneficiaries of the Pax Britannica for generations, but many of them liked to look on that form of order as vaguely immoral, and most of them refused to assume the slightest responsibility for it, or any other kind of order beyond American shores.

The men in the U. S. government by 1943 already knew that without active American participation no stable world could follow World War II. The American army and the Yankee dollar would have to replace the exhausted British navy and bankrupt English pound. During the war, the government could commit U. S. strength almost at will; anything could be justified as a war measure. The problem was how to get the same kind of acceptance for government interventionist policy when the shooting stopped.

One mistake of 1914–1918 was being avoided: men were worrying about the eventual peace ahead of time. But U. S. participation in such a peace would require an enormous break with American tradition. This was the problem worrying Roosevelt.

14

George Washington had spoken out against entangling alliances, and Henry Cabot Lodge the elder had scuttled President Wilson's dreams for the League of Nations. Franklin Roosevelt was afraid the mantle of Senator Lodge still waited in the Senate cloakroom for someone to try it on.

2.

The Lights at Dumbarton Oaks

IT IS GIVEN to the President of the United States, with the advice and consent of the Senate, to conduct the foreign policy of the Republic. And since the treaties made by Presidents become the law of the American land, no Congress tends to be completely free with its consent. The administration always has a free hand in proposing, but it is the Congress that, in the end, disposes. Many people, including all the strong Presidents, have not liked this arrangement, which was probably why the founding fathers insisted upon including it in the Constitution.

The original concept was to insure that the executive branch could do nothing overseas that was not acceptable to the people or their representatives. In practical terms, however, it came to mean that American administrations spent vast amounts of time and energy trying to avoid the will of Congress on foreign matters, rather than trying instead to sell programs that were not immediately popular.

The intent of the Roosevelt Administration in 1943–1944 was to avoid a direct confrontation with the people or Congress on the matter of a United Nations until the commitment was irreversible, and it was hoped, completely popular. During the war, public opinion on world problems was in flux. No one could be sure just how it would solidify, whether into internationalism or a new isolationism. In the meantime, time and tide waited for no one, not even President Roosevelt. He had to get the United States to sail with the tide or risk being left irretrievably behind.

He chose to sail. The early moves of the Administration aimed at making a permanent United Nations and keeping the United

16

States in it were made quietly, without fanfare. In 1943–1944 the government used the *de facto* commitment in global war to alter the *de jure* posture of the United States in the world.

The first problem was the Congress. The conduct of foreign affairs was left to the President, but since the League of Nations fiasco after World War I few foreign governments took American Presidents' proposals at face value until they had been certified by Congress. To free his hands in dealing with the important allies, FDR had to show evidence of Congressional support.

There was already widespread agreement among influential Congressmen and Senators that some new form of the League of Nations needed to be revived. Ironically, more League sentiment existed in Congress, which had killed the League, than in the State Department in the latter years of the war. There was a great deal of discussion at this time over the American withdrawal from the world in 1919, and how this had been disastrous to the peace. But what the Congress did not seem to recognize so clearly as the State Department was that the Peace of Versailles and the League would have failed with or without U. S. participation, for both were falsely postulated from the start.

One of the principal reasons for the success of a resurgent German belligerency after 1918 was the fact that France and Britain were always unable to agree on any common course of action. Had the United States, with its known ideals, stayed in the League, the disagreement would merely have been three-pronged instead of two, and the League could not have been any more effective. This, much later, was well recognized in Allied chancelleries. It was rarely broached, because it cast a discouraging light on the future that would follow World War II.

One real problem with which Congress was concerned was the possible resurgence of the Axis. Many otherwise informed and intelligent people had come to consider the problem of world order as a German problem, pure and simple. If the swine were kept from occupying the Rhine again, all would be well, or so some believed. The future weakness of Britain was dimly seen,

17

and many Americans agreed that U. S. influence would be necessary in Europe to keep the Germans from again making a comeback on the appeasement trail.

The French and British had proved they could not handle the Germans by themselves, and the Russians, to most Americans, were an unknown quantity. The anti-German sentiment, then, was definitely pro-American action to keep the Axis down. This body of opinion, however, showed no great interest in world order in general. Much of it was actually anti-European or anticolonial in outlook.

Thus, when Congressman Fulbright of Arkansas, an Administration stalwart, introduced a resolution in the House calling for the "creation of appropriate international machinery with power adequate to establish and maintain a just and lasting peace," it was interpreted in many quarters as a move to seal the victory, and there was no focused opposition. In the Senate a similar resolution offered by Tom Connally of Texas, Chairman of the Foreign Affairs Committee, passed as easily. Neither resolution had the power of law; they were merely American statements of principle.

With these resolutions in hand to show doubters that this time the United States meant business, FDR and the State Department now urged the governments of China, the USSR, and Great Britain to sponsor similar statements. Late in 1943, all four governments joined in a declaration that recognized the need for a new international apparatus after the war.

While these moves advanced on the highest diplomatic levels, a number of American-instigated and wholly American-financed appendages of a future world organization were brought into being on lower operating levels. These were the Food and Agricultural Organization, the United Nations Relief and Rehabilitation Administration (UNRRA), and the International Monetary Fund (IMF). On November 9, 1943, forty-four nations signed the UNRRA agreements at the White House. By March, 1944, FDR had signed into law Congressional acts giving UNRRA one billion, three hundred fifty million dollars. In July, 1944, monetary and financial talks were underway at Bretton Woods in New Hampshire. The Yankee dollar was coming into its own as a world force.

Meanwhile, the plans for the big one—the international apparatus to which all these appendages would be strung—were being polished and repolished in Washington. The staff briefings that had firmed the UN idea in FDR's mind in early 1943 were written into a "Staff Charter." This was revised into a "Draft Constitution of International Organization" by July, 1943, then completely rewritten in August. The final title was *Tentative United States Proposals for a General International Organization*, and this version was approved by Roosevelt on December 29, 1943.

It was presented to a Big Three conference called at Dumbarton Oaks, a mansion on the outskirts of Washington, D. C., August 21, 1944. This was a meeting of the diplomatic staffs of the United States, the USSR, and the United Kingdom. Its purpose was to draft the organization of a world peace-keeping apparatus and to delineate its powers. Over British objections, China was invited and joined the discussions a few weeks later.

France, although it had been one of the traditional big powers, was not included. At this time France was not really a sovereign nation; metropolitan France was wholly occupied by Germany, and the only French government was the Free French group headed by General Charles de Gaulle.

The makeup of the Dumbarton Oaks staffs was immensely significant. Only the four big powers—including China, which was given a sort of rain check—were invited. All allied, associated, or "united" nations had been parties to the declarations, relief, monetary, and financial agreements. The big powers reserved the organization of the future world security system to themselves.

This was utterly realistic. The allied big-power structure existed, and it was the rock upon which the Axis smashed. Without the Big Four it would have been Hitler's and Tojo's world, and every statesman in world politics from the smaller nations knew it. There was nothing like a shooting war to get men to face reality, though many still found facts unpalatable. Unless the new

19

league was to go the way of the old, the Big Four was the foundation of necessity upon which all hope of world peace rested. The big nations had the ships, the guns, and the money, too. In 1944, and later, nothing else really mattered.

The meeting of the Big Four staff at Dumbarton Oaks made it at once clear that the power realities of the 1944 world were being recognized. What was not recognized was the mythical "equality of nations." This supposed equality was not a historical fact, nor had it even been a historical custom. It first came into use as a diplomatic protocol—not a practical concept—during the interminable recesses that ended the Thirty Years' War. Then it was established that the ambassador of a small state should receive the same courtesies and protocol as the representative of a major power, but over some objection. The practice proved both comfortable and diplomatically profitable, and it was continued. No small power representative, however, at the conventions at Westphalia in 1648 or later, was ever given the consideration tendered ambassadors of major nations. His words were never so important, since he lacked the power to back them up.

The concept became dangerous diplomatically only when large numbers of men in the Western world came to equate the protocol equality of ambassadors with equality between the nations they represented. The fact that a man representing Liechtenstein and a man representing Russia were afforded equal diplomatic courtesies did not mean that their respective nations were equal, or would ever be treated as such. Under international law and custom, both nations had a right to a separate and independent existence. But separateness did not imply equality. In the rough and tumble of *Weltpolitik,* some nations, like the animals on Orwell's farm, were always more equal than others, and no amount of theorizing could change that fact.

Dumbarton Oaks realistically took the world as it was, and tried to make the best possible compromise under the circumstances to insure an orderly world. Here U. S. preparation and planning paid off. All four countries brought ideas and recommendations, but only the American plan was in final form.

20

Edward R. Stettinius, who headed the U. S. delegation, and whose main talent was getting people to go along, moved the conference to accept the U. S. proposals as the basis for discussion.

The United States, in keeping with the realism permeating Dumbarton Oaks, did not propose anything it felt the other powers could not accept. Sumner Welles and Roosevelt were practical men. They were quite aware that none of the great powers, including the United States, would permit any real restriction upon their freedom of action. No government involved had any real interest in seeking a legal or judicial solution to the broad gamut of world problems. They were out to insure international security, which to each staff at Dumbarton Oaks meant a system to insure the peace the Big Four was winning on the battlefield.

The U. S. proposals in essence called for a defensive alliance between the four powers against any resurgence of the Axis, or any other future threat of revisionism. This alliance would form the United Nations Security Council, and it would be vested with the entire executive power of the world organization. The Assembly, which was to be the other chamber, was to provide membership for all nations both big and small. It would thus be a forum. It was to have no powers beyond those of influencing opinion. The decisions of the Security Council, composed only of great powers, were to be binding upon the Assembly, as well as upon nations not included in the Assembly, such as the former Axis.

Some Americans have been amazed that there was no argument at Dumbarton Oaks. These people did not understand the U. S. position there, or the thinking involved. The Chinese had little to say in actuality; they were both enormously proud and humble at being invited into the new world power structure. The British found much of the American wording legalistic and involved. But the concepts boiled down into what the Foreign Office had in mind all along: a continuation of the alliance, and an order based on practical power. The Russians were also pleased. Like China, they had been, at one swoop, removed from a sort of pariah status in the West and asked to join the greatest council on earth.

The proposals in no way envisioned a world legislature or world government. They created instead a political organization completely dominated by four great powers, which could enforce common great power decisions. The lights burning late at Dumbarton Oaks were not beacons illuminating a coming millennium or a brave new world in which all the old rules were changed. The planners there saw a change in neither the nature of man nor the courses of his politics. Power of some sort would still rule the earth, but, hopefully, it would be power exercised by allied and seemingly responsible nations.

The State Department went out to get all that the staff figured it could get, and got it. The alliance was projected beyond the end of the war, and the framework for world order adopted. The Proposals, as they were now called, smelled more of the oil of efficient power machinery than of rosy ideals. They were released October 9, 1944.

There was an immediate protest from the chancellories of many smaller nations, from Australia to the Philippines. The smaller powers, by their size denied aggressive ambition, had genuinely accepted the Atlantic Charter. The Charter offered them peace and protection. They also thought they understood American hopes for the world. But neither the Atlantic Charter nor American idealism about the rights of small nations was embodied in what emerged from Dumbarton Oaks. They were implied—but not included. And the crystal-clear fact that the Big Four intended to keep the real power of decision in the future as they had held it during the war horrified many statesmen from small or weak countries.

The majority of the American people paid little attention to what happened at Dumbarton Oaks. There was a war on, and the release of the Proposals simultaneously in all the allied capitals drew only a few thousand letters, mostly from theorists at the State Department. It seems certain that very few Americans

22

understood the basic concept of Dumbarton Oaks, which envisioned a world ruled by national power and blueprinted a future in which four great powers would hold special police authority by sanction as well as by use and wont.

Machinery had been provided for this, but also for continuous consultation between great powers and small nations. The projected General Assembly and World Court, even without specific powers, were latent with political opportunity. Furthermore, the machinery permitted the great powers to join in the ruling group without relinquishing freedom of action or security. This last, which raised the hackles of both idealists and world government enthusiasts, was fundamental. Without such a guarantee, no great power would have agreed to Dumbarton Oaks, or even taken the first step toward international cooperation.

But there was too much optimistic language in the American press; too many people believed a real step toward genuine international cooperation had been taken. For its own reasons, the Administration not only failed to squelch the optimism, but encouraged it. The Administration never admitted that international cooperation could not actually be guaranteed, and that about all the United States could hope to do was to make a major place for itself at the bargaining table.

One unfortunate result was that millions of people, never bothering to read the text of the Proposals, got the idea of a new League of Nations that somehow could really change the nature of power politics. The State Department, whose top people knew better, was not permitted to enlighten them.

The Dumbarton Oaks Proposals offered the nations an opportunity for cooperation, but not a guarantee.

They also revealed one enormous flaw: there was no substitute for big power agreement. As *Time* magazine reported: ". . . The Proposals have many serious flaws, and they all add up to this: the plain reliance on Big-Power agreement is so desperate that no peaceful alternative is envisioned."

But *Time* had no alternative, either. The fact was, the peace of the world had always rested on Big Power agreement, and probably always would, as long as there was more than one big power.

The State Department and FDR were not wrong in their acceptance of continued big-power predominance as spelled out at Dumbarton Oaks. They were mistaken only in their optimism that nations would cooperate, and the fact that they fostered such optimism inside the United States. The fact that big-power cooperation was essential to future peace did not mean that the Russians or Chinese would always cooperate.

Congress accepted Dumbarton Oaks, with a few reservations. The public acquiesced. Ironically, the principal objection raised was not the immediately apparent flaw of required unity, but the clear intent to rely upon big-power politics to enforce future law and order. Millions of Americans, even in the middle of a war, were unwilling to accept what they called "power politics" as an international way of life.

This feeling could not be faulted in American moral terms. But its existence showed a remarkable misunderstanding of the world's peoples and governments. Too many Americans still saw the world at large in American terms, or considered the aims, morals, aspirations, and ideals of the English-speaking nations as universal. The man in Zanzibar was not much different from the man in Zanesville, Ohio, to this school of thought; therefore, a consensus could easily be reached between the two. The same people tended to regard Hitler and Nazism not as recognizable human manifestations, but as some kind of aberration. Their rejection of history, including their own, was profound.

The flaws in the thinking of this idealistic group could all be summed up in one phrase: they rejected the salient fact that all human political history was largely the record of power struggles. Further, rejecting the idea of the power struggle, they failed to recognize such struggles as eternal. They might deny the fact, but many of them really did long for the millennium: a time without trouble, a time without war, a time when human nature would change.

Not understanding the nature of power struggles, they looked

24

on Hitler as some kind of monster brewed up by black magic. They did not see him for what he was: a peculiarly unpleasant manifestation of the enormous pressures for revision of power and predominance structures within the industrial world. Germany, Japan, Italy, and other nations wanted to be first, in place of France and Britain. The desire and the drive were perfectly normal. The means used was not acceptable to the other powers, and provoked global war. The result, which some men could dimly see in 1944–1945, was not the triumph of the older European powers, but the actual destruction of the European state system itself. The collapse of that system in incessant, destructive wars was the spur that urged Roosevelt and others toward the establishment of some form of rudimentary supranational structure.

But the reliance on national power and "power politics" as the basis of the new League by the professionals inside the State Department—and the emotional rejection of both by millions of people unconnected with the realities of government—created a dichotomy between professional government and the American citizenry that was to grow over the next twenty years. This dichotomy caused confusion, on both sides.

Roosevelt himself reflected this typical American confusion toward the world. He was keenly aware of the realities of power; he knew how to use all the forms of power to get his way. But his Anglo-Saxon empiricism was inextricably mixed with North American idealism, too. He fervently desired a lasting peace to follow World War II. This was a finite, and reasonable, goal, and one toward which the U. S. government could strive. But he also seemed almost as interested in international "justice"—which was not definable in strict terms, and therefore had intimations of totality. No two nations in the world consistently agreed on what comprised "justice," which was one basis of the eternal power struggle.

FDR's immense prestige, and his ability to employ all the tools of personal and national power during the war years, kept the United States on an even, if erratic, keel. But because of his own basic confusion between desires for order on one hand and "justice" on the other, he was never able to create a coherent, lasting American policy that would continue beyond his death.

Even his use of diplomacy was erratic at times. Notoriously his own Secretary of State, FDR preferred using personal emissaries like Harry Hopkins or Judge Rosenman to the normal channels of diplomatic intercourse. In the early days of the war, when problems were immediate and finite, this system worked well. Later, when the American commitment had become worldwide, and long-range policy decisions had to be made, the personal emissary and the get-together over cocktails did not work at all. Deep-seated drives and historic ideologies, like that of the Soviet Union, could not be set aside by smiles or handshakes, or wrapped up over a kitchen table.

While the State Department career men were forging FDR a new tool for the employment of American power—not for aggrandizement, but for peace-keeping—in 1943 and 1944, FDR himself was thinking in terms of bringing American principle into the world arena. Anything less, Roosevelt felt, would result in no real improvement in the human condition; and the human condition, everywhere, was important to FDR. While the backroom boys wanted a useful vehicle to enforce world order, he wanted a more grandiose organization that could also insure American concepts of justice. Roosevelt's error was not in wanting this. It was in believing that any organization could achieve it, in one swoop.

Roosevelt had envisioned that his new international organization would forge the coming peace and, somewhat like a parliament of man, debate and set its conditions. Until late 1944, his timetable was well on schedule; the United Nations Organization was being made. But in the winter of 1944, the timetable began to go awry.

While FDR was channeling the U. S. diplomatic effort into the UN, massive Russian armies had entered Eastern Europe, beginning a historical process frightening to the British and disturbing to Americans. FDR's timetable had been too slow, and now the quickening collapse of German forces in Europe spurred him to belated action.

He had become obsessed with the idea that a genuine new world order was being made. Here he was correct. But by 1945 there was immediate concern for the shape of that new order. Roosevelt had been too much worried by the specter of 1919 and the fear that the U. S. Senate and people would not back him. Now he began to fear that the world body into which he had increasingly channeled his hopes and energies would not be completed in time.

The realization of an eternal truth—that new orders are made on the battlefield, not at the peace conferences that merely confirm them—was late in coming.

The original alliance between the United States, Britain, and Russia was purely one of convenience. It had been against Hitler, not *for* anything. Its immediate object had not been to make a new world order, advance human justice, or anything except the destruction of a common danger, the German state. In the hour of maximum peril there had been no discussion of eventual victory settlements or spoils. There had been the Atlantic Charter, of course. But while Britain had signed the Charter spontaneously, the USSR had really been bludgeoned into it.

The frightening realization that the Russians, via the Red Army, were already bringing their own version of principle and new order to Eastern Europe was transmitted from an alarmed Churchill to FDR. Roosevelt and his intimates, actually more worried than they dared admit, felt there was no time to waste on minor problems; they wanted all loose ends tied up quickly. The new UN seemed the one big answer to all the small problems. If an agreement could be secured with the Russians on the question of world organization, then it seemed all the details could be debated, and solved, at leisure. FDR, thinking this way, was entirely willing to bypass dangerous thickets to get what he considered would be a broad general agreement. He apparently failed to

27

understand that any agreement not based on enduring mutual interest was ephemeral, now and forever, and that the thickets would remain.

Hitler had failed disastrously in 1940 by not spending every shred of German nerve and muscle to conquer the thorny isle of Britain. Now American statesman, led by FDR, kept looking at the forest and missed the trees. They left equally dangerous and stubborn thickets behind them. Just as Britain, bypassed, remained to become a floating arsenal and launching platform for Germany's destruction, a whole generation of Americans would have to wrestle with the islands of people and principle abandoned in Eastern Europe by Rooseveltian diplomacy.

The British position, exhausted as the island was in 1944, was willingness to engage in power politics with the USSR, with the ultimate end of confining the Russians within their own historic borders. The British wanted Anglo-American armies to arrive in Central and Eastern Europe first, even if this cost an extra hundred thousand Allied dead. Churchill was not an insensitive monster; he was a man haunted by historic vision. But his vision was as unpopular and as unsalable in 1944 as it had been in the 1930's.

The American position was to reject British counsel, and to base everything on the hope of future Russian cooperation. The Russians, after all, had signed certain documents. Roosevelt did not want a confrontation, which was exactly what Churchill's plan would have brought. He preferred to concentrate on a future UN organization that, *after* the war, might have some success with putting the world back together again. The British had to acquiesce. Without U. S. power, they were as helpless against the Soviets as they had been against the Germans.

The Dumbarton Oaks Proposals had laid the groundwork for the UN, but that conference had postponed three extremely difficult questions for a later conference. These were (1) the representation formula, (2) voting provisions, and (3) colonial and

28

trusteeship matters. These, of course, lay at the heart of the proposed body.

By late 1944, FDR wanted a new meeting to iron out these details quickly. He felt there was too little time, with Russia overrunning East Europe, to arrange for this conference in the normal way. He requested Churchill and Stalin to meet with him personally. He hoped, at the highest level, to hammer out in a few days what the various diplomatic staffs could not get at Dumbarton Oaks during several weeks.

Churchill, deeply afraid of the Russian Communization of Eastern Europe that had already begun, was eager to meet with FDR and Stalin. But Stalin wanted no part of such a conference. He reported that his doctors would not permit him to leave Russia because of ill health. FDR—who was in far worse health—immediately replied that the meeting should be held in Russia, and agreed to fly to the Crimea. He was determined to secure a final agreement on the shape of the postwar world with the Soviets.

As 1945 dawned, he was not aware that it was already too late.

For the United States of America, remote in a hemisphere whose isolation the war had forever destroyed, World War II was mainly an expedition, a crusade of sorts to set to rights a world gone wrong. Many Americans equated the world's troubles with Hitler, Tojo, Mussolini—or some "ism"—and honestly expected that when the symptoms of the sickness were treated, a better day would surely dawn. Government propaganda, and even business advertising, continually bolstered this hope. It was an attitude among all parties, typically American, and in the light of American history and ethos, inevitable.

Because of its immense power, the United States assumed leadership of the war. It was the arsenal of democracy; it armed the allied world, supplied and clothed it, and to some extent even fed it. It sent millions of its young men overseas. But, the United States did not win the war alone, a fact often obscured in Ameri-

29

can thinking. The major allies, British, Russian, and Chinese, took and blunted the heaviest Axis blows. Out of a total of fifty million dead on the field of battle, only three hundred thousand were Americans.

But during this war the United States performed the industrial, organizational, and agricultural miracles that made all former progress seem small, and that transfixed the world. Those miracles, hardly understood by the men who performed them, gave the United States the basis for world leadership. In 1941 the United States had been a nation of great potential but no real power. By 1945 it was the greatest national power the world had so far known. Uniquely, of all the nations engaged in the war, only the United States failed to dissipate real wealth. The United States gained it.

Because the world of Napoleon, Bismarck, and Hitler—the traditional European state system—had repeatedly torn itself apart in a prolonged crisis of order, America suddenly dominated it. But as they gained power, Americans also raised a subtle but very real barrier between themselves and the rest of the world. They were suddenly the fat cats in a world of hunger. They were the rich in a world of rags and devastation. They were the powerful in a world of exhaustion and gray disillusion. Because of this, they were suddenly the leaders of a philosophical and political Western order for which they had never before acknowledged responsibility.

They were not unanimously happy with that responsibility.

Nor were they alone in the world of power.

While Western Europe, the former power center, devoured itself, and Britain, sinking, lived its finest hour, the Soviet society, with roots very different from the American, performed its own modern miracle. Attacked, overrun, and pressed to the wall by the German military machine, the USSR survived deep contradictions, hideous bungling, and a tyrannical leadership. Russians fought back from sincere patriotism, hardihood, and fierce peasant will, first to survive, then to get an advantage.

No one, seeing the Russian experience between 1941 and

1945, should mistake the real roots of national power, which have nothing to do with ideology or the kind of government a people happens to have. There is no single route to world power, just as there is no single road to the organization of human society. Variety can be infinite. The same forces, in different form, that catapulted the United States into prominence also served the Soviet Union.

Soviet leadership had wanted the war no more than American. The USSR had done everything within its power and polity to avoid a confrontation with Germany. Molotov had groveled to Ribbentrop, and Stalin had almost fawned on his arch-enemy, Hitler. But, with the chips down, the USSR could no more bring itself to surrender what it considered vital interests and ambitions in Eastern Europe than the United States could in the Pacific. If the United States could not do business with Hitler, neither could the totalitarian USSR. In each case, refusal to surrender provoked attack.

But once involved in it, the Soviet leadership never regarded the war as an end in itself. It was a period of danger and sacrifice, but it was also seen as a means to an end, and the end was Soviet world power. The USSR, with its recent history, national character, and current ideology, could not have desired a return to the status quo of 1937, and certainly not that of 1914. Americans should have seen this clearly, but did not. The USSR, as a nation, wanted a new order, like Roosevelt. But in this new order Russia would play the dominant role, and international justice had nothing to do with it.

Where Americans now faced the realities of power reluctantly, with the unhappy and historic bias of most English-speaking nations toward the exercise of power as either end or means, Russians understood nothing else. In the United States, neither the State nor the concept of national power had ever risen very high in the public scheme of things. Intelligent Russians dreamed of nothing else. There was a vast idealism in Russians, too—but it took different forms.

Once the USSR had been one power among many; by 1945 it

remained a survivor, like the United States, in a sudden power vacuum. The nation was terribly mauled, twenty million dead; and it had not grown richer. But it emerged into a shattered world with its power intact and sullenly disciplined by a Stalinic will.

The single greatest mistake of the American public during the war, which government did nothing to dispel, was its belief that the Soviet Union fought World War II from motives not unlike its own.

Some nations desire power, some seek it, and others have it thrust upon them. By 1945, there was no doubt in Russian minds about the reality of American power in the world. But there remained a very large question as to how Americans would use that power, or even if they would use it at all.

3.

The Toasts of Yalta

NOTHING MORE CLEARLY illustrated the shape of the coming world than the Big Three conference at Yalta. In that sense, the details are worth exploring.

It was not only Franklin Roosevelt but Roosevelt's whole generation who tended to be blinded by the roseate and rational outlook of the nineteenth-century Anglo-American world into which they were born. Not only FDR but men like Hull, Marshall, Hopkins, and Eisenhower suffered from a common failing to realize that while war sprang from ultra-rational causes, it was still a rational act toward a rational goal. The single persistent error that top American leadership, superb as it was, made during the war was the consideration that there was, or ought to be, a dividing line between war and politics.

It was clearly necessary once the fighting began for the free nations to move armies and armadas, not only to defeat the Axis, but to assure the new world order they envisioned. Ironically, Americans tended to look upon such moves to insure the kind of world they were fighting for as not only impractical but immoral.

Because the United States took a legalistic-moralistic hangover into the war—the enemy were not just men and women determined to overthrow an existing order and make the world over the way they wanted it, but criminals who had broken a natural "law" of nations—the main object of strategy became the capture and the punishment of the criminals who were responsible for all the horror.

This notion created a whole new dimension to war—and not a particularly happy one—but at the same time it sharply limited

33

war's possibilities. For it became morally assailable to try to mix the expediency of national policy with the higher motives and supreme sacrifices of the uniformed policemen bringing criminals to the dock.

Just as it had become immoral to permit individuals to make domestic profits from the war, it had become immoral for the U. S. government to seek foreign profits, even in pursuit of the highest motives, out of the death of its citizenry. Peace was one state, war another, and different rules were felt to obtain in each.

Inside America, the rule of law was firmly established. Abroad, it was difficult for Americans to accept the fact that there was no law as such; so-called international law was merely a civilizing set of conventions and protocols more often than not honored in the breach. Law cannot exist without common government. The relation of the various races, nations, and peoples with each other has always been, and has to be, a matter of political adjustment.

Americans had usually oiled the wheels of their domestic life with practicality; there was such a thing as the deal. But after the totality of the Civil War, they were never able to carry such pragmatism abroad. They had learned a lasting hatred, almost a fear, of violence for political purposes, and tended to lose sight of the practical ends for which the violence was all about. It was desperately hard for some Americans to see that while wars are sometimes fought for principles, international politics are always played for provinces.

Roosevelt and Churchill flew into Saki Airfield in the Crimea from Malta on the night of February 3, 1945. Churchill's plane landed first, followed by Roosevelt's *Sacred Cow*. Churchill watched Roosevelt lifted down. FDR had picked up some tan on the sea voyage out to Malta, where the American and British military staffs had agreed on the final strategy of the war, but to Churchill's eye the President looked frail and ill.

Churchill himself had recently run one of the fevers he was prone to on his travels, and he was accompanied both by

34

his daughter Sarah and his physician, Lord Moran. But as Stalin had said, pooh-poohing any frailty on the Prime Minister's part: "Churchill is the healthiest old man in the world, a desperate fellow."

Some of Roosevelt's intimates also thought he looked bad as he left Washington; he insisted, however, that he felt fine, and few on the American staff were concerned.

Now, a velvet-collared cloak fastened over his broad, flowered necktie, he inspected the Soviet honor guard from an open touring car, while Churchill, in the uniform of an RAF air marshal, walked along beside, and Stettinius, Roosevelt's new Secretary of State, incongruous in a gray double-breasted overcoat, light gray Homburg, and Air Corps flight boots, managed a sour smile for the official photographer.

Finished with the slap and crash of the honor guard, the Anglo-American parties proceeded to the airfield hospitality house, where Vyacheslav Molotov smiled behind his glasses, welcoming them. Josef Stalin, in a sleek gray uniform with a marshal's single broad star on the epaulets, looked very fit in spite of his doctors' protestations.

It is not possible for peoples of the world to deal directly with each other, despite certain democratic illusions; governments deal with governments, and leaders talk with leaders. These three, meeting, held almost all of the real power of the world in their hands, and all were aware of it: Roosevelt, worried but still optimistic, Churchill visibly glum, Stalin direct and hearty.

In Roosevelt's mind, as he revealed it then, was a deep concern for moral law among nations and human freedom, but no finite goals or solid plans either for America or the world. There was a certain uneasiness at the idea of settling the destinies of the world by summit conference—there was an American Senate, and an American public opinion—and Roosevelt had a real but mistaken hope that certain problems could be turned over to a future world organization for debate and solution. Coming into Yalta, Roosevelt showed himself more interested in securing

35

this organization than in the final prosecution of the war or in getting solid political agreement from Stalin.

Churchill came with the feelings bred in his British bone: a certain magnanimity toward the defeated, and an incorruptible belief in a balance of power. No man had smelled out Hitler sooner, and no man had battled him harder—but Britain defeats her enemies; she does not destroy them. Tomorrow, as the pragmatic English mind well understood, she might need them. The British, traditionally, had never so much wanted to rule the world as to assure that no one else ruled it.

Now, Churchill came bitterly aware of the British weakness in this meeting of giants, determined to fight for whatever Britain required to survive as a great power. Gloomily, Churchill saw all hope of a continental balance of power slipping away: Stalin's Red Army stood almost where the Wehrmacht had stood in 1939. Churchill had smelled out Bolshevism early, too.

Josef Stalin arrived from Moscow certain that in this world only power counts—visible power, as in armies; subterranean power, as in Marxist ideology—and comfortable in the knowledge that he possessed both. He could say, bluntly, to Roosevelt's protestations about world opinion and moral force: "How many divisions has the Pope?" It was the kind of question that angered Americans because it represented an attitude they sensed was wrong but were hard put to answer.

Stalin was a true product of the Soviet political cesspool from which he sprang; he had made himself supreme in a cauldron that constantly bubbled with contests for power. He trusted no one, and he kept his own counsel. Understanding the basis of world power, and the unsanitary world he lived it, Stalin between 1930 and 1939 lessened the comfort of the Soviet people but increased the production of Russian steel three hundred percent. The USSR did not bumble into prominence by accident.

Now, in 1945, Stalin's marshals, fat with victory, dripping medals, stood inside the doors from which Russia had long been barred. Stalin's keen eye, clouded only slightly by Marxist ideology, saw the ruin of capitalist society from Belgium to Bucharesti, and from Lublin to London. His seers and prophets foretold the end of that society, and Stalin could see the evidence. He stood at the head of the only genuine disciplined expansionist *movement* of the century, Communism, and he could almost hear the crash of the old order and of its institutions—capitalism and democracy.

Despite certain American oversimplifications, Stalin was never so sanguine as to think world domination was within his grasp. He did see and expect Eurasian hegemony, from which such domination might be built. To this end, Stalin had to insure the fragmentation of the German power basin so that Western Europe could never again dispute Soviet preeminence. He also wanted secure—that is, Communist —borders, and all the loot his exhausted nation and people could get. With these things, he could afford to await the future destruction of the outer world by its own internal contradictions.

But Stalin, of course, was no expert on the capitalistic world, or even on the real force that had saved his own Russian State—modern nationalism. Neither would act according to Marx, who had been equally uninformed.

He did not discount, but he had taken the measure of, Churchill's Britain, and he found it wanting. An undisciplined lot, the English, without the go-for-the-throat instinct in war both the Germans and the Americans seemed to share. There would be no conquering Britain, of course, but Britain was not likely to be able to interfere with the new Europe any more than it had been able to bring Hitler down.

The Americans were another matter. But the United States was far away. Moreover, America seemed only to issue forth like St. George to fight periodic dragons, then retire to a private funk of its own.

These then were the Big Three, whom Stalin jocularly

37

likened to the Holy Trinity, he the Father, FDR the Son, and Churchill the Holy Ghost. Each in his own way at Yalta would try to remake the world.

The conference opened on February 4, 1945. There was no formal agenda; there was agreement that any subject might be broached for discussion. FDR, in particular, wanted to keep the talks informal. It had always been an American tendency to hope that a nation's inevitable policy might somehow be altered over a cocktail party or by the laying on of hands.

Military questions came first. Here the military staffs of the three powers took over, smoothly and efficiently. From Malta, the Anglo-Americans had ironed out all mutual problems, and at Yalta they functioned as a team. All of the staffs, Soviet or Western, were composed of professionals. The generals and admirals of all three nations had been directed to win the war, and they were doing just that.

Each side had impressive accomplishments to relate. The Soviet January offensive had already advanced three hundred miles into Europe. It had swallowed German divisions wholesale. Russian troops were in Silesia, at the banks of the Oder, and within forty miles of Berlin.

The Anglo-Americans had nothing but awe for the smashing drive of the Red Army, and were staggered by the Russian losses, immensely greater than those suffered in the West. In return, the Soviet high command for the first time admitted that the Western strategic bombardment of Germany had produced some results, but of course not decisive ones.

The British and Americans detailed how the German winter offensive had been blunted in Belgium, and displayed the massive attacks they were preparing north of the Ruhr, with a secondary offensive to be launched in the south. The Anglo-American armies confidently expected to be across the Rhine in March.

Each side, with complete honesty, laid its military cards on the table. Both Russians and Westerners, above all, wanted the other side to continue to press the attack so that

38

the Germans had no respite to shift forces from one front to the other.

Actually, until this moment, the Russians and Anglo-Americans had each fought their own war in almost complete isolation from each other. Both were winning. While there was always a haunting fear in Moscow that the West might sign a separate peace and halt the Russian drive along the Vistula—in the West's shoes this was what Stalin would have done—the Russian military men never mentioned it. The European strategy discussions ended in harmony and a burst of mutual admiration.

The discussions then shifted to Asia, which was a horse of different hue. Stalin had already agreed to attack Japan in time; for several years the Americans and the British had been trying to persuade the Russians to join in that war. Now, Stalin agreed to move within ninety days of the final defeat of Germany. But he had his price, and here the wicket grew sticky. Here the Western allies made mistakes. The first, and probably unavoidable mistake, was the complete clamp of secrecy that surrounded these discussions. It was absolutely necessary that Japan be kept in the dark about Soviet intentions, but Stalin demanded, and received, territorial concessions as a price for involvement against Japan. These concessions came not only at the expense of the Japanese Empire, but of the Republic of China, and for expedient reasons, the Republic of China was not informed, nor was the American public. In fact, everything that occurred at Yalta was blanketed under security wraps, and as bits and pieces slowly emerged, they could only bring a bad odor to the whole conference.

FDR argued with Stalin on the Soviet demands in Asia, but Stalin was adamant. In the end, the United States agreed to support all Russian claims in Manchuria.

Since it had been agreed earlier that the Japanese Empire would be destroyed, the movement of Russia into East Asia could mean only the shift of the entire Asian balance of power toward the Soviets. The USSR would fill the vacuum the United States armed forces were creating, and which

China would be unable to fill. The British left these negotiations wholly to the American staff. They had already reached agreement with the United States on their primary area of concern, Southeast Asia, with tacit American consent to the British Asian empire. They regarded Manchuria, North China, and Korea remote from their own spheres of interest and deferred to the United States.

In retrospect, no part of the Yalta agreements came in for such criticism. In retrospect, no part could less stand inspection. The expansion of Soviet power into Europe had already come about, and could not be prevented, but the expansion into Asia was not only permitted, but solicited. The Yalta agreements led to immense American problems in the Far East, and the Soviet price was never worth the negligible benefits received.

But the United States government, in February, 1945, had its reasons.

The grave error here was that purely military considerations were overriding American policy and planning. The indictment, if returned, could not be against FDR, but an entire American generation that insisted upon separating warfare from *Weltpolitik*. It was inevitable that Admiral King and General Marshall, in the American tradition far removed from political considerations, should do so—but there was no real dichotomy between Marshall and Roosevelt or Hopkins, and the military men were allowed to subordinate all other questions to the actual prosecution of the war.

The philosophy that not one American soldier should lose his life for any reason not immediately concerned with the destruction of the enemy was, in its way, admirable. But it was also an attitude that lost sight of the real reason men died on the battlefields.

Just as it had hamstrung British action in two wars, the pressing question of casualties hampered American geopolitics at Yalta. American opinion supported casualties suffered in bringing the international culprits to the dock. It would support them for no other reason, even the pressing ones of state. It had seemed immoral to cause more Americans than militarily necessary to die by striking through the Balkans, meeting the Russians on the Vistula; it seemed equally immoral to allow more thousands to die by keeping the Russians north of the Yalu.

American planners did not foresee the early defeat of Japan. The best estimates gave the war at least eighteen more months. Japanese resistance in the Pacific had grown more and more fanatic, and almost all strategists assumed that the home islands themselves would have to be invaded and reduced foot by foot. The main Japanese ground forces, on guard in Manchuria, had not even been engaged. The shock of the heavy casualties suffered when the Wehrmacht was engaged in Europe still lingered, and Americans planning to invade Japan counted upon hundreds of thousands more.

The nuclear bomb had not yet been completed, and moreover, it was vastly underrated, even by its developers. In any event, strategy could not count on a "secret weapon" as yet unmade. The U. S. military staff was agreed that Soviet entry against Japan, striking against the crack Japanese Kwantung Army, would reduce eventual American casualties by one hundred thousand. It was the Soviets who, with enormous losses, had drawn the German teeth in Europe. It seemed reasonable to let them do the same with Japan, if they could be induced to do so, even at a price. The Americans at Yalta, from FDR down, could not realize how high the eventual price might be.

It was the military staff that prepared and approved the secret concession clauses, but they were fully ratified at the highest level. In complete fairness to FDR, it must be explained that it was always in his mind that Stalin had the power to move in Asia with or without American sanction. The attempt to bring the USSR into the war, and conciliate it at the same time, made a certain sense, particularly in the light of the fact that if a *modus vivendi* with the Soviets could not be arranged, the brave new world of 1945 was going to be bungled beyond recognition from the start.

It was, on the face of it, a reasonable bargain. Unfortunately, the United States was to find that some things are not for sale.

Asia was settled, and Winston Churchill was anxious to bring the discussions back to Europe. Trouble—serious trouble—had arrived with the Red Army.

It had already been discussed and agreed that the Soviet Union had a right to insist on friendly, or at least nonhostile, governments in the nations on its borders. There was to be no return of the hated *cordon sanitaire*—the ring of anti-Communist regimes and treaties to contain the Soviets—that France and Britain had drawn around the USSR in the 1920's. But there was a contradiction in terms not completely understood in the West. To the Soviet government the only nonhostile government was a Communist one.

After Poland had been overrun by the Nazi armies, a Polish government-in-exile had been set up in London. Although sponsored and abetted by the British, with whose forces the free Poles were serving in the Mediterranean theater, it was in no sense a puppet government. It was naturally anti-German, but traditionally, the Poles had had no more use for Russians than for their neighbors to the west, and there were few if any real friends of the Soviet Union among its ministers.

Whatever their actions might have been, the London Poles were never given an opportunity to restore the Polish government. As soon as Soviet arms had driven the Germans from Poland, the USSR had immediately sponsored and placed in power, backed by the Red Army, a Communist regime in Lublin. This regime repudiated, in the name of the Polish people, the exiles in London, and began making Poland into a Soviet state. The British, who had gone to war to preserve Polish independence in 1939, were concerned and deeply angered.

42

While Poland occupied the spotlight, as an ally of the West, the Russians were quietly accomplishing the same thing in Bulgaria. A new political entity was coming into being, the puppet or satellite state. The satellite had its own government, made up of its indigenous people, but on the basis of ideology and its dependence upon a foreign power it remained wholly subservient to that power. The Polish and Bulgarian regimes might be Communist, and represent only a tiny fraction of the total population, but they were Polish or Bulgarian governments, not occupation regimes. They posed not only a serious moral problem to the West, but a thorny legal and political one as well.

In Yugoslavia the Communist Tito was removing all Western influence, and gradually, after the war, the Soviets repeated in every Eastern European country what they did first in Poland. In Greece, however, where British troops had landed, the British occupation authorities put down Communist disorders with bloodshed—to the accompaniment of bitter criticism in most parts of the free world.

Because of their commitment to the London Poles, and their historic interests in Eastern Europe, Winston Churchill and the British were deeply disturbed at the apparent Soviet policy.

Churchill had anticipated the problem in 1943 and 1944, but he had never been able to arouse American support. Americans in high places refused to distrust Russian aims while the war against Hitler continued, and many tended to look upon the quarrel shaping up in East Europe as a purely Russo-British one, between two European empires with conflicting spheres of interest. Harry Hopkins, for one, made it known that he considered British ambitions almost as questionable as the Soviet. The British, after all, were in India, and a great many very intelligent Americans could not grasp the reality of a Soviet imperialism. Even in many Western minds, imperialism was synonymous, not with the spread of ideology or of national interest, but with capitalism.

In short, many Americans were willing to put down Hitler, but wanted no involvement in the future quarrels of a blood-stained Europe. There remained a lurking and haunting suspicion that the wily British were trying to play off Soviet interests against the American, to their own advantage.

It is quite doubtful that even the most intelligent Americans were seeing at Yalta what was already in Soviet minds: that there was a power vacuum, which in neither nature nor politics could long exist, and that the new world order must of necessity emerge in either an American or a Russian image. At Yalta the Big Three alliance was deep in corrosion, and the specter of World War III already hung over Europe.

FDR did not dismiss the Polish problem lightly. It worried him, though not so deeply as Churchill. What seemed really to bother him most was not the new continental hegemony the USSR was bent upon but the apparent Soviet betrayal of principle. This filled him with consternation, for all powers earlier had agreed that Poland should be free, and FDR had believed in the agreements.

But any reference to the Polish situation threw Stalin into an immediate rage. He would not discuss it; he made it exceedingly clear that in his eyes no territory that the Red Army had occupied was negotiable—from the Adriatic to the Baltic. He stated angrily that he had not interfered in Greece when the British had put down the Communists by force, or in Belgium, traditional Western-influenced areas. What happened in Soviet-bordered East Europe, then, was strictly Soviet business. If the West pressed, they would blow the conference—and Roosevelt could go home and take his precious UN with him.

Roosevelt pleaded with Stalin, but he did not dare to press the point. He sensed the deep impasse, but he wanted to turn this and other problems over to his world body. There, in open proceedings, he believed it could be debated and resolved.

Roosevelt and his staff were also disturbed by the proposed

44

Russian territorial changes in Eastern Europe. The USSR had already seized the three Baltic states, Estonia, Latvia, and Lithuania, and incorporated them into the Soviet Union, and the tacit acceptance of this was about as much as the American staff could stomach. The Atlantic Charter and all wartime commitments had pledged the United Nations to no territorial adjustments without the consent of the people involved. Americans above all wanted to prevent the fatal errors of Versailles, which in an effort to weaken the Central Powers had split off Germans, Hungarians, and others under foreign rule. But in 1945 the USSR was clearly bent upon changing the map of Eastern Europe to suit its own wishes, with no sanction other than the fact that the Red Army had conquered the area.

The Russians intended to annex into the USSR large areas of the former Poland, Czechoslovakia, and Romania, which bordered them. There was some historic justification for this: the areas had once been Russian, and the populations involved were either Russian or more nearly Russian than they were Romanian or Polish. In some cases these populations had been treated as oppressed minorities in the 1920's and 1930's.

But to recompense the Eastern European states for territories lost, the Russians had evolved a truly Machiavellian scheme. The Polish loss was to be made up out of German territory in East Prussia, Prussia, and Silesia—areas that had been Germanic for centuries. Poland and the USSR were to split the old German province of East Prussia, and the new German-Polish frontier was to be moved west to the Oder and Neisse Rivers instead of along the historic Vistula. With grim logic, the Russians had no intention of repeating one error of Versailles—the boundaries were being moved, but the former inhabitants would not be left around to make future trouble. They were being evicted, driven west as destitute refugees in endless streams of millions.

FDR had no sympathy for the ethnic Germans, or for the millions of individual tragedies to be enacted in the East.

The Germans had done their own despoiling in the area, and they had done it with the hubris of a supposed Master Race. FDR had even listened sympathetically to the intellectual idiocy of the Morgenthau Plan—a plan to make Germany into a purely agricultural state—and initialed it at Quebec, an act that was to throw the eventual American policy for Germany into the confusion from which General Clay had to rescue it. It could hardly be argued that the Germans had not sown what they now reaped, but the question of justice could not be entirely free from the question of practical world politics.

The Russians were not out for justice, or to serve as its instrument against German crimes. They were transferring former German lands to Poland, and the Sudetenland to Czechoslovakia with two very practical purposes in mind. One was to ease the surgery of the land the Russians themselves seized. The other was to bind the new regimes in East Europe tighty to Soviet policy, since only the USSR could guarantee these new frontiers.

But this was the kind of territorial wound that festered, and that throughout all history produced new bloodshed. The German people, historically speaking, were not apt to accept it. Secretary of State Stettinius, strongly representing the Department, argued vehemently against the imposition of the Oder-Neisse Line, and warned that sooner or later, that line would have to be defended by force of arms. The Russians, however, made it very clear they were not interested in American advise.

In the retrospect of twenty years, the Soviet acts in Eastern Europe were an immediate success but a long-term failure. In the short run, they provided loot, more people, and large chunks of territory for the new Soviet empire. But other results were not so favorable.

The rape and enforced Communization of non-Russian peoples produced lasting bitterness; the addition to Soviet power of the new Soviet satellites was more apparent than real. Even where Communism as a way of life took hold,

46

there was enormous nationalist, anti-Russian sentiment. The Warsaw Pact, without the presence of Russian soldiers not only to aid but to enforce it, was to be something of a joke. The tying of Eastern Europe to Moscow's apron strings had the same unreality as had cloaked the French encirclement of Germany after World War I: It looked good on maps, but would not bear close inspection.

And the final German-Slavic reckoning in Europe was not settled peaceably, as it might have been with German collapse, but merely postponed. For many years, at least, no strong German government could accept the fact of Oder-Neisse any more than any strong German regime could have accepted the fact of Versailles.

In Asia, the Soviet expansion caused similar trouble. The Sino-Soviet quarrel far antedated Khrushchev's "de-Stalinization," and among its historic roots were the Soviet entry into Korea and Manchuria.

But the worst result, from the Soviet side, of the rape of 1945, was that the actions hastened and sharpened American fears and hostility, laying the groundwork that in NATO doomed Stalin's hopes for continental hegemony. The continuing Soviet power plays in Europe inevitably drew American power back into Europe like water down a sluice. They not only put the world on the brink of total war, but ironically frustrated Soviet policy.

This was a result the Soviets might have avoided. The USSR, with its admittedly immense military power and the equally immense prestige won through the sacrifices of the Red Army, might have exercised a pervasive, persuasive, and yet effective domination of East Europe, somewhat on the order of their domination of Finland. The influence would have been real, but largely unseen.

Then, by the 1950's and 1960's, the USSR would have been just as powerful, but without the hampering ties of a restive, rebellious string of satellites, which could not be trusted as allies in the event of war, and which on at least two occasions—East Germany in 1953 and Hungary in 1956—had to be restrained by force of arms.

The fact that Soviet domination was ruthless and enforced by bayonets had a large part to do with the fact that American power eventually bristled along the East-West line, making continued Soviet domination all the more politically necessary, in Soviet eyes, and at the same time, hideously more dangerous. Another unfortunate effect—in world terms—was that Soviet ruthlessness left the Soviet people damaged morally before the world, and the damage would grow, with Hungary and the Wall in Berlin.

Stalin, fearful as only tyrants can be fearful, undoubtedly thought his course was the only reasonable one for Russia. He not only seized Eastern Europe, then, but tried to divide Germany. At Yalta he argued for permament dismemberment of Germany. For an interval, at least, he got that in the four occupation zones. But ironically, fearing above all else the revival of an armed Western Europe, Stalin unintentionally but inevitably insured it. Without Stalin's moves, Europe would have had no reason to rearm.

Now, on the border of darkness, with both Stalin and Churchill close to each other's throats, Roosevelt deftly steered the talks back to what he had had in mind all along: the last touches on his international organization. Leaving Europe and geopolitics, the Big Three turned to the matters Dumbarton Oaks had left unresolved. Voting was the first question.

Dumbarton Oaks had provided that unanimous agreement between the big powers was necessary for any Security Council action. This was, in effect, though the word was never used, the big-power veto. This was the provision that allowed all great powers to retain their freedom of action, and all powers, including the United States, insisted upon it. At Yalta the provision was reaffirmed.

But FDR felt the veto was too all-inclusive. He saw no

48

reason why it should apply to mere procedural matters. As he said, the American position was one of freedom of discussion —no one should be allowed to cut off debate. The Russians, quite logically, argued that since discussion could have no effect on an eventual veto, why allow distasteful cans of worms to be opened up? Only with great reluctance did FDR agree to postpone that matter.

Referring to the veto, Stalin made the point over and over again that no collective action must ever be permitted to take place without the consent of all three great powers. In other words, the veto would prevent the USSR from interfering in American interests; but at the same time, it would bar the United States from having anything to say about what Russia did. By this time, the American staff at Yalta was convinced that the USSR intended to accept no qualification on its sovereignity, UN or no UN, and so advised Roosevelt.

Representation presented another problem. Molotov began an argument for six votes for the USSR, in the light of actual Soviet power and importance. As he said, it was ridiculous to equate the influence of Abyssinia with that of Russia, and this was what one nation, one vote in the Assembly would do. The American staff didn't agree. They were imbued with the idea of one man, one vote, and to them it seemed to apply to nations as well.

Molotov then hammered away at the fact that the British Commonwealth—in both wars a single power bloc—was going to have six votes, because it comprised six separate sovereignties, in practice if not theory. He also fingered the fact that at least a dozen "sovereign" Latin American states were so American-influenced that they would always vote the American ticket. The deck would be stacked against the USSR in the Assembly even before the UN was ratified. He stated that in practice the USSR could legally have six votes, since it was theoretically a federal system of "separate" republics. When the American staff, this time, refused to give in, Molotov reduced his demand to a minimum of three:

one for the USSR as a whole, one for the Ukraine, and one for Byelo-Russia.

Here, for a change, Winston Churchill was sympathetic to the Russians. The multiple-vote system was then still current in Britain—an educated man, for example, got more votes than a laborer—and to Churchill the Russian argument made sense. Whether he liked it or not, he acknowledged that the USSR was a truly great power. And he reminded the Americans that the potential Western majority among the proposed fifty-odd UN members was secure whether the USSR got six votes, or ten.

Outnumbered, FDR with some reluctance verbally agreed to three votes for the Soviet Union. But his staff hit the ceiling, mainly over fear of the political reaction at home. One of the real, if unadmitted, reasons for the secrecy clamp that suffocated the Yalta discussions was to free FDR's hands from American pressure or opinion during the negotiations.

Now, FDR was advised that nothing was more likely to foster a rebirth of isolationist sentiment in America than to grant three Assembly votes for the USSR, while the United States got only one. FDR then immediately complicated his original error: he dictated a letter to Stalin, reaffirming three Russian votes—he had given his word—but now reserving the right of the United States to an equal number.

On this note the secret voting clauses of the proposed UN were firmed and signed on February 7, 1945.

There was still one more problem to solve: the trusteeship clauses of the proposed Charter, which concerned territories not ready for, or not capable of, self-government. And here it was Winston Churchill, instead of Stalin, who breathed fire and truculence.

There were several trustee-lands remaining from the first war and the old League of Nations: areas of Africa, Palestine and Syria, and a number of remote Pacific islands. Many of these had been mandated to the British, and the British ruled them. Generally, the mandate lands were more of a burden than a benefit, and Churchill was not really concerned with turning these over to international control. But the trusteeship clauses of the new UN had been written in very broad terms by their American drafters, and they did reflect a certain anticolonial bias in general. Under them, any people who were ruled by an outside power could bring into question that rule before the United Nations, and have it debated and acted upon.

Churchill now stated that it seemed to him that any trusteeship clause, and particularly the one that Roosevelt had in mind, was simply a disguised means to apply the skids to the British Empire. Churchill was at heart a believer in British colonialism; he made his position clear: His Majesty's Government would accept no provision under which any outside nation or assembly of nations could bring into question the British presence, position, or actions, in Asia, Africa, or anywhere else in the world.

Edward Stettinius, a born conciliator, stepped smilingly into the breach. He said, diplomatically, that no one had the *British Empire* in mind, just the Pacific island mandates the League had given Japan, and that kind of thing. Along with Japan, Britain, South Africa, and Australia had been made mandate-ruling nations, usually of remote and barren areas.

Churchill was mollified. However, because of his opposition the final trusteeship clauses of the Charter were gutted. They did not apply to European colonialism. They covered enemy territories, old or existing League of Nations mandates, and such other lands as might *voluntarily* be submitted to international regulation. The UN, then, was not going to be able to liquidate the European colonial order directly. That had to come about in other, and in some cases bloodier, ways.

The business of Yalta was now finished, and FDR suggested to Stalin that the time had come to call a world conference. Stalin asked why. Roosevelt told him it was necessary to discuss the security proposals and to ratify the United Na-

51

COLLEGE OF THE SEQUOIAS
LIBRARY

tions Organization. But Stalin replied that there was really nothing to discuss. The ruling powers had already decided the issues.

Stalin's point was entirely valid. Dumbarton Oaks had proposed a big-power strong-arm system, which would both enforce peace and allow each big power to remain dominant and independent in its own sphere of interest. Yalta had cemented it. At neither conference had the opinion of the small powers been asked. Why throw what had been already decided up to debate?

But this kind of thought was unpalatable to the American staff. They were used to back-room deals and committee trades and all that, but the deals were always afterward ratified in an open meeting. FDR grew insistent that such a meeting be called.

And the Russians grew suspicious and uneasy. Stalin felt that FDR was up to something, perhaps a chance to wriggle out of the deal. Stalin had no intention of allowing Dumbarton Oaks and Yalta to be set aside, even if every nation in the world voted for this. Meanwhile, FDR's genuine sincerity for an open meeting showed both American honesty and American confusion toward great-power politics.

While FDR was putting great store in the coming open conference, it may not have occurred to him that the real mechanism, the prime movers, and the be-all and end-all of his cherished United Nations already sat here in Livadia Palace, proposing and disposing. At the heart of the UN lay national power, and all the national power in the world was represented in the Crimea. Neither one open conference, nor a thousand, could alter that fact. A great, perhaps the greatest, political asset of the North American mind was that it believed in principle, but it sometimes believed in principle so deeply that it confused principle with power. And this is exactly what Roosevelt and the American staff did.

It was finally agreed, after much argument, to call a meeting of the United Nations beginning April 25, 1945, at San Francisco.

FDR, now tired and strained, told Stalin he "hoped it would be possible for the earth to have peace for fifty years, if not for eternity." This last night there was no business, only toasts. FDR praised the Big Three as "one big, happy family." Churchill toasted future glories for the British Empire and the world. Stalin said merely, "The difficult time will come after the war. . . ."

Then there were toasts to victory, unity, and peace. But even at Yalta the toasts had a hollow ring. Bargains are for the future, never in remembrance of the past.

4.

Senator Vandenberg and the American People

THERE WAS for some years a myth that at Yalta Roosevelt sold out the world to Stalin. Against this nonsense, as a sort of backfire, was set a counter-myth that FDR acted as he did, acquiescing to many unpalatable things, because he had to trust Russian good intentions, and was betrayed. Neither myth followed the facts.

Returning from Yalta, the President called Congressional leaders from both parties to the White House. After extracting firm security pledges, he explained the Yalta agreements to Senator Tom Connally of Texas, ranking Republican on the Foreign Relations Committee, Arthur Vandenberg, and Republican Representative Eaton of Illinois.

"I got the best I could get," Roosevelt told them.

Connally and the two Republicans immediately and acidly disagreed. The whole Yalta business sat very sourly with them, and each said so. But none of these men, then or later, sat in Roosevelt's chair.

It was true that the President could have been a great deal more stubborn on a number of issues, above all the Polish question, the Oder-Neisse Line, and the *de facto* Soviet conquest of East Europe. The fundamental error of urging the USSR into the Pacific war could not yet be seen by anyone (and it would be largely offset, except for the running sore of the Korean question, by Dulles' adroit maneuvering at the Japanese peace conference of 1952), but the tacit acquiescence to the Soviet conquests, and the secret voting agreements, directly violated professed American principle.

Roosevelt had fought a rearguard action against Stalin,

and he had not won. But Roosevelt had his reasons, and not all of them lay in the hope he held for the coming United Nations.

One was that while he went to Yalta commanding the greatest concentration of military and economic power the world had yet seen, he still had a poor hand to play world poker against the Russians. There were severe restrictions on FDR's employment of power.

The American delegation arrived at Yalta fully aware that the war alliances were in corrosion, knowing the British and Soviets were almost at each other's throats over the Poles, and that American principles and policies were being trampled. But in its peculiar wisdom the Administration had done its best to make sure that nothing of this seeped through to the public. It had been U. S. policy to see or hear no evil concerning the Soviets during the war; this policy had produced a predictable effect on the well-meaning American people, and now it hung like a hideous skeleton in the Washington closet.

By 1945 the United States needed to enter a new power struggle against a major power, this time its former ally. The power struggle did not suddenly appear; it had been shaping up since at least 1943. But the Western public was completely unprepared or unconditioned for it.

Both Americans and British were sick of war and jubilant at approaching victory. Neither public, each armed with the ballot, had really accepted the purely political motivation of World War II; both had, in modern democratic fashion, turned it into a struggle of higher purpose. By 1945 both lived in a certain dream world where the Russian state was concerned. There are, after all, only certain minds in any age that can face the fact that the battle is never done, and that eternal vigilance is always the price of success. Most people want the five o'clock whistle to blow so they can go home.

The American public in large numbers had accepted the Russians as comrades-in-arms, which they had never been.

The Russians had fought their own war, for their own reasons, in their own way, and for their own ends, exactly as the Americans had fought theirs. The only thing each nation had in common was the same enemy.

Horrified by the image of Hitler, Americans persisted in thinking in legal terms: the good guys against the bad guys, sheriffs versus outlaws. Since the Russians were fighting the obvious outlaws, they had to be at least deputized. Refusing to accept the fact that war is normally an extension of politics, and that good or bad is never exclusively concentrated on one side or the other, Americans did not see that circumstances forced democratic Finland to fight on the German side, and totalitarian Russia to ally with England.

Though alliances between governments are, by their very nature, unsentimental, publics rarely accept the fact. Publics do not like the fact that evil is relative, varying from land to land, and that there are no good or bad guys in the world —only an enormous number of varied human populations, with a varying set of ultra-rational ambitions and dreams, some of which they are willing to die, or kill, for.

To have expected a powerful Russia—or for that matter, a powerful France—to be grateful or to follow any course other than one its leaders thought in their best interest, was naive. Americans had always pursued their own best interests as they saw them, from the Mexican War to the Kellogg Pact.

This naïveté, plus war weariness, tied FDR's hands. For Stalin's mind could have been changed *only by force or the threat of force,* and force was a commodity FDR was not only unwilling, but not empowered, to use. As he had told Stalin, he did not even think American public opinion would support the stationing of U. S. troops in Europe more than two years beyond the war. In 1945 this was an intelligent assumption. The troops, Congress, and the public were already clamoring for the boys to be brought home.

Stalin, on the other hand, could dispose. He could order

the Red Army into Poland, and keep it there twenty years. Roosevelt, for all the national power behind him, could only propose; he could do nothing, once the war ended, the American people would not support.

He could, of course, have gambled; he could have torpedoed the conference by standing on American principle. He could have directed Stalin to relinquish Eastern Europe or face an advancing Anglo-American army. This Churchill had already advocated. He might have made it stick—the USSR was devastated, and the last thing Stalin wanted was a new trial at arms. But he could not have done it without firm public backing at home.

And would the critics who later raged against his sell-out have consented in 1945 to the indefinite dispatch of troops to China and Manchuria, or to the immediate threat of retaliation against the Red Army in Europe, even before the Nazi capitulation? The answer, resoundingly, is no.

The time would come, of course, when all this seemed highly feasible. The time would come when former Wehrmacht generals sat in allied councils and plotted the defense of Western Europe. But in early 1945, with the charnel houses of Dachau and Belsen newly opened, as one commentator remarked, it was not bloody likely.

If Roosevelt made serious mistakes at Yalta, they were these: he trusted that through personal diplomacy he might ameliorate the Soviet stand, and he hoped that if the Russians could be brought into the United Nations Organization they might grow respectable. But the truth was that the historic direction of the Soviet national policy could no more be changed at a congenial kaffeeklatsch than Hitler's might have been, and the Russians could not be bribed with club memberships.

Because American goals at Yalta were general and Soviet goals were specific, the Russians took most of the tricks. The Americans had to settle for promises, while the Red Army swallowed provinces.

FDR came back from Yalta, certainly, deeply aware of the Western-Soviet split. There is an enormous amount of evidence that in the ensuing weeks he seriously considered changing his viewpoint of accommodation and abandoning his policy of securing Russian cooperation through appeasement. But he did not; time was running out for him.

Through no fault of his own, Roosevelt by now was a very sick man, and at the most crucial moments of World War II this caused a certain aimlessness, a vague drift, in U. S. policy, which was a source of concern to many statesmen. Generally speaking, however, there was a myopic tendency to concentrate upon the last guns of the battlefield and to ignore the mounting evidence that the historic game of power politics was still in play.

At Dumbarton Oaks and Yalta, Roosevelt had channeled the United States into a certain course. After April 12, 1945, that course could not be gracefully altered. Only FDR, with his immense prestige and the trust and affection of a majority of the American people, could have changed it, and Roosevelt was dead.

Yalta not only infuriated Congressional leaders, it also damaged the image of the coming San Francisco conference. The miasma of secrecy that surrounded the talks—the official communiqués never, for example, revealed the deals on representation and voting—turned out to have been a political mistake. The American public did not willingly accept this kind of secrecy, and within six weeks the *New York Herald Tribune* sniffed out the whole story. The matter of the American capitulation on three votes for Russia was now exposed.

At a press conference Secretary of State Stettinius was asked bluntly, why this pretense of separate republics in the Ukraine and White Russia? These states were no more independent "republics" than the states of New York or California. Was this pretense going to establish a Russian ploy or fiction by which Russia might take over Poland and Bulgaria as she had absorbed the Baltic states, and yet allow these conquered states to maintain a fictitious sovereignty in the UN, while Russia "voted" them?

The saddest part of the press conference was the fact that Stettinius obviously felt he could make no reasonable reply. Stettinius already realized that something like this was going to happen, even though it was not directly concerned with the matter of a vote for the Ukraine.

One by one, to the immense embarrassment of the Administration, the secret deals were made public or admitted: no anticolonial stand in the trusteeship clauses, three votes for Russia, three votes for the United States. Many Americans and even more citizens of small nations were appalled. Foreign Minister Evatt of Australia, the classic little man's little man, was enraged.

The little nations had swallowed Dumbarton Oaks because they had to; it was obvious that the world would have to be ordered by big powers. But they had been promised an equal say in the forum of the Assembly. Three votes for each of the monster powers, USSR and USA, and the fact that the British Commonwealth had a tight ethnic bloc of six, seemed to make a mockery out of equality in the Assembly, too.

This small-nation reaction caused the United States to drop its claim to three UN votes. But nothing could be done about the three already promised Russia. Stalin had FDR's word, and the USSR was indifferent to its image on the issue. The USSR would keep three.

Now, as the aura of Yalta spread over the coming conference, the American and Allied publics for the first time began to understand what Dumbarton Oaks had really proposed: not a brave new world, but a world political order based on the ideas and interests of the Big Four. Suddenly alerted, all the forces that had never understood what had been wrong with the old League of Nations were in full cry. This put the U. S. government on the defensive at a bad time. The professionals like Mr. Welles knew that principle had to be blended with power in order to make each fruitful; the State Department had not been starry-eyed, but neither had they been fools. But large segments of the public did not agree.

In retrospect, the U. S. government's main fault—and this, seemingly, is endemic in a democratic country—was not what it had done but its failure to explain and propagandize the facts of life to its own citizens. Too many people had already decided that a war that had been fought for survival, nothing more, must in some miraculous way bring both human justice and insure permanent peace—as if war itself could ever end war.

Roosevelt, in his person, had combined the best of American idealism and pragmatism, and if he had lived out his fourth term, he still might have brought some balance between the "liberal" and "conservative" views of international affairs.

But the more idealistic or liberal body of American thought immediately seized upon the UN as a vehicle of insuring a world without war. The more liberal type of American mind was fascinated by words and charters, and put great faith in written law, whether it was backed by force or not. The more empirical, or conservative, opinion continued to believe that the war had merely changed boundaries and power balances, and that power would still be power, and that no mere Charter could really alter the facts of international life.

The groups split, and split badly, and the split would continue for more than two decades. The liberals would insist that Dumbarton Oaks be liberalized, but once it was, the empiricists pragmatically assured that the new international body would never assume the importance Roosevelt and its planners had intended. Out of this split, which ran into government circles and public both, came the wonderful hypocrisy by which American statesmen continually paid lip service to the UN and all its works, but artfully ignored it as unworkable during crucial encounters.

It seems likely the Russians never understood this inherent

dichotomy in the American soul. They were genuinely irritated when the United States agreed to a world in which power ruled in 1944, then reneged and wanted some kind of parliamentary world democracy in 1945. This did seem double dealing, but it was hard for Russians to grasp the difficulties of the State Department, which, unlike the Soviet Foreign Office, could not wheel and deal with no regard to public consumption.

Stalin had agreed to the San Francisco meeting only on the grounds that it be window-dressing for the power plays at Yalta. Stalin understood this sort of thing, actually; the Soviets employed the same principle in their "treason trials." But when Washington, under severe pressure and recriminations both from allies abroad and people at home, began to make noises about a truly free and open conference, Stalin's consternation was unfeigned.

To expect any Russian regime, whether Bolshevist, Czarist, Stalinist, or Revisionist, to transact serious business in American town-hall style was of course not optimism, but idiocy. Yet this problem was to be lasting, because Americans found it politically and morally impossible to hold secret conferences in peacetime, from Geneva disarmament talks to discussions on Cuba's future.

Faced with Washington's threat to throw the conference open for any discussion, Stalin countered by sending a delegation of obvious second-raters to San Francisco. This would convince the United States, or so Stalin hoped, that the conference had no life of its own. But all it convinced Washington to do was to beg that Molotov, the Foreign Minister, be sent too. Molotov was finally dispatched, along with U. S. Ambassador Andrei Gromyko, U. S. Secretary Semyon Tsarapkin, Arkady Sobolev, British deskman K. V. Novikov, and an admiral and a general, both "experts" on international law. Some of these men later became famous or powerful, but in 1945 they were young and unknown.

Because of this Russian diffidence, President Truman was

61

advised not to go to San Francisco to open the conference, and he agreed.

Other events also depressed the coming meeting. One was the belated crowding of cynical and unsavory neutral nations under the UN banner, such as fascistic Argentina. President Edelmiro Farrell, anti-American, anti-British, and a great admirer of German efficiency, announced that Argentina had taken the "grave" step of declaring war on the Axis in April, 1945. This made Argentina immediately eligible for admission to the UN, and at the same time relieved Colonel Juan Perón, the strongman behind Farrell's throne, of North and Latin American pressures for hemispheric "unity." Given Hobson's choice, Argentina was choosing the United States over Soviet Russia in the brave new world.

There was a great clamor for Argentina to be taken in, especially from the other Hispanic-American nations, none of which had supported the war in any serious fashion. Washington was sympathetic. For one thing, Washington thought it could count on the Argentinian vote; and secondly, too many Americans still placed store in the chimera of Western Hemispheric diplomatic solidarity.

This decision of the United States to support Argentina's crowding aboard the UN bandwagon offended many small countries, angered the Soviets, and, of much greater significance, presaged a highly dangerous deviation from the original concepts of Dumbarton Oaks. What had been considered a defensive alliance pure and simple was now taking on intimations of universality. In order for the United Nations alliance to prevent another major war, there was no need for every nation to be enrolled. All the UN required was a monopoly of power. In fact, the more universal the UN became, as Churchill feared, the less effective it could be. The monopoly of power had to retain a unity of viewpoint as well as freedom of action.

Many Americans, trying to compare the world outside with

the domestic scene within the United States, which was like comparing ostriches with whales, believed in universality for the UN. What they failed to comprehend was that divergent views inside America were really not very divergent. Republicans and Democrats staged terrible squalls over which plays to call in the running of the nation. But both played the same game, on the same field, for the same goal posts, and by the same rules. The outside world was an entirely different proposition. Having Europeans, Asians, Hispanic-Americans, and Africans lumped together in one world parliamentary body was not like having Democrats and Republicans on each side of the aisle. Such a mixed bag not only played by different rules, they even disagreed on the game itself.

But while Dumbarton Oaks had deliberately kept all real power in the hands of the proposed Security Council of great powers, American psychology and image-consciousness in 1945 tended toward diluting this power. Even while American policymakers realized that the United States would find it difficult to act in its own interests in the face of a loud and emotional uproar from powerless but vocal small nations, they could not restrain themselves from letting a situation develop in which the small powers would be both prominent and vocal.

Another depressant on the conference was the fact that the Russo-British feud over the new Polish government seemed to be reaching a point of no return. The U. S. government itself was trying to stay out of this quarrel.

With FDR's hand gone, and Truman still largely unbriefed as to what had happened while he was Vice-President, Washington a few days before April 25 was drifting toward the conference flapped, confused, and aimless.

The fact that the United States emerged from post-Yalta confusion, and in a world already again falling apart went to San Francisco with reasoned hope and optimism to give American principle another chance, was due in tremendous part to Senator Arthur Vandenberg.

The existence and course of American Midwestern isolationism in the earlier decades of the twentieth century has been well publicized. A certain portion of this feeling rested on factors of history and geography. There were large elements, like the German and Irish immigrants, who hated the British hegemony of the nineteenth century, and who joined with other native groups and classes in an instinctive distrust of the more suave, moneyed and Angophilic internationalism of the East. But the mainstream of American isolationism in the century had a solid basis in another factor not so well understood: Midwestern idealism. Many of the attitudes of 1939–1941 were forged in the searing disillusionment of 1919.

Arthur Hendrick Vanderberg was born in the year 1884, in the predominately Dutch town of Grand Rapids, Michigan. His grandfather was one of the men who nominated Abraham Lincoln. His father, a harness maker, had flirted with the conservative Democrats, and had been wiped out in the Cleveland panic of 1893. He told young Arthur: "Always be a Republican." And through many changing allegiances and attitudes, Arthur Vandenberg never swerved from that party.

He had a flair for oratory, and his high-school classmates called him "Senator." After a single year of college, he went to work as a reporter on the Grand Rapids *Herald*. With a solid, Dutch, middle-class philosophy, Vandenberg stated, "I'm here to stay," and he was. In 1907 he became editor, and eventually owned *Herald* stock worth half a million.

He grew into a heavy, round-faced man with horn-rimmed glasses, a thick cigar always in his teeth. As editor, he paid little attention to the circulation, news, or features of the *Herald;* smoking furiously, he wrote editorials. It was reported that he often threw his butts behind the ancient radiator in his office—but the editorials he turned out brought him national prominence. In 1920 he was already listed in *Who's Who in America* as an opinion-maker.

For Vandenberg had one uncanny genius—what he thought, and said, was almost invariably in the mainstream of the American thought of his times. He did not make opinion; he rarely followed it. He reflected it and crystallized it, by some process of his own. From the chair of the *Herald* he boomed Prohibition, plugged capital punishment, raged against *Elmer Gantry,* and thundered against Bolshevism. A generation possessing only the sophistication of hindsight should remember that the vast majority of Vandenberg's good-hearted countrymen agreed.

He approached Wilson's war in 1917 with all the fervor and evangelism of the American spirit, with a dictionary on his left and a King James Bible at his right. Of Wilson, he said: "The greatest revival the world has ever known since Christ came upon this earth." He received awards for selling Liberty Bonds, and a commendation from the White House.

But on March 4, 1920, Arthur Vandenberg expressed his bitterness, and the bitterness of the mainstream of America, toward Woodrow Wilson:

"He has toppled from his pedestal. His European interference has won him European hatreds and his American autocracy has cost him American friends. His erstwhile foreign wards stand appalled at his posture. . . . He must always be gratefully remembered for his magnificent spiritual leadership. He must also be remembered as the man who all but lost the peace."

American foreign policy, and isolationism, must always be evaluated in the light of the false hopes stirred up in 1917, and the disillusionment that sprang from them.

It was inevitable that Vandenberg, so deeply interested in public affairs, went into politics. He got to know Warren Harding, even while he was writing a bit of fiction and three books on Alexander Hamilton, and while he was continuing to reflect the American attitudes of the day: "Nationalism—not internationalism—is the indispensable bulwark of American independence."

In 1928 he went to the U. S. Senate, and after reelection

in 1934—a very Democratic year—he never had much trouble at the polls.

He was always a Republican, but he voted for Social Security, the SEC, and price control. He opposed TVA. But with the majority opinion he protested Supreme Court packing, and he—not the New Deal—was the father of the Federal Deposit Insurance Corporation.

In 1939 the remembrance of 1917 was still strong. He told his constituency: "I do not think this is our war, and I think we should stay all the way out."

He associated with men named Wheeler, Bennett Clark, Nye, and Fish. But the mind of Arthur Vandenberg never set or fossilized. It probed, and flowed irresistibly where the majority of decent American opinion flowed. Before Pearl Harbor he had doubts about neutrality, departing from the likes of Ham Fish.

After Pearl Harbor, the change was not sudden. The latent idealism, wanting a better world, had always been there. It was, as he said, the German robot bomb that turned him into a "fanatic" on responsible internationalism, when the first V-2's flew, Vandenberg recognized them as birds of ill omen for American safety.

While the Dumbarton Oaks talks had been limited to diplomatic staffs, Vandenberg had become the central Congressional figure in the earlier briefing discussions. Vandenberg approached the idea of a new world order in much the same way he had approached the New Deal—with great dignity, firm opinions, but with an innate sensitivity to the need for accommodation.

In his diary, on November 24, 1944 he recorded:

"My chief complaint . . . has been that we . . . through the [new] League guarantee the ultimate status quo in the post-war world even though the status quo shall prove to be wholly unjust (as seems clearly threatened by a new dismemberment of Poland). I have been constantly told by students of the [Dumbarton Oaks] Agreement that these

66

peace table decisions would not be within the jurisdiction of the new League. I put the question squarely to Stettinius and Pasvolsky today. After much discussion, they finally answered (to my amazement) that if any state is aggrieved as a result of the peace decisions, and it causes friction and unrest . . . the new League can take jurisdiction."

Soured, like almost every thinking American of his time, by the Franco-British insistence upon the status quo after Versailles, Vandenberg believed that no peace-keeping functions in the new world should be wedded to the peace treaty. It had already occurred to him that the peace treaties with "our enemies" might have to be revised to fit a changing world situation. To Vandenberg it appeared that the job was no longer suppressing German, Japanese, and Italian militarism; that was being destroyed on the battlefield, and needed no emphasis. He felt something very few others could see: that the nature of 1945 would be as ephemeral as 1919, and no peace treaty, or new league, could chart the course of the world for twenty years.

But in 1944 it was not chic in government circles to talk candidly of certain disturbing symptoms: the USSR's selfish intentions for Eastern Europe; Egypt's sullen determination to repudiate all its treaty agreements with the United Kingdom, and to throw the rascals out; the French government's brooding fear of reduced French grandeur.

What Vandenberg wanted above all were two things, not legal, but political and moral: clauses allowing for the review of unjust treaties, not only for the Axis, but for every power; and something written in the Charter to foster the observance of human rights and the fundamental freedoms as he saw them. None of this had come from Dumbarton Oaks.

This was the faith, as Arthur Vandenberg would try to keep it.

On January 10, 1954, Vandenberg, feeling that U. S. policy was drifting, and that the United States was rushing to the end of the war and the end of an era in a vacuum of its own ideals, made a speech that perhaps changed history. He stood up in the Senate and told his colleagues it was time the nation quit talking about collective security and a brave new world, and did something about it.

He said: "I do not know why we must be the only silent partner in this Grand Alliance. There seems to be no fear of disunity, no hesitation in Moscow, when Moscow wants to assert unilateral war and peace aims which collide with ours. There seems to be no fear of disunity, no hesitation in London, when Mr. Churchill proceeds upon his unilateral way to make decisions often repugnant to our ideas and ideals. . . .

"Honest candor compels us to reassert in high places our American faith in the Atlantic Charter. These basic pledges cannot now be dismissed as a mere nautical nimbus. They march with our armies. They sail with our fleets . . . they sleep with our martyred dead. The first requisite of honest candor . . . is to relight this torch.

"I am not prepared to guarantee permanently the spoils of an unjust peace. It will not work. I am prepared by effective international cooperation to do our full part in charting happier and safer tomorrows."

A decade, or even one year afterward, not many Americans would understand the crucial importance of this speech, or grasp its impact. Even Vandenberg, at the rostrum, was surprised at the immediate favorable reaction. He brought the issue of American participation and power in the postwar world into the open—something the Administration had been half afraid to do, partly for fear of the reaction of powerful men like Vandenberg.

Vandenberg was the first influential politician to state flatly that both the destiny and the foreign policy of the United States had, and ought to have, changed, and that both political parties were agreed on it—even if what they agreed on was still somewhat inchoate. As Arthur Vandenberg thundered, the mantle of Henry Cabot Lodge continued to gather dust in the Senate Cloakroom. Vandenberg had crossed the aisle, and America, hardly understanding the fact, had crossed its Rubicon.

FDR took fifty copies of that speech to Yalta, in a hopeless attempt to prove something to Stalin. And he made Vandenberg a delegate to whatever conference the United States would call.

Vandenberg had studied Dumbarton Oaks long and hard. Now, that study paid off. He became the balance of power in the Senate, which was suddenly the most important parliament in the world. It was the body which would ratify or repudiate Franklin Roosevelt's law of nations. And now, Vandenberg wanted above all to infuse into the clear, bureaucratic, oil-smelling clauses of Dumbarton Oaks a light of justice, perhaps even some kind of Bill of Rights, for the world.

With Vanderberg, six other Americans were appointed to go to San Francisco: Edward Stettinius, Secretary of State; Tom Connally and Sol Bloom, chairmen respectively of the Senate and House Foreign Affairs Committees, and Congressman Charles A. Eaton of Illinois. Virginia Gildersleeve, head of Barnard College, was added to represent the woman's viewpoint; and Commander Harold Stassen, the balding boy wonder of Minnesota politics, was brought in, still in uniform, because of his recognized and vocal One-Worldism. There was also a top-drawer level of advisers: John Foster Dulles, who was actually to be the number two man at the conference, under Vandenberg; Hamilton Fish Armstrong, who might have been Secretary of State had Dewey won the Presidency in 1944; Nelson Rockefeller from the Latin-American desk; and Dr. Leo Pasvolsky, the State Department technical expert on the language of Dumbarton Oaks.

The day the delegation left Washington for San Francisco, all Senate eyes were on Vandenberg. He got up and made a simple speech, without notes.

"I have no illusions that the . . . Conference can chart the millennium. Please do not expect it of us . . . but I have faith that we may perfect this charter of peace and justice so that reasonable men of good will shall find in it so much good and so much emancipation for human hopes that all lesser doubts and disagreements may be resolved in its favor."

The Senate cheered and adjourned. Arthur Vandenberg and the American people, in a world where power still ruled, would at least try to keep faith with their vision.

5.

The Fogs of San Francisco

WHEN, AT 4:30 on the steamy afternoon of April 25, 1945, Edward R. Stettinius rapped a gavel on the stage of the San Francisco Opera House, and said, strongly: "The first plenary session of the United Nations Conference on World Organization is hereby convened," it was a moment filled with a certain grandeur.

The stage of the Opera House was set: flags of forty-six sovereign nations hung in brilliant floodlighting against a blue backdrop. Four great columns, representing the Four Freedoms, rose from the floor. Around the stage in plush red seats sat delegates from fifty countries, representing the greatest military and economic alliance the world had ever seen.

The stage of the world was set, too. The most destructive war in human history was ending in fire and blood. All world order had collapsed during the past five years, and it was waiting to be restored.

This hour was a culmination of many years, many plans, many events. It could, in its bloodless way, be an hour as decisive as Marathon, a day as long-lasting as Waterloo. There was, perhaps, too much hope, for all was not well in the midst of this glittering ceremony.

The golden voice of Franklin Roosevelt, who had lived for this hour, was gone. FDR was dead, carried through Washington to the sound of drums, buried at his ancestral home at Hyde Park. Roosevelt might have given a meaning to the hour beyond the words and oil of politics, but there was no one, and nothing, now to take his place.

71

Already corrosion ran deep. No great man, no heads of government, no major chiefs of state, came to San Francisco. There were instead two hundred seventy-nine delegates and the foreign ministers of the Big Three, already overshadowed by the realities of global power resting on their shoulders. It was not men, but realities and corrosion that would dominate San Francisco.

There was, in the stillness of the Third Reich's defeat, no call to glory that men could heed. There was no theme like the Legitimacy agreed upon at Vienna, no watchword like the Democracy Wilson took to Paris.

The world had already been made on the battlefield. Roosevelt might have wrought changes, but these men could not. There was forty-four-year-old Ed Stettinius, the steel man who succeeded Hull, his dark eyebrows contrasting demonically with his pure-white hair; Anthony Eden of Britain, Tory politician, gray but still handsome enough to make women look again; Vyacheslav Molotov, the Hammer, Old Bolshevik, eyeglasses glinting, iron-faced but usually affable in public. These men each had orders to ratify, not create.

The men from lesser powers were aware of the realities, too, but in different ways: Bidault of France, hatless, submerged by the failure of France on the field of 1940; Canada's Mackenzie King, umbrella balanced between his knees like his nation's policy was balanced between America and the world; florid Evatt of Australia, his workingman's identification with the underdog outraged by the eternal unfairness of life; Romulo of the Philippines, brown and articulate for the weak and emerging.

Around these men sat a horde of Hispanic Americans, Asians, and Arabs, each nursing his own dreams, his own resentments. These, and their governments, were most interested in discovering where power lay, then accommodating to it, with grace or without it, as became them.

To begin, Harry Truman's voice was piped in from Washington. He wished the conference well. Then Stettinius spoke, and Eden and Molotov. Eden spoke best, though nothing anyone said would survive. The words, the ceremony, were merely rites as old as man, almost without meaning.

After the opening ceremonies, the crowd drifted out to waiting cars, taxis, Army sedans, and gray Navy buses. The three princes of the blood of Saudi Arabia, gaudy in flowing robes, climbed into limousines sent by a thoughtful Standard Oil. Industrialist Henry Kaiser of the United States walked out with Senator Vandenberg, uncomfortable in a new Homburg. Behind them came Commander and Mrs. Harold Stassen, she with a pink corsage. The sullen sky glowed redly against the general staff tabs on Jan Christian Smuts' drab tunic.

Six hundred San Franciscans, mostly women, had watched them arrive. No one saw them depart. There was a war on; the world might be made or unmade, but San Franciscans had better things to do.

Soon the parties would begin.

At the St. Francis Hotel, one of the U. S. Navy buses skidded to a screeching stop as its redheaded WAVE driver stamped the brakes. "St. Francis Hotel! Brazilians, French, Russians, and so forthski! And Gawd bless you all!" The blue-suited Russians smiled. Two of the elegant Latins shuddered.

The world was hardly going to be remade at San Francisco. But if men were to conquer despair, they had to try.

The Conference was a mixed bag of power politics, muddy thinking, official hypocrisy, high idealism, keen good sense, legalistic nonsense, compromise, and false hopes. Men could take from it almost anything they wanted.

The delegates varied as widely as the countries sending them. Many represented the genuine power structures of their society and its dominant thought. Many did not. Too many had been chosen simply because they had been connected in some way with the old League of Nations. These

73

men and women carried over into the UN worm-eaten concepts like the "harmony of interests" or a hatred of power politics.

However, the unspoken rivalries, the petty legalisms, the interminable quibbling in committee rooms for the next sixty days did not come from mere human foibles. These were symptoms of real problems.

There were three genuine obstacles to world order at San Francisco. They affected everything that did or did not happen. One was a rising ethnic consciousness; men were more aware of their differences than ever, and the idea of ethnic sovereignty was coming into vogue. Another was ideological separatism, with its resulting clashes. The Communist Russian-Western hostility was indicative of something deeper than mere national rivalry. Finally, no nation or its people, big or small, was prepared voluntarily to surrender sovereignty to *any* international organization. The big nations got all the blame for this attitude. But the small nations felt just as deeply about their independence, and were determined as far as they could to make any Security Council control unworkable.

Dumbarton Oaks envisioned that the Big Four would be required to surrender no sovereignty to each other or the Organization, but that all other powers would have to surrender freedom of action to them when they were unanimous in demanding it. This would, of course, continue the security of the Big Four, which was precisely what the framers had in mind. In the light of the events and the atmosphere of 1943–1944, this did not seem unreasonable; what was good for the Big Four then was in a very real sense good for the whole world.

But by 1945 things had already changed. The United Nations no longer had anything to organize *against*. The destruction of its Axis enemies and the universality of its membership meant that any future danger had to come from within the organization itself. Almost all human societies

74

or organisms are held together partly by outside pressures, or fear of a real or fancied danger. The U. S. Constitution was eased on its way by thirteen weak colonies' fear of European colonial power. The Big Three alliance in World War II could never forget Hitler. But the UN now had nothing whatever to fear except itself. This made cohesion and agreement virtually impossible.

The seven U. S. delegates themselves varied widely in background and political creed, but as a group they were much more closely knit than most other groups. The French, as usual, were split across the political spectrum from Left to Right. The British delegation was hopelessly divided between Old Leaguers and empiricists like Eden; people who wanted to abolish world realities and those who wanted to use them to their own interests.

Because the U. S. Administration was Democratic, and because official Washington was still fearful—despite Vandenberg —of a Republican uprising similar to the one Lodge waged against the League of Nations, the delegation was heavily slated with Republicans, namely, Eaton, Stassen, and Vandenberg. The same flavor extended deeply into the second echelon, or actual working areas, with Foster Dulles and Ham Armstrong.

According to protocol, Stettinius was chief of the delegation, and Tom Connally outranked Vandenberg in both Committee and Senate. But in actual practice, it was agreed that Vandenberg and Dulles were to be number one and two, respectively, at San Francisco. These two were not technical experts, like Dr. Pasvolsky, but no one else on the delegation had the same powers of mind, or had done half so much homework. And Stettinius and Connally realized that Vandenberg was the real balance or power in the Senate.

When they had left Washington, President Truman had told Stettinius and Vandenberg to run their own show at San Francisco—they did not have to check with Washington to make decisions or speak in the name of the United States. And actually,

Vandenberg, Dulles, Stettinius, and Truman were all agreed on four major planks, several of which already went beyond the wording of Dumbarton Oaks.

These were: (1) retention of the American veto; (2) recognition of sovereign equality among nations; (3) justice, with special regard to Eastern Europe; (4) specific machinery, beyond Dumbarton Oaks, for the peaceful alteration of a changing status quo.

In these aims could be seen the heart and mind of Vandenberg and Dulles. Vandenberg's—and for that matter, the American people's—attitude had not changed basically from 1918. The goal was a decent order, in which all nations and peoples could pursue their own ends without fear from abroad, free from aggression or the pressures of power politics. The difference between 1918 and 1945 was that Americans now understood that the machinery of the League was imperfect, and the decent order, for all its idealism, still had to rest upon some kind of world power. That power was embodied in the big nations; the problem was to bind the big nations to the goal of decent order.

As the pragmatists of the Big Three had put the framework of the UN together at Dumbarton Oaks, it was not really a world organization, for it excluded many nations. It was never intended as a superstate; the Dumbarton Oaks UN possessed no sovereignty in itself, nor was it a legal organism, with a recognized legal life. It had been a careful, and not very daring, plan to avoid or at least postpone the next war by a continuation of the Grand Alliance, and it was definitely an attempt to perpetuate the power balance that would exist at the war's end.

This was not enough for Arthur Vandenberg or Foster Dulles. Dumbarton Oaks, for obvious practical reasons, had avoided all mention of the Atlantic Charter or political freedom; and both men were eager to write this concept into U. S. foreign policy. The notion, significantly, had already achieved great popularity both at home and abroad.

Now, Vandenberg and Dulles had to face two ways. They were saddled with Dumbarton Oaks and the Yalta formulas; the United States had pledged its word. But they were determined to do as much as possible to make the UN a forum for justice, in the old, bold—if sometimes irresponsible—American tradition. Dumbarton Oaks had pumped oil into the gears; Vandenberg and Dulles wanted to add life's blood.

Significantly, though lawyers dominated American government, legal minds were not predominant at San Francisco. Vandenberg had no faintest interest in international law or legal pitfalls. Dulles, though he was the nation's highest paid corporation lawyer, had said he was deliberately relegating the ideas and concepts of law to the sidelines; he saw no "legal" or judicial solution to the world's problems. Haunted by Versailles and the League's failure, he saw the real problems of the coming era as political, and the real function of the United Nations Organization as facilitating peaceful change.

Both he and Dr. Pasvolsky, the round-faced, bespectacled language expert, agreed privately that there should be no attempt to write new international law. The rule of law could not apply abroad; the first thing a lawyer learns, or ought to learn, is that there can be no law without government. And the UN was not conceived as, nor would it ever be, a world government.

The UN, in Dulles' view, was to be a political mechanism to help carry out American national aims. And American national aims, coming from a society without foreign ambitions, were to insure peace and justice, and reasonable adjustments of the status quo, which, in Dulles' mind at least, included not only the Soviet but the French and British world empires.

The distortions—the legal terminology and world government connotations—that crept in later were never Dulles' fault. But while Dulles could put aside legality in the interests of justice, he could not put aside morality as he saw it

77

in the pursuit of order. Nor could, hopefully, the American nation.

Stettinius' suite at the Fairmont Hotel, loaned to him by Mrs. James Flood of the Comstock millions, was soon buzzing with midnight strategy. Blue cigar smoke obscured the magnificent view of San Francisco Bay. The four bedrooms were littered with flung-down coats and jackets. This was an American conference called on American soil; America was the greatest power on earth; and Stettinius' delegation never forgot this. Here Stettinius straightened out his strategy with Vandenberg, who chewed denicotinized cigars.

Tom Connally, both a bit concerned about his Texas constituency—eventually, his Chairmanship of the Foreign Relations Committee would bring him to ruin and bitter retirement in Washington—and consciously in over his head, voluntarily took a back seat. Harold Stassen was too busy answering his fan mail—fifteen hundred letters a day, for in the public eye he was the glamor figure of the conference—and dealing with local Republican organizations to take a hand. Congressman Eaton, a good and solid nineteenth-century liberal of the kind called "conservative" in the United States, primarily disliked Bolshevism and kept saying so as his addition. Dean Gildersleeve had brought kind intentions. Congressman Sol Bloom, as *Time* magazine put it, was also present.

Pasvolsky and Ham Armstrong pored over the fine print, muttering and rewriting. Archibald MacLeish, who was reported as vague on Bolshevism but liked Russians personally, presided over a horde of restless intellectuals on the U. S. staff who wanted to influence the fate of the world but argued about how to do it. Nelson Rockefeller, in charge of the Latin-American desk of the State Department, began to resemble a scoutmaster trying to get his chattering troop to march in step. Handsome Alger Hiss, brilliant young career officer of whom the world would hear later, kept the mountainous conference machinery running on schedule. He was International Secretary General.

Ed Stettinius, the figurehead around whom the conference inevitably revolved, was a man of splendid character and seriousness of purpose, but of small intellectuality or political sense. He was dwarfed by Vandenberg and Dulles, but intelligent enough to be glad he had them along. Stettinius' real job was to act as front man, and this he did splendidly, as he had done all his life.

He was friendly, a first-name caller to the frostiest diplomats. He chewed gum and smoked cigarettes in conference. He knew better than to try to conceive, but he had a real genius for presiding and getting men to agree. At the University of Virginia he had earned only six credits of a needed sixty in four years; he never graduated. He had made grades of 54 and 57 in the two courses in Government he had endured. After leaving college, he had begun in the stockroom of General Motors at forty-four cents an hour in 1924. Seven years later he was vice-president in charge of public relations. He was not quite the poor boy made good. His father had been of the House of Morgan, and president of Diamond Match.

Myron Taylor, the head of U. S. Steel, met Stettinius and recognized his genius in certain fields. Taylor, who was later FDR's man at the Vatican, also understood the coming importance of fostering the right image in the American mind where American business was concerned. Stettinius projected a very good image indeed; men instinctively liked him. Taylor was able to get him away from General Motors, and placed him on the Board of U. S. Steel. Here, at the age of thirty seven, he became Chairman at a salary of $100,000 per year.

He presided over the Board, and his handsome, tanned features with the pure-white widow's peak charmed. Meanwhile, Ben Fairless, an entirely different breed of industrial genius who was not so likable but got things done, made U. S. Steel blow and go.

It was entirely natural that Stettinius became one of the

79

so-called "tame capitalists" who made up FDR's Business Advisory Council. He was recommended by Harry Hopkins. And Stettinius, who was no intellectual but anything but a fool, saw early that the New Deal was not really a revolution; it only looked like one. The New Deal's roots might lie deep in Western Populism, and some of its measures were certainly a continuation of Wilson's search for middle-class justice, but Stettinius also sensed that the reforms were also an extention of Theodore Roosevelt's efforts to control a rapidly changing industrial machine. He felt he, or any other alert businessman, could not only survive but even prosper with them. And he did.

Harry Hopkins was also responsible for getting Stettinius into government when the war began. He had a series of jobs, including running the Office of Price Administration. Stettinius, however, had small talent for administration or management. He only found himself when he entered the State Department as Undersecretary of State for Cordell Hull. A great many people in the Department felt that the professional, Sumner Welles, should have got this post. But Stettinius was a born conciliator; he could make any meeting run smoothly; he was not intellectual, and therefore reluctant to intrude his own ideas. Under his guidance Dumbarton Oaks went well, and when Cordell Hull retired in late 1944, Stettinius moved up. He still did not try to intrude his own ideas on Roosevelt, who continued, as with Hull, to act as his own Secretary of State.

Stettinius told his associates privately that it had required a certain bravery for him to fly to San Francisco. He was supposed to be running the show, but he did not have any personal, burning ideas to put across. It was a foregone conclusion that some kind of charter would come from San Francisco, of course, but the actual shape of that charter was not decided until Hull retired and FDR died. By leaving Ed Stettinius in charge, they assured that the United Nations Charter would reflect much more of Vandenberg and Dulles' moralistic thought than the original pragmatism of the faceless men who had worked for Sumner Welles.

There were 282 delegates from fifty nations, with a few more waiting in the wings. The Argentines had not yet been invited, and the Poles could not be seated until the West made up its mind which government was the real Republic of Poland. The International Secretariat, recruited mostly in the United States, numbered 1,058. The newsmen, continuing a wartime inflation that was not to end, outnumbered everybody else. There were 2,636 of them. To support this horde, the U. S. armed forces lent 2,262 personnel, who were assisted by 800 Women's Volunteers, 400 Red Cross workers, and 800 Boy Scouts.

Between all these groups, supporters and supported, there began a daily outpouring of half a million sheets of paper, 78 tons in all. A favorite joke was that a "middle power" was a national delegation with access to a mimeograph machine.

The cost of all this came to two million 1945 dollars, which the United States as host paid in full.

It took only a few days of meetings in this open discussion the United States had called to show that San Francisco would never stamp an age in the manner Vienna had done. The San Francisco shag would never replace the 1815 Viennese waltz.

If the world of 1945 was more tightly drawn than that of 1815, it was also immensely more various. The statesmen who gathered at Vienna came from the same class of society, born into a Europe where that class differed little from the Shannon to the Volga. This is not to say that Castlereagh and Metternich, Talleyrand and Alexander, were all the same. They were not. But they came from a basic civilization that still had a vital unity, and from governments universally willing to oil the wheels of justice with expediency. They could talk the same language on the dance floor and in the committee room, and the tongue was French. Since France, in 1815,

81

was the defeated enemy, this was much as if the communication a hundred and thirty years later in San Francisco had been German. The fact that statesmen in 1815 still talked in French told much about the post-Napoleonic world, and its ordering.

Since 1815, however, the world had changed. In 1945 each delegate suffered in varying degree from the great disease of the century: acute national consciousness. It was impossible, in this present world, to coin a watchword or concept acceptable from China to Peru, or from Riyadh to Moscow. Everybody wanted peace and security, or so they said. But there was no formula for achieving them that all nations could or would recognize as valid. The men of 1945 not only spoke different languages, they did not even apply the same meaning to common words. With a variant history, ethical sense, morality, and polity, American and Russian negotiators could not even agree on the meaning of a word like "democracy."

It was bad enough that the great powers bent on ordering the globe were so different. But now, an enormous number of Hispanic and non-Western societies that had not counted in the colonial order at Vienna had to be counted, too. The only thing West and non-West really had in common by the middle of the century was the patina of Western technology; oil drums, machine guns, and typewriters, wherever made, were recognizably similar. But artifacts, as always, bridged the cultural gap faster than thought or custom. Aircraft had brought the continents closer only in military and strategic terms—which some men failed to understand.

The amazing thing was that anything at all, even words on paper, was achieved at San Francisco. There was, as Vandenberg put it, "quite a fight." And while it was not permanent peace or genuine world order, something did emerge.

Dumbarton Oaks was changed. And these changes, as time would prove, ironically became the nexus of the United Nations, for the assumptions of Dumbarton Oaks, brilliant as they seemed in 1944, were hopeless from the start. They were flawed because even had the USSR and the United States found agreement, the United States, half empirical but always half idealistic, could not have accepted and promoted big-power rule. Neither could it have maintained the hands-off attitude of the big powers at Vienna, which had dealt serious blows to democracy, self-determination, and mass sovereignty. Dumbarton Oaks envisioned great-power cooperation—but it also envisioned that any great power could behave as it pleased in its own sphere.

It was very plain at Dumbarton Oaks that Stalin had no intention of interfering in U. S. gambits in Cuba or Mexico; the British Empire would be free to control the Middle East; and also, if the USSR decided to sterilize the Poles, it was their business. The United States, as Vandenberg and Dulles saw, could not live happily in that kind of world.

It was not the small nations, clamoring for attention and changes to Dumbarton Oaks, that forced the changes. It was Vandenberg. He was soon regarded as the small-powers' champion. But Vandenberg could not change the framework of Dumbarton Oaks, nor did he want to. The small powers would not get all they wanted, because as Vandenberg told them, "true collective security, or the guarantee of sovereignty for every people are simply not in the cards."

The best Vandenberg could give them was a Charter, and a forum for justice, and the promise of a certain amount of cultural and educational cooperation.

6.

A Charter Is Born

A DUTCHMAN, of the race that builds dykes from both dreams and dirt, summed up what was happening at San Francisco as well as any. Eelco van Kleffens, the Netherlands Foreign Minister, said: "The world expects too much from San Francisco. Dumbarton Oaks meant only that the great powers would go only the smallest way in the direction of cooperation.

"We will go as far as we can go here. Later, we will try to go farther. We have no choice but to support whatever degree of world organization, no matter how small, the great nations will permit. In spite of all the bitter, tragic lessons, the great powers prefer to rely on their own strengths rather than upon world government. . . ."

While Great Britain, weakest of the powers, genuinely liked the idea of collective security, and might have surrendered some sovereignty toward it, neither the United States nor the USSR could move an inch in that direction. The U. S. government, one eye on the Senate, the other on the people, had never dared. Neither the Senate nor the people had any idea of scrapping the Army and the Navy and putting everything to a vote. That also was never in the cards. The United States wanted a United Nations partly to assist its own security, partly to foster its own notions of justice, in which men like Vandenberg and Foster Dulles felt lay the best hope of world peace. The USSR, also, had its own reasons, and none of them involved an open world society.

Most of the in-fighting in San Francisco centered around the demands of the Little Forty-five—France, for old time's sake, had been lifted out of the ruck to official Security Coun-

84

cil status—to soften the proposed strong-arm system. But in the end, as Kleffens predicted, all they could do was argue, then agree. But it was not the clamor of the Little Forty-five that chilled the optimism of the conference very soon. It was the obvious, and growing, big-power split that yawned during the first five days.

The British government was not rocking the boat at San Francisco; it was determined to continue the wartime alliances and especially the Anglo-American relationship and to stake as much of its vital policy as possible in backing U. S. positions. But the USSR showed immediately that Stalin could not care less what American policy was, if it conflicted with his own ideas.

Molotov's first speech, in all the high-flung optimism and good cheer, was a chiller. France and England, he said, had had the job of securing the peace prior to 1938, and they had bungled it. While they were botching it, the USSR had been abused, insulted, ignored, and shunted aside both at ministries and the League of Nations. But those days were over. The USSR was a big power, now, and it intended to take a major role in the world, and it would have a major say in everything that went on, whether anybody liked it or not.

Molotov's mood was not improved by the first floor vote. The United States, perhaps unwisely, had made up its mind to seat Argentina, and when Nelson Rockefeller gave the signal, the Hispanic-American chorus of assent was deafening. Also, every member nation except the USSR, Greece, Yugoslavia, and the Czechs went along. The lopsided vote proved something Stalin had feared: the Soviet view was not likely to prevail in open assembly, even when, as now, the USSR had an excellent case. The vote convinced Molotov the question of future admissions had to be kept in the Security Council, where it would be subject to veto.

At San Francisco it was the Russians, odd, mysterious, and somehow repellant, who caught the public attention. A Soviet

85

ship anchored in the bay, and some of the Russian delegation lived aboard it. The ship served merely as a communications center for contact with Moscow, but rumors flooded the Embarcadero that the vessel was jammed with caviar and vodka and wild things were said to occur aboard.

Unlike the Western nations, the Soviet State had taken all the aid it could get from its allies but had done nothing to remove the deep-seated Russian fear of foreigners or suspicion of the outside world that had pervaded Russian society for centuries.

Wherever Russians went, their big, blond security police went with them. The agents tried to be inconspicuous, but in their ubiquitous blue suits, smoking long brown *papyrossi*, they could not be. They gave everyone the clammy eye, and they annoyed the hell out of the San Francisco police, whom the State Department ordered to lay off, concealed guns or no concealed guns.

No Russian of rank went out without his bodyguards. Moscow demanded a bullet-proof sedan for Molotov. This also annoyed Americans, used to seeing their own officials like Stettinius and Vandenberg walking freely about hotel lobbies. The Soviet agents checked rooms before scheduled conferences, frisked reporters for arms at press meetings, and generally made an enormous nuisance of themselves. They gave foreign uniforms, like that of Field Marshal Smuts, close scrutiny before allowing them to pass, but fortunately no serious trouble arose.

As April passed and May lengthened, the Soviets kept proving they had arrived, the small powers kept crying emotionally for reason, and the Hispanic-American states thumped in committee for more attention to the economic and social aspects of world order, to wit, more aid. One of their members called UNRRA "Unhappy Nations Receiving Ridiculous Assistance." Vandenberg, who, in spite of being an idealist and supporting foreign aid, was still a Republican, told them:

"The United States is not rich enough to become permanent almoner to the whole earth."

Ridiculous assistance or not, while the committee rooms were wreathed in smoke and delegates writhed through speeches, San Francisco was doing a roaring business. Taxis and restaurants, already war-crowded, boomed. The delegates reportedly brought $10,000,000 to town, and they left most of it behind. Europeans went wild over rayon lingerie and hosiery they had not seen for years, and almost broke into tears when they found Americans had not bought up all the Homburg hats. Everybody wanted to look like Eden.

Zionists and NAACPs, idealists and other assorted groups tried to get the conference's attention. Six Canadian Iroquois staged a demonstration against the Indian Act of 1927. Mrs. Pandit, whose brother Jawaharlal was in a British jail, went from room to room challenging the right of Indians with British titles to speak for India. Jan Christian Smuts, normally a man for all seasons, at last cried, "Let us bypass issues raised by men with a passion for reforming the world in general." The United States had asked for an open conference, and that was what it got.

But in spite of it all, something was getting done.

Elsewhere, it was a bitter spring.

Across the Pacific the Japanese Empire was being extinguished in flame and agony. Japanese soldiers died by the thousands on Okinawa, in Burma, and Luzon; the greenwood and plaster cities of Japan itself roared day and night with fire and explosion and the screams of victims. On the plains of Kyushu young men painted their faces corpse-white and wore their shrouds in the cockpits of old aircraft. The Divine Wind was rising, but both the young men and the rulers of Japan, the *Gumbatsu,* would find that the will to die was not enough.

Apart from the actual battlefield the millennia-old fabric of Asian life was being ripped beyond repair from Manchuria to Malaysia. Western hegemony and Western rule were destroyed. The economy and social institutions of China, after a generation of warlords and eight years of Japanese armies, were in dissolution. The Japanese gambit for empire had failed, but in failing it had brought down the structure it had sailed against, from Indonesia to India. Asian society would not soon again be ordered, even though the order had been only a patina of Western rule.

Thousands of miles to the west, in Central Europe, another centuries-old order was ending in the cold spring rains. The German Reich was being killed inch by inch in blood and rape and degradation. On the soil of old Prussia a Russian commander marshaled more men and guns on one front than the world had ever seen, or was likely to see again. Anglo-American armies had burst the ancient barrier of the Rhine. The German watch had failed; German armies fought fanatically in the east, sporadically in the west until they died, ran out of ammunition, or passed into the prison pens. The German Wehrmacht was running out of territory; it had run out of honor a long time before. As the Reich's executioners passed Erla, Belsen, Buchenwald, and Auschwitz, they learned the extent of the trauma modern civilization had suffered.

In Europe as well as Asia, the economy was ruined. The Nazi grip had been hard, but it had been efficient; it had organized Europe as a whole. In soil-rich France, with organization and German nitrates gone, there was hunger. In Belgium transport broke down. In the east, beyond the gates of the Danube, civil life disintegrated, and there was mass horror. Only in North America and Australasia, remote from the destruction, was there enough to eat, or enough of anything else.

The monsters who had menaced the world were being killed, but because the world was still the less, no man could escape diminishment. Nevertheless, the bodies of men were tougher than even man himself believed, and the urge to build was at least as great as the urge to destory. Man would survive.

War ended in Europe. No nation in modern times had been so thoroughly devastated as Germany, no continent so utterly disrupted. But it was over at last.

In London jovial crowds thronged the gates of Buckingham Palace, shouting: "One, Two, Three, Four! What the hell are we waiting for? We want the King!" Eventually, the King appeared.

Paris was calmer. Parisians had exhausted all their emotion with the Liberation last August; it was raining, and they were hungry.

In ferociously neutral Dublin, students of Protestant Trinity College broke out UN flags, while Irishmen booed. The riots began only when some students, reckless, began to sing "Britannia Rule the Waves." Few Dubliners liked Hitler, but the realization that Saxons had won again was enough to drive the town to drink its own Irish whisky.

In Münster, Count Clemens von Galen, the Catholic Archbishop, who had been a fearless critic of Nazism, told American soldiers: "My uppermost concern is the spread of Communism." He had little patience with the Americans' old-fashioned preoccupation with the Nazis who still lived.

In Berlin, a German-language edition of *Pravda* appeared on the shattered streets.

One order had ended; another had begun.

Back at San Francisco, people were getting a bit impatient with all the talk. It was time to move or get off the pot.

The Big Powers were interested in moving, but not very far. The Russians felt they had bought a good thing in Eastern Europe with the blood of the Red Army, and they weren't going to give it up. The British had had the war forced on them; they wanted nothing out of it. But they would not have been human if they had not still looked upon the Empire with a happy, pukka eye.

89

The United States, able to be broadly internationalist and idealistic toward all foreign empires, took an equally idealistic view toward the Monroe Doctrine. This, in short, was perfect. Its perfection was revealed first when all Latin countries voted for Argentina's membership, secondly, when Argentina and all her friends swallowed three votes for the USSR when Rockefeller smiled.

"What we are creating here," Mexico's Alfonso García cried, "is a system of order in the forest which will keep the mice in order, but not the lions." García had the message, all right—but after all, who was there to bell the cats?

Because of the U. S. insistence upon open meeting, each clause of Dumbarton Oakes had to be forced, openly, down some small powers' throats. What had emerged from the war was three power centers, three regional blocs: Russia-East Europe, British Empire and Commonwealth, United States-Western Hemisphere.

The power centers within each bloc, Britain, Russia and the United States, saw no world problem of security—yet—just regional ones. Each power center, jealous of its own, had to have the veto for its own protection. The one thing the small nations wanted most from San Francisco, a means by which they could bypass the veto, was not and could not be in the cards.

The "fighting" Vandenberg described went on, while the Russians regarded the whole business as extreme, if not dangerous, nonsense. It was the Yalta voting formula, Article 27, that raised the most hackles. The room where it was debated, with Tom Connally presiding, soon was called Madison Square Garden. And Room 223 of the Veterans Building, where some seventeen nations held out for adoption of a way around the veto—what would later be called the Acheson Plan—had its own battles. Some of the arguments made sense. Some did not. Australia and the Philippines could see the immorality of the Big Power veto, but they saw nothing whatever wrong with a system in which the United States and

Luxembourg's three hundred thousand peasants had one vote apiece.

Stettinius was informed that the Big Five were being placed above the law. Stettinius, getting frayed around the edges, asked, to just which law did the gentleman refer? Patiently, he argued that the Charter was allowing the Big Five no powers they did not already possess. But the Charter, as it was now being amended, was placing far-reaching responsibilities upon them. Tom Connally stated, "I am confident that the great powers will not betray the trust that has been placed in them by using their right of veto willfully or maliciously." But Old Tom could speak only for the United States, and all the small powers knew it.

It should be made clear that even Vandenberg never considered sacrificing the U. S. veto. As he pointed out, the question could not be considered simply as a moral matter. The U. S. Senate, Democrat and Republican alike, had made it plain it would not accept a vetoless Charter. Therefore, it was going to be a Charter with a great-power veto, or none at all. Connally illustrated the fact plainly in the middle of a bitter session in "the Garden" by holding up a copy of the proposed Charter, ripping it in half, and letting the pieces fall. "You may, if you wish, go home and say you've defeated the veto. But what will your answer be when you are asked, 'Where is the Charter?'" There was no answer to that, and although Evatt roared like a wild man, the conference voted thirty to two, with fifteen abstentions, to accept the Yalta voting formula as it stood.

But Vandenberg made a change elsewhere. He inserted an amendment by which on purely procedural matters before the Security Council, seven affirmative votes of the eleven would carry, with no provision for veto. It did not matter which four voted no, or abstained.

This brought the Russians out of their corner. Until Vandenberg inserted this provision for free debate, Russians and U. S. aims were in convergence, and the Russians had let Vandenberg and Connally carry the ball. Now the Russian delegation argued strenuously that the veto was all-inclusive, and it applied to anything and everything brought before the Council, including mere discussion. Vandenberg countered that this was gag rule.

The Soviets said that since as soon as any discussion was ended, any great power opposed to it could effectively veto any and all proposed action, why allow things to be stirred up in the first place? In logical terms, the Russian position was well taken. But Vandenberg, going by American logic, could not accept this. He unquestionably placed a great deal of faith in world opinion. He felt that free debate before the Security Council, even if action was stymied, could be valuable in the cause of justice. It did not occur to Vandenberg in 1945, of course, that world opinion might not always be on the side of the American brand of justice.

The Russians, who knew opinion would be against them in coming days, deadlocked the conference over this issue.

Molotov had long since left the conference and gone home. Andrei Gromyko, who had taken his place as chief of the Soviet delegation, now proved he could be as stone-faced and unyielding as the Old Bolshevik. This was the first, and only serious problem the conference encountered. Stettinius worriedly called on Washington for help.

Washington tried one more shot of the personal diplomacy so much in vogue in FDR's time. Sick and weary Harry Hopkins, whose personal world had been blasted by Roosevelt's death, was asked to fly again to Moscow, and to intervene personally with Stalin. Hopkins was a good choice. No American had more prestige in Moscow. He was one of the few Anglo-Americans who had believed the Russians would win over the Germans in 1941. More important, he had been instrumental in getting U. S. aid sent to Russia, at the time over the firm opposition of the U. S. State Department.

In Moscow, he called on Stalin, and simply asked the Russian dictator to modify the Russian stand on the veto as it affected procedural matters. Even though Stalin saw each attempt to modify Dumbarton Oaks as a direct threat against the new Soviet empire in Europe, he agreed. He was not giving up anything of real importance, because the Dumbarton Oaks and Yalta formulas actually guaranteed Russia a free hand within its own sphere.

The trouble was that when the U. S. staff had drawn up Dumbarton Oaks it had not anticipated the Russian conquest of Eastern Europe, or the Russian insistence on spoils. The system of great-power veto had been designed to permit the United States a free hand under the Monroe Doctrine, and the British to keep their empire, but it also allowed the Soviets to reorganize Eastern Europe to their liking.

There was no way out of this trap in 1945. Over Arthur Vandenberg's deep reluctance, Article 2 of the Charter in effect confirmed the new Soviet empire. But Vandenberg and Connally were able to insert a power of free discussion into the generally powerless Assembly:

"The General Assembly should initiate studies and make recommendations for the purpose of promoting international cooperation in political, economic, social, and cultural fields to assist in the realization of human rights and basic freedoms for all, without distinction as to race, language, religion, or sex and also for the encouragement of the development of international law, [and further,] The General Assembly should be empowered to recommend measures for the peaceful adjustment of any situations, regardless or origin, which it deems likely to impair the general welfare . . . including . . . violation of the Purposes and Principles set forth in this Charter."

Connally said happily that "without regard to origin opens up to discussion in the Assembly almost any question that has arisen since Adam and Eve were in the Garden. I think it is very wise . . . and very good. . . ."

The liberalization was considered primarily a blow at the USSR and the colonial powers in 1945. The time would come, however, when a United States forced to man the walls of world order would be far less sanguine about all the diversionary gripes—such as the South Africa question—this language opened up. Article 14, as adopted, assured against a completely static world; and Foster Dulles, with his fears of a new Versailles, was satisfied.

The UN Charter now presupposed both a great-power security system, and a public forum, and an organization that could take limited action in the social, economic, and welfare fields. This was all that Vandenberg, who knew well enough the facts of the world, really hoped to get. He had wanted to assure the freedom of Eastern Europe, but this had already been pledged away; he had no powers to change that.

If there were millions who hoped for more, who hoped that in a world where there were still impassable gulfs between Englishmen and Egyptians, Ukrainians and Americans, Hindus and Chinese, armies were going to be abolished and everything put to a vote, the fault was not that of the framers. The Charter had to be written for a world of power, but it was tempered with a little reason. It also came from San Francisco with a preamble, and a sincerely written, if unenforceable, dedication to the ideal of human rights.

The language itself of the Charter reflected too many cooks, unfortunately. There were inserted phrases from the League of Nations Preamble, the Kellogg Pact, Abraham Lincoln's writings, Pope Leo XIII, and the Chinese and Russian Constitutions. The final document was overwordy, repetitious, and shot through with compromising language. No one, not even its framers, considered it a great document.

The Dumbarton Oaks Proposals were substantially liberalized through the efforts of Vandenberg and the U. S. delegation. The first vision of the UN was that of a powerful Security Council, to enforce security. The General Assembly of all nations, and the international Secretariat—the organization needed to operate the machinery—were thrown in almost as afterthoughts. But at San Francisco, at American insistence, the Assembly was given greater importance, and it was placed squarely into the economic, social, and humanitarian fields.

In one important area the Security Council was weakened. Dumbarton Oaks had spelled out a right of the great powers to intervene in the domestic affairs of smaller nations where world peace or security seemed threatened. This was watered down into a general principle.

Security Council decisions were still binding on everyone, subject to a Big Five veto. The Big Five—Nationalist China, France, Britain, the United States, and the USSR—were assigned permanent seats on the Council. Six other powers were to be elected periodically by the Assembly. Significantly, the Council's powers were pointed toward the prevention of aggression rather than the maintenance of a legal order. The trusteeship clauses had been weakened at Yalta to the effect that any nation could treat its colonies, dependencies, and wards as domestic matters beyond UN jurisdiction.

The Council could vote on only three matters: procedural, political, and quasi-judicial. A majority of seven was required to carry on procedural matters. On all other matters not only was a majority of seven needed, but all of the Big Five had to vote in the affirmative. A negative vote by any one of the Big Five on anything but a procedural matter killed all action or discussion. This was the big-power veto, by which each great power retained its freedom of action.

"Political," as defined in the Charter, included the determination of whether or not a threat to the peace existed, the use of force or sanctions, the furnishing of armed forces to UN causes, or any question concerning arms regulation or disarmament. But the term was also broadened to include such questions as the admission of new members, expulsion of the old, appointment of the Secretary General, and amendment of the Charter. Thus, the right to veto was protected forever; any great power could veto a proposed change.

The veto, of course, had certain ridiculous aspects. With it, for example, France could prevent negotiation in the UN between Greece and Turkey, even if the interested parties desired it, or the USSR could block settlements between two Western Hemisphere nations in cases to which it was not even a party. Of course, such cases could be taken outside the UN and solved elsewhere, and this was the procedure that the veto actually forced on UN members.

The Security Council, the peace-keeping arm of the UN, emerged designed for only two functions: *to prevent wars between small powers, and to crush any renewed threat from the old Axis enemy.* This was all. The framers had to recognize and live with the facts of life, and these included great-power sovereignty. National sovereignty, since the Peace of Westphalia in 1648, had been considered as absolute in theory. When it was combined with national power, as the case of the USSR, it *was* absolute. National sovereignty buttressed by real national power could be bound or regulated only by two things: a sense of responsibility, or a fear of consequences. There was much discussion of laws applying to nations at San Francisco. But the fact remained that there were none, and the Charter recognized this.

The small nations complained that under the Charter it was possible for a big nation to attack a little one, then block UN action with its veto. This was correct. Other big powers might still take action against the aggressor, but what then would ensue would be war, no matter what name was put on it. It would not be a UN action. Many people never understood what Stalin had tried to emphasize at Yalta: the Security Council could not prevent conflict between the great powers themselves, if one or more of them were determined to disagree.

The incisive changes made to Dumbarton Oaks at San Francisco, however, did not affect the Council so much as the Assembly. *These changes lay in a successful attempt by the small powers, in which the United States joined, to shift the emphasis of the UN from a police system for regulating the world from the top, to an organization duty-bound to*

96

promote welfare, justice, and international cultural cooperation.

This change in emphasis was shown by the fact that the Assembly, at first a mere forum and appendage of the Council, was broadened into a continuing body, and it was given a much wider list of functions than the Council. Besides the political arena, the Assembly could enter the social and economic fields. It still had no legislative powers and no power to bind any decision, but the economic and social areas were destined to be critical in coming years. San Francisco assured that the Assembly was to play a preeminent part in the UN.

Overall, the UN Charter stated high principles, set up a machinery for certain kinds of political action, and offered the nations opportunity to take action. The Council met only on call, but the Assembly was a continuing body that met most days of the year. The UN, however, was not an automatic constitution. It did not create a superstate, or anything even approaching world government. It had no actual existence outside its member states; there was no such thing as a separate UN that could operate outside the framework of national governments.

Nor did the UN Charter create new international law, although some American observers tried to talk as if it had. The Charter was not a legal document, nor was it binding the way it was written. No nation was guaranteed perfect security. But all were provided an opportunity and a means, as the international community had never had before, for international cooperation if they wanted it.

Very few of the delegates were wholly satisfied with this Charter. Jan Masaryk of Czechoslovakia, already trying earnestly to act as a bridge between the Russians and the West, said: "I feel like the father fondly awaiting the birth of a son. The baby finally arrives, and it turns out to be a girl. At first the father is disappointed, but he soon learns to like her just the same."

On June 25, 1945, the Charter was signed in the auditorium of the Veterans Building in San Francisco by representatives of all nations present at the conference. To create the United Nations Organization, all that was now needed was ratification of this Charter by twenty-eight nations. This was already assured.

During July, 1945, the Senate of the United States was asked to advise and consent to the UN Charter. In its time-honored way, the Senate moved slowly, seeking comment from one and all.

There was very little opposition within the halls. The Democratic Administration had proposed the Charter; the Republican opposition had rewritten it into compromise. Even maverick Bob LaFollette, who had denounced San Franscisco as late as June, glumly agreed he would vote aye. It was not easy to be against peace, justice, welfare, and social cooperation, especially with a veto handy. The response from the public was remarkably favorable. Burton K. Wheeler, unreconstructed isolationist, muttered: "We might as well vote for it, because in itself it means nothing."

But there was at least one fracas in the Senate hearings.

Mrs. Agnes Waters, of the National Blue Star Mothers of America—the names change, the notions never—testified that the Charter would set up a world government for Communists and "make this nation a feeding trough for the have-nots."

"Have-not" was 1930's terminology for what the more delicate-minded were now calling the "underdeveloped" or "emerging." But the Committee understood.

Tom Connally, in charge, listened politely.

Mrs. Waters continued, "The real war criminals are sitting right in this room. I name Mr. Stettinius, the former international banker—"

Ed Stettinius, the former chairman of U.S. Steel, blushed, while Senator Connally roared for Mrs. Waters to be thrown out.

At the door, hair flying, she screeched: "I'm not afraid of all

98

the devils in hell! What this country needs is a good old-fashioned American revolution!"

After Mrs. Waters departed, the Senate advised and consented, 89–2. President Truman ratified on August 8.

But then, as later, a certain number of Americans who had no fear of hell or whatever devils might inhabit it, remained thoroughly frightened by world welfare and justice, and the novel notion of international cooperation.

Part II

THE FAILURE

7.

The Edge of Darkness

IN 1945 no one wanted to think about more trouble. From San Francisco to Sverdlovsk, U. S. and Russian diplomats toasted each other. American Army bands blared forth the stirring strains of "Meadowland," the Red Army's song. Russian peasants called to the colors—the Soviet armies did not demobilize—nostalgically sang what they were told was the American soldier's song, which went to the tune of "I'll Hang My Heart on the Weeping Willow Tree." The last thing the common man, anywhere, wanted to think about was another war.

Liberal thought was ephemerally dominant in every Western country. This opinion railed at domestic "fascists" who tried to explain the real nature of power struggles, or who hinted that the millennium was not just around the corner. That kind of thinking had been invented by Haushofer—the German who had invented geopolitics, then prostituted a truly brilliant concept of national actions and strategies into a justification for German conquest—and it had surely gone out with Adolf Hitler. When American or British generals spoke cautiously about keeping the defenses up, they were equated with their late colleagues of the Wehrmacht. With war disciplines ended, there was a wave of strikes in the United States and Europe. Otherwise sensible men called Henry Ford a fascist.

In such a period of confusion, both public and private, it was natural that millions of Americans as well as Europeans began to look to the United Nations Organization for the peace and security all craved, and to read something into the UN that had never been intended.

Having staved off disaster by force of arms, the West had some-

103

how come to the idea that principle, rather than force, was a better basis for peace. The trouble was, publics took an "either/ or" attitude toward the question; few stated that force without principle was sterile, but that principle without force behind it was powerless. The great trouble with classic liberal thought and classic liberals is that they have no trouble conceiving principle, but enormous trouble understanding how it must be implemented.

The United Nations came from San Francisco a political vehicle that men could ride to the stars, or push through the mud. But it was always a political vehicle, and it was never self-powered. It needed gas to go.

Instead of gas, the UN got window-dressing. From some hopeful corner of the American mind, tired of alarms and wars and chaos, came notions of international law, and even more startling, impossible connotations of world goverment. George C. Marshall, one of the most splendid Americans who ever served his country, was also unfortunately the first to refer to the "rule of law as being at the heart of the Charter and the structure of the UN." He was already confusing the UN with the American Constitution and the American body politic.

This notion of "international law" being behind the UN increased the inclination to look on it as a world government. In fact, in 1945 and 1946 the idea of world government had its greatest vogue. A proposal to make the UN into a world government was placed on a Massachusetts referendum. It carried, seven to one. Fourteen American state legislatures passed similar resolutions; eighteen members of the new Republican Congress of 1946 pledged themselves to work for universal law.

A *Newsweek* poll of October, 1946, showed that 52 percent of those interviewed favored the scrapping of national armed forces, 32 percent opposed it, and 15 percent abstained. But a solid 54 percent concurred that the UN could easily be made into a world government, and an enthusiastic 63 percent wanted the UN to create immediately a representative world congress empowered to "solve all international problems."

Liberal opinion on international affairs outran government

planning in the United States and elsewhere. But such opinion was strong for panaceas, without really taking into account the nature of man, peoples, and governments. The vision of world government was, of course, a shining one. But what was tragic about all this was that nobody, not even liberal opinion, really wanted world government. What was wanted was a world without war. And even the vision of world government was an impossible one. Sociologists believe that viable government can exist only where and when there is a common history, common language, and most important, a common sense of future destiny. Government may be imposed where one or more such factors do not exist, but then it is either imperial, colonial, or tyrannical. After World War II, the world was fragmenting into more, not fewer, sovereign states.

Ironically, the rosy-hued dreams of peace and world government aroused a backlash from those people who were afraid of losing national identity or national sovereignty in the United States, and so dubious of the UN's pretensions that they came to fear and hate it as a symbol of what they despised. Both world-government rooters, and its haters, actually created problems for the U. S. national government that continued to exist. Both had a distorted view of both the real world and the UN, and they tended to be vocal and noisy.

The vision of world government, unfortunately, took time, attention, and needed energy away from more urgent causes in the West. The trouble was that the USSR, beginning with World War II, had started to advance its own concept of world government with more action and less debate.

History does not really repeat. No two situations separated by time or place are ever the same, and no two nations, races, or peoples respond to similar stimuli in exactly the same way. But this does not mean there is no continuity to history. The men who say there is no pattern really mean that they are unable to see the pattern.

One reason some patterns are indistinct is that no one wants to see them. Some men always reject the historic logic of their times. The West was unable to see the historic logic in the rise of Hitlerian Germany and adventurist Japan. In some respects, the world of 1945 seemed as blind to the apparent logic of its day as that of 1919. The world of 1919 grew out of events begun in 1870, and the enormous crisis of order between a rising Germany and the older powers.

The dominant pattern was Western weakness in the face of challenge. The mainstream of Western civilization, after 1870, was able neither to conquer nor to accommodate the Germans. The first world war was a logical German attempt at the domination of Europe, and the Allied response was a successful rejection of that hegemony—but apparently at a cost of will and moral strength too great to bear.

Western society had to bear the cost of Flanders fields—or a dozen Flanders fields—or go out of business. It was not the first great civilization to be challenged, from Marathon to Cannae Plain. And as Dean Acheson once explained to a disbelieving college audience, the first duty of any society is to survive. What it survives as is not so important as the act of survival itself. Concern for the image and content of that civilization, while good, unfortunately tends to weaken the will to survive.

The inability to reach a new European consensus in 1919, coupled with certain weaknesses in the West, made a new war in 1939 inevitable. And this time the West was even less prepared to defend itself than it had been in 1914. As late as 1944, the British still hoped for a peripheral war. They had no real enthusiasm for the Second Front, in spite of the American advice that they could fly over or sail around the German *Festung Europa* till doomsday without putting Hitler and Company out of business. It was not entirely due to American power and industrial strength that the United States assumed direction of the war, and Western moral leadership as well.

And if Western weakness, material and moral, between 1919 and 1939 raised Hitler, Western weakness between 1939 and

106

1941 conjured up its own new monster. All historic logic pointed to the fact that the West had to contain *both* Hitler and the Communist aberration.

Instead, the West was forced to choose between them. Because the far richer, more populous, and decent societies of France, Britain, and the United States did not stop the German and Japanese challenge in time, and stopped it only with great difficulty and with the help of the USSR, the West was going to have to live with a new demon.

A large part of the ending of World War II was foreordained by the circumstances of its beginning. For the destruction of the Nazi regime, and the death of Hitler in his bunker, or the brightness of a thousand suns over Hiroshima, did nothing to change the nature of man and his societies or the course of his politics.

On April 27, 1945, Hitler said, "As long as I live, there will be no conflict between Russia, America, and England. They are united in their will to destroy me. If I am dead they cannot remain united. The conflict must come. . . ." Hitler was insane, at the last, but mad as he was, he understood the logic of his times.

The Russian entry into Europe on the heels of the collapsing Wehrmacht recreated the menacing power structure that Hitler originally forged in 1939. One national, expansionist, alienated power was again so predominant upon the Eurasian continent that no European state, or coalition of states, could hope to offset it. The European balance of power had collapsed, and the one great fear of all English geopoliticians—Eurasia under a single rule—seemed certain to come about.

Germany had been so thoroughly defeated in 1945 it was no longer a menace. Even German ambitions seemed likely to be ended for many years. Germany thus might be reintegrated with the West, and was.

The historic and deep-seated hostility between the Western powers and had the USSR remained, however. The Bolshevik Revolution of 1917 did more than just topple the Russian government. The Russian revolutionaries attacked not only the structure but also the very bases of Western society and philosophy; they took Russia again out of European civilization not only physically but spiritually as well. The disaffection was deep, on both sides. The Stalinist era, in which the original premises of Marxist humanism were diverted toward national socialism and national power, accompanied by bloody purges, pervasive tyranny, and utter disregard for humanity, did nothing to heal the breach.

In 1939 Chamberlain, the English Prime Minister, said: "I must confess to the most profound distrust of Russia . . . and I distrust her motives, which seem to me to have little connection with our ideas of liberty, and to be concerned only with getting everyone else by the ears." Soviet statesmen at the same time were saying things like Dmitri Manuilsky's hope: "Not a stone of the accursed capitalist structure will remain. . . ." Russia in 1939 was as completely alienated from the West as Hitler's Germany.

There was, however, a large minority viewpoint on Russia in the West, which found the Soviet experience appealing. European history since the Middle Ages had settled into roughly hundred-year patterns of crisis, dissolution, rebuilding, stabilization, and renewed despair. Christendom shattered in the Reformation. The Ancien Regime fell in French Revolution, and bourgeois democracy collapsed in the funks of 1919.

All stabilizations have their own unfairnesses and contradictions; modern Western society had these, and Marxist ideology appealed to many persons who had come to despair of the present. Communist thought also appealed strongly to many European intellectuals who despaired of the fact that life seemed to be a power struggle between the nations, resulting in the continual and bloody crisis of Lenin. The triumph of Marxist society seemed the only escape from national wars, to these people, for one of the early and ironic premises of Communism was that it would do away with nationalism.

Ironically, the mind that could see plainly the jealousies, rivalries, vested interests, class conflicts, vote-buyings, and racism latent or rampant in every Western society tended to see only the dreams of Marxism on the other side: pure equality, brotherhood, humanism. They never saw that the *institution* of Marxism inevitably distorted Communist life just as some Western institutions distorted human values. In Russia, Marxism meant slave labor, heresy hunts, degradation of all human values, and violent national expansionism. But the minority viewpoint, which in critical times and critical places caused every non-Communist Western government trouble in dealing with the specter of a rising Russia, refused to recognize the reality of Communist experience in the USSR.

At the beginning of World War II, the West had to choose between Stalin's totalitarianism and Hitler's. But the USSR had to make a similar choice. At first, in the volatile and dangerous atmosphere of 1939, Stalin sought a détente with Hitler. The result was the notorious Russo-German Nonaggression Pact, which doubled in spades the inept Franco-British attempts to turn the two European giants against each other.

The Soviet-Nazi détente was completely cynical. Both sides needed it for different reasons. Hitler wanted a free hand against the West; the French campaign was already planned. Stalin, fearful of a German drive toward the Ukrainian bread basket, an old German dream, was perfectly willing to free Hitler to become involved in the West. Stalin's strategy was the old business of "let's him and you fight"; and he intended to stay neutral, strong, and ready to pick up the pieces. This apparent about-face by Russia in the Nonaggression Pact showed that if Russian strategy did not change, tactics could and did change daily. During 1939 and 1940, Stalin stinted the Russian people to provide food and raw materials for the Nazi war machine, out of expediency.

But this détente was an immense Soviet miscalculation. It had not settled the basic argument of whether Slavic or Teutonic power was to dominate south of the Danube, although the Polish question was uneasily solved by partition. In East Europe, Nazis and Soviets were still like two scorpions circling each other, and by allowing Hitler to attack and defeat France without interference from the East, Stalin almost sealed his own fate.

The Soviet High Command never anticipated the rapid German victory in France in 1940; they were counting on another repetition of the trenches of World War I. But France fell and Britain was isolated, and by early 1941 an uneasy Soviet staff watched German power march through the Balkans, and German armies deploy along the Soviet borders. When the full might of the Nazi war machine turned on Russia, Stalin could only blame himself.

The months of the Nazi-Soviet détente should have taught Western statesmen much about Soviet strategy, but many of them were too busy eleswhere. In 1941 almost the entire U. S. State Department opposed aid to Russia. During the détente period, American diplomats had found themselves regularly humiliated and ignored by Soviet leaders who made no attempt to disguise an anti-Western bias. The cynical partition of Poland between Germany and the USSR also shocked Americans. Most of the men on the spot could see no difference between Soviet Red and Nazi Brown. But the professionals were overruled by the amateur opinion of both FDR and Cordell Hull, who acted on Harry Hopkins' advice. All three agreed with Winston Churchill that Hitler was the greater demon.

This could not be called a strategic error at the time. American military men assured FDR that England would not be able to hold out, and FDR's main purpose in aiding the USSR was to prevent a strengthened Hitler from taking Britain after an Eastern conquest. He too hoped the Germans would bog down, just as Stalin had hoped Hitler would trip himself on the Western Front. And in that sense, like Stalin, he helped build his own new monster.

But attached to the pragmatic decision to assist the Soviets against the Nazis were two real errors. One was, in typical American fashion, to put aside all political considerations

110

until after the war. The other was to try to fit the image of the Russian bear into the sort of "holy" war Americans and British liked to fight. Publicly, the U. S. government began to act as if Russian and American war aims were identical; the Soviet tyrannical image was cleaned up. Films were distributed in which the Russians were heroes, and the Russian way of life not too undemocratic.

This was remarkable for a government that was informed of the German-Soviet protocols dividing Eastern Europe and must certainly have understood Soviet ambitions. There was some Russian dissembling. But Americans, many on high levels, pulled their own wool over their own eyes.

The United States, Britain, and the USSR agreed on the structure and importance of world power. All the professionals played the same game. But the Russians played by vastly different rules. Many of the things the United States did in Hispanic America, or the British in Africa or Asia, were amoral, a blending of national interest, basic good intentions, and the evil of power-backed action. But where the democracies used a combination of cajolery, bribery, veiled threats, and honest bargaining to win their way, the Soviets used the naked fist. It was the crudeness of Soviet power plays that caused so much trouble. Finland illustrated a case in point.

In 1945 the West acquiesced willingly to Soviet pressures, reparations, and domination of Finland. Finland had been a German cobelligerent. But the USSR had also attacked Finland without provocation in 1939, and Finland had genuine friendships in the West. The ready acquiescence to Soviet indemnities, and Soviet bases and veto power over Finnish government and foreign policy—no anti-Communist regime was to be allowed to return to power—came because the Soviets did not overrun the small country, loot or rape it, or impose a Communist puppet government by bayonets. They dominated Finland, got their way by threats and a show of force, but left the economy and local government to its own affairs.

111

Realistically, the State Department of the United States was prepared to accept Russian influence over Eastern Europe after the war. So was FDR. But the way the USSR went about imposing such influence violated both the Atlantic Charter and wartime pledges. Russia showed itself willing to smirch its new image in America and even scuttle the Big Three alliance in pursuit of these goals. Such action could not help but bring about trouble with the West.

Harry Truman came to the Presidency thoroughly unprepared. He had not even been told the truth about the Yalta agreements on the day FDR died. American domestic institutions are such that it does not make an enormous difference who is President, or what philosophy he holds—but foreign policy is almost wholly the preserve of the President. The President, and the kind of men he puts in office, soon put their own peculiar stamp upon the overseas affairs of the Republic.

Truman was a very different kind of man from FDR. He would not, and could not, change the historic imperative of the Democratic Party as it had been firmed by Roosevelt. He continued its domestic policies. But overseas, there were changes. Truman, as Vice President, had developed two pet hates: the palace politics so beloved by FDR, which kept Cabinet members and others jockeying for position; and the personal diplomacy of the sort that based decisions on Hopkins' reports and kept him uninformed of Yalta.

From Missouri, Truman was more in the mold of early nineteeth-century Americans than the intellectuals who had crowded around FDR. He did not like the true New Dealers; no man of his background or sentiments could. One of his first decisions was to get rid of them. Judge Rosenman, Morgenthau, Hopkins, Robert Sherwood, and Leon Henderson were sent packing, one by one. Stettinius had to go, too, not because he was unacceptable, but because under current law he stood next in

112

line for the Presidency. No one, least of all Ed Stettinius, himself, considered him qualified. Assistant President James Byrnes, who was qualified, went to Secretary of State, while Stettinius went to the United Nations as Ambassador.

Truman did not possess apocalyptic vision; he did not see the truth always marching on. But as far as he did see, few men saw more clearly. He knew he had his limitations, particularly in high-level international affairs. These he began to leave to those professionals in the military and State Department whom he considered best suited to handle them.

Ironically, on his accession all Washington agreed that the man from Missouri was a caretaker President, who would never go down in history. *Time,* by no means alone, printed flatly that "HST would not be a great President."

And in his early days and months Truman was not. No man so unprepared for awesome responsibility could be. Truman felt he could only continue FDR's policies without any changes, and for critical months the drift Vandenberg had noted went on uncorrected.

When Churchill demanded that Truman make a public policy declaration on the Soviet rape of East Europe, Truman refused. He also refused to consider another Churchill proposal: that the course of Anglo-American military action in Central Europe be tailored to overrun Czechoslovakia, seize Berlin, and bar the Red Army from all of Austria.

Truman refused partly due to following FDR's policy of restraint toward the USSR, partly on the basis of advice he received from the wartime leaders who had served Roosevelt. The record shows that Marshall—toward whom Truman felt a deep respect—Admiral Leahy, and Secretary of War Stimson all disagreed vehemently with Churchill. These men, highly influential in Washington, did not want the United States to become involved in the European power game, on any side.

George C. Marshall had more to do with winning the war than the public would ever realize, for he was an unassuming

113

leader. But he had not understood the nature of totalitarianism in 1939, and his education on the true logic of the twentieth century came long after 1945.

Truman did, however, summon Molotov to the White House on his way to San Francisco, and tell him that Soviet-American friendship could not be a one-way street. Molotov, emerging stiff-faced from the meeting, indicated that Soviet policy had not changed.

The "final solution" of the Polish problem was illustrative of the way each great power thought in 1945. The war ended in Europe with no agreement, and at San Francisco Poland became a UN member, but no delegation was seated. Sixteen members of the London Poles, in desperation, flew back to Warsaw to see if something could be salvaged from the Lublin-Communist takeover. Nothing was heard from them after that.

During the San Francisco conference, at a sumptuous dinner that Molotov threw for his colleagues Eden and Stettinius, amid the rich food and drink and smiling photographs, Molotov suddenly announced that the West could stop worrying about the London Poles. They were in a Russian jail. All of them had engaged in "diversionist activities" against the occupying Red Army—which meant they had protested the forced Communization and satellization of Poland. Eden, sixteen years a diplomat, left the party coldly polite. The next morning he issued a statement claiming an obvious Russian betrayal of a democratic Poland—but Stettinius refused to back this, and there the matter ended.

On the day of German surrender Churchill again made a proposal to Washington. He now saw the agreed-upon partition zones of Germany as a cover for Russian domination, and he wanted the Anglo-American armies to hold in place, even where they stood on German soil pledged to the Russian zone. Washington said no. It was not a good year for Winston Churchill.

Few men in Washington were open to such suggestion.

There was indeed a vast mistrust of Russian ambition, but no practical politician, Truman included, dared suggest counter-moves that would require the maintenance of large U. S. forces in Europe. The American public, unaware of the looming geopolitical crisis, demanded that the boys come home, and since the public was armed with the ballot, the boys were going to come home.

Americans in the mass, spouting hopes of world government and lasting peace, were quite slow to understand the geopolitical morass into which they were moving. They did not understand the British weakness; they did not understand that order is not kept by Charters but by powers behind those Charters, or that some nation would have to take the failing Great Britain's place.

Above all, they remained confused about the true aims of the Soviet Union. The fatal image of a "not too undemocratic Russia" inculcated during the war was responsible for Americans ignoring the obvious virulent suspicion, enormous hostility and wide ambitions of the USSR.

If the crisis was not immediate, but looming, it was because the Soviets were too weak to make any move to push the West out of its vested areas. The symptomatic trouble spots —Trieste, Greece, Poland, Korea, Austria, and others—remained only trouble spots, because only the steel will of Stalin kept the war-battered USSR in the power game at all. There was a realistic respect for American power which in 1945 was enormous. Further, Josef Stalin still believed his prophets. The Marxist strain had become virulent all over a war-disillusioned Europe. One third of the Italian people were Communist-leaning, a quarter of the French. Time seemed on the Soviet side.

Unknown to most Americans, the world had emerged from Hitler's night only to reenter the edge of darkness.

8.

The Whale on the Beach

IF POLAND and Bulgaria were nagging worries in the post-war wings, the whale on the beach was Germany. In May, 1945, there was more than a scent of victory in the air; there was a hint that the Nazi carcass was going to infect the new peace. As *Le Canard Enchainé* put it, "At Potsdam the Germans divided the Allies into four zones."

Time magazine reflected that the four occupation areas in Germany were certain to make administrative difficulties. But neither *Time* nor Washington saw that the Russian determination to dominate Germany, or failing in that, to keep the German nation eternally prostrate and divided, presaged deep trouble. The Slavic-German rivalry was as old as European history, much older than the flash-in-the-pan Teutonic-French unpleasantness. Twice in the century German power had penetrated deep into Russia, and the Russians would have been inhuman if they were prepared to let it happen again.

There was a large body of opinion in the West—which had had its own mauling from the Huns—supporting the Soviets. Germans had twice overrun France, and two German wars had reduced Britain from the world's dominant power to a second-rate nation. Not only the French and English, but also millions of Americans had come to see the modern world problem as a German problem.

A substantial number despaired of any real democratization or demilitarization of the German state. Influential men such as Morgenthau and Vansittart demanded nothing less than the abolition of Germany. In the shadow and stench of Belsen and Dachau, their arguments made a certain grim sense. But

116

these men, deeply involved in the emotions of their times, were equally lacking in the historical sense that might have told them that the *furor Teutonicus* was as apt to be a passing phase as the furor of Napoleon, and that the problem of power struggle springs eternal.

At Quebec, surprisingly for so intelligent a man, FDR had bemusedly initialed the Morgenthau Plan calling for an agricultural Germany, thus adding confusion to American German policy for some years. For the Vansittarts and the Morgenthaus did not come to grips with two salient facts of European life.

Germany was the geopolitical and industrial heart of Europe. In the twentieth century Europe was tightly interlaced, and a stable and prosperous Europe demanded a stable and productive Germany. The chaos experienced by the various West European economies when the iron German hand was relaxed in 1944, and the immense feats of production of the whole conquered economy during the war years, were not lost on many European planners from Brussels to Rome.

In compact Europe, a dying Germany tended to infect the whole. France needed German nitrates, Italy needed German steel; both remained impoverished without them. This the supposedly fanatical Communist Soviets saw much more clearly than the Americans and the British. The Soviet determination to keep Germany prostrate was based partly on fear of German pugnacity, but also on the Russian realization that German impotence diminished the whole subcontinent and allowed Russian political aims more opportunity.

At the war's end, three main lines of Russian policy were already apparent:

(1) Overall collaboration with the West in the United Nations to prevent any resurgence of fascist power, and to protect the interests of the USSR so far as they could be protected in a world organization.

(2) The creation of a special interest and special security bloc in Eastern Europe—a new Soviet empire.

117

(3) The prevention of any rebirth of military or political power on the entire European continent that might, now or a hundred years from now, threaten the USSR.

The first two policy lines were not really incompatible with the West; they could be lived with, and the United States was prepared to live with them. But Washington and London had their own geopoliticians, and these men, like Spykman of Yale, argued that while the Eurasian heartland, now controlled by Russia, did not threaten the United States, control of the European rimlands did.

The third policy line involved genuine trouble with the West, because the USSR felt safe only on a continent it controlled. The movement of Russian power or ideology westward from the Elbe or Danube could only bring the USSR into violent confrontation with the North Atlantic civilization. And the United States had twice taken to crusade to prevent the consolidation of Western Europe under single-power hegemony.

If Russia should prove as messianic as Germany in the pursuit of its national goals there would be war, *and ideology would have nothing to do with it.*

U. S. policy, as delineated at Potsdam in July, was to accept tacitly if not officially the creation of the Soviet Empire, and to trust that the USSR would cooperate in the new world order. This was an enormous surrender of principle as it had been enunciated on the *Augusta* and at San Francisco. The United States had become, in the words of Senator Vandenberg, the "eunuch" among the great powers. The decision was partly drift, partly a facing of certain realities vis-à-vis the USSR. But it was also, as no critic should ever forget, based on the refusal of the American public to put their power where their mouth was. If the American people truly believed in principle, it did not matter if the boys came home for twenty years.

And when the United States returned in force to Europe, as Soviet ambitions and agitations inevitably drew it back like

118

water down a sluice, it would not be in defense of the principle surrendered at Yalta and Potsdam but in protection of the United States' vital national interest.

When the Western allies marched into Germany in 1945, the Americans were surprised, the British were disgruntled, and the French were horrified to find the Germans generally unrepentent and, instead of exhausted, eager to go to work again.

Germany had been bombed, defeated in battle, and overrun as no other nation in modern times, but it was not in the chaos the Allies expected. Strategic bombing had killed one million German civilians as compared to 60,000 killed in the Battle of Britain, and it had burnt out the hearts of seventy cities. It had left approximately ninety percent of German industry intact, although the transportation system was wrecked, and certain critical bottlenecks had been created here and there.

Europe was beginning to starve, but Germans were still well fed, partially because they had looted Europe, and almost equally due to the fact that German organization still held, where other nations and their economies had dissolved in chaos. This situation the occupation authorities were soon able to correct. The resulting mess might have lasted even longer than the three years it did had the Russians not made serious diplomatic blunders.

General Lucius Clay and others, including almost the entire professional diplomatic staff of the United States, were aware that the Morgenthau Plan was intellectual idiocy. But they were able to approach the problem sensibly and allow German recovery only when the new Communist peril had replaced the old Nazi one in the public mind.

By 1945, only five potential centers of world power remained. One was the United States, both an island and a continent geopolitically, having the resources of its broad area, but largely addicted to the strategy and mobility of its ocean site.

The second was the Soviet Union, which had become, with transportation and industrialization, the land power par excellence. The other three were all war-damaged, but still potentially powerful, because they retained homogeneous, highly skilled, disciplined populations as well as vast basic industries. These were Britain, Germany, and Japan. Neither France nor China were great powers, or potentially great powers in the immediate future. Both lacked discipline and organization; France's power base was too small; and China, with enormous resources, lacked almost all industrial skills.

In 1939 the alienated USSR, whose hand because of history and a warped ideology was against every man, looked out from its great land masses on a discouraging situation: all of the other power centers were in unfriendly hands. By 1945 the situation had improved greatly. Japan had disappeared as an immediate power and threat; its military and industrial potential had been damaged by the U. S. forces; its vital Asian resources severed by the war and Yalta. Japan was not destroyed, but it was neutralized. Unfortunately, from the Russian view, it had fallen into enemy hands. Ironically, the Soviets were as short-sighted as the United States in thinking that with the collapse of Japan their one great Asian rival had disappeared. In 1945 neither could see that another power, inevitably, must try to replace the Pax Japonica with its own.

The other island empire, Britain, was victorious in the war, but strained past endurance. Its overseas resources were intact but threatened by immediate dissolution. Without its overseas possessions, Britain would resemble no other nation so much as Japan—a tight, homogeneous, highly skilled island, important culturally and economically, but no longer a prime mover in world affairs. Britain, also, was enemy territory.

Thus three of the world power basins including the apparent arch-enemy United States were hostile or potentially hostile to the USSR.

The final power center was Germany. It was in Soviet eyes

120

the most dangerous of all, for it was not only an historic enemy, it was also closest to the Soviet homeland. Because of the war, the German basin was neutralized and fragmented, and the USSR intended to keep it that way. With control of Germany, Russia could hope to rival all the island powers combined. Without Germany, the USSR might hold its own. But with a restored Germany in the camp of the island powers, the USSR was eternally overmatched.

Russia's European policy, then, was clear. It had to be based on control of Germany. But if a rearmed and revenge-hungry Germany gave Soviet statesmen nightmares, the reverse had exactly the same effect in the West.

Marching into Germany, Americans had no intention of remaining; they had counted on keeping occupation armies on German soil no more than two years. But once involved in Central Europe, and understanding Soviet motives and ambitions, the U. S. government did not dare depart. Gradually American officialdom began to accept the fact that some problems, like that of Germany, defied any quick solution, and that the price of continued security or success had to be eternal vigilance.

The immediate *de facto* solution to the problem of Germany, splitting it in two, mollified each power bloc's fears but created an unstable status quo. The situation was acerbated by the rape of Eastern Europe and Soviet pressures in Germany, and also by the tentacle of Western power that remained in the city of Berlin, far within the Russian occupation zone. This was always, as Khrushchev put it later, a bone in Russian throats. The image of a Western free Berlin interfered with the Soviet consolidation of their empire.

Millions of Americans found the whole Soviet attitude of hostility and suspicion of the West illogical. The United States and the USSR were both almost self-sufficient, self-centered, and far apart. They had no natural frontiers where power clashed. Americans had trouble understanding that Russian hostility toward the West grew out of Russian historical logic; it was not irrational but ultra-rational logic, and it would never

121

be changed by conferences or personal contact. To Russian minds, trained to see all political life as a power struggle, the mere existence of a powerful United States was a serious, ever-present threat to the Russian state.

The Soviets went to Dumbarton Oaks with the idea of arranging a world alliance that would permit them to do as they pleased in their own sphere, which in their eyes was most of Europe. They were prepared to let the Anglo-Americans do pretty much as they pleased elsewhere, having no real power to act otherwise. And the United States acquiesced to this, to a very great extent at Yalta and Potsdam—but only after so much objection that Soviet minds were far from convinced the United States intended to.

Stalin made it clear many times that the USSR tried to separate spheres of diplomacy, propaganda, and reality. The first two were tools to the Soviets, and should not be allowed to influence the last. The Soviets rarely understood the American backing of Atlantic Charter principles, and some Russian diplomats tended to feel that American statements of principle masked American ambitions or threats against the USSR.

Any real détente between the Russian and American state, given the Soviet attitude and fears, could have nothing of idealism or principle in it. It would have to be an empirical, amoral agreement, if it came, and this was the very thing Americans found most difficult. Agreement between Soviets and Americans meant that the United States had to acquiesce to Soviet ambitions and control of much of Europe. And this Americans could not really do, especially when it came to Germany.

The advent of the nuclear bomb in 1945, which some men hoped would insure future peace, merely forced immense changes in geopolitical tactics. General or total war no longer was a rational instrument of policy; the messianic forces unloosed in 1914 or 1939 had to be damped. The Soviet dream of greater world power, therefore, had to seek different channels from the

122

German. Any mass conflict like the two world wars was ruled out.

All the logic of 1914, and again that of 1939, pointed to a trial at arms between the contending powers. But the logic of the postwar world pointed elsewhere. No one seemed to understand this better than the Russians, whom World War II had almost destroyed. In this one case, at least, Soviet minds were more flexible than American. Russians accepted the power struggle inherent in the American and Soviet positions, and wanted to continue it, but with a different type of war. They accepted Clausewitz, who wrote that strategy never changes, while tactics and techniques must change to meet new situations.

Within a few months of the collapse of Nazi Germany, the United States and the USSR would actually be at war, over the carcass of the beaten enemy. But this new war would take a form the century had not yet seen.

9.

Mr. Bevin's Britain

THE STATUS QUO of the postwar world broke down into three broad entities: Western civilization, composed mainly of a cluster of nation-states around the North Atlantic; the Eurasian Communist empire; and the decaying European colonial order spread over most of the rest of the earth. All three elements, not just two of them, were actually mutually hostile. If Britain and the USSR were clashing over Poland, Egypt and India and others had their own sullen resentments against the United Kingdom, as logical and as historical as the first quarrel.

The first thing that had to be understood about this world was that there was no world society as such. There never had been. Only the predominance of Great Britain, in an informal partnership with Americans and Frenchmen, in the nineteenth and early twentieth centuries, had made it seem like there was one. Under this predominance, British and Western ideas of law, government, morality, and commerce had spread thinly around the earth, generally without taking real root. When the Western predominance vanished, the ideas and institutions, for the most part, would disappear, too.

The so-called Pax Britannica—the colonial peace enforced by the British Navy—in this respect was like the famous Pax Romana, which ended all the local quarrels of the ancient world. But a great many nations and peoples had no more respect for the Pax Britannica than the ancient Jews had for the Pax Romana, because the Pax was not exactly in their favor. This is a fact many Americans forgot.

In this sense, the great German revolt against the ordering

124

of the Western world, and the continuing revolts of lesser powers that were to follow 1945, were more human than essentially evil. Germany and Japan failed in their attempts to gain control of the old order, but in the failure they effectively destroyed that order. A Europe that fought itself could not continue to dominate the world.

Americans—who were a real beneficiary of the British world stabilization, or empire—never quite understood its beneficial nature as far as the Atlantic world was concerned, at least not until it had begun to disappear. When British power cracked, the British Peace ended. Around the world, dozens of areas that had been ruled or overwhelmed by British power and influence would return to the instability, disruption, and petty wars they had known previously. Only now, this instability offered opportunities for Soviet influence.

The idea at Dumbarton Oaks was that there would be a coalition peace, rather than a purely British, American, or Soviet one. But Britons and Americans tended to forget one fact: that moral standards, and standards of government, are never universal. Domestically or worldwide, they are usually the standards of the dominant power structure. But the UN that emerged did not represent a single dominant power structure.

The old order was destroyed in the main by three things: two great, internecine wars with Germany (without Germany, Japan could have been overawed, and Italy never was a real power) that eroded the European power bases; changes in technology, which reduced the value of sea power and increased the importance of aircraft and missiles, thus returning military power from the "islands" to the vast continental nations; and finally, a rising ethnic and national consciousness, which set almost every population in the world on a course as narrowly nationalistic as that of Germany and Japan.

The founders of the United Nations anticipated the disintegration of the colonial order of Asia and Africa, and allowed for it, though nothing was done, in the face of British

125

opposition, to hasten it. What was not anticipated was the extreme and rapid decline of British power immediately following the war, a decline that gave the Russian expansionists immediate opportunity for meddling.

There had been many virtual wards of the British hegemony, such as Greece, Turkey, the Arab States, and Iran. In these areas, the tentacles of British influence and British subsidies kept other influences at bay. But British influence required a powerful and wealthy nation and economy behind it. A Britain that had once sent gunboats and millions of pounds quietly around the world, by 1945 had run out of both.

All signposts in London pointed toward retreat. The new Socialist government, looking backward to nineteenth-century panaceas for its twentieth-century domestic ills, still rode with this tide more gracefully than the Conservatives or Churchill might have been able to do. The new men who took over Whitehall had never been the beneficiaries of the Empire, or of the wonders that capitalism had wrought from Cape Town to Calcutta. This attitude made the surgery they were required to perform much less painful than it could have ever been for a Churchill or an Eden. The Socialist attitude toward the British power position and toward the idea of collective security under the UN was probably more logical than any Tory's would have been. Eden later proved this at Suez.

Otherwise, the British misjudged the future badly. They emerged from the war with enormous moral prestige, but bungled a chance to align with a Western Europe in their own image. Ironically, Labor, which was not Imperial, was also inherently antiforeign in outlook.

The decline of British power began to leave a vacuum, which Soviet noses were keen to sense. But because the United States, Britain's great partner in world hegemony, in 1945 and 1946 was still not prepared to become the reluctant watchman on the walls of world order, Britain still had a few more hours to play upon the world stage. In Ernie Bevin, it had an actor for the part.

126

The United Nations Organization, now organizing, met in London in January, 1946. At this time the Russians were consolidating their grip on Eastern Europe, doing their best to make the joint occupation of Germany unworkable, and shooting both agents and propaganda abroad like flights of arrows. It was a time when Bidault of France, sitting on the Security Council, seemed paralyzed by the French Communist vote, and when Jimmy Byrnes, who hated Communism but still held too much of the prewar American viewpoint, was determined not to let the United States become too deeply involved in an untidy world. He sent Ed Stettinius to London as UN Ambassador, with instructions to straddle the fence between Britain and Russia.

Stettinius served well. He was able to maneuver two Latin American states, Mexico and Brazil, onto the Security Council to make the Western preponderance overwhelming, since only Poland and Russia represented the Communist world. The United States repeatedly backed Hispanic-American seats, expecting the countries to the south to recall on which side their tortillas were margarined, which generally they did. At the same time, Stettinius was eager not to engage in open acrimony with the Russians, or to offend in any way the liberal vote at home.

In January, 1946, only Ernest Bevin, Socialist Foreign Secretary of Britain, came to Church House prepared to fight both for King and Country and One World. It was a sane and simple paradox, which few in 1946 could see.

Bevin was born in the West Country. He was orphaned at six, and one of his earliest memories was the sound of Christians arguing whether or not his Nonconformist mother should be allowed a churchyard burial. As a grubby, big-eyed child, Ernie Bevin learned to hate that form of cruelty known as subtlety. At ten, he was put out to work on a farm at sixpence a week. As a grown man, like his Socialist colleagues, he never believed in economic opportunity, because in the Britain of his youth he found none.

But there are some men who cannot be held down. Bevin was rude, strong, and energetic. One by one, he worked through many jobs. He learned the way the world was, and for a laboring man in Britain, the way was rough. He went into the Labor Movement, and in time he became head of the million-member Transport and General Worker's Union, and his was a voice heard in the land.

He entered Parliament, and Winston Churchill made him Minister of Labor in the coalition government of 1940. When Labor carried at the polls in July, Bevin wanted the Exchequer. But because of his strength, Atlee made him take the Foreign Office. Short, pudgy, and flat-nosed, he took the office with no humor and less geniality. He made no friends, and soon the F. O., when he was not around, was chanting, "Life is real, Life is Ernest." And to Bevin it was.

But Ernie was not stupid; he kept all the career people, who knew what to do, at their desks, and in the bad old days of austerity, he clamored for a pay raise for his new union. Somehow, with only growls and never a smile, he won the Foreign Office's hearts. He was not, like most Labor politicians, ridden with doctrine or dogma. He could succumb to childishness on occasion, but he was always practical. He did not suffer from Labor's emotional rejection of old British values; he loved the land he came from. Also, for Bevin if an idea or practice did not seem to work, then he wanted no part of it, even if the idea was a dogma of the Socialist religion.

He began offering up large chunks of the Empire to independence or trusteeship: Tanganyika, Togoland, Jordan, and the Cameroons. This made him a world hero. But Bevin did not repudiate the idea of the Empire. He said, "If the Empire fell, the greatest collection of free nations would go into the limbo of the past."

He tried to see the world as it was from the Foreign Office. He could see the pious cruelty of much of Western capitalism, but he could also, unlike his party or many Socialist

128

intellectuals in 1946, see the even more pious and immensely greater cruelty of Communism. His British instinct told him that the gap between the kind of socialist democracy he believed in and Russian state totalitarianism was unbridgeable. He stated further something that horrified many people, but that was soon to become demonstrably true: if all Europe or the world went Communist on the morrow, the same national rivalries and problems would remain.

Believing in the West's own brand of pragmatic, largely dogmaless freedom, Ernie Bevin looked on the United Nations as a purely political organization, not a glorified egg palace where foreign ministers pussyfooted about. When the expanding Soviet power in East Europe and Asia came into confrontation with the declining British sphere of interest in those areas, it was Bevin who first began to call the spades by their real handles.

In January, 1946, the UN was still in a formative stage. It was seeking a permanent site, selecting members for the various councils, and personnel for the Secretariat. But it still had the diplomatic spotlight. All major international diplomacy was being channeled through it.

President Truman and Secretary of State Byrnes were acutely aware of the threatening difficulties with the USSR. In recent months the Russians had been increasingly suspicious, sullen, and given to diplomatic insult behind the scenes. But Truman and Byrnes still did not want to make the looming quarrel public; they still hoped that someway, somehow, it might be damped. In the UN Stettinius kept striving for a mood of compromise. This was a typically American position, and taken for the best of motives.

But this attempt to stand between the Russians and the British, as during the Polish crisis, was not only inherently futile, it was basically an error. The root of the trouble was Soviet determination to extend Russian influence into areas that were British-allied, or British dependencies. These included Greece, Turkey, and Iran, and it was as vital to future American security as to British that Soviet power be contained, although the American realization of this fact in 1946 had not yet crystallized. The assumption that the United States could act as moderator, rather than a prime mover, was based on an erroneous estimate of British power.

Because American leadership had not yet grasped the fact that Britain was rapidly failing, power-wise, American policy seemed indecisive, impractical, and even fearful. The American reluctance to get involved directly was always understandable, but it was not always admirable, nor did it reflect the best judgment. There were some games the United States did not dare keep out of, and any dangerous expansion of foreign power was one of them.

The Security Council meeting in January, 1946, had been expected to be routine. Instead, it was handed a fused bomb.

Old Ebrahim Hakimi of Iran, with Stettinius trying to shut him up, and Bevin determined to spur him on, came before the Council with a formal complaint that the Red Army occupying northern Iran was reluctant to fold its tents and go home.

Iran was ostensibly an independent kingdom. But for almost a century it had been divided into two great power spheres of influence—British in the south, including the capital Teheran, and Russian in the north. This arrangement alone guranateed Iranian independence; it had restrained both British and Czarist Asian expansion since the 1800's. The arrangement had survived the Russian Revolution, and during the war it was confirmed by the Tripartite Treaty—which gave Anglo-American forces control of the south, Russians occupation of the north. The Treaty, however, fixed a deadline for all parties to withdraw March 2, 1946. The Anglo-Americans withdrew in 1945.

Now, there was a strong separatist movement in the Iranian province of Azerbaijan, bordering the kindred Russian Azerbaijanian Republic. Iran sensed a Soviet gambit to detach the province and attach it to the USSR. But since Russians controlled the north, the central government in Teheran was helpless to interfere.

130

Iran took the matter to the Security Council, in an atmosphere of great instability and palace politics at home. The move was unquestionably precipitate, and done for domestic reasons, as well as at British urging. Iran had not exhausted all private negotiation with the USSR. The deadline had not arrived. The abrupt Iranian charges of Soviet interference chilled the members of the UN, and greatly disturbed the not-yet-elected Secretary General, Trygve Lie.

The shark-smiling, white-haired Vyshinsky ceased to smile. He was angered because the first security violation of the new world was filed against the USSR, and also because he smelled a British plot to embarrass him. Vyshinsky denied the charge savagely, then went on to reveal what would be the Communist reaction to all such charges—accuse the other side of the same thing, bring in extraneous charges, and thoroughly muddy the track.

Vyshinsky filed a complaint of security violation against the United Kingdom, on the grounds that British troops were still in Greece. Similarly, Dmitri Manuilsky charged the British with interfering with the new independence movement in the Dutch East Indies, where British troops had landed at the end of the Pacific war.

Later, all these charges and countercharges might seem minor and laughable to a world grown accustomed to the cleavage that was to come. But in 1946, they were new and sounded deadly serious; they had to be taken seriously. Stettinius was appalled and, by some neat footwork, got the Council to pass a resolution that approved the apparent willingness of the USSR and Iran to negotiate outside the UN, and requested them to do so, and report back the result.

This was the first, but by no means the last, Security Council bypass, for the one thing the Council could not handle was big-power friction.

The Greek charges, however, did not bypass so easily.

In 1941 Churchill had sent British troops—which could not be spared—to the aid of the Greeks being overrun by the German army. Churchill felt he had to honor a British commitment, even if it meant sacrificing British lives in a hopeless cause. And in 1944, as German power receded, British troops again landed in Athens. But now, in November, 1944, the Greek Communist Party staged an armed coup to seize control of the Greek government.

Churchill reacted swiftly. He authorized the British forces in Greece to put down the EAM, the Communist Party, by force of arms. There was a blazing gun battle in the streets of Athens, and the EAM was crushed. At the time, Allied newsmen, dodging bullets in hotel rooms, had painted a highly unfavorable picture of Churchill's action.

At the end of the German occupation, a Greek referendum recalled the exiled King, George II. George, ethnically German, had won something of a hero's status when the German armies had invaded by his ringing calls for defiance. He had not, like a later Rightist hero named Grivas, displayed pro-German sympathies.

George II was a reserved, quiet, decent man. But he had grave political liabilities. For one thing, he had tolerated, as a constitutional monarch, the dictatorship of Metaxas before the war. Greece, the birthplace of ancient democracy, had never been able to forge a viable democracy in modern times. It had remained torn between extreme leftist and rightist elements, with the middle group ineffective. George himself was deeply conservative, and now he again tolerated a rightist regime, which, as *Time* magazine put it, under leaders like Constantin Tsaldaris and Napoleon Zervas was more reactionary than conservative. Worse, it was also inefficient and corrupt. It made more opponents daily, to add to those already professedly Communist and determined to tear up all Greek society by the roots.

Balked in 1944, the Greek leftist rebels retreated into the mountains of North-central Greece. They received men, money, and arms from the bordering Communized nations of Albania, Bulgaria, and Yugoslavia. By 1946 they were waging full scale guerrilla war against a tottering royalist regime, with forces estimated at 25,000 in the field. Only the presence of a small British military force, and some hundreds of millions of dollars in British money, kept the Greek royalist regime in power. It *was* a civil war. But it had ramifications of the kind that were henceforth destined to complicate most wars of this century.

The Greek government had no ambitions against any neighbor; good or bad, it was no threat to world peace. But the Communist-led rebels were determined to take the country behind what would later be known as the Iron Curtain. They represented a thrust at the existing power balance, and the expansion of Communist doctrine and dictatorship into areas it did not inherently control.

Vyshinsky now opened fire on Bevin in the Security Council, with all the expertise of Soviet dialecticalism: "British troops have no necessity for being in Greece, other than to exert pressure on Greek political affairs—a circumstance . . . frequently used by reactionary elements in Greece against the democratic forces of the country." Vyshinsky snarled that the Greek government was "fascist scum" and branded it, and its British allies, as a threat to peace and security.

From the Soviet viewpoint, the charge was true. The British were refusing to permit a power vacuum to develop, which Communist power could fill—even if a Labor government had to support a tottering, and rather corrupt, monarchy to prevent it. But this was a position that much liberal thought in the West had trouble understanding—just as it had trouble comprehending that all of the pressure, and thus all of the danger, of war stemmed from the determination of Communist forces to expand.

There was in the West then, and there remained, a large body of opinion completely ignorant of the realities of power plays and the nature of the developing power struggle. This opinion failed to recognize countries such as Greece, or later, Korea and Vietnam, as highly important pawns. It also placed greater importance upon the internal workings of a "pawn" society than

133

its place in the world's political power structure; in other words, it tried to break nations and peoples down into "good guys" and "bad guys," and argued that political actions should be carried on with them on such a basis.

This opinion, ironically, was not restricted to the liberals. In a reverse sort of way, it also infected the right. If Western liberalism was offended in 1946 by Western support of a reactionary Greek regime, Western conservatives equally failed to see the geopolitical opportunities inherent in nationalistic splits between Communist countries, such as that between Titoist Yugoslavia and Stalinist Russia.

Ernie Bevin and the realists in the British Foreign Office were aware that the Greek regime was no trade unionist's dream. But they considered it a far better regime, according to the interests of the trade unionists of the West, than any Soviet-dominated Communist regime that might displace it.

Bevin saw no reason why Stalin should be treated with gentleness, particularly while Soviet diplomats were impugning British honor. He was not the man to smile and simper and plot a devious revenge. He stood up in the Security Council and roared for conviction or acquittal, put up or shut up, stand up and be counted.

He harpooned Vyshinsky and, as Trygve Lie admitted, said some things that needed saying. However, to Lie and others whose greatest hope was that the great powers would lie down in friendship, Bevin's immediate counterattack on Soviet propaganda almost made him, not Vyshinsky, the villain. He did hurt the Russians, but he put both Stettinius and Byrnes on the hot seat. And to some, it seemed that the old situation of Munich, where the West had to choose between war and surrendering another province, was approaching. This was almost too depressing to think about, and ironically again, to these minds it appeared that Western resistance, not Soviet ambition, was shaking the peace.

But while Bevin might have shaken the peace, he also performed a signal service. He was destroying the myth that Soviet hopes for expansion would go away, or be appeased, if they were only ignored.

The British did have certain interests to maintain in Greece, as well as India. Bevin admitted this. But he shouted: "Have I, or my government, been endangering the peace of the world? The danger to peace . . . has been the incessant propaganda from Moscow against the British Commonwealth!"

Vyshinsky, smiling sourly, returned a Soviet attack upon the Western imperialism of the past. "When these words were uttered here . . . from the seat occupied by the British delegation, all we Soviet representatives felt a sudden cold breath of the un-happy past." Vyshinksy tried to capitalize on the fact that nine-teenth-century Western imperialism was now discredited, while the new Soviet-style imperialism was not yet understood. Vysh-insky showed the new Soviet ploy: to obscure Russian ex-pansion and Russian tyranny by direct and repeated reminders of former Western imperialism and the Pax Britannica, of which the West had grown ashamed.

It was to be an effective gambit. It seldom failed to strike moral doubts, in the same way that Hitler's, or Fidel Castro's, hammering at the injustices of the past paralyzed democratic will toward certain contemplated injustices of the totalitarian fu-ture. Moral doubts are always expensive in world politics, and unfortunately, in the post-1945 world, only the democracies seemed to have any.

The fact was that Britain, the United States, and France were firmly status quo in outlook. They were not reactionary, nor were they unwilling to accept some compromise. Their posi-tion thus was inherently peaceful. China as yet did not count. France, under its first de Gaulle government, was beginning to show signs of what would come later; de Gaulle was demanding military budgets, muttering about French pride and grandeur, and being intransigent on questions concerning the French em-pire. For the most part, however, France, and particularly the Anglo-Saxon powers, were not only satisfied but willing to make reasonable adjustments.

None of the three Western powers had any real international ambitions, and therefore none posed any threat to the status quo or world peace. There was a growing demand for revision from many smaller powers, such as Egypt, which grew its own ultra-rational dreams and ambitions in the Islamic world. But the smaller powers could not bring about an international holocaust even if they wanted to, and in general the West was prepared to meet their demands.

The real sourness came solely from the ambitions of Communist power, first in Soviet Russia, later, more aggressively, from Red China. The Communist powers were *not* status quo in outlook. They were not prepared to accept the world as it was. As Molotov had made clear at San Francisco, the USSR demanded a far greater role in the world than it had ever been allowed previously. The USSR was determined to get it, fair means or foul.

The West had demobilized by 1946. British and American military power, except for a few nuclear devices, had been liquidated, a perfect sign of peaceful intentions. Massive Red Armies, however, still stood in Europe. They were needed, of course, to hold down Russian conquests—but they also posed a threat difficult to ignore. And spreading out from these areas, Soviet influence supported every manner of disruptive and subversive movement, anything which tended to damage or destroy the status quo.

For all its faults, the Pax Britannica had been a decent state of affairs. A Pax Sovietica, by which the USSR hoped to replace Anglo-American supremacy, had an entirely different odor.

Not much came of the Greek and Indonesian debates before the Security Council in 1946, except that Bevin did clear the air, especially for some Anglo-American officials. The Greek and Indonesian questions were shelved by the device of appointing commissions to study them. These commissions upheld the British position in Greece, but not in Indonesia. Here the fact was that British commanders, true to their own instincts,

136

had interfered with a genuine, if highly unpalatable (in Western eyes) native independence movement. The British, however, quickly withdrew from Indonesia, leaving the Dutch to handle the situation as best they could. And after a brief and futile colonial war, the Dutch acceded to East Indian independence. The world was changing, and the old order with it.

While the razor strokes and hammer blows of the Greek debate were still ringing, a fourth complaint was brought before the Security Council, this time by Syria and Lebanon, and against France and Britain. This action was immensely more significant.

Both Syria and Lebanon were Arab states severed from the Turkish Empire by World War I. They had been League of Nations mandates administered—not always gently—by France. During the second war, Britain had wrested them from Vichy control by a military campaign, and de Gaulle's Free French promised both areas full independence. There had been, during and after the war, some Anglo-French friction in the occupation of these states. On one occasion, de Gaulle had been humiliated by Churchill and FDR over a disagreement, and this was a fact that would come home to roost later. But Syria and Lebanon had been invited to San Francisco, and both were original signatories of the Charter.

The occupying powers, for one reason and another, were slow to pull out in 1946. The Arabs went to Trygve Lie, the newly elected Secretary General of the UN. Lie said they had a good case. He told them he trusted Anglo-French good intentions, and advised them to air the case before the Council.

As Lie guessed, the case was heard not with rancor but with sympathy; an open airing was enough. Seven nations, including the United States—while France and Britain abstained—voted for a European withdrawal, for arrangements to be made privately between the nations and results reported back. France and Britain prepared to implement the resolution without protest.

It was a memorable milestone toward world order. Charles

Malik of Lebanon said wonderingly: "It is certainly an historic event when two small states can, through the action of the Security Council, obtain satisfaction for their claims solely because they have a right to it." This was the kind of UN Franklin Roosevelt and Sumner Welles had envisioned, and Vandenberg and Dulles had guaranteed against a static world—a governing body in which the great would be responsible, and in which necessary changes could be effected before they reached the boiling point.

Vyshinsky coolly vetoed the resolution, to which the USSR was not a part, on the grounds that it had not condemned France and Britain as imperialistic aggressors.

The Soviet veto, cast deliberately and with irresponsible maliciousness, did not wreck the European-Arab settlement. This was immediately taken outside the UN, and adjusted amicably. But the implications of the Soviet veto torpedoed the UN. As a possible order-keeping body in the way that Roosevelt and Welles had forged it, it was dead. The USSR showed it would halt any action of which it disapproved, for the most trivial of reasons.

When the first UN meeting ended on February 15, 1946, Trygve Lie wrote in private papers that the positions were hardening; dialog had turned into invective; and there was a growing refusal, on all sides, to participate in the give and take of normal diplomacy—even on nonessentials.

It did not yet have a name, but the Cold War had begun.

10.

A Policy Called Containment

NEITHER THE RUSSIANS nor the Americans were the cleverest people, or the most experienced, in the world that followed 1945. The French were rather more civilized, the British more knowledgeable, and even the Italians at times more practical. But if you have the ships, the guns, and the money, too, cleverness or experience is not really necessary. Even a reasonable amount of blundering can be survived.

All this was brought home painfully to the world of Napoleon, Wellington, Bismarck, and Hitler in the decade that followed war's end. Because of incessant internecine warfare, Europe had surrendered control of its destiny, and possibly even of its independence, if the Soviet empire could extend west.

Meanwhile, the United States was still criticizing the old Pax Britannica, and yet acting as if that peace still held. But mistakes are fatal only if an opponent takes advantage of them.

If the United States was waiting for the world to right itself and return to the good old days, the USSR confidently expected it to go to hell unaided by much effort on its part.

In early 1946, the movement of the UN headquarters across the Atlantic to New York illustrated the dramatic shift of power westward. The UN Charter was incompatible with Swiss neutrality; Geneva as a UN site had been ruled out. Moscow was equally impossible, for different reasons, and finally, over much West European objection, the UN Secretariat settled in New York. At first it took up quarters in Hunter College, then at Lake Success, on Long Island, while its permanent site was being built at Turtle Bay.

The move was logical. The UN was American made; it was, and would continue to be, largely American financed, and the United States would continue, indefinitely, to be its most influential—if not, after 1950, its dominant—member. But while the UN apparatus moved to New York in 1946, the lessons of the London sessions remained lost on most of the American people.

One reason, in the face of Soviet intransigence, was the spasm policy of the USSR. The "spasm" policy contained rapid transits from aggressiveness to relative sweetness and light; its purpose was to keep the other side off balance. If the United States had been the aggressive fascistic monster Soviet propaganda accused it of being, the first Soviet spasm would have produced war, or at least a situation in which the USSR would have been backed into its own borders. But because it was a truly status quo power, concerned only with peace and order, the rapid transits of the USSR produced instead continuing confusion.

Russians by history were chess players. The surface game, as in chess, was important, but not vital. The real game, for power, control—all the marbles—was the thing. Americans, as a people, did not care for chess. They preferred a ball game, and this was what the USSR would not play. With no greater game in mind, Western policy always fell into the trap of watching the current score, the needs of the day, and the passing scene, never the future. It put more store in ephemeral diplomatic gains than real, if hidden, shifts of power.

In the power game, the United States, not realizing it was playing, surrendered all its cards save the trump—nuclear energy—early. Soldiers and seamen who never understood what World War II was all about clamored to go home, sending the prestige of the United States in Moscow plummeting like a shooting star. They wanted out, and they got out. The inductees of the U. S. Army learned what the poor of old London had learned in earlier centuries, and the depressed and

140

discriminated-against of modern America would learn in later years: if you make enough noise in a democracy, eventually you get results.

The war was over; the troops went home, but they scared the Congress and tied the hands of the Presidency at a time the United States needed to show extreme strength. The U. S. government had not yet learned that what the people want in international affairs is important, but cannot always be paramount. But that lesson the government, from Harry Truman on down, was learning. What the people wanted was weakening the United States, not as a free and decent nation, but as a great power.

Within twelve months of total victory and unconditional surrender, the West had retreated almost back to where it had been in the 1930's. Armed forces disappeared. The massive outflow of U. S. money—$45,000,000,000 into Western Europe alone during the war—ended with the shooting. The withdrawal produced symptoms similar to those that aided Hitler. Europe had rich lands, developed industrial economies, and highly skilled populations, but they were in temporary disorder. And they would probably not in this century again assume the importance they had once had in the world. Europe was a power vacuum, and the USSR held a real power monopoly on the continent.

If the USSR had wanted genuine accommodation with the West, on reasonable terms, it would have demobilized. The West demobilized and withdrew first, and Soviet intelligence could not mistake the fact. But the USSR neither disarmed nor withdrew, and eventually the question of what meant this martial array, in the words of Patrick Henry, again had to come into question.

There are such things as great men, and sometimes they are never given rest. The new warning was sounded, as the old one had first been many years before, by a man named Winston Churchill.

141

He was old in the March winds of 1946, seventy-one, and not so erect as he had once been. He carried a gold-headed cane, and he needed a slug of brandy now and then to warm his bones. But he could still chomp a cigar that would have made most strong men sick, and he could down five Scotches before dinner and still be the clearest mind at the table. His voice was strong as ever. His eyes were older, but as far as they saw, no eyes saw more clearly. He was a private citizen now, no longer numbered among the great. But he had been the man of the century, and his words still carried weight.

He came to Westminster College, which few men had heard of, at Fulton, Missouri, which had the same distinction. Accompanied by President Truman, he came to make a speech. Most of the undergraduates who heard him would have no idea of what he spoke, but because of former greatness, and because Truman sat beside him, nodding, the old man would again change history.

Churchill still had the qualities that had made him great—love, honor, courage, the high sense of duty. But he also had the pugnacity and the realism that once brought him to power, and now made him almost a figure of scorn. Modern man, especially modern urban intellectual man, without a sense of history or blood soil—the words Hitler's distortion made anathema—understood poorly the seemingly inexorable cycles of human conduct. Men such as Churchill, nonintellectual but brilliant, were not cleverer than the best minds of the West. But they tended to see what was, and not what should be.

At Fulton, Churchill began to describe the world of 1946 as it really was.

"From Stettin in the Baltic to Trieste in the Adriatic an iron curtain has descended across the continent."

That curtain portended something to Churchill. The USSR, apparently, did not seek war, but it sought "the fruits of war and the extension of their politics."

"If the Western democracies stand together in strict adherence to the principles of the United Nations Charter, their in-

142

fluence for furthering those principles will be immense and no one is likely to molest them.

"If, however, they become divided or falter in their duty, and if these all-important years are allowed to slip away, then indeed catastrophe may overwhelm us all."

He said the world of the twenties and thirties was repeating itself, and the present trend, unchecked, would lead to a new 1939.

He knew the talk of a European "third force" was greatly premature.

He knew the Security Council and the powerless Assembly as now organized could not of themselves defend the Charter that brought them into being.

He called for a fraternal association among the English-speaking peoples, plus an all-Western security arrangement outside the UN—but in defense of it.

To those who still put their hopes in the UN, he said: "Special associations between members of the United Nations which have no aggressive point against any other country, which harbor no design imcompatible with the Charter . . . far from being harmful, are beneficial, and as I believe, indispensible."

The West could not work on narrow margins offering temptations to a trial of strength.

"Great Heart must have his sword and armor to guard the pilgrims on their way." Churchill, quoting Bunyan, knew faith alone never defended the Holy Grail.

Thucydides, long before, had written: "War is a bad thing, but to submit to dictation of other states is worse . . . to those of you who call yourselves men of peace, I say: You are not safe unless you have men of action at your side."

The West had an old man at its side: his name was Churchill.

He finished the Fulton speech, *The Sinews of Peace,* had a quick shot of old brandy, and five full Scotches before dinner. Afterward, he sat with his cane and papers, reading the world reaction. It was universally bad. To a world sick of sacrifice and power politics, longing for its own utopia, everything that

Churchill said was horrifying. But in a year or two it would all come true.

Almost all American newspapers, isolationist or liberal, editorialized against the Fulton speech. Some even cried alarm. A great many otherwise intelligent men argued heatedly that this kind of thing was what made the USSR hostile. Not one single U. S. Congressman would publically agree with anything Churchill said. It was almost as if Churchill, singlehanded, had himself diabolically created the Communist danger.

The British Labor government, even now angling behind the scenes for an Anglo-American alliance, was completely gutless in the face of its public's wrath. It repudiated the speech as that of a private citizen. Afterward, the Labor party forced Ernest Bevin to disassociate Britain not only from the speech, but from the views as well. It broke Ernie Bevin's honest British heart.

But amid all the repudiation and all the uproar, one significant fact was largely missed. Harry Truman sat on the platform with Churchill. He had read and approved the speech beforehand. He had deliberately encouraged Churchill to send up a trial balloon presaging a shift in American policy, and a return to world politics outside the UN. That balloon was shot down, but Harry Truman remained tight-lipped when questioned about his own views on it.

No pressures, Democrat or Republican, could make him criticize or repudiate any part of it. Harry Truman, and the men around him, were learning the necessity of acting first and talking later. Harry Truman was learning there are times when peoples have to be saved whether they want such salvation or not. Within short months, from the ideas behind Fulton would come the Truman Doctrine, the Marshall Plan, and the North Atlantic Treaty Organization, whether the American people wanted them or not.

As a bitter Churchill, grim-faced and silent, went home, there was a significant event in Nuremberg, where the trials the legalistic-minded United States had insisted upon were getting under way. The British had settled Napoleon's hash politically, merely exiling him to St. Helena; they proposed to do the same with Hitler's gang. But the United States would have none of that; it was convinced it could dredge up enough out of international law to make it all legal and aboveboard.

Now, relaxing over a drink with his Western colleagues, the Soviet prosecutor discussed Churchill's speech. "Your papers are saying this means war. I don't believe it. It merely means the Western powers are going to use the same strategy we have been using all along. Don't you have an old proverb, 'You must meet force with force?'"

"Fight fire with fire," an American told him.

What Churchill had also said at Fulton—"It has been the dominant lesson of history that mankind is unteachable"— might not always be true.

Franklin Roosevelt's power and prestige as President had helped put the United States out into an alien world, but the blueprint he left behind to guide its path in that world was insufficient. By 1946, it was clear to most Western governments that the UN as originally conceived not only did not fit the new world, it also could not work. The blueprint could not anticipate the complete polarization of power between Washington and Moscow, nor did it allow for the Cold War.

The great-power veto, which paralyzed the security arrangements of the Council, had not been unrealistic. It was merely a sublimation of the veto power actually held by powerful countries in the field of action, in the same way that ballots are not sacred, but only a sublimation of clubs or bullets, in the domestic arena. The veto was demanded by *all* great powers, the United States included. There could have been no Charter without it. The only thing which made the UN unrealistic from the start was that it was organized as a house divided.

In April, 1945, the United States had made the UN a cornerstone of policy. For more than a year the United States had tried to channel all international affairs through it, and for many years the various administrations would continue to pay lip service to that idea. But to be effective, American power could no longer be channeled into it alone. With a Soviet veto used wholesale, the Security Council had become a dead-end street.

By late 1946 Truman's administration was dominated by the thought that it had to take American policy-making and actions outside the UN, if it were to cope with actual problems. Practical politics, on a world scale, demanded more action, less debate, especially since the USSR was willing to act outside the UN.

The first great watershed of American policy came under Roosevelt, with the realization that American security and the security of other nations were intertwined. That shift had created the UN at the same time that it destroyed the old isolationism.

The second great watershed, which was more a governmental than a public one, was initiated by Truman. In the forties the United States did not surrender its basic idealism or drop its pledges under the Charter. But it began to act more as a great power than as a powerless moral force.

Truman set a vital pattern that, with only small changes, was to be carried on for two more decades. Truman's outlook and policy became the fundamental policy for the United States from Marshall to Acheson, to Dulles, to Rusk, although millions of Americans never quite understood it and millions more disagreed with it.

The deadly weakness of the Democratic administration under Truman was that most Democrats were either indifferent to, or utterly idealistic in, the field of international relations. The great coalition of underprivileged or alienated domestic groups that FDR had forged was generally not interested in either foreign policy, or world order. They were preoccupied with domestic problems.

The Democratic intelligentsia, to a surprising extent in the late forties, seemed to have a poor grasp of actual world politics. Truman, on taking office, had a deep dislike of out-and-

146

out New Deal intellectuals such as Rosenman, Hopkins, and Henderson, and got rid of them.

This does not mean the out-of-power Republicans were better equipped. The opposition had brilliant minds and effective men in Vandenberg and Dulles, who had, or thought they had, real alternatives to the policies Truman developed. But businessmen, who still dominated most party councils, were still pretty much as the elder Lodge had once described them: less fit than any to assume direction of international policy. The powerful Taft wing was still isolationist and confused about things across the water.

First Truman drove the old Roosevelt men out of government. And with the end of the war, businessmen of the kind who had made policy for both parties since 1865 refused to serve; the heavy salting of wartime Republicans left Washington.

An odd and perhaps fortunate thing happened. What might be called the mainstream of American intellectual thought and American idealism passed from government. Truman, of himself, could attract no such coterie as had FDR or would John Kennedy. And in retrospect, it was probably a very good thing, for Truman turned what seemed a fatal weakness into an enormous asset. Truman's administration did something no American government had since the War Between the States: it fell back, out of necessity, on the professionals in government service.

This mixed breed—professional soldiers, career diplomats, and, strangely, some great foundation and international bankers—had generally been outside the mainstream of the American business and political community for generations. But they were all, unlike most Americans, already deeply involved in foreign affairs; they all had had to adopt a world view; and perhaps more significant, the very nature of their jobs required that they be empiricists. Bankers, soldiers, and diplomats learn early to see shades of gray, and not black or white, or they do not last. Bankers are uninterested in moral postulates but do

147

like collateral; soldiers and diplomats know that good intentions alone never won a battle or a war.

The men who remained, or now came, in the government service—the McCloys, Clays, Forrestals, Marshalls, Bradleys, Murphys, Rusks, Achesons, and Kennans—were by no means a common breed. They did not all agree. But within their wide divergences of viewpoint and disagreement on tactics, they had certain attitudes in common. Most, like Dean Acheson, had agile minds. They would put their stamp on policy so firmly that it would not soon be erased.

These men, generally, had no real interest in domestic affairs. They did not care one way or the other about the extension of Social Security; they had no position on farm policy (except as it affected foreign trade), small interest in labor legislation.

But if they were cool toward domestic Democratic aspirations, they were equally isolated from middle-class Republicanism. They believed in the usefulness and the exercise of governmental power, and federal power in particular.

They were professional in outlook, often patrician in background, and tended to be conservative—but this was conservatism in the ancient Roman or British Tory sense, never the nineteenth-century middle-class liberalism that would be called conservatism in the time of Goldwater.

They were brilliantly equipped to act, but not to make a differently oriented American public opinion understand what they were doing. They created a lasting dichotomy between the Administration and the people on foreign affairs, as well as a similar dichotomy within the party itself, between themselves and the party politicians who kept them in office.

All of these men, instinctively, had no use for Communism. But they could not regard it as a sin; they saw it as Churchill did, a mortal political danger. They had nothing against it as long as it stayed home; but when it tried to expand, that was something else.

Their real, if not openly expressed, attitude toward the idea

148

of the United Nations was probably best summed up by State Department career man Robert Murphy, who wrote that he regarded the UN as an organization that might on occasion be useful to the United States in the conduct of its foreign policy. When the UN was not, they carefully and deliberately ignored it.

This policy was called containment. When it was being built, it was a very controversial thing. It angered moralists, like Dulles, who wanted the USSR to be forced to disgorge; it infuriated idealists and intellectuals who were determined to find détente with Soviet power, then and later. Ironically, it angered Americans who wanted to get along with the USSR, and Americans who wanted to smash it.

Containment could be called, in simplest terms, the Soviet foreign policy in reverse. It did not seek war, but sought to deny the Soviets the fruits of war. In this sense it was a reaction to Soviet policy, and sterile. But there is a season for all things, and when containment came, it was already overdue. If it had come about in 1944, the shape and nature of the postwar world would have been very different; the world that was confirmed at Yalta would have never been.

None of this could have come about without the personality and strength of Harry Truman, a one-time insignificant man whom history would probably rank in at least the second tier of the hierarchy of great Presidents. When the man himself faded, when the image of partisanship, bad temper, unfashionable clothes, and Missouri accent were gone, and only the acts remained, Truman's place would be secure.

Almost unnoticed at the time, Truman showed his qualities early. At the time of the San Francisco conference, the United States had to make a commitment on the Pacific bases it had wrested from Japan. Truman's military staff told him Okinawa was obviously vital to American security in the Orient and the future control of Japan. But at the same time many nations were looking to the United States to develop the trusteeship and self-determination principles for all colonial areas. In FDR's

149

councils, U. S. thinking on the subject of retention of Pacific bases remained confused and even somewhat shamefaced.

Truman listened to both sides, then said colonial areas were one thing, military bases another. International trusteeship could not be applied to U. S. bases no matter where located, from Panama to the Pacific. Saying, "It is so ordered"—a phrase he had learned while presiding over the Senate as Vice-President—Truman settled the question, and the United States kept its hard-won bases.

It was fortunate if a President could be a great moral leader, like Roosevelt; it was good if he could create a favorable international image, like Kennedy. It was also nice if he could be intellectual and communicate, but it was not necessary. What an American President needed to be from the day the United States became a great and involved power was a decision-maker. He must be able to set the nation quickly and unerringly on a course of action overseas, without fear of public opinion or personal doubts or qualms. The Constitution gives him the power, and duty demands it—whether he or his party are ever elected to office again.

Correct decisions, as military history has proved, are not usually hard to recognize, whether in Lincoln's time or later. What is hard is to select the correct course in the face of opposition. If Harry Truman made mistakes, he never passed the buck. He did not hesitate when Acheson reminded him, in 1950, that "your decision to intervene in Korea may not always be the popular one."

It was no accident that *every* Truman foreign policy decision was removed from popular or Congressional control, and presented to Congress and public only when it was irreversible. The debate on Truman policy was always *ex post facto*. In the climate of the forties, domestic and foreign, there was no other way. Truman's policies had very little popular or intellectual support; some might have lost in public airing; and at any rate, after thorough Senate discussion, it would have been too late.

150

This did damage to traditional American democracy. If the Presidency, with its new power of decision overseas, was now an almost intolerable burden, it had also begun to overshadow all American life, in a way the founding fathers never contemplated. The President, in the nuclear age, held the fate of all Americans in his hands.

But without the willingness to commit national power immediately, and to commit it first and seek domestic support later, the policy called containment could not have been forged. Without this willingness there would have been no Truman Doctrine, no Marshall Plan, no broad entangling web of alliances, like NATO, to hold Soviet expansion in check, and no decision to meet force with force in Korea. Without it, Stalin's prophets who foretold the fall of the West might have been correct.

COLLEGE OF THE SEQUOIAS
LIBRARY

11.

Shifting Sands

THE POLICY called containment grew out of the obvious threat of Soviet expansionism, a Churchill speech, and the decline of Great Britain as the world's foremost order-keeping power. Containment, as a policy of the U. S. government, was given real form by a group of men in the State Department, headed by George F. Kennan, who were ordered to study world conditions and make recommendations for future U. S. actions. Both the studies and the recommendations were done almost without public knowledge. The reason was simple: a large segment of the American public, particularly the intellectual fringe, showed no signs of willingness to accept world realities between 1945 and 1947.

In fact, when Kennan, under the pen name "Mr. X," published a study of the motivations of Soviet policy in *Foreign Affairs,* the reaction was swift and bitter, so bitter it caused the Administration to stop advertising its beliefs. It seemed a very large proportion of the American and Western intellectual community were simply not prepared to accept the fact of Soviet ambition, or Soviet hostility to the West. It was an almost religious belief that would linger on, cropping up again when Red China's determination to dominate East Asia appeared in the 1960's. Many people would not face this fact, either.

But containment did not emerge full-blown as a finite, coherent plan of U. S. action. Truman, the decision-maker, did not order: "Contain Communism!" and the Executive branch, increasingly aloof from the Congress, did not move immediately to make it so. Containment, as a recognizable policy, was put together out of a series of challenges and responses.

152

The basic challenge was that Communist power seemed determined to expand its influence anywhere it could. The basic response was that the U. S. government recognized such expansion as hostile to its fundamental interests. This action and reaction formed the framework, the bare bones, of the entire political spectrum of the postwar world. And because this involved the collision of two great powers, the United Nations could play no effective part in it.

By 1947, it was clearly evident that the United States, which had inspired, named, founded, and was largely supporting the UN, had already been forced to move the implementation of its world policies outside that organization.

The first move was called forth by the imminent collapse of British power in Greece and Turkey. Here, since 1944, only British influence had held back the flow of Soviet influence into the region—if not an actual Communist takeover.

World order had been synonymous with European imperialism in the past century, and Communist propagandists were able to carry the analogy forward with a great deal of success. Any use of force by Western powers to enforce order was immediately branded as imperialism. Unfortunately, for a variety of reasons—one of which was Western pacificism and unwillingness to accept a difficult burden—some of these charges stuck.

In 1946, in Iran, the Soviet policy-makers had held a bad hand. They were in a region where British nerves were sensitive; Iranian oil was vital to Western Europe. The Red Army itself was involved, on foreign soil where it did not even have the theoretical right of conquest it enjoyed in Central Europe. Stalin understood the vital stake the Western world had in the Middle East and was fearful of going too far. Understanding that U. S. power would back the British in this region, he pulled his troops back from Iran in early 1946, but not before the Soviet delegation staged a temporary "walkout" of the UN over the issue of Anglo-American pressures.

But while holding the dam in Greece and exposing the new

153

Communist game there, the British began to take a terrible propaganda beating around the world. Here no Russian troops were involved; it was the British who were on foreign soil. By preventing an indigenous Communist movement from taking over, they were now accused of standing for Empire and reaction. Bevin's vehement defenses of British policy in the UN were branded as dangerous to world unity, rather than revealing of a disunity that already existed. Cops, in any uniform, are never popular.

In Greece, unlike Iran, Russian-inspired pressures were doing very well. Here there was a pattern that was to become familiar in the coming years. Russian forces were not involved, nor, to the casual observer, was the USSR involved. But Greece's civil war had turned into what the Communists called a "war of national liberation." Local dissidents, Markos Vafiades' 25,000 guerrillas, had turned into foreign instruments of Soviet policy.

Defeated by British troops in 1944, the Communist rebels had been armed and aided by the Soviet satellite states of Albania, Bulgaria, and Yugoslavia. They trained north of the Greek border in the privileged sanctuary required by all guerrilla movements; Communist arms trickled southward through the Macedonian hills. It looked like civil war—but if a Communist-armed and-dominated force took control of Athens, the USSR through it would effectively control Greece and flank Turkey, all without the cost and terrible danger of a third world war, which an overt march of the Red Army might bring.

The British government, bankrupt at home, by 1947 had spent about $250,000,000 keeping Communism at bay in Greece. Only this money, and the British troops still garrisoned there, held George II and his rightist ministers in office. The Royal Greek Army and the royal Greek economy, meanwhile, due to ineptitude at management levels, as well as historic graft and corruption, were at the point of collapse.

At the same time Turkey, a nondemocratic but Russian-hating bastion that barred Soviet entry to the soft underbelly of the Near East, was equally approaching collapse. Turkey had no

154

domestic Communist movement of any consequence. But its economy was as badly managed as the Greek; modern economies were simply not a Near Eastern art. An agricultural nation, Turkey had maintained 600,000 men under arms all during World War II and afterward. This force was proof against both German and later Russian adventures, but it cost $150,000,000 a year. This burden, on top of a mismanaged agrarian economy, was too much. Yet the Turks did not dare to disarm.

Immediately after the war, the Soviets calculatedly began making demands for the Dardenelles—a historical Russian goal. They also pressed claims for three Turkish provinces on the Caucasian frontier, where the Turkish-Soviet border split certain Georgian ethnic groups. Russian army corps continued to hold large-scale maneuvers near Turkish soil; a latent threat of invasion was kept foremost in Turkish minds. In this way, Russian pressures were forcing the Turks to bring their country to the point of collapse.

It must be remembered that Turkey, a neutral during the war, was diplomatically isolated except for Britain. Only British money, comfort, and promise of support kept the Turkish cabinet strong against all Russian pressures. And British money, comfort, and troop support were wearing thin. If the British lost out in Greece, and Communist power was sucked into the vacuum, Turkey would then be surrounded on three sides. Turkey then would almost certainly have to make an accommodation with Russian notions of the brave new world.

In December, 1946, the Greek government laid formal charges before the UN, claiming interference in its national affairs by the Communist powers of Albania, Bulgaria, and Yugoslavia. These charges were later completely substantiated by a UN commission. Arms and men were crossing the Greek border from the Communist powers to aid the KKE, the Greek Communist front. Ethnic Greeks who lived north of the border were being recruited to the Communist cause.

The United States government, in 1946, had agents and missions in both Greece and Turkey. Official Washington was well

155

apprised of the situation. But official Washington really pre-ferred to take no responsibility, even though it was increasingly apprehensive of encroaching Soviet influence. On February 27, 1947—long before the news was made public—London quietly passed the word to Washington. His Majesty's Government was too strapped to continue manning the walls in Greece and Tur-key. Yet the walls still needed to be manned. Did Washington want into the great game of world order?

This was the first real step in what was to be a long British retreat from the world's ramparts. It was the first step in what was to be the changing of a British to an American guard. Wash-ington did not really want to play—but as Kennan, heading the containment policy board, and George Marshall, now Secre-tary of State, forcefully argued, what other choice was there? It seemed vital that both Greece and Turkey be kept out of the Soviet orbit.

As one nameless diplomat snapped: "Stop this damn gabble about pulling British chestnuts out of the fire. To hell with the British. Forget the British and their problems. Can't you finally understand this is *your* problem, too?"

The matter of the stupid and reactionary Greek regime was broached, in typical American fashion. There was no answer to this, the policy-makers argued, but that it would have to be shored up until something better came along. It was, indisputa-bly, better for the United States than a Communist regime.

With receipt of the British notice of withdrawal, the reaction of the Truman Administration was swift, sure, decisive, and true to its empirical instincts. Truman proclaimed what was to be called the Truman Doctrine—before he cleared it with either Congress or the public. Truman pledged the United States to sup-port both Greece and Turkey against all internal rebellion or for-eign aggression, and then, as a sort of afterthought, asked Con-gress for the money: $400,000,000. Congress, which if given a chance to debate the matter might not have gone along, was backed into a corner from which, luckily, there was no escape.

Significantly, the U. S. Ambassador to the UN was not even

informed of this monumental shift in U. S. policy until the news of it was on the radio. Truman's men had no illusions as to the UN's ability to act in the Greek and Turkish crisis. Both Trygve Lie and Arthur Vandenberg were horrified. Neither opposed the action; Vandenberg, like the growing class of internationalists, was highly in favor. But both men were obviously depressed by the fact that the United States was abruptly removing the implementation of policy from the UN.

Public and intellectual reaction to the Truman Doctrine was far from adulatory. There was immediate war-fear: it had almost become implanted in the public mind that any real opposition to Communist expansion was warlike. In Chicago, there was talk about "getting out the old uniform again."

Here, in 1947, patterns became evident that were to influence and haunt all future American international order-keeping. Opposition did not stop the government, but it was pronounced. Throughout all the opposition was threaded the old American fear of "getting involved in someone else's quarrels." Americans did not like to get involved unless there was a clear-cut, black-white moral issue, such as Americans had thought they had against Kaiser Bill in 1917, or against Hitler, or the Japanese after Pearl Harbor.

In Greece and Turkey, and in most future operations, there were no such clearly delineated issues. Neither the Greek nor Turkish ruling parties were demonstrably good guys, threatened by obvious monsters. Aiding Greece and Turkey showed a clear acceptance of a world power struggle that went beyond purely moral terms. And millions of Americans' nonacceptance of that struggle was to linger and grow, from Greece in 1947 to Cuba in 1961 to Vietnam in 1965.

Opposition centered in three main groups. First, there were the pacifists, a ubiqitous and never quite submerged group, sometimes numbering as much as twenty percent of the population. They wanted no trouble; they wanted no sacrifice or service, for any reason, except perhaps an invasion of North America. Their feelings were humanly understandable, but ignorable.

157

Liberal-intellectual opinion was automatically outraged by the pragmatism of the move, and by the nature of the regimes being aided. George II of Greece had become a sort of liberal whipping boy on college campuses, where the incessant terrorism of the Greek KKE and Vafiades' army—which murdered political opponents as deliberate acts of terrorism and abducted women and children—were generally passed over. This body of opinion, also, never seemed quite to understand the nature of man, and the courses of his politics, which frequently result in vast power struggles—for the sake, at times, of power. It was one thing to decry power struggles. It was quite another, as George Kennan and George Marshall knew, to be defeated in one.

But there was also a certain gloom on the American right. Many influential men, like Joseph P. Kennedy, father of the future President, were opposed. These men felt that the Truman Doctrine would lead to prodigal spending overseas and, with continual involvement on the executive level, to the eventual destruction of domestic American democracy. These men also felt that Communism overseas was destined to conquer anyway, and there was little the American republic could do about it. This, ironically, was an argument that would be seized upon by American liberals opposing action in Vietnam almost twenty years later, when it would be argued that Communist China was destined to dominate Asia no matter what the United States did or did not do.

Bernard Baruch agreed with Kennedy. Walter Lippman also had a great many arguments as to the danger of this kind of empirical action. But Harry Truman—in retrospect, wisely—confronted the nation with an accomplished fact. It is probably safe to say that most of the arguments in themselves were specious, sincerely as they were proposed. They reflected what John F. Kennedy would later put into words he was unable to use at Dallas, Texas: that the United States had become the watchman on the walls of world freedom not through choice, but necessity, and a great many people preferred, for a great variety of per-

158

sonal reasons ranging from money to the draft, not to mount those walls.

At the end of World War II, the realities of world politics forced the United States to act, for the first time in its history, as a responsible and responsive great power. Order-keeping is never all imperialist beer and skittles, as both the British Colonial Army and the French Foreign Legion discovered. And as Americans were to discover, it requires money and, sometimes, blood.

In both Greece and Turkey the new policy begun by Truman produced demonstrable results. It had never been designed to make either place a human paradise, but to balk the flow of Communist power. And this it did.

The Greek Royal Army, with American funds, was raised from 60,000 to 132,000 men, and 50,000 more militiamen were recruited and trained. The flow of dollars corrected economic deficiencies, in spite of the continued ineptitude of Greek leaders like Tsaldaris and the new Premier, Demetrios Maximos. It may have been money down a rat hole, but the rat hole was saved for the West.

The Greek Communist rebellion was not destroyed by American aid alone, but by a combination of circumstances. At the same time that the Greek Army was retrained and refurbished, Yugoslavia, under Marshal Tito, broke out of the Soviet bloc in 1948. Tito, really at the point of a cold war with Stalin, closed the Yugoslav border to Greek guerrillas, almost at the time when the improved Greek Army cut them off from the Albanian and Bulgarian frontiers. The KKE (called Koo-Koo-Ay) was denied a sanctuary to retreat to under pressure, and a source of outside help. This was an immensely damaging blow.

Secondly, the guerrilla leadership made a historic mistake, one the Communists would try to avoid in the future. They took the war out of the hills before they were ready, and tried to meet the more heavily armed royal forces in conventional battle. The Greek army, with American advisers, defeated them.

159

Meanwhile, the guerrillas had estranged the bulk of the Greek population—even many who hated the royalist regime—through their terror tactics. Rebel raiders killed women without compunction, and carried small children off north of the border to Bulgaria. When the strengthened Greek National Militia began to give real protection to Greek towns and villages, this terrorism backfired. The people turned against the KKE. The rebellion was finally stamped out.

In Turkey, likewise, the pressing economic problems were eased. U. S. money paid for the large standing army, and reequipped it, and the standing army stood on the borders implacably. Turkish diplomatic isolation was ended; Turkey came into the Atlantic world under American sponsorship. U. S. backing gave Turkish leader Celal Bayer all the freedom he needed to defy the Russian threats. Soon, the Soviets stopped making them.

Moving onward from this historic crossroads (which, perhaps, was too easy, and created a certain false confidence that the future task might be easier than it was), the United States discovered serious handicaps to what some already called a new Pax Americana. Americans were now accused of all the crimes the British had once been accused of, although it was easily demonstrable that the United States had no personal ax to grind in supporting foreign regimes against Communist takeover. There was no profit, only cost, to the United States, which had to be charged against American security.

The United States was now accused, and not only in Russia, of supporting reactionary governments that oppressed their own peoples, of interfering with legitimate protest movements, and even of increasing the dangers of a big war. Again, these arguments were specious: no government could be so reactionary as a Communist one in the twentieth century; the United States had no quarrel with any protest movement unless it were infected with or included Communists; and the tragic spectacle of the 1930's should have proved forever that wars are not caused

160

by refusal to accommodate aggression, but rather the opposite. But human nature is not built that way.

All Harry Truman, George Kennan, and George Marshall had in mind was the containment of *expansionist* Communism, and the kind of world order in which the majority of Americans believed, a world in which no nation was allowed to enlarge its border or *span of control* by any kind of force, including subversion. Actually, Truman's Cabinet had no quarrel with Communism itself—*if it stayed behind its prewar borders*. As Kennan was tacitly to admit, what Russia did within its own historical borders was as much Russia's business as what the federal government did in Missisippi was Americans' business.

It was noticeable that the British, who had passed their own subsidies quietly and totally without fanfare, were a bit shocked at the way American aid was trumpeted and proclaimed. But then His Majesty's Government had always called "foreign aid" by its historical name of "subsidy."

The Truman Doctrine was the first move in a vast design that later became formalized in the European Recovery Act (called the Marshall Plan), and in 1949, NATO, the North Atlantic Treaty Organization. The causes of ERA were the same: Russian pressures on Europe. The reasons were similar: to put Western Europe back on its feet as the first step toward allowing it to resist Communist subversion. The three billion dollars for the Marshall Plan was announced in the same way as the Truman Doctrine: Truman announced the plan, backed Congress into a corner, then asked for the funding money. But ERA met less opposition, for it made economic as well as strategic sense. Between 1947 and 1950 the results of ERA were spectacular. After 1950 Western Europe exceeded postwar levels of production and even living standards, and a voluntary turn to Communism in Europe was unthinkable.

NATO, just as much as ERA, grew out of Churchill's Fulton speech. NATO was the mere formalization of a strategic situation that already existed. By 1947 the United States was prepared to go to war with the USSR if the USSR invaded Greece, Turkey, or Western Europe. The signing of mutual alliance treaties and the slow rearming of Western Europe, as Churchill had called for, informed the Soviet world of the West's intentions as nothing else could have done. It also had a certain side effect: for a number of years the alliance, and the fear of Russia that hastened it, accelerated the integration and consolidation of Western Europe.

But if NATO had a great fault, it was that some Americans, even on high levels, tended to think of it as being forever. But treaties, unlike diamonds, are called forth by changing circumstances, and all alliances—as "perfidious Albion" knew—are changeable and friable.

If and when the Russian threat receded, NATO might become as irrelevant as the Marshall Plan became after European Recovery. Whatever happened, in the years between 1949 and 1962, NATO served its purpose, as its chief architect, Dean Acheson, was well aware. Ironically, no man ever did more to contain expansionist Communism than Acheson. But like Kennan, because he could not take an evangelical attitude toward Communism's admitted evils, eventually no man was ever more crucified as Secretary of State.

Between the years 1947-1949, while European Recovery and NATO were forged, the United Nations had met and failed its first great test. Its failure lay in the fact that it was never called upon.

Soon after the Greek crisis, the British began another great withdrawal from world-order keeping, this time in Palestine. Here again, for entirely different reasons, the UN failed. But because it did become involved, and because the United States refused to take the kind of quick, decisive action it had taken with the Truman Doctrine and European Recovery, the result was a certain tragedy.

Palestine had been, like most of the Arab world, a Turkish province until World War I. In 1917 and 1918 British forces occupied it in the war against the Turks, and in 1922 the League of Nations mandated Palestine to Britain at the same time that Syria and Lebanon were mandated to France. But Britain began the mandate with already unsolvable problems—some of circumstance, some of Britain's own making.

For the whole period of thirty years of British rule, the British made a mess of the mandate. In extenuation it can only be said that Palestine was not the kind of situation that British order, pragmatism, and the spirit of fair play could handle. Truthfully, British policy in Palestine was always ambiguous. The trouble was that the British, like Americans in Hispanic America, really wanted only order, but did not ever learn how to bring it about.

The trouble began in 1916, when Dr. Chaim Weizmann, a Russian-born, German-educated, British-naturalized Jewish chemical genius who was also a Zionist, rendered immensely valuable services to the British war effort by synthesizing acetone, a vital ingredient in the making of smokeless powder. Weizmann had no interest in the British honors or rewards offered, but he was deeply imbued with the Zionist dream of founding a national home for world Jewry.

When Lloyd George's government asked how it might repay him, Weizmann insisted that Britain back his plan for establishing Palestine—the ancient home of Israel, from which the Jews had been scattered by the Romans about A.D. 135—as a Jewish national refuge. In this, Weizmann was more clear-sighted than leaders such as Theodor Herzl, who was pressing for Uganda. Weizmann believed that in Palestine, the ancient Israel and Judaea, modern Jews could find not only a physical but a mystically spiritual sanctuary.

Thus, in 1917 while Palestine was still a Turkish and therefore an enemy province, the British government issued what came to be called the Balfour Declaration. This officially recognized the implicit right of Jews to establish residence in Palestine, and pledged British support in allowing world Jews to immigrate there.

163

But the British promised something they could not deliver. The province was occupied by more than a million Arabs, largely nomadic peoples who had lived in this land for centuries, and who reacted to the idea of a Jewish national state carved out of their territory with nothing but hatred. Between 1918 and 1922 and later, many Jews were settled in the coastal areas of Palestines, under the British mandate. But Britain had to renege on the idea of a Jewish state. And it soon had all it could do merely to keep Arab and Jew from each other's throats. A measure of the problem was that as early as the 1930's Great Britain had to keep an entire army corps tied down in Palestine on peace-keeping duties.

Here the governing British were caught between two wholly messianic, emotional, ultra-rational, and irreconcilable forces. There is usually no answer to religious wars except mutual extermination, or mutual exhaustion. Almost from the first there was steady trouble, terrorism, and fighting. Arabs created atrocities, and Jewish extremist groups were formed to repay them in kind. There could be, in such a situation, no clear-cut right or wrong.

The Jewish refugees from many places in the world had a desperate need for a refuge or national home. They were also, generally, European and better trained and organized than the nomadic Arab tribesmen who inhabited Palestine. They made better citizens and did more to develop the land. But Palestine had been Arab for as long as the tribal legends ran, and to the natural Arab determination to hold on to what was theirs was added a burning fear: although the lands set aside for Jews were small and restricted, Arabs feared the better education and organization of the Jewish communities. They realized they might be crowded out of their ancestral sands and overpowered politically and economically. All this heightened normal religious animosity.

Each side was obsessed with its own fears or visions. British arguments for reason and compromise were futile. But as Sir Ronald Storrs, a British Military Governor, wrote in his memoirs:

164

"No monopoly of errors can be ascribed to any one of the three interested parties: the Jews, the Arabs, and the British."

The British made bad errors, trying to play off one side against the other, making promises that could not be kept. But it should also be remembered that an equally empirical and level-headed race, the Roman proconsuls of the first century of the Christian era, had no better luck against the same kind of ultra-rational forces. The British, as even condemned extremists on the way to gallows admitted, were inherently more decent than the Romans had been. They did not exterminate anybody, and kept trying to the last for a reasonable settlement.

In 1936 a commission under Lord Peel investigated Arab-Jewish fighting and called the mandate unworkable. Peel requested partition of the territory, stating it was the only possible solution. But the Arab answer was the often-shouted: "Drive the Jews into the sea!"

The Jews, particularly after the Hitlerian persecutions swept Europe, refused to honor British laws restricting immigration. They smuggled thousands of coreligionists into the mandate, inflaming Arab hatreds and fears even more.

Arabs attacked and massacred Jewish communes: Jewish terror groups, like the Stern Group and Irgun Zvai Leumi, shot down Arabs of all ages and sexes. Ironically, both attacked any and all British peace-keepers who got in the way. Jewish terrorists blew up a hotel where British officers, Arab leaders, and Jewish compromisers were meeting. Arab tribesmen waged continual guerrilla war against British patrols. Two teenage Jewish terrorists, in 1944, murdered Lord Moyne, the Resident British High Commissioner in the Near East.

The Hitlerian persecutions dramatized the plight of world Jews, and won them immense sympathy in their desire for a national state in Palestine. At the same time, rising Arab nationalism in the states carved out of the old Turkish Empire—Egypt, Iraq, Jordan, Syria—put great pressures on the British, who had large interests in each country, to contain the Jews. Chaim Weiz-

165

mann, all these years, worked indefatigably toward his Zionist goal, winning increasing sympathy and support in America and the West.

Acute ethnic consciousness made the situation impossible. The British, with a profound pro-Arab bias on army and civil service levels, but with strong Zionist pressures at home, tried to behave neutrally in practice. As usual, they succeeded only in infuriating both Arabs and Jews. At the same time that Arab nationalists were accusing the British of sneaking in uncounted thousands of Jews "to build a pro-British, Jewish Western state" on the shores of Galilee, American commentators such as Walter Winchell, wholly pro-Zionist, went so far as to accuse the British soldiers in Palestine of emulating the German SS.

Understandably, at the end of World War II the British only wanted out. Their League of Nations mandate expired May 14, 1948, and they would have preferred to hasten the day.

Palestine was then outside the defined boundaries of the Cold War between East and West. Since there was seemingly no security interest at stake, Britain considered the logical move was to take the Palestine question to the UN. In a situation where two parties each demanded independence from Britain and also from each other, in a country where both were inextricably mixed, an international solution seemed necessary. In its founding, the UN had been designed for just this kind of problem.

In 1947, Sir Alexander Cadogan, the British Permanent Undersecretary for Foreign Affairs and delegate to the UN, told the Security Council: "We have tried for years to solve the problem . . . having failed . . . we now bring the question to the United Nations, in the hope it can succeed where we have failed."

The British Colonial Minister went further: "We hope by our withdrawal and relinquishment of authority, that the naked realities of the situation would be better appreciated by all concerned. . . . British administration of the mandate has brought down upon our heads the execration of the Jews and the bitter resentment of the Arabs; it has made us the butt of malicious criticism throughout the world."

166

It was the kind of thing order-keeping brought forth, as the United States, intervening later in Santo Domingo or Vietnam, was to learn. But as the Minister also said: "We have played our part to the limit of our resources." Britain no longer had an army corps to keep in Palestine.

The Security Council had been organized and empowered to take action in just this kind of matter, to prevent bloodshed or a breach of peace. The USSR, under Stalin, regarded the Arab East, with its vital Western oil interests, as too sensitive for Russian meddling. The USSR was not prepared to hamstring any Western effort here, and the Soviet delegate made this clear. The other nations, listening to the British case, voted to take Britain off the hook.

A UN commission was appointed in 1947. It made an extensive study on the ground. It reported back that a coalition Arab-Jewish government of Palestine was impossible in the light of the emotions aroused by mutual terrorism. Like Lord Peel eleven years earlier, the commission recommended partition.

A resolution for partition passed the General Assembly 33-13, with ten abstentions. The USSR and the Communist bloc joined the United States and Western Europe in voting for it. Only the Moslem nations—still holding out for Jewish extinction—voted no.

Although the UN resolution proposed to allow the new Jewish state only one eighth of the territory promised in the old Balfour Declaration, the Jewish leaders in Palestine acquiesced to it. The Arab groups—still a majority of the Palestinian population in 1947—noisily refused, and were supported by the neighboring Arab nations.

The power centers of the world, through the UN, had spoken. To keep peace, and prevent killing, they had made a political decision to divide Palestine. But it was now obvious that force was going to be needed to make the decision stick.

And here, the whole mechanism of the UN broke down. The Charter of the UN envisioned that one or more of the great powers would enforce UN decisions. But now, with much spout-

167

ing of pious words, each of the great powers refused to become involved.

Britain, as an interested party, was in no position to be the implementer of the UN mandate. Further, Britain, with enormous interests in the Arab world, was in the most ticklish position as far as enforcing an unpopular decision down Arab throats was concerned. Britain passed, and everyone understood. The ball passed to the United States, the organizer and indisputably the greatest power sitting in the UN.

But there had been a bit too much light and far too much heat generated domestically on the Palestine question inside the United States. Nineteen forty-eight was an election year, and American emotions were also aroused. American-Jewish voters in strategic areas had somehow identified with extreme Jewish factions in Palestine, who wanted more territory. American oil companies, with strategically large amounts of campaign money, were making urgent phone calls to Washington, urging it to do nothing that might irritate Arab sentiment.

Washington, belatedly, had nightmare visions of stepping into the same kind of stew the British were gratefully getting out of. The U. S. government, which had been making self-righteous pronouncements over the twists and turns of British Near Eastern policy, suddenly turned slippery itself on the whole question.

Now the terrible and salient weakness of the Truman Administration was illustrated, if not illuminated. Truman's men, rational, dispassionate, and utterly devoted to American interests in the broad view, worked effectively only when they did not have to work in the limelight, and when they did not have to tell an emotional American public what they were doing. Truman was a policy- and decision-maker, not a great popular leader. He and his closest advisers liked to work in a vacuum of popular opinion and attention—to do what they felt had to be done, and then present the public with a neat package, irretrievably wrapped. They were not only, in the main, like Acheson, poor public salesmen; they deeply resented having to explain the facts

168

of world life, federal power, or national self-interest to a fickle public.

Truman's policy-makers and implementers were great international bankers, professional diplomats, and career soldiers. All of them were loyal Americans, but none of them were politicians. In fact, few of them gave a damn about domestic politics, Republicans and Democrats included. To them, America's emergence as a great power into the world was the salient and only important fact of the age.

But when both Zionists and oil moguls descended on Washington, each with their own brand of threat, the political weakness of Truman's Administration was revealed. The domestic, or political side, of the Democratic Cabinet was frightened when the ruling party was threatened with the loss of New York (which it turned out later they did not need) and with the loss of needed financing. The demand was that the United States stay aloof from Palestine.

The uproar forced the watchman on the walls to turn his back. The empiricists in Washington, who were completely unenamored of both Arabs and Jews, but who knew a world situation was being allowed to go to hell, were unable to cope with the situation. They did nothing.

Warren Austin, the white-haired, florid Republican running the U. S. show at UN headquarters in New York, suddenly made a complete turnabout. He was acting on instructions from Washington, where the domestic politicians had seized ascendancy. One minute he was debating in favor of partition. Now, he blandly put forth the new opinion that the Security Council really lacked any and all authority to *enforce* any kind of decision in Palestine.

Trygve Lie saw this U. S. shift as treachery. It was a terrible blow to him and to his Secretariat who had worked so hard, with U. S. backing, to resolve the crisis. Lie was infuriated, and, as few people knew at the time, was barely dissuaded from resigning at once.

Now, as Easter 1948 approached, the British, in a sort of self-righteous stew, began to pack up and move their troops out. The United States, as one observer said acidly, did a great deal of equally self-righteous shouting and screaming, but nothing else. The Arabs and Jews, left to their own devices, began a civil war.

The day following Easter Sunday there were a dozen engagements. At a place called El Kabri, 250 Arabs ambushed a Jewish convoy trying to run supplies to isolated Jewish communities in the desert. Forty Jews were killed. Near Bethlehem, a force of 3,000 Arabs descended on a Jewish area and killed about twenty in a day-and-night gun battle. It was hardly all one way, however. Jewish gunmen littered the streets of Haifa with Arab corpses, and photos of this massacre ran in many newspapers.

The British regulars on the ground gave up trying to stop the fighting, and tried only to referee. The British refused to employ real force against either the Arab or Jewish armed bands. The world was treated to spectacles of Highlanders acting as intermediaries between Arabs who had bottled up Jewish terrorists, and British Tommies arranging safe conducts for Arabs attempting to flee coastal cities. In a grim and tragic sort of farce, Arab militia, Jewish Haganah, and British soldiers all moved side by side, heavily armed, in a terrible Alice in Wonder-Holy Land.

As May 14 approached, even the referee prepared to leave. Meanwhile, U. S. representatives at the UN broached a new idea in New York: how about a new international mandate to rule Palestine—but one in which the United States, unfortunately, could take no part? This approach got the answer it deserved: utter silence.

The Zionist leaders in Tel Aviv understood their own self-interest if American leaders did not. They now made the only logical move they could make. David Ben-Gurion and twelve other prominent Jews met in the Tel Aviv Museum at almost the same hour as the Union Jack fluttered down the flag pole at British Government House on the Hill of Evil Council in Jerusalem. They formed a Jewish government, and proclaimed the Jewish State of Israel. The aged Chaim Weizmann saw his great dream come true. He renounced his British passport and was sworn in as the first President of Israel. The tough, white-fringed Ben-Gurion was made Premier. Israel prepared to fight.

The Israeli proclamation of the new nation was generally in accord with the UN resolution of 1947, though it overstepped it in some particulars.

In the UN at New York, the U.S. delegation was still engaged in desultory debate for some kind of international control of Palestine when a member rushed in, shouting that the radio had just announced U. S. recognition of the new State of Israel. That, at least, ended the debate.

In Palestine, there was now war. More than a million Arabs, less organized than the largely European Jewish community and badly served by their own propaganda shouting news of Jewish atrocities, fled toward the Arab countries. These were the people who became homeless refugees, and created the festering human problem of the Arab world. Ironically, had they stayed put, the very weight of their numbers would probably have prevented a truly Jewish religious state from coming into being, except along narrow lines. But Jewish power flowed into the areas they left behind, and Jewish opinion, understandably enough, was never amenable to returning them. The State of Israel, therefore, grew much larger than the UN had ever contemplated.

On May 15, 1948, just as the American delegation at Lake Success had lapsed into a sort of incoherency, the UN received a telegram from the Royal Government of Egypt: "Egyptian armed forces have started to enter Palestine to establish security and order. . . ." This was not, of course, the kind of order the United Nations had in mind.

King Farouk and his ministers were ill-advised in invading Palestine. The Jews were better organized, better armed, and tougher than any Arab thought. The Arab countries of Iraq and Syria, also declaring war, had made even more noise than Egypt at the formation of Israel. But now these nations suddenly realized their own internal situations were so unstable—as always —that their governments dared not send more than token forces against the Jews. For that matter, only King Abdullah of Jordan had an armed force worthy of the name.

Abdullah's British-armed, Glubb-Pasha-led Arab Legion of 8,000 was the only decent Arab military instrument in the Near East, and the one the Jews most feared. The Legion itself was no match for all of Israel, but it attacked west, overrunning a third of Palestine and reaching Jerusalem. The city was split in half between Legion and Jewish fighters: the capital of Solomon would not rise again.

But Abdullah was playing his own game. His forces did not cooperate with the Egyptians; and the Syrians, Iraqis, and Lebanese had no real liaison with each other. Israel, like most new nations, was born in blood and iron, but it was born. The Arabs were stopped. The Jordanians were held to a draw; Abdullah, who was receiving a British subsidy of $8,000,000 per year for his Legion, eventually proved amenable to British pressures for him to desist. The Egyptians, boasting the biggest Arab state and largest army, were ignominiously routed.

As soon as this war began, Secretary General Trygve Lie took the legal and correct attitude that Palestine was still a UN responsibility under the Trusteeship Clauses, and declared the Arab invasions aggressions. Lie had a strong feeling against letting these aggressions succeed. The Arab weaknesses in May, 1948, were not then apparent, and Lie felt that if the Arab states were allowed to destroy Israel the UN would be damaged disastrously. This kind of war, above all, was exactly what the UN had been organized to stop.

Lie approached the U. S. delegation, asking it to take some initiative toward achieving an immediate cease-fire in Palestine. But, as he said, "At the Security Council meeting in the afternoon of Saturday May 15, the day of the Arab invasion, the United States did not say a word." It was possible that Warren Austin and his cohorts were still stunned, or maybe, in the Soviet fashion, awaiting the word from the top. But Lie also said: "There seemed to be a conspiracy of silence reminiscent of the

172

most disheartening head-in-the-sand moments of the Chamberlain appeasement era."

The whole weekend Lie and his staff tried to get action out of someone. He held meetings with the Secretariat, wrote personal letters to the members of the Security Council. Warren Austin frankly told Lie he had troubles, not only with Washington, but with the British on the whole Arab-Israeli question. Austin had talked with Mr. Rusk in the State Department. Undersecretary Dean Rusk mentioned that the best policy would be "to wait and see." Mr. Marshall, the Secretary of State, was unavailable.

Meanwhile, Ernie Bevin and the British Foreign Office had been scandalized by Washington's abrupt and almost flippant recognition of the State of Israel, even while official U. S. policy was arguing for the internationalization of Palestine. Also, Britain had found itself in the uncomfortable position of subsidizing the Jordanian army and being in over its head in the Arab sands generally. Washington grew bitterly critical of Bevin's early refusal to order Abdullah to break off his military action against the Jews, though, as already noted, British pressure finally forced Abdullah to withdraw. Meanwhile, Washington still refused to accept any responsibility at all, even while urging it on Britain. The almost pitiful thing was that two great powers were paralyzed, one by fear of its oil interests, the other by domestic politics. The fighting went on.

By May 27, the Arab states had rejected four toothless UN appeals for a cease-fire. But on this same date, Britain and Bevin, under strong urging, agreed to endorse UN sanctions against either Israel or any Arab state that refused to comply.

The next UN order, backed by a threat of sanctions, got more attention. The UN, after some discussion about Paul Van Zeeland of Belgium—who refused the job—appointed Count Folke Bernadotte of the Swedish royal family as a special UN mediator. Bernadotte flew to the East, and while the shooting was still proceeding, got all parties to agree to a truce that went into effect June 11.

173

Bernadotte headed a Truce Commission of about five hundred men, mostly drawn from the officers corps of the United States, Belgium, and France. These men were armed only with a blue and white UN arm band, and they stationed themselves along an uneasy truce line between Arab and Israeli forces. Seven, eventually, were killed.

Crossing lines tirelessly, Bernadotte tried to hammer out some kind of agreement. The Arabs were adamant, and when the first truce period expired on July 9, they again attacked. But the attacks failed badly, and by July 18 the Arabs were willing to accept a new truce. It was impossible to iron out a real peace. The two sides were too far apart—and each of the Arab states was playing its own selfish and unilateral game, not even cooperating with its allies.

During this shaky truce, Folke Bernadotte was murdered along with Colonel Serot of the French Air Force by Jewish terrorists in Jerusalem. Some Israeli groups had been infuriated by his refusal to play favorites with either side; Bernadotte was not pro-Arab, but neither was he pro-Israel. The murder came as a great shock to the Israeli government and the UN Secretariat.

The assassins were never punished—it might have been almost politically impossible to seek them out; but Moshe Shertok expressed the feelings of the Israeli government in terming the killing an abomination. Probably, it helped that government to curb its own armed terrorists, who at the time seemed likely to influence or even dominate Israel during the passions of war.

Ralph Bunche took over after Bernadotte died on September 17. Bunche, a distinguished American Negro, fearlessly continued the impossible job. Again the battle erupted. But this time the Israeli army repelled the attack easily, then began to advance. It seized more territory—and the final realization by the Arab states that they would not, could not, win, at last allowed Bunche to hammer out an armistice. For this tremendous, thankless effort, Bunche was awarded the Nobel Peace Prize for 1949.

But the war never ended. In 1965 members of the UN Field Service were still on guard, observing the armistice terms at

174

places like Government House in Jerusalem. Once it had been allowed to begin—the initial and tragic mistake—that war showed no signs of being settled during the century.

The final result, as far as the outcome of the fighting in 1948-1949 was concerned, was partition, just as the UN had originally proposed. Partition came along lines different from the peaceful settlement suggested, however. Israel, as the result of a successful campaign, expanded greatly. Jordan, another winner, swallowed up more than one third of the old Palestine Mandate. Eight hundred fifty thousand Arabs who had once lived in Palestine were made homeless. These people became tragic pawns. Israel refused to accept them back, or to indemnify them. The Arab nations to which they fled also refused to resettle them or integrate them, mainly to keep a burning political issue against Israel, whose continued existence they did not accept. Fifteen years after they were uprooted, most of these people still lived miserably in displaced-persons camps near the Israeli borders—a source of continuing misery and burning hatred toward the new nation. They existed on UN and other doles, and remained a festering trouble spot in an already bitter sea.

Israel itself, understandably, took in too many immigrants in the succeeding years, which both unbalanced its economy and kept Arab fears of eventual Israeli expansion green. Israel, although efficient and hardworking, remained dependent on American capital. While the United States eventually came to guarantee its borders, its future was unstable.

Egypt was the big loser among the Arab powers. Egypt was defeated disastrously on the battlefield, with high losses; worse, Egyptian inefficiency and corruption in government were demonstrated clearly. Egypt's prestige, never very high, plummeted. Out of the shock of this defeat and loss of prestige came the Egyptian revolution of 1952, which swept Farouk and the pashas out, a new clique of military officers in.

But the revolution was not just a military coup. It turned into a genuine social revolution, which developed a deeply national-socialist tinge. Creating incisive changes in the two thou-

175

sand-year-old pattern of Egyptian life at home, Colonel Nasser, who eventually came to power at the head of the young officers, also turned toward foreign adventures. The shift in Egypt took the country out of the nominally pro-Western column and changed the whole power structure in the Middle East. It set off rampant Arab nationalism throughout the region; and Egypt became the leader of this violently emotional, socialist, and antiforeign Arab movement.

In this way the Egyptian revolution threw a discordant and highly dangerous influence over an already unstable area, making eventual solution of Arab problems even more difficult. Worst of all for the West, even though the USSR was never able to exploit the inroad, the Egyptian revolution by its neutralist bent opened up the Middle East to Soviet penetration. By the 1950's, lands that Stalin had once considered Western preserves, Khruschev found to be fair game.

The Egyptian revolution was a direct consequence of the Western failure to keep order in the Middle East. The Egyptian revolution, and Nasser's rise to power, in turn became the cause of trouble in Jordan, Syria, and Yemen; and it fomented the Iraqi revolution of 1958. All these actions further damaged Western influence. The Western powers hurt their long-range interests immensely by permitting the Arab-Israeli war to occur.

The fighting also damaged the United Nations. Those people who claimed the UN had no powers to intervene in Palestine, or to stop the fighting once it began, or to partition the area by force at the beginning, simply never read the UN Charter. Such powers were specifically reserved to the great nations on the Security Council—this was the fact that had worried the Little Forty-five so greatly at San Francisco.

Other people, who later tried to show that the UN was responsible for ending the fighting once it had broken out, never studied the ebb and flow of the war on the ground. Folke Bernadotte and seven members of the UN Commission gave their lives, and Ralph Bunche and hundreds of others risked theirs in damping the combat and hammering out a truce. Truces, partic-

176

ularly on the Arab side, were acceptable only after exhaustion had set in, and became permanent only when the Arabs clearly saw they had far more to lose by continuing the war than by ending it. In this way the UN and its Commission were convenient agencies to achieve an armistice, not prime movers in forging one. The problem was that Bernadotte and Bunche, except for the rare time when the Council threatened sanctions, had no real force backing their efforts. The UN, in Palestine, merely worked to ameliorate an already hopeless situation; it did not prevent a war. That war was allowed to take its course, and Israel was born, not by peaceful UN decision, but out of military victory.

The UN was damaged not so much in the popular mind around the world, which never really understood the ins and outs of the situation, but in the minds of the statesmen concerned—where such damage counted.

The UN—both Vandenberg and Dulles made this amply clear in 1945—was forged as a political, not a legal, instrument, through which the great powers could *enforce* political security decisions. The League failed because it lacked power, and moral suasion was not enough. But men were already trying to use the UN as they had once used the old League: as a moral, and not a military or political, force.

In Palestine, the USSR did not involve itself. There was no Cold War complication to hinder a United States-Great Britain political agreement. But it takes both willingness and responsibility to enforce anything, even discipline on a child. The British were unwilling, and the United States was clearly not eager to accept any responsibility at all. Both nations, with Nasser and continuing troubles in the Middle East, got very much what they deserved. Power without the will to employ it is no power at all.

If the Palestine war had been prevented, certain pitfalls might have been avoided. There would have been no million Arab refugees whose plight could not be settled. There would have been far less searing hatred among the Arabs than that which afterward surrounded the State of Israel. With a clear under-

177

standing that the great powers of the UN backed Israel's existence—which they did, and only later admitted formally—no Arab state would have dared attack in 1948. Facing gun muzzles, even Arab politicians tend to be realists. The Egyptian revolution might have been avoided, or taken a different turn. The shape of the Middle East might have emerged much differently.

The UN, then, as a moral force, was less than satisfactory. Its orders, as the first few weeks of Israel-Arab fighting proved, had to be backed by force to be heeded. On paper, the UN was nothing. It was only as strong as the sum of its greatest powers. And without the United States, its largest power, it was wholly ineffective. By 1948, no one, including the Arab states, expected the British to enforce anything.

The Palestine tragedy showed several things clearly:

(1) A great, order-keeping power, whether it was the United States or Britain, had to be powerful enough to enforce its national will without taking any sides in disputes that threatened the peace. Its government, therefore, had to be strong enough to make decisions in the national and world interest without regard to domestic politics. This, in the case of democracies, made order-keeping extremely difficult. After all, it had been the popular will in the 1930's *not* to rearm, and the Western democratic peoples had refused any responsibility toward controlling the revisionist fascist powers—until too late. This inability to act—for which no one could blame the mechanism of the UN —was to result in containing disorder and continuing tragedy, from the Congo to the blood-stained soil of Cyprus.

(2) It was pointed out by many people that the UN, in a strictly order-keeping function in which the Soviets put no sand in the gears, had failed to take effective action. The denigration of the UN, in American and British and French statesmen's eyes already begun, was far advanced. On the other hand, the corollary that the UN could be effective *only* when great powers worked through it, using it as an instrumentality, was overlooked by millions who still believed in its powers and purposes. It was clear by 1949 that if the big powers, attempting to remain un-

178

involved, continued to try to devolve the responsibility upon UN Commissions, Canadians and Swedes wearing arm bands, and world "opinion," the UN must continue to fail in reality. Commissions were simply not capable of policing world trouble spots that might lead to larger wars.

(3) Finally, the Palestine crisis proved that Truman's instinct to isolate all his great foreign policy decisions from popular or political control in the United States was inherently wise. The first great watershed of American policy in the century—from the inchoate idealism untouched by any feeling of real responsibility for world affairs of the 1930's to the measured, responsible use of American power in the Truman Doctrine, the European Recovery Act, the NATO alliance, and the Korean War, none of which had any powerful domestic political, intellectual, or vocal support—could never have been accomplished by debate, even at the national level.

The 1948 Palestine crisis did not actually shake the world. But it showed ominously that if the United States and the United Nations could not take quick, effective action here, they might not take quick, effective action anywhere.

12.

The Only Game in Town

IF THE actual shape of the postwar world was decided on the battlefields of 1945 and not in San Francisco, the politics of the age were firmed three years later, in the summer of 1948.

Americans, who think things happen suddenly, or without historical logic, such as the attack and response in Korea, see only the violent color of events, seldom their pattern, and almost never their texture.

The continuing presence of Soviet divisions in Central Europe and the hysterical turmoil of Communist parties everywhere in the middle forties had already sucked American concern and power back into the rimlands of Europe by 1948, but the real catalyst was Czechoslovakia, and the touchstone was Berlin. Czechoslovakia was the first nation to try to balance between East and West, with finally disastrous results.

In 1939 and again in 1945 the Czech Republic was the single genuinely democratic society in Eastern Europe. In both eras the Czech position, intellectually and emotionally oriented to the West, but surrounded by hostile power, was intrinsically hopeless.

Aged President Benes and T. G. Masaryk's son Jan could hardly forget, after the war, what had happened at Munich. Their desperate attempt to build a bridge between the two worlds, and to live with both, was understandable. The Czechs were essentially a bourgeois nation; they were middle-class and democratic, and Charter signers of the UN. But they lay well within the Iron Curtain, and in 1945 they signed a military alliance with the USSR. And they let their native Communist parties flourish. Some observers have tried to show that Czech Communism arose out of the Czech experiment with a socialist economy in 1945-1946. Few things could be farther from the truth. Because of the long Nazi occupation, which withered traditions of government and destroyed the Czech intelligentsia and disrupted the economy, forty percent of the population voted Communist in the postwar years. But this figure, in 1947, was the high-water mark of Marxist influence. By the same year it had become obvious, especially in Moscow, that Czechoslovakia would not vote itself behind the Iron Curtain. The Czech's democratic leanings were too strong, and Communism was actually waning domestically two years after the war. This worried Soviet rulers, who looked upon Czech democracy as a dangerous contagion, and a viable Czech Republic as a possible finger of Western influence bordering the Soviet heartland. To further the Communization of the country, the Russians held two trump cards: the fact that Czechoslovakia was completely surrounded by Soviet military power, and that it was economically dependent upon the rest of satellite Europe.

Jan Masaryk understood this. At San Francisco the Czech Foreign Minister worked tirelessly to ease Molotov's suspicions, and to bridge the gap between East and West. The bald, articulate, cultured Czech tried to be a true European, and to bring his nation under genuine collective security. Masaryk realized that Czechoslovakia needed the UN to survive. But the Cold War doomed the country, and killed Masaryk, because in their own way each side insisted that the Czechs make an impossible choice between them.

In 1946 American UNRRA funds ceased. The 1947 Czech harvest failed. The Czech economy, like that of Western Europe, foundered, and Masaryk asked the United States for entrance into the Marshall Plan. Washington agreed to this. But Moscow let Masaryk know that the USSR would not stand idly by if he made such a move. The problem was that Masaryk's people needed Marshall aid, especially food, but the bulk of Czech trade was and had to remain with satellite East Europe.

As winter came, the nation did not have enough wheat to survive until the spring, and the democratic Czech government

181

quivered on the brink of extinction. The Communist leaders, Klementis and Gottwald, had the promise of 300,000 tons of Soviet grain—but only if they were taken into the government. They did not want all the government, just the ministry of the interior, with its internal police powers.

Neither Masaryk nor Benes were fools. They denied the request and spurned the wheat, but they requested the United States, in the light of the Russian intransigence, to make an informal grant of aid, to allow them to last the winter and to stave off Russian pressure. Washington, however, was obdurate. If Masaryk wanted U. S. aid, he would have to sign with the Marshall Plan formally, stand up and be counted. The only charitable thing that can be said of American policy at the time was that most men in government did not understand Masaryk's true position, and above all, were still living in a dream world where Soviet ruthlessness was concerned.

Masaryk went to friends in the UN, where he had many. He begged Trygve Lie, whom he knew well, to try to communicate with Washington or London. "Washington and London," he said in despair, "have failed completely to understand my position. They are making a serious mistake in not granting my request for funds or material assistance." Trygve Lie, who at the time was regarded by some people as a "Goddamned Communist," was not able to help him.

Masaryk came bitterly to the conclusion that his friends in the West had written him off. And so they had—but the West had not yet learned what such a write-off anywhere, from Korea to Czechoslovakia, meant.

With the Czech factory workers going without bread, Masaryk and Benes took the Soviet offer of wheat, and put the Ministry of the Interior in the hands of the country's Communist bosses. Soon, news accounts carried stories of demonstrations in the streets, with rioting. Instead of putting these down, the Communist ministers began to arm "militia" to maintain "law and order." In a crisis of will, half of Benes' democratic ministers resigned.

182

The Czechs, as a people, were democratic, but they had lost a certain toughness and will to resist. They had wept in 1939 when panzers rolled in, while Yugoslavs took to the hills, and later, even though Marxists, they told Stalin to mind his own business. Now, they were to weep again, watching mass Communist parades and demonstrations. But if the Czech spirit had been shattered, a double betrayal by the West might have had somthing to do with it.

What now happened came to be called the classic Communist coup. The Communist minority went outside the law, creating an artificial crisis on top of the festering economic depression. The government was paralyzed; its loyal ministers resigned. Armed from outside, the militia took over. Communist ministers took office, passed new laws. Masaryk, a thoroughly life-loving type, was reported to have leaped out a window. Thousands of other Czechs soon joined him, or went to the mines.

The United Nations, and the United States, could take no action. It was all, once the new laws were passed, quite legal. In fact, the West and the UN were never able to come up with any kind of counter to the Communist ploy of the satellite state. Czechoslovakia went immediately behind the Iron Curtain Churchill had described.

But some good came out of this tragedy, at least for the West. After February, 1948, it became increasingly difficult to maintain that Russian aims for the world were not inimical to those of the West. It became also hard to argue that local Communist parties were free agents, or only misguided or sincere reformers with no provable link to Moscow. For whether or not controlled or directed out of the world Communist center, such parties immediately made alliance with that center upon achieving power— *which made the end result the same.* A Czechoslovakia or a Cuba allied or sympathetic to Moscow, or later a North Korea or North Vietnam allied to China, was as utterly dangerous to Western aims and interests as a satellite wholly controlled from Moscow or Peking. After all, in the great alliance against Hitler, the United States, Britain, and the USSR had worked effectively

183

for German destruction, each without being wholly controlled by the other. Similar aims were enough.

It was significant that after the Czech affair no Western European power ever again allowed known Communists into any ministries with national or police powers, whether their voting representation called for such inclusion or not.

It was also obvious, in hindsight, that coalition governments, such as General Marshall had innocently but ignorantly urged upon the Chinese Nationalists, were fatal. Communists and democrats—or any non-Communists, for that matter—simply could not mix. Very probably, if the combined Communist-Nationalist government that Marshall had tried to arrange in China in 1945 had come about, the Communist takeover would have come earlier, and even legally. As it was, the Nationalists refused, and the end result was decided by a vast civil war from 1945 through 1949, with the more disciplined and far more dedicated Communists eventually winning. The United States would not propose such a course again, at least not soon.

The shock waves from Czechoslovakia reverberated belatedly through Washington. Almost too late, they crystallized U. S. policy in Europe. While forging containment, U. S. policy-makers had had to proceed nervously and cautiously in the face of "liberal" thought, which still held Communist-Western aims compatible. Many genuinely sincere Westerners had continued seeking accommodation where it could not be found.

In 1948, each Western nation with large and noisy Communist minorities was badly frightened. They moved closer together, and consciously closer to Washington, the only power center that could defend them. NATO, then, on both sides was easier to forge than it would have been otherwise. It was fear, not a spirit of cooperation, that brought NATO into effective being.

Finally, ironically, the Czech coup added to the Soviet empire, but shattered all Soviet hopes of achieving domination of the European continent. It changed both European and American thinking toward Germany. It marked the end, if not in the popular mind, at least in statesmen's minds, of World War II and most

184

of its issues. Statesmen facing the USSR had something new, and far more urgent than Nazis, to think about.

To the demonologists still picking the ruins of Germany came new orders. U. S. Prosecutor Jackson at the Nuremberg trials was ordered quietly to finish up. However unpalatable, with Nazi crimes still ringing all over Europe, Western policy-makers already knew there was going to have to be a new Wehrmacht, this time on the side of the West.

General Lucius Clay, the military governor of the American zone in Germany, and later High Commissioner for Germany, had reported what most thinking people in Europe now saw: that effective European economic recovery was contingent upon German recovery. Germany was the economic as well as the geographic hub of Europe. It had been morally satisfying to keep Germany prostrate as a sort of economic pesthole with a cigarette currency, but by 1948 it was obviously hurting Frenchmen and Luxembourgers almost as much as Germans.

Oddly, many of Clay's arguments and ideas grew out of his own Georgia boyhood. A career soldier, and a capable engineer general, he had grown up on stories of the rape of Georgia by Union armies during the American Civil War. He had an underlying but very strong dislike of the occupation of one people by another, even his own people, and he carried a hatred of inflation from the same source—the destruction of Confederate credit and money, in which his own family had suffered enormously in 1864-1865. Clay was by no means insensible to the horrors of Nazism. But he had no sympathy for an occupation of Germany that did not make immediate economic and human sense.

As soon as he had taken over from General Eisenhower after the war, Clay and some of his staff had made moves to ameliorate the isolation of Germans from their own government, and to employ minor, functional Nazis in the U. S. zone where such hiring aided the U. S. authorities. Ironically, while Washington rarely acquiesced to this, the other occupying powers hired ex-Nazis almost from the start.

The British, soon after the war, tended to regard the division

185

of Germany as permanent, while the French made move after move to try to assure it. As men on the spot said later, the French and Russians continued to be incongruous allies upon this point. Both did everything in their power, for generally the same reasons, to prevent the rebirth of a powerful Germany in Europe. Both feared a German revival. However, after 1947 the French came slowly and reluctantly around to the American viewpoint. In those days France was in no real position to defy American thinking. The USSR remained adamant, and Germany was to remain the principal bone of contention between the two giant powers.

The occupation of Nazi Germany had begun with men in the American military government who could not speak a word of German, and who were forbidden by their own rules from having any contact with German nationals. As Robert Murphy remarked, even separate rest rooms were set aside for Germans and Americans in German governmental buildings—a sort of extension of American "Jim Crowism."

However, it gradually became more and more obvious that some sort of German regime had to be set up; no occupation could last forever. Clay wanted a responsible one, and one that could pull its own weight as well as be allied with the West. He did not win immediate approval from many official Americans, who in Clay's eyes were trying to follow the defeat of Germany with something approaching the Reconstruction of the American South between 1865 and 1876—a time when lasting bitterness was sown.

Clay and his staff worked out ideas for a new German currency by 1947; they considered it ridiculous that an industrial nation had no real monetary system. They also developed a plan for merger of the British and American zones into Bizonia, into one self-sufficient economic unit. The French agreed to join in the monetary reforms, but not to merge their zone. Only later, in 1949, after the Czech coup frightened Europe and Bizonia was a demonstrated success, did France join her occupation zone to the other two, creating West Germany.

186

As soon as Clay had achieved the British-American zone merger, he placed a German economics professor in charge of Bizonia's money and credit. This man was Dr. Ludwig Erhard, a believer in free enterprise and governmental noninterference in economic affairs. As soon as Clay had informed him of the appointment, Erhard, a fat, amiable-looking ex-artilleryman, stopped his official sedan on the way back from Clay's headquarters. He bought the biggest, fattest cigar obtainable at that time in West Germany. It was a symbol of the things he had in mind.

Erhard abruptly ordered the cessation of all economic controls. This angered both Allied occupational authorities and many Germans. Production was low, absenteeism high, and there was a shortage of almost everything. Prices immediately rose—but so, as Erhard had gambled, did production. The new, sound money turned the trick. Erhard's policy was simple: "More work, better work, more productive work." He regarded the devaluation of the British pound in 1949 as a palliative, not a cure, and said so. His comments, and the fact that Britain still had rationing, did not endear him to British authorities.

With economics under control, Clay began steps to form a permanent German government.

Konrad Adenauer, born in 1876, a former mayor of Cologne, had been ousted from that office by the Nazis. He had spent his silver wedding anniversary in an SS prison at Brauweiler near Cologne, and only luck had prevented his execution as the Nazi regime crumbled. At the end of the war, Adenauer, as an anti-Nazi and a man with strong personal qualities and experience in government, came to prominence in the American administration. He was eventually chosen to draw up the constitution of the Federal Republic of Germany that was proclaimed in 1949, and, largely as a result of Erhard's successful economics, Adenauer, leader of the German Christian Democratic Union political party, became Germany's first postwar Chancellor. Erhard himself got a cabinet seat out of the same victory.

Adenauer, an old man and an authoritarian one despite his democratic leanings, called in German industrialists and labor

187

leaders in 1948, as the framework of the new Germany was being laid. He told them the good news: that the occupiers were going to permit a free German government. Then he told them the bad. Germany was a ruined nation, and Adenauer simply informed both labor and management of the facts of life. Because both groups were Germans, they heard and obeyed. But also because they were Germans, they went out and worked. The Germans, and European, economic miracle was made here.

But while the Western powers were consolidating their positions in Germany and beginning to allow it to regain its feet, the Russians in the East zone refused all cooperation. And in 1948, after the West began to move unilaterally—there was no longer any attempt, after three years, to wring concessions from the Soviets—there was a Russian reaction. There came that sequence of cause and effect in European affairs that Machiavelli had recorded four hundred years before. Czechoslovakia produced Western fears, and hastened the creation of West Germany. West Germany angered the USSR, and produced the first Berlin crisis.

In the summer of 1948 the Russians began cutting off the access routes to the city of Berlin. This was a pure and simple power play, undertaken with two Soviet hopes: first, to strangle the showcase that Western policies and reforms were already making out of the Western enclave, and second, to prevent the formation of the Adenauer regime, which was already on the drawing boards.

Two-thirds of Germany, containing the Ruhr and allied with the West, could be construed only as a Russian defeat in Europe.

The highly technical questions of access to Berlin—a jointly occupied city two hundred miles within the Russian zone—had been bypassed by the Western allies along with other thorny thickets in late 1944. For this reason the Soviets, who physically controlled the routes on the ground, could apply a blockade piecemeal, quasi-legally, and do it in such a way as not to provide an outright act of war. But the meaning behind such a blockade was clear. It was pressure.

188

Fortunately, the Soviets imposed the blockade of land routes slowly. They telegraphed what was coming, thus giving Washington time to think. The access arrangements in use since 1945 had been by verbal agreement with the Soviets. The Western powers used one main highway for truck traffic, and had one railway line from West Germany set aside for their exclusive use. Only the three air corridors in which Western aircraft flew into Berlin had been confirmed in writing, however. The Russians could close down Berlin to Western access except from the air any time they chose to ignore, or supersede, verbal agreements.

When the Russians first began to delay Allied convoys or trains into Berlin, on the pretext of making "inspections," General Clay and Murphy, his principal political adviser in the American Military Government, warned Washington. They wanted a clear-cut policy adopted as to what should be done. The warning was made several times in the winter of 1947-1948, and Russo-Western relations in Germany deteriorated.

There was disagreement in Washington. Holdovers from the Roosevelt war days still wanted to try to work things out with the USSR. A few pragmatic Truman advisers said that the currency reform, and a West German government, all done without acquiescence by the USSR, might be provocations better avoided. It might be better to let Germany continue to go to hell rather than antagonize the USSR; Murphy was told this on a trip to Washington. A certain number of military men saw that Berlin was militarily indefensible, and urged it should be abandoned. It was George C. Marshall, Secretary of State, who finally gave Clay the go-ahead for German reforms, regardless of what the Russians did. But Marshall did not issue coherent instructions as to what to do in case of a Russian blockade of Berlin.

The currency reform went into effect in all three Western zones on June 20, 1948. This was more than two years after many American experts, including Clay and Joseph M. Dodge, had stated such reforms were "urgent." The Russians had been interfering with Berlin access for several months—delaying trains, blocking highways, returning barge traffic. The Western powers had done no more than protest. But on June 24 the Russians halted all traffic to and from Berlin because of "technical difficulties." At the same time, all electric power, except for the small amount generated in West Berlin, where there was coal enough for only two or three hours per day, was shut off in other sectors of the city. Berlin, with two and one half million inhabitants in the French-British-American sectors, had food and fuel for only about one month.

As the Soviet barriers crashed down, and roadblocks were placed across highways—at Helmstedt on the East German border the block was only a wooden pole across the road, attended by two Mongolian privates—Clay and Murphy were flown back to Washington for consultation. There was no definite Allied policy as to what to do.

There was a great deal of doubt and uncertainty in all Allied circles. The British showed that their own policy had come full circle. For two years they had led the fight to oppose Russian expansion. Now, they recognized their own weakness and war weariness. The Socialist regime wanted no confrontation with the USSR over Germany, and further, no confrontation between the United States and the USSR in which Britain might be mauled. They advised Washington to evacuate Berlin now, before it became a matter of Western prestige not to do so. As a British general said, in military and strategic terms a defense of a Berlin deep in Communist territory made no sense. But the salient fact about Berlin was that the issue was psychological, and political. Not military possession of a city, but the future control of all Germany was actually at stake.

Robert Murphy, who was close to Ernst Reuter, the heroic mayor of Berlin, was convinced by Reuter that the Communists were bluffing. Reuter, a stubborn little man who had himself once been a Communist, stated flatly that the Russians were not prepared for a major war, and would definitely back down if a show of force were made. In retrospect, Reuter's evidence and advice seem correct. At any rate, both Clay and Murphy pressed for a show of force, and asked that an armored column be sent through

190

Soviet blockade posts at Helmstedt in assertion of Allied rights. If the Russians chose to fire on it, what happened then was on their own heads.

But the new breed of Washington policy-maker, Truman's containers, instead decided to plan and take action according to their own instincts. They refused to see Berlin, or Germany, in the light of a military problem, which Clay contended it was. To a majority of the American National Security Council, which included General Marshall; General Bradley, Chairman of the Joint Chiefs of Staff; Averell Harriman; and Truman, Berlin was more a pawn in the game of world politics. The crisis was seen for what it was— not an apocalyptic challenge, demanding an immense showdown, nor a moral confrontation between right and wrong, but a pure and simple clash of great-power interest. These men in Washington wanted to hold on to their position, but at the same time to throttle any possible escalation of the conflict.

The British were going to be no great help, and the French, having one of their quarterly crises, had no real position except a vague anti-Americanism. But the British were now the Greeks in the new Roman Empire of the American ascendancy, as Harold Macmillan had said, and the French were powerless as yet. It was up to Washington to make, and enforce, its own decisions.

Harry Truman's courage at this time was obvious. He faced very bleak reelection prospects; even in his own Cabinet the smart money was all on Dewey. Anything Truman did might be damaging to him. But Truman stated flatly that if his Council advised him to send an armored column through Russian roadblocks, he was prepared to sign the order. Or not, as the case might be. Truman was not passing the buck. He was deferring everything but the responsibility to the men he considered expert in a field where he was not.

Here, however, on July 20, 1948, in the first Berlin crisis, began another policy that went hand in glove with the policy of containment: a pattern of responsible reaction, which was to be repeated again and again. It was a policy that understandably pleased few people, for it was neither wholly defiant and militant,

191

nor wholly conciliatory. It devolved into the meeting of limited force with limited force, while seeking a compromise or standoff. It was never surrender, as many men thought. It was always, whether performed by Democrat Truman or Republican Eisenhower, a form of "brinksmanship." It began in Berlin, with the logic of the postwar age.

The entire logic of 1914, and again of 1939, had virtually demanded a showdown at arms. The entire logic of the world that followed 1945 gravitated against a major war. General war was simply no longer an effective instrument of national policy, even without the intrusion of nuclear weapons. But the nature of man's politics, and his incessant urge to engage in power struggles, had not changed—only the struggles themselves had to take a different form.

The National Security Council, with General Marshall, Bradley, and Mr. Harriman dominant, felt even the relatively small risk of war that might be provoked by overt military action, such as crashing through Soviet barricades, unacceptable.

The old policy of America, from San Juan Hill to Hitler's bunker in Berlin, had been to remain uninvolved as long as possible, but once goaded too far, to pull out all stops. It was very much a policy like that of accepting no responsibility at all for law and order until the criminals had taken over the streets, then to cry havoc and order up the vigilantes. Then, with war, came the philosophy that anything went—from fire bombs to nuclear incineration. After all, the bastards over there had started it. The other side tended to become the devil, the American side the right. Evil was smashed, and then the chips were allowed to fall where they might. It was not considered the American job to pick them up again, or prevent them from falling in the first place.

This apocalyptic view of war rejected all notions that war itself, or power struggles, resembled both business and poker games. At one swoop, Americans always removed war and the use of force outside the scope of politics, refusing even to consider that war always arose from a purely political condition. Sometime between 1945 and 1948, however, many Americans in high places for the first time in a century seemed to realize the fact.

The Berlin blockade could easily have been construed as an act of war under international law. The United States had gone to war with Great Britain in 1812, and twice with Germany, under far less direct provocation. But in 1948, for the first time, the United States possessed transcendant power; and power, perhaps, bred responsibility.

Ironically, when the decision on what to do in Berlin was made July 20, 1948, Robert Murphy, Lucius Clay, and a spectrum of thought throughout the State Department agreed with Henry Luce, the publisher, who felt belligerence was the answer. These men, unknowingly, represented much of the old view: they saw war, and politics, in black and white.

But it was the military men, above all Marshall and Bradley, who advised restraint. The reasons were diverse. One thing the Joint Chiefs could not forget was the terrible weakness of American armed forces on the ground. This was a continuing weakness that would haunt all American leaders after 1945, from Truman to Johnson. The American nation was simply not willing to match Soviet ground strength; it sought solutions cheaper in terms of service, or in case of fighting, human life. Bradley and the Joint Chiefs, facing a demobilized America, stated that it would take at least eighteen months after war began before the United States could hope to hold its own with the USSR in Europe. If the barricades were cracked, and the Red Army marched, it would probably crack the Rhine. Bulgaria alone had more ground divisions—and probably of as good quality—as the United States in Europe.

And if Europe were overrun, atom-bombing the Russians out of it would be a sticky business. In fact, on the historic decision-making day, those who were there stated that the American monopoly of nuclear weapons was never mentioned. One thing the

193

leaders knew, and the public then and later never quite understood, was that between the USSR and the United States the logic of the age argued against all use of nuclear warheads. It was vitally necessary to have them, and equally necessary, in the peculiar workings of human politics, not to use them.

But to try to meet the Russians with force, Truman's Joint Chiefs explained, would require M-Day plus two years. To avoid defeat, once such an action had begun, would require immediate use of the atom bomb. In their eyes—hysterical as the thought made some professional anti-Communists—this immediately ruled out any use of real force against the Soviets.

But it worked both ways. If American weakness on the ground ruled out a conventional brawl à la St. Lo or Château Thierry, the American nuclear superiority virtually stopped any deliberate act of war by the Russians, unless there was a gross miscalcuation. There were equally enormous reins on Soviet strategy, too, if anyone cared to look. They could not afford to back the United States into a corner.

There was no indication at all in 1948—and again in 1950, or 1962—that the Russians had made preparations for general war. The reason there was so much doubt in so many quarters in the United States was that millions of Americans simply could not bring themselves to understand that world politics, and warlike moves, have much in common with poker. In fact, millions of Americans, having come to regard war as something out of the ordinary or transcendental, even thought any such view immoral.

Truman's strategists sensed that the Russians were playing some sort of game in Berlin. They were hot for the fruits of war, as Churchill had warned, but without the risks and agonies of war. They were playing chess—some called it slicing salami—a favorite Russian pastime. It was a game, a very deadly and dangerous game; and the stakes—the world—could be no higher. But it was still a game. The men to whom Truman had entrusted the safety of the nation decided not to kick over the checkerboard, but to sit down and to try to learn the game. The thing to do seemed to be to hold one's cards, or kings, swallow a certain

194

amount of invective—Russians, like New York taxi drivers, were just like that—and keep one's nerve.

A second reason for American restraint lay in the nature of the men in the policy-making slots themselves. Aside from a realization of conventional weakness and a shying away from using hard radiation, the professional viewpoint was being required to delineate policy for the first time in a hundred years. It should never be forgotten that one of the outstanding characteristics of the Truman Administration was its dependence upon career soldiers, as well as career diplomats and international bankers. Truman appointed a dozen top generals as ambassadors, and several held the most sensitive cabinet posts all through his tenure.

The American military lived, to put it simply, in a world of grays. It was taught to go for the throat in war, but also to keep its world untinted with black and white moral notions. Few men reached stars without the ability to see shades of gray; this was part of military life. Able to see it in their Army or Navy world, they had no trouble in seeing it in the larger world—something they were rarely given credit for. The professional soldier almost never hates his enemy, or thinks of him as a devil incarnate. The enemy is, after all, only a poor damn Kraut or Chink or Russian, who has had the same kind of training, and has his own stinking job to do.

And because the United States has always been an essentially civilian nation, the military were forced into an inherent sense of responsibility found neither in soldiers of nations like Germany, nor in civilian statesmen of the kind who made American policy from the Civil War through the time of FDR. Being members of an establishment that by law, custom, and instinct was always subordinate, and also being North Americans, generally from the small-town middle class, they could hardly have been otherwise.

Truman placed more responsibility on generals' shoulders than any President before or since. He really placed too much: at times he asked soldiers not only how they would fight a war, but whether it should be fought at all. He asked soldiers, for example, if the United States should stay or get out of Korea in

195

1947, and what it should do in Berlin. These were essentially political, not military, decisions. Military men such as Omar Bradley were never happy with having to make them. There is overwhelming evidence that Bradley and Marshall were uncomfortable at having to make them. Later, in the fifties and sixties, this power was again removed from the military. But it had its day —and it shaped the American world posture.

The only unfortunate aspect was that perhaps on several occasions the generals let military considerations, such as how many divisions the United States had, overweigh more important psychological or political factors generals were not trained to understand. This happened on the withdrawal from Korea in the late forties, and was a factor in the decision not to intervene in 1954 in Vietnam. It was certainly a compelling factor in the first Berlin crisis—where actually, to give Robert Murphy and Ernst Reuter their due, the United States might have had an unconditional victory and settled the question of Berlin access for all time.

But such policy-making as the generals were forced to do showed that they brought both enormous forbearance and restraint, and the ability to see the world power struggle for what it was, rather than some sort of contest between St. George and a changing cast of dragons. The men who normally see military hysterics are usually ex-privates, who, if they wore stars without thirty years of military conditioning required in American life, might well themselves behave as they think generals do. There have always been more hysterics in American political life than in its military.

It was, or should have been, instructive, that in 1948 a Bob Murphy, the "diplomat among warriors," was bitterly disappointed that the decision not to rip down the Soviet barriers went against him. Omar Bradley, one of the greatest field soldiers the United States ever produced, was not half so ready to blow and go. The same would be true in the Cuba crisis of 1962, and the Vietnam embroglio of the middle 1960's. The military were never so sanguine as the State Department, or so warlike.

196

Soldiers do not like war; only a generation of military men, that of 1914, which had never seen a war, was eager for one. But soldiers do understand the exercise of power. Some men of rank love power, but so did John F. Kennedy and Lyndon Johnson and FDR. Love does not mean abuse, but often quite the opposite. But soldiers, like the best politicians, know that power is amoral, useful for either good or evil. And soldiers, like Communists, much prefer to gain the fruits of war without being shot full of holes.

Amid argument, much internal disagreement, and no little doubt and controversy, the triumvirate of soldiers, statesmen, and bankers upon whom Truman relied hammered out a coherent military policy to go along with the broad outlines of containment. It had approximately six premises, some of which, naturally, were more valid than others.

(1) The USSR was not bent on precipitating a general, and therefore nuclear, war with the West. At the final whistle, American nuclear superiority offset Soviet divisions.

(2) No interest of the West or the United States could be served by engaging in a war with the USSR (or China, in later instances) if such a war could be avoided with honor.

(3) The USSR, however, must be contained, and its politics confounded whenever they impinged on the West. Fire had to be fought with fire.

(4) Because of political weakness in the West, the Soviets would be able to maintain conventional-arms superiority, which would be balanced by Western nuclear superiority.

(5) With time, the bipolarity of power in the world would change, and a more normal situation develop: a revived Europe and other powers would offset Russia.

(6) Again with time, and frustration, the aggressiveness of the Communist power center might diminish, permitting détente and a reasonable world order.

The great fault of such Western thinking, of course, was that it was defensive. It left the initiative always to the other side. However, it was almost impossible in human terms for the West not to be status-quo minded. The West was ahead in almost every respect.

What had begun was a world power struggle that ruled out general war. This meant the struggle would take odd turns. The enemy, allowed the initiative, had to take some points. Score had to be kept over decades, not just in election years; in fact, it would be difficult on occasion to tell who was ahead. It was that kind of game.

It would also be a mistake to develop any fixed manner of play. The dealer, in this game, could change the rules. Emphasis could shift from one part of the world to another, and from one type of pressure to a different kind, such as from subversion in Europe to support of wars of national liberation in Africa or Asia. Each move required entirely different responses.

The new game, and the new American response to it, was at once unpalatable to many Americans. A great many people shuddered at having to play nuclear roulette with Russians all their lives. This particularly bothered the intellectual community whose imagination was more highly developed. Other people disliked the realization that eternal vigilance was still the price of success, and that there might never be any relaxation of pressures in their lifetime.

Republicans tended to dislike Truman's policies on principle. An equal number of Democrats never understood them. American public opinion remained demon-haunted, and not amenable to the idea of power struggles. And one reason policy remained unexplained was that it was admittedly difficult to explain a policy that, even while it supported the UN Charter, went strongly counter to so much former American thinking and experience.

Vandenberg until his death never agreed. Containment, and the theory of war games did not work toward the victory of American principle. John Foster Dulles, who took over Vandenberg's mantle, wanted a much stronger policy, with more pressure on the Communist powers in the name of principle. But the policy was fixed—and certain events, like the exploding of a Russian H-Bomb seven months after Dulles became Secretary of State, made Dulles' stronger stands academic. Even Dulles, the strongest American Secretary of State in a century, was forced to play the game of limited response, and brinksmanship. He was even mistakenly accused of inventing the game.

The great problem from 1945 through 1965 was that new ideas, new approaches to world order all sounded good, but all ran up against the stone face of Communist hostility and divergent world aims.

A large, if largely unadmitted, problem that Truman's Secretaries, Dulles, and eventually Rusk all had to face was that Germans and Mickey Spillane were not the only people who thought a straight line was the shortest distance between two points in politics and that you could get more business done with panzers and pistols than with political deviousness. Millions of Americans felt the same way, just as other millions went too far in the other direction.

Much to the disgust of men like Murphy and Clay, the Berlin blockade did not become a testing ground for American and Soviet wills. The National Security Council ordered that only the access routes guaranteed in writing by the Soviets—the four air corridors—be used. This was challenging the Soviet move obliquely, staying in Berlin while at the same time avoiding a direct confrontation that might devolve into a game of "chicken." After all, the United States was seeking only stalemate and the status quo.

When Clausewitz wrote that the offensive always wins, he might have been right. However, Clausewitz had never been to a demonstration at Bikini.

The primary countermove to the Soviet road and rail blockade was what became the most spectacular air lift in history. The U. S. Air Force surprised even its own Chief of Staff, General Hoyt Vandenberg—who opposed the idea—by supplying a city of two and a half million wholly by air through a European winter. General Curtis LeMay, the Air Force chief in Europe, performed miracles; food, coal, and even electrical-power-station equipment was flown into Berlin. Four-engine planes landed at Tempelhof every twenty minutes; thousands of tons of supplies were unloaded.

None of this could have been accomplished, however, without the phenomenal discipline of the Berliners under the leadership of Mayor Ernst Reuter. The Berliners rationed themselves even more severely than the Military Government asked. They put their best minds to work assisting the flow of supplies, and utilizing efficiently the supplies they had. The entire city understood clearly what a takeover by the Soviets meant, and cooperated wholeheartedly to prevent it.

It was ironic that three years after the war ended, Americans and Germans were in effect allied in a Cold War action against the USSR, a former ally. Later treaties only formalized what had already taken place during the airlift. The Berlin Airlift began what was to continue as a peculiar symbiosis between American government and the citizenry of Berlin, and turn the Germans into America's principal allies on the continent of Europe.

The British, with their limited resources, cooperated completely in the airlift. The French did not participate, though French forces in Berlin were supplied by American and British aircraft.

The airlift was a spectacular military, logistic, and propaganda and political success. It vitiated the blockade, though at great cost.

The second Western response was a counterblockade of East Germany, where the Soviets had set up their own version of a German Communist government. This counterblockade hurt badly, since East Germany was dependent on the West for many economic items. The result, after some months, was impasse.

In the twentieth century, the world had come to expect inchoate idealism, notions of international law, no understanding of world politics, and periodic belligerence from the American people. American allies would have been horrified, but not surprised, had Berlin produced the same pattern. Even when it did not, all European allies were not completely convinced. Their confidence in American responsibility had to be renewed regularly, from Truman to Kennedy, from Dulles to Rusk. Fortunately, since the Communists cooperated with fresh pressures every few years, each American administration had its chance.

The United Nations had no means of coping with a United States-USSR confrontation like the Berlin blockade. Its peacekeeping machinery depended on big-power cooperation. But if the UN Security Council was powerless to handle this kind of crisis, in 1948 the UN showed that it had the means of ameliorating the crisis by adding a new dimension to international diplomacy.

As the Berlin situation reached stalemate, the UN provided a neutral ground for some backroom negotiation that neither the United States nor the USSR dared conduct in the open. The UN's murky corridors and antiseptic conference chambers were suitable for quiet meetings and secret bargaining.

Philip Jessup, a former career diplomat and expert on international law, served as alternate U. S. delegate to the Security Council while on leave from a professorship at Columbia University. As the Berlin crisis lengthened, Stalin made a remark to an American newsman in Moscow, indicating that the Soviets might negotiate. Dean Acheson requested Jessup to take aside Jacob Malik, who had replaced Gromyko at the UN, and see what might be done.

Malik was the usual type of stone-faced Soviet diplomat, who smoked endless *papyrossi* and never smiled. But in private he did show some signs of a sense of humor. If anything, this tended to lead Jessup astray. No private, personal relationship reached with any Soviet leader in any way was even allowed to influence Soviet policy. This was desperately hard for Americans—who often did business on the strength of personal relationships—to understand.

Malik, after showing some signs of private unbending, proposed outrageous conditions for ending the blockade. But then, after many weeks, he backed off, which seemed to indicate Soviet concessions. In the end, the Soviets conceded nothing—the access question was left exactly where it had been in 1944—but the USSR, now playing a bad hand, graciously ended the blockade on May 12, 1949.

But there was some value to the UN negotiations. Malik and Jessup talked without a spotlight; there was none of the touchy protocol of a Geneva convention, with reporters and public breathing down diplomats' necks, stiffening their backs. In fact, the talks were so secret even General Clay, chewing his fingernails in Germany, was not informed of them. Clay actually first heard about them from a British colleague.

While the blockade came to a quiet end—a draw—there was no settling the entire Berlin or German question. That could only await the end of the power struggle called the Cold War. But the current crisis was damped, and a suitable disengagement worked out. Eventually Russian barricades were lifted, and Western boycotts ended.

The summer of 1948 was the Soviet high-water mark in Europe. It hardened and formalized the Cold War, and after that, Europe was never again so vulnerable. But UN influence in easing the Soviet danger was vastly overrated in some quarters. The UN itself had had nothing to do with ending the crisis. But the UN site had provided a valuable service just by being in existence. It was neutral ground. For this reason alone the UN was proving worth the money—two-thirds of its entire upkeep—the United States poured into it. But now, as each American administration continued to advertise the UN as a cornerstone of its policy, almost always for political consumption, it was practicising a certain hypocrisy.

American policy-makers and implementers had removed all real action outside the UN. The big moves of the later 1940's, ERA and NATO, were accomplished outside the structure of the UN, though in accordance with those portions of the Charter that permitted regional alliances, arrangements, and solutions. This was never made entirely clear to the public, mainly for domestic political reasons. The UN did reflect what was taking

202

place outside it. But reflections and cornerstones are two different things; one is of glass, the other of rock. The UN had moved from prime mover to mirror of the world.

The hard fact was that the cornerstone of American policy was now a series of military and political alliances with fifty-odd nations. All were conceived for one purpose: the containment of expansionist Communism. There were those who argued that the United States should have continued to rely on the UN rather than military alliances. These people always overlooked a salient fact: that the UN had proven itself unable to contain Communism from the first.

Thus, as a new geopolitical nightmare unfolded in front of American officialdom's eyes, there was a lessening of the former American idealism as well as traditional American belligerence. The United States had never been used to taking foreign insults. But from the Russians the United States took more insult and calumny than it had ever permitted Hitler. Ironically, this showed a growing American world responsibility rather than a growing cowardice.

In the late 1940's there was a certain American coming of age. Like all adolescence, it was painful, unsure of itself at times, and it had an acute awareness of its image. Like some teenagers, America spent too much of its time before the mirror, alternately admiring and despairing of itself. But since neither knight-errantry in 1917 nor demonology in 1941 had saved the world, there remained only secret diplomacy, war games, and all the dangerous and untidy practices of the exercise of world power.

The policies forged by Acheson, Kennan, Harriman, Marshall, and Bradley, and men in the second rank like Rusk, Clay, and McCloy, were first of all based on the idea of American preservation. It would have been all to the good if this fact had been better publicized. Policy-makers had already forsaken the idea of perpetuating a beautiful world society in the American image—which never existed, and could not exist for a number of historic, geographical, and political reasons. There was no reason, except childishness, to expect gratitude from rescued allies. Alliances

203

are for convenience, and bargains for the future, as FDR learned too late.

Containment of Communism could not be the sum and future of America, however, and this was one thing that worried many thinkers. The policy was sterile. But perhaps there was a season for all things, and what Truman began did much to save the world as Americans desired it. After all, the policies that had made tyranny tremble in the old days had also been inherently sterile, too, since they had accomplished very little.

In the nineteenth-century world of the American frontier there had been three postulates, which the famous scout Kit Carson once stated: Life's a fight; there's no such thing as luck; and the price of success is eternal vigilance. The men and women who had erected the American republic from sea to shining sea saw nothing odd, outdated, or despicable in such notions. They reflected life. After 1900 the American frontier was no longer the vanished West, but the whole turbulent world—a region in many places as alien, and as harsh, as the old frontier. Frontiers themselves change, but the rules for living on them do not.

Emerging into the world as a great power, the United States had three choices. These did not include enforcing worldwide adherence to the principles of the Atlantic Charter, or rolling back the USSR. If there had ever been any chance of that, it had been let slip by 1945.

One option was to retreat as it had in 1919. The United States could then let the world take its own course, and do nothing until some new threat came knocking on the Pearl Harbor door. But after the V-2's flew, few Americans saw logic in this. The next knock would be on New York or San Francisco.

A second choice was to accept a contest at arms with the powers that had divergent aims for world order, and by opposing, end them. This appealed to large and not necessarily warlike segments of the population: it was moral, and it was neat. But this choice had immense hazards. Even if victorious, a bloodied, battered, impoverished, and probably spiritually diminished people returning from a great crusade against Communism might

204

have found the fruits of "victory" to be ashes. For this would not change human nature, or settle the courses of the world forever.

On the horizon, surely, maybe in the south, perhaps in the east, conscious of sudden power and opportunity in an exhausted world and long sullenly unhappy with its lot in the old one, a new monster would have risen. In a world in which the northern hemisphere was destroyed, it would be impossible to laugh at a Nkrumah or a Sukarno, or whatever current junta ruled Brazil. Power is relative. And whether China or Brazil, the result would have been the same. The fight that is human life is never over. New frontiers replace the old, but the world would never be made. For if it were, the pattern of modern life had shown clearly that someone would unmake it again.

The United States took a third option. In the middle of the century in a time of satanic weaponry, demonology ended. The United States stepped in, not too well prepared, to play the enemy's very human game from Saigon to Berlin.

Short of Armageddon or surrender, it may have been the only game in town.

13.

A Cloak of Many Colors

THE UNITED NATIONS Organization had fallen into incoherency and relative disuse by 1950. But it was to get one more chance. Briefly, it would even be what it had once been intended to be—an order-keeping mechanism—at the start of the Korean War.

By 1950 the American policy of containment and limited response to Communist aggression had succeeded brilliantly in Europe. The spasm of Russian expansion had retracted in Germany, though it still jealously guarded all it had won, and this created the usual feeling in the West that the Russians were settling down at last.

Unseen, and in Europe of little concern, the emphasis of Communist expansion had shifted to Asia. Here, American policy had remained indefinite and even confused. Japan had been stabilized by occupation, but for the rest of Asia the United States still clung to a policy that actually was unfeasible. At one time, this policy had been called the Open Door. What the Open Door in China or elsewhere actually meant was that the United States desired no single power to be predominant in the area, or to establish its own "peace and prosperity sphere" over the Far East. It did not matter what particular power had ambitions; the United States automatically was predisposed to resist such ambitions.

In the early 1900's Theodore Roosevelt had backed the Japanese against what seemed the most dangerous Asian power of the day, Czarist Russia. The Japanese, who stopped the Russians in 1905 in the Russo-Japanese conflict, were considered heroes not only in the United States but also in England. But in the normal course of human events, Japanese ambitions merely replaced Czarist dreams.

206

As Japan industrialized, it must be admitted that neither the United States nor the dominant European powers recognized legitimate Japanese needs. America and Europe had their own continental marketing areas, or preferential colonial empires from which other nations were excluded.

Japan, a few islands with about the total area of California, soon had 100,000,000 people, and it came too late on the world scene to secure its own colonial territories. As an industrial nation, the Japanese had to trade somewhere and somewhere secure the raw materials they lacked. Except for trinkets and junk goods, which did not compete, Japanese industry, however, was barred from the United States, and from every European colonial area in Asia, which meant, outside of China, almost all Asia. The Japanese internal combustion was predictable, and it was utterly logical that Japan joined the German and Italian demand for world revision in the 1930's. But Japan was only a minor great power compared to such industrial states as the United States or Britain, and when the Japanese voyaged forth against what they considered an unfair world, the venture was hopeless from the start, and Japan's utter defeat was also predictable.

However, the Japanese, fighting with the tenacity and ferocity only homogeneous peoples can achieve in war, only seemingly lost World War II. Japan was damaged, defeated, and occupied as thoroughly as Germany. But in the process Japan destroyed the European colonial empires, from India to Indonesia. They were never reconstructed, and Japan had destroyed the economic web that had bound her in. By 1950 Southeast Asia was open to Japanese economic penetration and trade, and by 1950 the fact that a large Japanese population enjoyed a higher standard of living than in 1940 was hardly the result of U. S. aid. The Japanese, like the Germans, became politically apathetic on the world scene, and devoted themselves to economy building and hard work. Japan, like Germany, ceased to be a great power, but like Germany became a relatively rich nation.

But as Japan continued anesthetized, the power vacuum created in the Far East had to be filled. The Pax Japonica had been destroyed, but the Pax Americana did not immediately rush in to fill the gap. The trouble was that large parts of Asia were considered fringe areas by the West. Neither Japanese, American, nor European power rested firmly. These areas became, and had to become, inviting targets to the new revisionists loose in the world.

One problem was that in this part of the world the West faced an entirely different cultural and social system, and Western standards did not apply. The day would come, no matter how unpalatable the idea was to some, when the Allied-German wars would be considered internecine, almost civil wars within the same basic culture. The same could never be said for Western-Asian conflicts.

Japan had been vulnerable to the West not only because it was an island, but because it was industrialized and could be controlled like Germany. The rest of Asia was established on a village culture four thousand years old, agricultural, and could be policed only by men on the ground. No idea was less palatable to either American citizens or American policy-makers at the close of World War II.

The fact was soon evident that the Chinese Revolution, which Eden predicted in 1943, could have been neutralized or stopped only by the use of American ground troops, as the Wedemeyer Report stated. But Wedemeyer's conclusions were stamped secret. Washington saw no purpose in releasing something that was politically impossible to implement anyway. China, which was a fringe area for the West in 1945, by 1949 had become the second most important Communist power.

What should have been clearly foreseen, and was not, was that China inevitably would take up where first Russia, then Japan, left off: it would try to establish its own Pax Sinica over East Asia, and to become the dominant power, in an expansionism in which both Marxist philosophy and nationalist sentiment were irretrievably mixed.

And the Chinese Reds fostered a deliberate hatred for the

208

United States from the very beginning of their days of power. Ideology had something to do with it, but not all. Mao Tse-tung and Chou En-lai, the Chinese leaders, saw as clearly as Ernesto Guevarra of Cuba would see later that Communist aims for their area of operations could never be realized unless the United States were first neutralized. American policies persisting in trying to keep Asia "open" inevitably brought the Chinese into protracted conflict with the United States.

Actually, *any strong Chinese regime with an element of nationalist pride would have found itself in conflict with the United States,* just as de Gaulle of France found it impossible not to oppose the United States on principle. It was as logical for the largest power in Asia, no matter who it was, to consider that it ought to be dominant upon the continent as it was for the United States to consider itself dominant in the Western Hemisphere and to take steps to make that consideration a reality.

The U. S. opposition to any Asian domination by a single power was based both on idealism and self-interest. Ideally, a very good case could be made that all the small powers of Asia from the Philippines to Thailand preferred to remain undominated by anyone, and had a right to be free. And it could not be argued that American economic and geopolitical world interests were not far more secure where there was no hostile, or potentially hostile, power to challenge them.

At the end of World War II, Korea, an ancient ethnic kingdom, had been a Japanese province for forty years. Earlier, the Japanese had pushed out both Chinese and Czarist influence. In the last days of the war in 1945, both Russian and American troops entered Korea, the Russians from their contiguous border on the north, the Americans from the Philippines to the south. As a matter of convenience in implementing the Japanese surrender, Korea was divided into two zones along the 38th parallel.

It was no more anticipated here than in Germany that this temporary line of demarcation would turn into a hard political frontier. But here on the edge of Asia the Cold War followed exactly the same course as in Europe. The Russians took control of their zone, refused entry or cooperation with the Americans to the south, and tried to extend their influence and control over the whole peninsula.

After two years of military occupation of South Korea, the U. S. Joint Chiefs of Staff recommended pulling American ground strength out. American policy did not seek commitments on the ground in Asia; in fact, it was a cardinal principle of American military policy not to engage in any kind of ground conflict on the continent of Asia. During the wartime Big Three conferences, FDR, Stalin, and Churchill had agreed on Korean independence no later than 1950. But with the Russians refusing to cooperate in any way toward forming a single Korean government except on their own terms—which meant a Communist state—the United States in 1947 placed the Korean question before the United Nations.

The Assembly, acting under American influence, immediately accepted responsibility for all Korea under the trusteeship clauses of the UN, which provided for UN action, custody, and control in areas either unready or unable to achieve self-government. Such a resolution was voted over strong Soviet opposition; the Soviets termed the resolution "illegal." The UN voted that at the earliest possible date a true Korean national government should be formed through national elections, which a UN Temporary Commission on the ground should supervise. This government, once formed, would take over from the Russian and American military governments in the North and South, respectively.

There was only one problem. The Temporary Commission was welcomed in South Korea, but it was turned back at the border of North Korea by Russian bayonets. The Soviets stated that the UN had no jurisdiction over their zone, and that—unless the UN wanted to go to war with the USSR—was that. The Commission, balked in repeated efforts to enter the North, at last recommended that free elections be held only in the American zone, where the "atmosphere was held to be free enough for free elections," as Trygve Lie wrote.

Elections were held in the American zone on May 10, 1948. A right-of-center party headed by Syngman Rhee was brought to power, with Rhee as President. The UN confirmed these elections and Rhee's government by a vote of the General Assembly, and further continued the UN Commission in Korea as a hope of eventually facilitating the unification of the country.

The Soviet reaction was quick and predictable. Denouncing Rhee as a puppet, the Soviets established their own "People's Democratic Republic of Korea" in the North. This was a typical Communist satellite state, or "tank democracy," in which the top one hundred political posts were held by Soviet citizens of Korean ethnic ancestry, some million of whom had fled Japanese occupation into Siberia a generation earlier.

North Korea was quickly organized into a disciplined, if thoroughly unfree, rump nation. The Soviets were assisted by the fact that almost all the industry and mineral wealth of Korea lay north of the 38th parallel, while two-thirds of the Korean people and their problems were in the South.

There was no historical or ethnic justification for the division into two nations. Koreans were simply caught between two great power systems in a titanic power struggle. The West acted according to its own institutions and customs, the Communists according to theirs. Half of Korea became reasonably free, though democracy in the Western sense was foreign to the Korean experience or ethos; the Northern half remained a slave state.

In this same year, 1948, the Cold War had reached a form of respectable permanency in Europe and was even beginning to function along certain ground rules. But Communist policy now began pressures on the Asian periphery, seeking more fertile ground. Along with pressure against Syngman Rhee's regime, which consisted of continual propaganda attacks, espionage, and subversion, and even border raids and armed guerrilla action, there was increased Communist activity all over Asia.

211

In Malaya, the ruling British found a genuine rebellion on their hands, led by Communist-infected Chinese. This insurgency quickly turned into a major operation, threatening a significant Western supply of tin and rubber. The British and Malayan authorities, however, were able to contain the rebellion for several reasons. One was the fact that the Communist guerrillas were virtually isolated from outside help, and could be bottled up in large sections of Malaya. Another was a wise and far-sighted policy of restraint on the part of the British, who let the other side commit all of the terroristic activities. They took their losses, but did not reply in kind against the civilian population, which was terrorized by or supported the guerrillas. As a British officer said, "You do not win friends by using a red hot poker on people when you want information about insurgents." The most important, and most ironic, factor in the British victory, however, was the fact that the rebels were Chinese, immigrants into the Malayan area. The British very successfully turned the dominant Malay population against them, successfully using in reverse a Communist tactic of turning ethnic group against ethnic group. At that, the insurgency was not ended for ten years, until 1958. And not until almost that time was it clearly recognized in the West that this insurgency had been instigated out of the Communist world power centers.

At the same time, 1948, Communist doctrine called for strong measures against the French in Indo-China. Russian and Chinese Communist money and arms flowed south to Ho Chi Minh and his General Giap, and within a few months the French authorities had a war on their hands, which it turned out could not be handled even by the Foreign Legion. For in Indo-China the Communist situation was highly different. For one thing, the fall of China to Communism placed a contiguous Communist border next to rebel areas, which could not be sealed off. Even more important, the French, who unlike the British in Malaya had not turned over significant areas of government to the Vietnamese, and who had not scheduled independence for the area, were the ones isolated from the population. The French were fighting Communists and trying to defend a colonial order, and the combination was fatal.

The Communists, sometimes acting in concert with the great power centers of Peking and Moscow, sometimes developing purely indigenously out of the turmoil and tragedy of the underdeveloped world, were beginning to confront the West with tactics and situations with which it had no experience. In Asia, the war of national liberation, as it was called, was something new. It represented not only Communist ambition to extend power, but incorporated all the frustations of impoverished and admittedly often abused peoples. It wanted to destroy not only the foreign European or American presence, but the Western economic and power structure as well. It employed both clever propaganda and the most brutal terror.

Waterloo and the Battle of Berlin had been decisive; they had ended eras. But those battles had occurred in Western culture. In Asia, insurgents could lose a thousand battles and still continue fighting. The only way they could be controlled was by immense numbers of policing troops on the ground itself, until they accepted defeat psychologically as well as tactically. And immense numbers of troops stationed in Asia was the one thing the Western powers would not, or could not, contemplate.

The British used more than a hundred thousand troops in Malaya against only a few thousand Chinese bandits. The French refused to draft national armies to fight in Vietnam, actually wisely, since their cause there was politically hopeless. But the loss in Vietnam was not only a result of the revulsion of the populace against the French. The French never had anything like the actual policing strength needed to combat insurgency. One good guerrilla, in proper terrain, can tie down at least seventeen regular soldiers. Neither tanks nor nuclear bombs are any advantage.

Prophetically, General Giap, who defeated the French at Dienbienphu, said that unless the West found some new way to combat such "wars of national liberation," their whole world position was doomed, from Asia to Africa to Hispanic America—because such wars were feeding not only upon Communist ambition but

213

all the frustrations and hatreds and miseries of a world in which only the Western citizenry could be considered generally fortunate; and a world in which the Western power structure and its wealth, by its very existence, set up a shining target to destroy. In such a world, issues of right or wrong, morality and immorality, grew very vague.

This pattern began to be set in 1948. But in Korea the Communist powers made a very grave tactical mistake, one they are not likely ever again to repeat. One measure of the success of old, cantankerous, and autocratic Syngman Rhee was that his government stood strongly against all attempts to unseat it. Frustrated in what they considered a vital area—Korea was a dagger pointed at the important islands of Japan—Communist world leaders met in Peking in January, 1950. It seemed to them that since the United States had pulled all its troops, except a few advisers, out of South Korea, a war of Korea against Korean might be passed off by the West as a genuine civil war, in which the West had no excuse to interfere. The United States had clearly refused to combat Communism in China on the ground; it might take the same course again.

It was always odd that while the United States, in NATO and in strengthening European ground armies (it would soon have 250,000 soldiers stationed in Germany alone) had accepted the idea that European Communist expansion must also be countered on the ground, it refused to face a similar need in Asia. The reason could only have political roots: Americans in large numbers balked at the idea of ground commitment in Asia. And every strategic loss the West suffered in Asia from 1945 through 1965 stemmed from this refusal. Containment in Asia could only be won by a certain amount of blood. This was a brutal, but inescapable, fact.

But in 1950, the United States had not written off Asia. It was then merely refusing to face both the fact that power vacuums in Korea or anywhere else cannot exist, and that whatever the UN might be, it was not a power center.

On June 25, 1950, a North Korean army of 100,000 men,

214

armed with Russian weapons, tanks, and aircraft and containing a cadre of 30,000 veterans of the Chinese Communist Forces —ethnic Koreans who had been brought up in North China— crashed over the 38th parallel. Their object was the conquest of all Korea.

The Communist mistake was the fact that the act was overt aggression, not subversion or a "war of national liberation" that might be passed off as a civil war. It was taken against a UN ward, and a nation to which the United States still had a commitment.

Faced with this kind of situation, the West could act.

When Adlai Stevenson, U. S. delegate to the UN Preparatory Commission meeting in London, cabled a rotund and obscure Norwegian politician on Christmas Day, 1945, he started a chain of events that exploded dramatically five years later.

The United States had decided on Trygve Lie, then snowed-in in a Norwegian hunting lodge, for the post of President of the General Assembly. But while Lie was willing, Spaak of Belgium beat him out on the balloting. The vote was close—28-23—and Lie was offered a consolation prize, the Secretary Generalcy. This was, as a few people saw in 1946, a much more important post.

Lie, like Lincoln, found the executive branch with certain inherent powers, and left it with those powers vastly increased by precedent. Lie's powers as Secretary General stemmed from the Charter and the consent of the great powers. But he considered himself no lackey. He felt he was first and last an executive, and not just an executive agent of the Security Council. Lie, reading the Charter as carefully as any Presidential staff reads the American Constitution to see what may be squeezed out of it, felt he could stir any matter, propose, direct or ask for support.

Dear to his heart was Article 99 of the Charter, which read: "The Secretary General may bring to the attention of the Security Council any matter which in his opinion may threaten the maintenance of international peace and security." The Charter also reserved to Lie the exclusive right to make all appointments to posts on the Secretariat, freed him from responsibility

215

to accept the instruction of any government, and guaranteed that no government had any right to influence him in the discharge of his duties.

Lie took all this seriously, and it is safe to say that in his first five years he at one time or another completely infuriated every power on earth.

Logically, every nation tried to influence his appointments—the United States belatedly, when Congress questioned the leftist leanings of some Americans on his staff. Lie had asked the U. S. government to screen all American applicants; it had piously refused. Now, when it asked him to fire some, Lie refused. As he said, with complete honesty, he would never knowingly appoint an American Communist, just as he would not knowingly appoint a Russian deviationalist—because such men would not be representative. But, once he had picked a man and found something good in him, Lie was thoroughly capable of telling Truman, Congress and that ephemeral third force in the world, Senator McCarthy, to go to hell.

He was inexperienced, not suave, and certainly unintellectual. He belonged to that great spectrum of Western Socialism that included Ernie Bevin, Australia's Makin and Evatt, and Belgium's Spaak. But like Bevin, he was above all a European; he could not think in terms other than European. He was not, as time went on, able to communicate with men like India's Nehru. A carpenter's son, he was, in the words of a top diplomat, "a man with guts, but no political or other culture." In Lie's job, guts were perhaps more important.

The British did not like him, even the Labor government. The Russians had troubles with him. Some Americans were convinced he was a Communist. He was not, however, provocative or quarrelsome.

The problem was that while no government had a right to influence him under the Charter, no government, including the United States, ever stopped trying. When he decided a procedural question in favor of the United States, he was immediately a great democrat and far-seeing statesman. When he took an

216

opposite position, from evidence or conscience, he became a "goddamned Red."

Lie first had visited Moscow in 1921, and he tried to keep on good terms with the Russians. He felt that his primary mission—peace—depended on this. But being Norwegian and a democrat, he could never swallow the Czech coup. Masaryk had been his friend.

In the world of the Cold War, it was actually impossible to remain neutral without also remaining indifferent. Yet this was demanded of the Secretary General. Hammarskjöld, a very different kind of man, who followed Lie, had the same trouble. Even had he lived, his effectiveness was ruined by the position he was forced to take against Soviet policy in the Congo. Only when a neutralist sat in Lie's chair would the office be free from certain pressures; but then, of course, it would also be even more ineffective, and more and more a voice crying in the wind, unheard by either great power. As Lie wrote in his diary, the job was impossible.

No man worried more about the Cold War, or worked harder to bridge the East-West split. But *in extremis* Trygve Lie's neutrality did not exist. When the news of the Communist invasion of South Korea was phoned to him on his Long Island estate on June 25, 1950, he exploded. "This is war against the United Nations!" And so it was.

With the news, Lie saw not only the world crisis, but the terrible danger to the UN organization itself. This was not a long-festering localized sore, like the Israel question, which could still be contained. This was a direct confrontation between the power and authority of the UN itself and a Communist state. And there was no question in Lie's mind or anyone else's about who pulled the strings and supplied the arms in North Korea.

In Czechoslovakia, China, and a dozen other Cold War actions, the UN had had to sit by, paralyzed both by the veto and the fact that it could construe no legal right to intervene. Lie knew that if the UN could not meet this challenge, the open crossing of borders with armed force, in some effective way, the UN's

217

days were numbered. It would live on, as the League of Nations lived on after Manchuria and Ethiopia, but it would be dead in the hearts of men.

Lie went into action immediately. Using the authority of Article 99, he convened the Security Council at 2:00 P.M., June 25th. There he did not wait for big-power direction. He placed before the Council his information on the Korean invasion, and he termed the North Korean move aggression. He asked the Council to do something about it. Within four hours—a record —the Council proposed, debated, revised, and adopted a resolution calling for a cease-fire, withdrawal of North Korean forces, and for assistance to the Republic of Korea.

The United States, for its own reasons, actively supported Lie, and Nationalist China, Cuba, Ecuador, Egypt, France, India, Norway, and the United Kingdom voted for the resolution. Only Yugoslavia, at this time precariously hostile to both the West and Stalin's Russia, abstained. The Western influence on the Council, and in the entire UN, in 1950 was still overwhelming, as Russia had always feared.

But only an accident of history permitted the Council to get away with it. Had Andrei Gromyko been in his seat that Sunday, there would have been no UN action in Korea. There would have been a Korean War; that had already begun. But the war would have taken on a very different cast. Gromyko had walked out of the UN on January 10 over the issue of seating the new Communist government of mainland China. The USSR had continued the boycott in the hope of hamstringing the UN until it gave in —but being absent when the North Korean invasion broke was an enormous tactical error.

The USSR had not expected the American reaction to be as violent as it was. It had expected the United States to stand by, to wait for the dust to settle as it had stood by in the Chinese civil war; and without U. S. action or support, no other Western power was likely to do anything. As the British had made clear at Yalta, Korea was outside their sphere. The Russians had mistakenly

218

believed that U. S. policy-planners had excluded it, too. All that the superior North Korean forces needed was a few days, and the whole peninsula would be in Communist hands. Moscow expected Washington to recognize a *fait accompli* and sit still for it.

But Moscow had not reckoned on either Trygve Lie or Harry Truman. Lie, acting on his own initiative, gave the United States an enormous propaganda and moral advantage. Lie asked for action, and the United States immediately supported him, and the other powers went along. If either Lie—or the United States—had hesitated, if Washington had approached the Korean muddle in the same way it had approached Palestine, or would later try to ameliorate the Cyprus crisis, South Korea would have passed into limbo.

Truman met on Sunday with important members of the State and Defense Department at Blair House, across the avenue from the dismantled White House. And U. S. policy in Asia solidified, as it had in Europe in 1948. The real, *if still publically unadmitted,* policy of the Administration was containment of Communist expansion. All Cabinet members agreed it was time to start containing.

Lie's request for support, and the overt nature of the Communist move—this was no coup, or infiltration, or guerrilla action, but a painful aggression across a recognized border—freed Washington's hand. South Korea was both a United Nations and a United States ward. Both had to take action. There was a clear-cut moral issue to do so. And the UN resolution gave the United States a moral and legalistic mandate under which it could move.

There was a further effect, of transcendent if ephemeral importance. The shock of brutal armed action by a Soviet satellite sent a thrill of fear through all the non-Communist members of the UN. This seemed a new Manchuria, the beginning of a slide toward war such as had occurred in the 1930's, when the League had failed to act. The fear produced a moment of fusion within

219

the UN such as had not been felt since Hitler's death. Truman was prepared to support South Korea with arms, men, and money. The other nations were agreed in principle.

But the Korea decision—no one, in June or July of 1950, realized how difficult the job of stopping the aggression would be— must be viewed in the light of the Berlin crisis of 1948. There the pattern of U. S. action had been set. Aid to South Korea, even armed forces, in no way implied a decision to accept hostilities with the USSR. The earliest dispatches sent to American commander Douglas MacArthur in Tokyo clearly stated this. The world, at Berlin, had been accepted as a checkerboard. There the play had been with aircraft, tonnages, and counterblockades. Here the pawns, unfortunately, had to include men and American blood. The same considerations that restrained U. S. policy over Berlin restrained it over Korea.

By June 27, it was apparent that the North Koreans were going to ignore the UN resolution of June 25. Now the UN became, in its moment of fusion, the most effective tool possible to the United States in its determination to halt the Communist flow.

White-haired, portly Warren Austin, the New England Republican representing the United States on the Council, had no trouble getting what Washington instructed him to get: a resolution authorizing any measures necessary to repel the aggression.

The Resolution of June 27 read, in part: "Recommends that the members of the United Nations furnish such assistance to the Republic of Korea as may be necessary to repel the armed attack and to restore international peace and security in the area." The words *repel* and *restore* were significant. This was containment, not counteradventure. In this way, the United States was able to weave a UN cloak around its own national Korean policy.

In 1950, and later, there was only one government that was capable of preventing Communist chaos or Communist world hegemony. It was never the UN, but U. S. power working through the UN, that met Communist force with force, and repelled the invasion. The UN was always the sum of its member powers, and without the United States, the sum was always very small.

The UN had passed a resolution to partition Palestine and prevent war, but no great power would stand behind it. There the UN failed. Now, briefly, with the United States wearing it proudly, the mantle of the United Nations was a many-splendored thing.

14.

The End of Credit

TRYGVE LIE and the American government hoped for a majority of nine to sustain the Security Council Resolution of June 27. But the vote to brand the North Korean state an aggressor was only 7-0. Soviet Russia had still not gotten its man in New York back to minding the store. The three abstentions showed a hint of future trouble.

Yugoslavia, Marxist but anti-Russian, was still suspended between both blocs. But India and Egypt were non-Communist nations. They were not influenced by Marxist ideology or Russian friendship. However, they were also non-Western, and had no intention of being drawn, in the Cold War, into the Western camp. The vote, then, was on purely political lines. Cuba, Ecuador, France, Norway, and Great Britain were all treaty allies of the United States. The United States cast the sixth vote. The seventh, and carrying vote, came from Taiwan, by now no longer a great power but an American protectorate.

The abstentions showed, for the first time, that a large part of the world did not see the Cold War in apocalyptic terms, free world against tyranny, but as a pure power struggle in which many nations wanted no part. They rejected, as far as they could, the bipolar nature of the postwar world. Americans should have seen nothing odd in this fact.

The greatest force influencing men in this century was not ideology, but nationalism. Each nation had its own ends and its own determination to act independently. Because of the nearness of the Soviet danger to them, Western European countries had fused with the United States, in NATO. This was a logical but not necessarily an inevitable process. NATO was an alliance of convenience, not a mystical brotherhood. It would last only as long as it was convenient to all parties.

It was true that the majority of the NATO nations shared a common culture and a generally common Western experience, except for Greece and Turkey. They were also tightly interconnected commercially and economically; Western Europe and Great Britain were America's and Canada's best customers, and vice versa. Again with the exception of Greece and Turkey, the NATO countries—the United States, Canada, Iceland, Norway, Denmark, Netherlands, Belgium, Luxembourg, France, Italy, and Germany—shared very similar ideas of government and politics. The shores of the North Atlantic were the great spawning ground not only of Western culture but also of popular democracy.

But in the face of nationalism and separate languages, separate histories, and separate notions of destiny, all these similarities could not be carried too far. After all, the bloodiest war in modern times was between the northern and southern American states. And the greatest wars in human history had been fought in the twentieth century between the major nations that comprised the North Atlantic Treaty Organization.

In these terms it was no more incongruous to consider that the day might come when Germany and the United States might be allied against France or Britain than it would have been to state, in 1943, that some day Germany and France would be allied against Russia. The great tragedy of human history is that moments of fusion between peoples and nations are rare, and then are seemingly called forth *against* something or someone. Except in extremity, the normal stance of any alliance is disarray, which in the early 1950's, a time of supreme danger, many Americans, new to entangling alliances, forgot.

In the years after the Czechoslovakian coup, the Red pressures on Berlin, and the onslaught in Korea, Western Europe and the United States stood closely together. It was greatly in Europe's interest for them to do so. But other nations of the world, not so much under the Soviet or Red Chinese gun, wanted

223

no dangerous entanglements they could avoid. Egypt had its own ambitions, one of which was to break the British hegemony in its part of the world, a determination that sprouted long before Nasser. India wanted regional solutions that excluded all non-Asians from Asia—Churchill's Asian policies in reverse.

A prominent diplomat summed up the attitudes of what would soon be called the uncommitted, or neutralist, world, which from 1950 onward grew spectacularly. Almost all such nations were new, or at least undeveloped or disadvantaged. They depended upon massive aid from the industrial nations, and they did not care whether the tractors were made in Ohio or the Ukraine. They wanted aid, but no dictation.

They had two great fears. One was that the industrial nations would go to general, or nuclear, war. Even if they were not involved in the fighting and destruction, the impoverishment of the world would affect them grievously. The other fear was that the East and West would find a workable détente and divide the world between them. In a world where both the United States and the USSR wanted stability—and enforced it—the ambitions, and even the aid to, lesser nations faced a cruel future.

The Cold War, like all previous power struggles, was the great stimulus to modern subsidy. Just as the Roman Empire had sent enormous sums of silver abroad, buying good will on its frontiers, and Louis XIV had kept the King of England, Charles II, in funds, hoping to assure his amity or at least neutrality, both East and West, jockeying for advantage, ran their own subsidies. All great powers before them had done the same. Only the Americans had to call subsidy by another name, and thus confuse things.

The very diversity of the world in the twentieth century, growing not less but greater, was painful to all proponents of world order whether democrat or totalitarian. Even the so-called blocs were porous. "Free world," applied indiscriminantly to the United States, Britain, France, Spain, and Dominica or Taiwan, took on a nonsensical sound. "Communist," when applied equally to Lenin in 1920, Stalin in 1945, Tito in 1948, or Mao in 1957, was anything but monolithic. If it was an axiom of Marxist dogma that true Communism could not succeed until it was universal, —then true Communism was torpedoed from the start.

But ideology was not the real cause of the power struggle. Too many Russians and Americans blinded themselves to the fact. Ideology was a Russian tool—which sometimes went dull, as in China—and which acerbated American fears. But it was perhaps necessary to keep the power struggle going. The minds of ordinary men, concerned with making a living to the exclusion of geopolitics, had to be filled with something.

After the vote of June 27, the United States rushed aid—at first aircraft, later ground forces—to Korea, and Russia hastened Gromyko back to the Security Council. The Russian decision on the Resolution was that it was illegal, and the USSR would not be bound by it.

The Nationalist regime on Taiwan had cast the deciding ballot, and the Russian position was that the Chinese seat, as spelled out by Dumbarton Oaks, rightfully belonged to Peking. However, the Communist powers could only ignore the resolution; they could not defy it, without taking an enormous propaganda beating.

It should be remembered that the two June resolutions had not been framed as political commands—which the Council was empowered to issue—but as mere recommendations, which the powers could support or not as they chose. The USSR, supplying North Korea, was thus permitted some flexibility of action, but not much. Active Soviet intervention, as North Korea collapsed under American armed might, was politically impossible. It would require complete Russian defiance of the UN, and probably force the USSR from that body.

No such restriction applied to China, however, which the United States, for more emotional than practical reasons, still blocked from membership.

One important action the USSR could take was to drop the

boom on Trygve Lie. From this time forward, they boycotted him, and finally destroyed his usefulness. A Secretary General in a bipolar world had to be able to traverse both poles.

Lie's intention was to keep the UN actively engaged in the direction of the Korean police action. This plan Washington, for perfectly logical reasons, opposed. The thought of a UN committee or commission in the middle of the already over-extended U. S. chain of command gave Pentagon personnel gray hairs, and Warren Austin was instructed to block any such moves in the UN.

Warren secured, also, authority for the United States to command and direct the war. The UN ordered South Korea to place its forces under American command, and gave it the right to fly the UN flag.

The Resolution of July 7 in effect gave the United States carte blanche to conduct the Korean operation as it saw fit. The only condition was that General MacArthur was required to report back to the UN headquarters. As it turned out in practice, Lie often read MacArthur's UN communiqués in the papers before they crossed his desk.

The U. S. determination to keep control was understandable; after all, ninety percent of the aid and forces going to Korea would be American. But it was also a tactical error.

The United States anticipated a small police action. In time it got a major war, with a need for very large ground forces. When this happened, the United States was eager for more UN participation; but each member, frozen out in the early days, had an obvious, if rather tenuous excuse, not to provide it. Fifteen members sent armed forces to Korea, but with the exception of the British, all were token. The United States had asked for a private war, and this is very nearly what it got. And in the first months, it almost blew that.

American policy had been committed to the noncommitment of U. S. ground forces on the Asian continent, and these forces were unprepared. Only a combination of South Korean sacrifices, a desperate stand, the predominant air and sea power the United States could apply, and MacArthur's brilliant counterstroke at Inchon prevented the UN presence from being ejected. If it had been, after the United States was committed, it might not have been possible to keep the demon in the bottle.

Faced with a choice of humiliation or holocaust, Truman would have had to blow the whistle. In Korea the United States learned, or should have learned, that to keep ahead in this great game you have to have white chips—conventional troops—as well as the nuclear blue ones.

It was touch and go for a time, but by September, the U. S.-UN forces had defeated the North Korean invaders and sent their remnants fleeing back across the 38th Parallel. It had taken blood this time, but again the wonderful mobility of the U. S. air and amphibious power was able to flank an enemy effort, and stalemate it.

On September 30, Trygve Lie circulated the draft of a new resolution that he felt would end the Korean embroglio. Called "Suggested Terms," it proposed the following:

(1) Complete North Korean withdrawal (now largely accomplished).

(2) Demobilization of North Korea.

(3) Permission for UN commissions to enter the North.

(4) Free elections to decide the final fate of the peninsula.

(5) *De facto* jurisdiction of the North Korean regime until after such elections.

(6) No UN forces to cross the border until after the same.

Lie's views aroused interest among the smaller nations, all of whom wanted the war to end on the old status quo. They were optimistic—it was not likely that North Korea would permit free elections. However, North Korea had absorbed a stunning defeat, and it seemed perfectly logical that the peninsula could be neutralized.

Significantly, Gromyko asked for a cease-fire on October 2,

and a return to the old borders. But the U. S. government was not seeking neutralization of Korea. It was seeking final solutions. The aggression had been "repelled" and Korea "restored," but it had been a bloody fight. The United States wanted to send its own and South Korean forces north to destroy the Communist regime. The problem was how to get the UN support for such a move. Once it had wrapped its policy in the UN flag, the United States could not just ignore the body. It wanted its carte blanche continued. But Gromyko was not likely to leave the store untended again, and a Soviet veto would stop any such UN resolution in its tracks.

The United States decided to try to transfer the action to the General Assembly, where the West still had a comfortable majority. It was impossible, of course, to transfer any real powers as delineated by the Charter to the Assembly; the USSR would block that, too. But it was possible to make certain administrative changes in the Assembly, and this was done.

These changes, now called the Acheson Plan, had been discussed since 1944. They permitted the Assembly to meet within twenty-four hours after a vetoless vote of the Council that it should do so, or simply upon the concurrence of an Assembly majority, to discuss security problems. And more significantly, the Assembly was now empowered to make *recommendations* on any matter blocked in the Council by veto. The recommendations had no force; they could be followed or not. But if a great power such as the United States backed and implemented them, they would have the same effect as the Council resolutions of June 25 and 27.

This, of course, opened Pandora's box in a way Mr. Welles had never imagined. When the Western majority shrank, it would present the United States with some very embarrassing resolutions on matters such as South Africa, colonialism, and the like. But in 1950 it seemed the only way around Gromyko's *Nyet*. The resolution the United States offered the Assembly under the newly adopted Acheson Plan undercut Lie's proposed solution. In fact, it knocked it out the window.

The Assembly resolution of October 7 called for "all necessary steps . . . to ensure conditions of peace throughout Korea, and further, United Nations forces entering North Korea [the word *enter* was construed by the American staff to be their authority for such entry] should remain only so far as necessary for achieving objectives."

Anticipating the passage of the resolution, American forces massed on the 38th parallel. They crossed on October 7.

The United States really did not have to pressure the resolution through. There was much sentiment for it in the UN of October, 1950. There were strong legalistic grounds for an invasion of North Korea: the UN had passed a resolution in 1947, and again in 1948 and 1949 calling for the reunification of all Korea, moves that died when the Soviet Union, with troops on the border, ignored them. The North Korean regime had invaded the South, and caused great loss of life and damage. Limping home, it showed itself completely unrepentant. It continued propaganda barrages against the United States and the UN, and the North Korean leaders refused to answer or treat in any way demands or inquiries from MacArthur's headquarters. In terms of the UN, North Korea had no legal or moral sanction for continuance as a state. It had been created purely by Communist power. And as it turned out, that alone was still sufficient to keep it in being. All calls broadcast from UN headquarters for a North Korean surrender were ignored. Kim Il Sung shrilled defiance of both the UN and the world.

In the halls of the United Nations in New York in late 1950 there was a sort of euphoria, a sense of high and successful purpose, as Lie wrote. The first overt aggression other than Palestine since the end of the war had been halted and defeated. Korea had not become another Ethiopia or Manchuria. For the first time since the Charter had been signed, the ghost of Geneva no longer seemed to haunt the shores of Lake Success. There was even an ephemeral willingness to dare and do.

All members of course were aware that the United States was going to do most of the daring and deeds, too. It was now openly

229

said that the UN resolution of 1948 had died like so many others because no great power had been prepared to back it up, which was perfectly true. And it was now argued by some members that if the United States was at last willing to carry the UN ball, it should be given running room.

The decision to invade North Korea and unite the Korean people under a free and independent government was a just and perfectly logical one. It was even, for the United States, excellent geopolitics. There was, however, one thing wrong with it. The invasion was a gambit into territory the Communist powers considered theirs. It was a gambit launched by force. The United States and the United Nations had to be prepared to make it successful by force.

But there are times, unfortunately, when justice is expediency. And carte blanche, like any other credit card, can be withdrawn.

In Korea the U. S. government had been faced with a limited assault. The play was for provinces and not really in pursuit of principles. The Communist thrust could not be ignored, and it had not been. But the response was tuned to the challenge. The United States defended the borders of Korea, rather than declaring war on the instigating powers, Soviet Russia and Red China. Now, when the United States in fusion with the UN hurled a new challenge northward, that riposte was again met in kind. The Chinese escalated the war by sending in "volunteers."

The Korean War, therefore, was merely an extension of the Cold War into the field of limited combat. It was a very dangerous acceleration, of course. Shooting, even limited shooting, inflames tempers. And there is always trouble when a popular democracy is faced with the situation of getting its citizen soldiers killed for limited goals.

The Korean conflict resembled in many ways the limited wars of the European eighteenth century, when ambassadors had met and smiled over refreshment and lied to each other while in far corners of the world native armies with white officers overran provinces, and European warships meeting each other on the high

230

seas cannonaded each other to the bottom—all without total war, or any passions that enveloped the general populations.

In these limited wars, fought between professionals for finite goals, the wealth of nations was won or lost. But in civilized Europe, after the religious wars ended, it was considered bad form to try to exterminate each other. What many non-historians forgot was that the Peace of Westphalia, which forged the broad outlines of the settlement ending the violent wars of religion in 1648, did not bring either religious or national peace. At Westphalia Europeans of different faiths tacitly agreed to stop trying to exterminate each other, and to accept a form of coexistence. But limited conflict went on, and it was never bloodless, as for almost a century Catholic and Protestant powers still jockeyed for predominance and position.

There were certain resemblances in the struggle between the Communist and non-Communist powers. Mutual extermination was not desired, on either side. Predominance was; and the score was being counted in societies influenced, governments won, and provinces secured for one side or the other.

Even the ten percent (a New York *Times* estimate) of the American public who intelligently followed foreign affairs had no ancestral experience or remembrance of Europe's limited warfare era, and they were hard put to understand the trend in Korea. To many, the fact that the world seemed to be still playing the old "balance of power" game, first invented in the 1600's, was depressing—it showed that the nature of man and the courses of his politics had not really changed.

Acheson, Bradley, Truman and Company, the architects of the Korean policy, could and did take quick and efficient action when necessary. None of them was much good at selling the reasons for such action to the public. Acheson, for one, had never learned to evangelize in the old American tradition, mixing platitudes with rabble rousing, or even to talk turkey. In spite of the fact that Acheson was hardly an intellectual but an actual "hardhead," a custom-suited variety of Missouri Truman, he could not communicate. One of the most anti-Communist of men, and the man who, as much as any other, had made NATO, actually ended up being branded Communistic by the American right wing.

Truman could not successfully isolate foreign policy from domestic politics during the Korean crisis, especially once conscript soldiers had to be used. This was not unusual. Britain in her most powerful hour had experienced the tug of war between Gladstone and Disraeli, one trying to involve Britain in order-keeping, the the other determined to withdraw. The trouble with containment as a policy was that too many Americans rejected the basis premises. Millions still wanted the United States to be the hope of the world. Others still dreamed of a Fortress America, to which the United States would withdraw and defend only its own shores. Both groups, at a time when Truman needed help, gave Truman only trouble.

When the Chinese armies entered the Korean War in late November, 1950, they did more than frustrate a total UN victory. The action put the world on the brink of a major war. By any precedent of custom or international law, the United States now had justification to pull out all stops and engage China in total conflict.

It was almost foreordained that General MacArthur, of the generation and school of Stimson, Hull, and Roosevelt, would see only the old crusading path. He was affronted by Communist crimes, enraged by Communist defiance, and determined to bring the malefactors to the dock, exactly as Hitler and Tojo had been. MacArthur was not a warmonger. He was a man who believed deeply that the limited course Washington eventually set was immoral. He could not accept the mere repelling and restoring as sufficient.

The tragedy of General MacArthur, one of the greatest Americans who ever lived, was that he outlived his time. If Wilson, or even Roosevelt, had been President in 1950, MacArthur most likely would have got his way.

232

But to Truman, and Truman's men, the move into North Korea had always been a gambit, nothing more. They had no feeling for crusades. They were aware that if Korea was a dagger pointed at Japan, it was also a tentacle reaching toward Manchuria. It was a bridge, and for that reason East and West had split it in half. If the West had a right to intervene, under the rules of *Weltpolitik* the Communists had the same. If the gambit to take the whole bridge failed, it was a gambit Truman would willingly abandon, and did.

For what happened in North Korea was that American arms, still unprepared to fight on the continent of Asia, suffered their single decisive defeat of the century. Had the Chinese been defeated on the ground, Asian history could have been very different. China would have suffered a disastrous loss of face and power. The Communist world would have been handed an enormous setback, which might have curbed its appetite for adventure for decades, if not forever.

But to have defeated the Chinese with nuclear arms would almost undoubtedly have enlarged the war. The USSR, as Acheson believed, could hardly have stood by. There was never any evidence that the Soviet Union intended to take the war beyond Korea, unless the United States did. But the UN flag was trampled under an avalanche of Chinese bodies, and while the U. S. forces came out in good order, they had to come out.

Ironically, there was less panic in Washington chambers than in UN chancellories in December 1950. Washington ordered American forces in Korea to hold the South, and to continue to confine the fighting to Korea, until American policy could be cleared through the UN.

There was a strong feeling among the Cabinet, and in Omar Bradley, Chairman of the Joint Chiefs, that the nature of the Korean action had not changed. Its magnitude and the antagonists had. But it was still a gambit, on each side. No one had yet said aloud, why not victory?

Time magazine shrilled, for all the world to read: "It was de-

233

feat—the worst defeat the United States had ever suffered. If this defeat were allowed to stand, it would mean the loss of Asia to Communism. The policy of containment was dead. There remained only the policy of retaliation and positive action by the United States and its allies to damage Communist power at the sources from which aggression flowed." But *Time* was old-fashioned, and it had often been wrong before.

The meeting of the U. S. Security Council on November 28, 1950, as the Chinese Communist Forces drove the UN out of North Korea, was instructive:

General Bradley advised the President that despite Mac-Arthur's pessimism, the situation in Korea was not such a disaster as some newspapers allowed. Bradley was confident that a mechanized UN army of 250,000 was not going to be run into the sea. Bradley's quiet evaluation put the crisis in perspective and calmed things down.

Another professional soldier, Secretary of Defense Marshall, said that in his opinion this was no time to go off half-cocked. Instead of new military moves in Asia, the United States should act in concert with the United Nations. The architect of the Marshall Plan had learned, since Yalta, to blend his war and politics.

The three Service Secretaries all agreed that the United States and the United Nations should not, if it could be avoided, get in a big brawl with Red China. The reasons were practical, political, and strategic: China was the wrong enemy, at the wrong place, and this was the wrong time. The United States had really nothing to gain, except a lot of dead people and a certain morose satisfaction at having won. Without several million American ground troops marched permanently into China, there was not much chance of enforcing the United States will over that monster.

The Service Secretaries, Army, Navy, and Air Force, saw China as a serious threat to peace—but not, then or later, as a serious threat to U. S. security if the United States only contained and kept calm.

234

Acheson, Secretary of State, mentioned that there must be some diplomatic way out of the mess. The North Korean gambit had backfired. Averell Harriman said that here careful consideration should be given to the opinions of all U. S. allies. Truman, nodding, rasped drily that it might be hard to convince the world that the United States was going to stay calm in the face of the shrieks and "distortions" of some of our biggest publishers.

The final decision was to hold South Korea, and not to enlarge the war unless the UN so ordered. This was the decision that drove MacArthur into insubordination.

Having carefully wrapped its policy in the UN cloak, the United States now found, if had it wanted to, no easy way out of those folds.

Meanwhile, back at Lake Success, the UN was in a ferment of agony and indecision. There was suddenly great doubt as to just where the United States had been leading the world. If it is true that nothing succeeds like success, the corollary is that nothing so upsets the troops as failure. All at once, all the old ghosts of Geneva had returned. The League had failed because in the final analysis, the Japanese, Germans, and Italians had scared the democrats. And now, plenty of democratic nations were again running scared.

In all fairness, most of the diplomats of the UN could see the Korean War for what it was—not a confrontation between St. George and the dragon, but a regional power play. They were, perhaps, excessively timid in the face of Chinese power. But five years after the most destructive war in history, Europeans and others were reluctant to accept any new sacrifices except in a last-ditch defense of their homes. Had Russia moved in Europe, it would have been different. But Korea was far away.

They were also free of the tangled American emotions that had surrounded American-Chinese relations since 1945. China, red or yellow, had developed domestic lobbies in the United States, much like Palestine, and with much the same disastrous result

235

toward clear-headed policy making. It did not occur to most Americans that they would have come into confrontation with *any* strong Chinese government after the war, just as they came into a kind of confrontation with Charles de Gaulle.

The rise of China faced the United States with problems similar to the rise of Japan, or later, of the USSR. But the Chinese chronic overpopulation, lack of organization, and general backwardness made China much less dangerous—if the United States kept its nerve.

The UN, examining the alternatives of getting out of Korea or accepting a bigger war with China, was leaning rapidly toward getting out. At a press conference on November 30, 1950, Truman brought matters to a head. He made a moderate statement on U. S. policy, and then, with one remark, touched upon the sorest nerve of the latter half of the twentieth century and stampeded the show.

He said, at first: "Recent developments in Korea confront the world with a serious crisis. . . . We have committed ourselves to the cause of a just and peaceful world order through the United Nations. We stand by that commitment. We shall meet the new situation in three ways. We shall continue to work in the United Nations for concerted action to halt the aggression in Korea. We shall intensify our efforts to help other free nations strengthen their defense. . . . We shall rapidly increase our own military strength. We shall exert every effort to help bring the full influence of the United Nations to bear on the situation. . . ."

Then, in answer to a question about the atom bomb, he affirmed that the United States still had one. And if the UN authorized such action, Chinese bases in Manchuria and elsewhere would be bombed. Under U. S. policy, Truman as President would pass such authority to MacArthur, and the General could pick his own targets. Within three hours, there was a diplomatic explosion. Nobody paid much attention to the moderate statement. Everybody heard only the words about the bomb.

The New York Times reported: "The President's mention of the atom bomb caused consternation and alarm in Britain and

236

brought from France official disapproval. Most UN delegates were agreed that it would be politically disastrous to use the bomb in Asia."

The fact that approximately one million Caucasian Germans had been bombed, blasted, and burned to death from the air in World War II never made any impression on Asia. The fact that two nuclear devices, developed only after Germany surrendered, were dropped on a nonwhite nation, did. Communist propaganda during the days of the American nuclear monopoly, now ended, played this to the hilt.

In one sense nuclear bombs were only gunpowder, an extension of industrial society's already present capability of killing itself off. But they were of almost uncontrollable dimensions, and a psychological horror had been wrapped around them by 1950. The UN members were right; it was about as impossible politically to employ them on Asians now as it was to use another once highly respectable practice, burning at the stake.

As the *Times* continued, "Nothing so awakened the French Assembly as mention of the bomb. . . ."

A London dateline read: "Britons dismayed by Truman's talk —Atlee will fly to Washington to discuss crisis with President." The London *Times* editorialized, "[Truman] touched upon the most sensitive fears and doubts of this age. . . ."

The press generally, from Communist rags in Italy to the staid Conservative sheets in Australia, now took the position that the U. S. armies should not have marched to the Yalu—no great deduction, in December—and that a North Korean buffer must be left between U. S. power and the Communist heartlands. Winston Churchill rose in the House of Commons and warned against emotional involvement in Asia at the expense of vital areas elsewhere. Even Socialists cheered.

Without quite meaning to, Harry Truman had cleared the air, and also clarified where three quarters of the world stood on the China question. That opinion would not back a war with China, except in the continuing defense of South Korea. There were people in the United States who fought any war to win. The people of the world asked, Win what? The game did not seem worth the candle.

Without waiting for Acheson to lead, thirteen Arab-Asian nations drafted a UN resolution calling for a Korean cease-fire. Under the Acheson Plan, the Assembly passed it overwhelmingly.

Acheson, who had unwittingly opened Pandora's box with the revised rules permitting security matters to go to the Assembly, now found himself and U. S. policy wrapped in a different kind of UN cloak. Instead of responding to U. S. appeals for help, the Assembly, dominated by frightened nations and neutrals, was ordering an end to the war on almost any basis. Without the sheerest display of arrogance and hypocrisy, there was no way out of this entanglement for the United States. But a certain number of American diplomats and government officials made a mental note about again wrapping U. S. policies in a UN cloak.

On February 1, 1959, with heavy fighting continuing between UN and Chinese forces in Korea, the Assembly expressed only a mild indictment of the Red Chinese intervention. A resolution was passed 44-9, with 9 abstentions, which called for continuance of an effort to hold South Korea, affirmed the UN intention to bring about a cease-fire, and named China an aggressor. The resolution did not apply sanctions or any other UN measure against the Chinese, however. The resolution also reiterated the objective of the October 7 resolution—the unification of Korea —but in effect it abandoned this objective by specifically stating that any such unification must be accomplished by "peaceful" means. Expediency had become justice where Koreans were concerned.

A few days later, Washington circles leaked hints to the press that the official U. S. policy toward unifying Korea was being changed, and that the United States would explore the possibilities of a peace in line with UN resolutions.

First, however, the Chinese had to be prevented from conquering all South Korea. The Chinese Communist forces had punched through over the 38th parallel, deep in Syngman Rhee's republic. But now, in February, 1951, the tide again turned. Lieutenant General Matthew B. Ridgway, commanding the Eighth U. S. Army, ordered a stand at Chipyongni, and here and at Wonju massive Chinese offensives were blunted and turned back with enormous slaughter. It was proved that the Chinese could not meet the U. S. forces in open battle, openly arrived at, as General Bradley had predicted. During the spring of 1951 the Communists attacked again and again, determined to win an enormous psychological victory by driving the UN forces into the sea. But the UN defense remained ascendant, and in each engagement the Chinese were severly mauled. Hundreds of thousands were killed or wounded.

By the end of March, Ridgway had retaken Seoul, and two months later the Chinese forces in Korea tottered on the brink of disaster. They had been driven back across the 38th parallel, and South Korea was virtually cleared of all Communist troops. The Chinese were exhausted, and probably unable to prevent a UN drive to the Yalu.

But the United States, wrapped in UN policies, was in no position for further northern adventures. Truman had never felt strongly about the advance into North Korea or Korean unification, and these were policies he abandoned readily. The United States was ready to accept a return to the old status quo, provided the Communists were.

The problem was to find a way out, with some honor on each side. Both sides had made it fairly clear that they would not accept a major defeat without a contest that went beyond the immediate desires of each. As in Berlin, the result was impasse.

On May 26, 1951, Lester Pearson of Canada, the Assembly President, made the marvelous understatement that a surrender of the Chinese might not be necessary in order to end the war. He was heard.

On June 1, Trygve Lie noted that the battle line had reached the old 38th-parallel border; the war was back where it had started. Lie said, making his meaning clear, that the UN resolution of June 25 and 27, 1950, could now be considered carried out.

The bad dream of October 7, which had taken the United Nations into the never-never land, was forgotten. Also forgotten was Korean unity, and freedom for the North Korean population. There were times in great-power politics when justice was expediency, and when unlimited credit cards such as the United States had received had to be withdrawn.

Dean Acheson, with some neat footwork, now divided the Korean problems into two: he said that the long-term political approach of the United States was still to unify and free Korea, but the immediate military problem was to end the shooting. Under severe questioning by a Senate Committee—he was spending more and more time there—he repeated on June 7 that any reliable peace based on the 38th parallel would be acceptable to Washington.

The USSR was also amenable. It was aware of Chinese exhaustion, and also aware that Communist intransigence could push the United States too far, UN or no UN. On June 13, almost a year after the first aggression began, Yakov Malik made a speech in the UN that, at his request, was publicly broadcast. Speaking as a sort of *amicus curiae* for everyone—the USSR had remained officially uninvolved—Malik vituperated the capitalist powers for a spell, then got down to business. He said that if the belligerents could open discussions, the war could be ended.

In a tradition that had already sprung up at the UN and that Lodge and Stevenson would carry on, nobly, the man in the white hat, Warren Austin, asked Malik to put up or shut up. From Washington, in more diplomatic language, Truman said the same.

On June 30, General Ridgway, the UN commander in the Far East, radioed Communist commanders: "I am informed that you may wish a meeting to discuss an armistice. . . ." This came less than a decade after Americans had demanded unconditional surrender from the Germans and Eisenhower had refused even to

240

speak with Nazi emissaries. Now, Americans sat down with Communists. But if a certain haunting innocence was lost, perhaps the United States had at last grown up. But perhaps America surrendered its principle too soon, and grew up a bit too late. In millions of Americans' mouths, a very bad taste remained.

The Korean War ended for all practical purposes in July, 1951. But the fighting and the dying continued for two more years along a stalemated line because first the United States and the UN took a certain naïveté to the truce table. It had become an uncontrollable reflex of the democratic, genuinely peace-loving states to relax whenever things looked up or the Communist side cried uncle. The Chinese, under terrible pressure, were perfectly sincere in asking for a cease-fire. But they were only surrendering for a day, and it was Communist practice sensibly to salvage everything that could be salvaged at the truce tables.

The immediate relaxation of UN pressure on the Chinese troops when the truce talks began in July, 1951, was a mistake. It allowed the massive Red armies to dig in and reinforce. Then, when the sticky prisoner-of-war problem blew up, the Communists in secure positions, could procrastinate, delay, and continue the war and pressures on the West for two years.

Actually, by November, 1951, the geography and terms of the cease-fire were settled; the final cease-fire line was drawn. But an unforeseen complication developed. The UN had taken a hundred thousand North Korean and Chinese POW's during the fighting, and a majority of these men requested asylum in the free world rather than return home.

This was unprecedented, and a propaganda blow the Communist world could not accept. They delayed the armistice, and in the spring of 1952 instigated riots and disorders in the POW camps on Koje-do. But the disorders were put down without a mass slaughter, as the Communists had hoped, and neutral commissions clearly established the fact that the POW's were sincere, and not forced into their actions by UN or U. S. pressure. The fact that about 80,000 North Koreans and some 12,000 Chinese eventually were resettled in South Korea or Taiwan was, with the subsequent Berlin Wall, one of the most damaging psychological blows the Communists ever took in the war for men's minds. It showed clearly what many Asians thought of the brutal Communist system, which ruled by force rather than consensus.

Over the refusal of the Communist side to accept defeat on the POW question, the war dragged on until the summer of 1953. Here, two things happened. One was the restiveness of the United States, caught in an increasingly unpopular action. It became apparent even to the Chinese that the United States would not fight trench warfare along the proposed cease-fire line forever. Secondly, Stalin died in March, 1953; and the iron will that had held the Communist world together disappeared. Soviet Russia entered a period of domestic power struggle, and a respite was needed from foreign adventures. On July 27, 1953, a cease-fire was signed.

The Korean War, never officially declared, was never officially ended. More than a decade later troops still watched the cease-fire line in Korea, and incidents were still reported. The whole question of a Korean settlement, was, like the German question, left to await the end of the Cold War.

From Korea the West seemingly did not learn, perhaps was incapable of learning, that the Communist tactic of retreat under pressure never implied a real surrender. The Communists, unlike American thinkers, saw no separation between peace and war; they accepted without question Clausewitz's dictum that there could be no separation, and that war was nothing more than an extension of international politics onto the battlefield. Men trained to look on life as a power struggle and who came to power only by means of a struggle—no Communist leaders were ever "elected"—could not help but regard such struggles as endless.

But they were marked by peaks and valleys. Today the struggle might be intense, tomorrow relaxed. And again it might be on a certain "hot" battlefield, like Korea, Malaya, or Vietnam, or continued just as well over a table, or over the air waves. Everything, "peace" or "war," was part of the whole, and part of the game.

242

Given the Western background and mentality, it was hard for Americans to continue implacable enmity, take a view embracing decades, and to refuse to consider any separation between violence, propaganda, and true diplomacy. In the West, means were important, because men were taught that ends were inherent in the means. But that was a purely Western moral view, which Communism did not accept.

The Korean War revealed that in spite of the mountainous piles of modern weaponry each side was amassing as symptoms of the tension, there was a complete reluctance to engage in general or nuclear war. There could be no real disarmament as long as the tension existed. But there did not have to be big war.

The Soviet bloc, which with Stalin's death was rapidly ceasing to be a bloc and turning into a grouping of powers immensely hostile to the West but only slightly less hostile to each other, had a heightened realization of the dangers inherent in small wars. Too many men in the United States had figuratively frothed at the mouth over Korea, and the United States several times seemed ready to enter the twilight zone. Afterward, both the USSR and China would proceed more slowly down the same path. They surrendered no goals of expansion, but no more armies would cross defined boundaries. In Asia, subversion, insurgency, and support of revolutions and wars of national liberation on the periphery might just as well serve the Communist purpose. Any disorder, *even where it was not Communist instigated,* furthered Communist interests and world aims.

The Communist power centers, Russia and China, in unison or acting singly, could hope to extend their influence only through the creation of disorder and the resultant power vacuums that disorder developed. In this way, sometimes even a completely non-Communist revolution in the underdeveloped world, if it shook the existing commercial and political framework, damaged the West psychologically or economically and served Soviet or Chinese interests. To remake the world in a Communist mold, the older orders had to first be destroyed.

But following Korea a prime objective of the Communist powers was to prevent another open confrontation from developing. Khrushchev, who finally came to power in the Kremlin during the five-year power struggle that followed Stalin's death, defined this neatly, with his "peaceful coexistence." Peaceful coexistence meant the tacit avoidance of nuclear or general war, but it meant open season and continual skirmishing on all other fronts. Above all, the Communist aim was to aid and abet the "war of national liberation" that, however justified, always chipped away at the Western power position. Khrushchev made this very clear, and his toothy grins were as dangerous as Stalin's heavy frowns.

This kind of peace was not clearly understood by everyone in the West. Khrushchev, when he allowed the Cuban confrontation to develop, erred because he had grievously misjudged the quality of America's response.

The Korean settlement, then, continued the practice that had begun at Yalta. In the interests of expediency and to avoid great-power conflict, the Soviet-Chinese conquests in North Korea were confirmed. There was no treaty, but the Communist powers were left in full control. The United States again showed that it would sacrifice the principle of self-determination—which was, in the minds of many American officials, unworkable—and abandon the interests of minor peoples to avoid war. The Koreans, north and south, were the real losers of the Korean conflict.

But if the Communist powers had grown more wary of overt aggression, the United States had become even less enthusiastic about ground commitment in Asia. The Democratic party paid a painful price for Truman's stand. The old desires for an immaculate war, in which Asians fought Asians while Americans fought only from the sea or air in support, emerged stronger than ever. Two years after the Korean War ended, Admiral Radfort and others pushed this course strongly. This thinking, almost irresistible to some Western leaders who did not dare risk the political implications of high casualties in ground police actions, continued to hamstring American policy in Asia. Ironically, it was supported by many who had not thought out the possible consequences of reacting to infiltrations or minor aggressions by aerial

244

bombs, nuclear or otherwise. In some eyes, general war seemed more morally acceptable than limited war.

The world hammered out on the battlefields of 1945 went on. It had not turned out to be the kind of peace millions had hoped for. It had grim aspects, and moments of both tedium and great fright. But as the challenge and the response in Korea showed, things might not be as bad as free men thought as long as they kept their courage.

And meanwhile, the mantle of the United Nations was sent back to gather dust in its New York closet.

Part III

THE FUTURE

15.

Dag Hammarskjöld and the Spirit of '56

THE YEARS immediately following Korea were relatively quiet ones for the UN. The East-West split continued, with Russia gaining prestige and power vis-à-vis the United States through scientific, economic, and weapons advances. The colonial order continued to collapse from its own weight, increasing the neutral or uncommitted strength in the Assembly, until it eventually approached a majority.

The term "neutral" was always a misnomer. The powers like Yugoslavia, which blazed the trail in 1948, and Egypt, which followed in 1952, were never neutral. They had their own aims and aspirations, and many of these countries were essentially hostile to the West and everything it stood for. These nations wanted to be a third force in the world, but their effectiveness was sharply restricted by their lack of real power.

They settled into the United Nations Organization, noisy and demanding, because in no place else—with one nation, one vote —could they attract so much attention or wield so much influence. And because the United States and the USSR, the two dominant powers, were running out of fringe areas and had already arrived at a stand-off, they assumed an importance in men's minds they never actually had. In a world in which either great power had full control, a country like Egypt would have had its teeth kicked in for insolence, one way or another. But in a world in which neither had control or felt secure, the Egyptians were actually courted by each side with offers of aid, and every kind of Egyptian intemperance and interference was tolerated, all in the hope of "influencing men's minds."

It turned into a tidy situation for Colonel Nasser and many another leader, such as Nkrumah of Ghana or Sukarno of Indonesia. They were children who were not only seen, but heard—incessantly. Vandenberg's UN had given them a forum in a way he never envisioned.

The UN was also serving in a way that had not been contemplated but was extremely useful: it was the organization, and the only possible organization, that could have put the stamp of world approval on the emergence of states from European colonies to sovereign nations. Acceptance of former colonies as UN members immediately gave them both a "legal" and a visible membership among the nations and greatly eased the transition. In fact, the whole passage of some fifty separate dependencies out of the colonial order into nationhood, even imperfect and uneasy nationhood, relatively peacefully, was a remarkable phenomenon of the postwar world.

It was accomplished partly because of the stability and good sense of the European powers, partly because of the immense influence of the United States, which wanted it done, and partly because the UN provided a ready-made mechanism to help accomplish it.

But the changes in the world map were inevitably changing the UN Assembly from the Western alliance that had defeated Hitler into something very different: a vast amorphous body with no common ideals, ideas, or aspirations and with very conflicting ambitions.

The emergence of Dag Hammarskjöld, the new Secretary General, as one of the two or three best-known men in the world, illustrated the changes taking place.

Trygve Lie had been destroyed by the Russian boycott, even though he had been reelected for another term. No one knew this better than Lie. Also, Lie was generally unable to communicate with, or gain much sympathy from, the emerging Afro-Asian world. Lie was too European, too Western, and too eternally committed to his own inherent beliefs. This lack of support from the emerging majority eventually caused Lie to resign in November,

250

1952. Dag Hammarskjöld of Sweden, from an officially neutral nation, was elected to replace him.

Hammarskjöld was of a very different breed from his fellow Scandinavian. Lie was the son of a working man; Hammarskjöld was a descendant of the old Swedish service aristocracy. The ability to see grays instead of blacks and whites was steeped in his bones; the family had been bureaucrats for generations. He was also deeply reserved and dignified where Lie had been ebullient, cautious where Lie had stamped and stormed. He preferred, above all, to smoke his small dark cigars when he sat in Council Sessions and keep his peace. But that did not mean he was ineffective; far from it.

He was to carry Lie's initiative under Article 99 even farther than Lie had taken it, and to do it almost unnoticed. For Hammarskjöld was that rare mixture of mystic, visionary, and coldly practical politician that so frequently occupies the world stage. After his death, his writings revealed his sense of Christ-identification. During his life, his actions showed his superb sense of realism in a world he quite probably considered mad.

Hammarskjöld understood from the first Lie's weakness with the rising Afro-Asian states. Lie had never been able to communicate with Nehru, or Nasser, or even the Emperor of Abyssinia; there was a complete cultural block. Hammarskjöld set out at once to correct this. He struggled to see and understand the underdeveloped powers' views. He learned to talk to Afro-Asians and got across the point that in him they possessed a friend.

Hammarskjöld saw his job as Secretary General as one that required that he be scrupulously neutral between each of the super powers, but keep the confidence of both, and meanwhile, necessitated his leading and being responsive to the emerging numerical majority. This he eventually did with consummate skill. At the start, he enjoyed three quiet years in which to build confidence in himself, from April, 1953, through the beginning of 1956. Then, the two great crises of 1956 showed Hammarskjöld's concepts most clearly.

The Palestine crisis still smoldered in the Middle East. Arab pressures and provocations against the Israeli state continued and grew worse. These were led by Egypt, which, after Nasser's national socialist revolution was secure, strove to lead the entire Arab world. Egypt took the forefront in proclaiming the destruction of Israel, since nothing so pleased the Arab world; and at the same time, in its own nationalistic interest, worked through propaganda and subversion to try to bring down the generally pro-Western monarchies that still made up most of the area.

Egypt followed no Communist path, however; Colonel Gamal Abdel Nasser proscribed his native Communists and jailed them whenever he could identify them. Nasser aided the Soviet Union, however, by doing his utmost, for his own purposes, to undermine the Anglo-French power structure that still kept a tenuous control over the Middle East. His reasons were typical of all national action: ultra-rational, religious, and nationalistic. He wanted both a new Arab empire, with Egypt, ruled by himself, at the head of it. He sought arms aid from the USSR and got it; he hired ex-Nazi scientists and German engineers; and he tried to get economic aid from the United States. Nasser, quite humanly, strove for the best of all possible Egyptian worlds.

And he became absolutely intolerable to France and Britain, and eventually to Secretary of State Foster Dulles of the United States, while he kept the Israelis standing to arms day and night.

By 1956 the Arab tensions were approaching the boiling point. In January, the Security Council heard charges that an Israeli force had attacked Syrian soil. While the attack was in reprisal for undeniable provocations by the Syrians, Israel was warned. France, Britain, and the United States, in 1950, had issued a statement to the effect that they guaranteed all borders in the Middle East. The act had been aimed at Arab encroachment on Israel, but it cut both ways.

But by 1956 it had become obvious that Israel's patience was limited. It was about to embark on the old Biblical course of an eye for an eye, and with justification. Egypt was instigating deliberate murder raids by the so-called "fedayeen" or Palestinian

252

refugees across its borders, and shelling the Gaza Strip. Egypt was building up immense piles of Soviet arms along the borders, behind the UN Armistice Demarcation Line of 1949. On March 26, the United States called the Security Council into session to investigate this buildup and the one Israel was also starting. The Council ordered the Secretary General to investigate and report back.

This trip and mission were then unique. It was the first time the Secretary General of the UN went forth as a diplomat in his own right, to see what might be done to relieve tensions. Hammarskjöld was able to accomplish nothing, but he did take soundings and made contacts that helped him later.

In the summer of 1956, as the situation grew more tense, the United States cancelled a previous offer of economic aid to Egypt —the building of the Aswan High Dam. Nasser's whole economic future was based on this dam. The cancellation was to be much criticized, but Dulles found Nasser's provocations and trouble-fomenting intolerable. Nasser soon accepted a Soviet offer to replace the U. S. aid, but one week after Dulles' move he did something a great deal more explosive. He nationalized the Suez Canal, using the cancellation of Aswan Dam as an excuse. The international waterway had been built and run for almost a century by an Anglo-French company, and it was absolutely vital to both France and Britain. Most of their petroleum from the Middle East passed through it on the way to market. Nasser had touched a very sensitive nerve.

France, Britain, and Egypt tried to work out an acceptable solution to Egyptian control of the Canal, but no agreement was reached. For one thing, Egypt closed the Canal to all Israeli shipping, and this was intolerable. For another, Nasser's attitude in dealing with the European powers was intolerable to them. Nasser was trying to make up in one summer for a hundred years of what he keenly felt was Egyptian humiliation at their hands.

The question came to the UN in October, 1956. The Council debated various international solutions, one of which the USSR, suddenly alive to opportunity, vetoed. And while these UN negotiations were in progress, Premier Mollet of France, Prime Minister Anthony Eden of Britain, and Ben-Gurion of Israel, each for his own reasons, entered into a weird and secret alliance, aimed at ridding the world of one Gamal Abdel Nasser.

Israel, understandably, could never feel secure while Nasser bought piles of arms from the USSR and filled the radio with hate for Jewry. Britain, even before the vital Canal issue, had had enough of Nasser's fomenting trouble in its Middle Eastern protectorates and essential oil preserves. France was angry over Nasser's aid and abetment of emerging Algerian rebels. Nasser preached burning hatred of all three countries, and he had given each of them more provocation than was usually needed for retaliation.

But what they did was in absolute violation of the UN Charter, which forbade the open aggression of one power on another. On October 29 Israeli forces suddenly attacked into the Sinai Peninsula, Egyptian territory. To the surprise of the world, and certainly of Nasser, the Israeli Army cut through the massive and well-armed Egyptians forces like a hot knife through butter. The Egyptians were as inept as ever, and this easy advance gave the French and British leaders a false impression that all that was needed now was a little of what had once been called gunboat diplomacy. The world, however, had changed.

The ex-colonial Egyptians were still poor shakes at fighting, but they rallied behind Nasser, with none of the panic or confusion they had shown at the approach of Rommel's Panzer Afrika Corps in 1942. This, the British above all did not expect.

Both the United States and the United Nations were thrown into confusion. Dulles and Eisenhower held a meeting, and Dulles publicly called attention to the fact that the United States was pledged to take action against *any* aggressor in the Middle East. The U. S. ambassador in London called on Selwyn Lloyd, the British Foreign Secretary, to discuss a joint Anglo-American resolution calling for Israeli withdrawal. Now, Lloyd dissembled. He failed to mention that Christian Pineau, the French Foreign

Minister, was arriving within the hour to draft an ultimatum to Egypt, which permitted the Israelis to advance within ten miles of Suez, but which stated that French and British forces would land if the fighting went on.

On October 30, this ultimatum was issued as a "solemn appeal" to the Egyptians and Israelis to halt the war, or else Anglo-French forces would intervene and seize the Canal to assure its remaining open. The language fooled no one. The French and British were out to retake the Canal and rub Nasser's nose in it.

President Eisenhower blew sky-high. He used violent language not heard since Grant's day. He was enraged at a number of things: the British deception, what he genuinely considered British immorality, and the fact that Eden had done this to him a few days before the 1956 election—especially since he had gone to the futile 1955 Geneva summit conference only to assist Eden in the British elections of 1955.

Dulles was equally enraged. The action presaged a violation of the Charter; and Dulles, from the days when he had served Wilson at Versailles, had in his heart believed in the right of colonial peoples to self-determination. This the British Foreign Office had not sufficiently understood. Dulles despised Nasser; but he was not pro-British, either. When he had come to office in 1953, there had been subtle changes in the Anglo-American relationship. Dulles had never been a member of the old Anglo-American wartime team; he tended to regard Anthony Eden not so much as a mystic partner but a rival advocate before the world's bar.

Earlier, Dulles had been in favor of Anglo-French evacuation of Suez. He considered this Egypt's right to demand. And he did not think humiliation of Nasser by the coalition as a proper answer to the Middle East problem. He was generally unable to sympathize with the Anglo-French viewpoint.

Dulles saw almost everything in perspective to the East-West struggle, which had absorbed his later life and energies. He was interested in the Suez embroglio only in its relation to the Soviet-United States standoff, a fact that almost drove Eden crazy. And

Dulles was wrapped in a cold fury at Britain's blatant use of gunboat diplomacy for the simple reason that this weakened the West's moral position in a world that Dulles was trying unsuccessfully to rally against the USSR and China. Worse, Eden had as much as lied to him in planning the secret moves.

World reaction, understandably, was immediately bitter toward the two colonial powers and Israel, which the ex-colonial world liked to regard as a Western puppet.

The real tragedy of the Suez fiasco was that Dulles and Eden were unable to communicate; they disliked each other, and neither could really see the world from the other's vantage point. Eden clearly saw Britain's interests; but Dulles saw only the grand design against world Communism, in which Britain was only a small part.

On October 30 in the Security Council, Ambassador Cabot Lodge of the United States read the message he had been instructed to deliver: "Failure of the Council to react at this time would be an avoidance of the responsibilities that maintain peace and security. The government of the United States feels it imperative . . . to have a cease-fire ordered immediately, and to obtain the withdrawal of Israeli forces behind the frontier lines. Nothing else will suffice."

With deep irony, the United States and the USSR were united on the idea. Each, for entirely different reasons, found itself on Nasser's side.

Britain and France, with Australia wringing its hands beside them, tried to delay the vote on the U. S. resolution ordering Israel to withdraw. But the United States and the USSR together forced the issue. The resolution carried—but France and Britain vetoed it. Here, not only the UN but the great design behind it reached the end of the road.

The USSR now presented a resolution condemning Israel. The Anglo-French team vetoed this, while the United States abstained.

What began to occur now was complete confusion. America's

256

first reaction was violent and bitter toward the three attackers. But France and Britain were America's principal NATO allies, the European prop of containment. And Israel, although the seeming aggressor, had enormous American sympathy; the old pro-Israel elements in American society went immediately to work on Washington. U. S. policy, in a sense, began to flutter in the wind. Dulles recognized the immense idiocy of joining the USSR in a drive against the European powers; yet at the same time the United States could not back, or acquiesce in, the European-Israeli move without agreeing to violations of everything it had stood for since the end of World War II.

U. S. policy was forced into some painful acrobatics. What Dulles did now was mentally to prepare himself to accept a British-French accomplished fact, in case the Anglo-French forces occupied the Canal and deposed Nasser. The United States could not agree to this, but it could accept the result, if not with humor and grace at least with equanimity. Nasser was an enormous pain in the ass—the words of one U. S. diplomat. Dulles, privately, was even resigned to pulling the Russian bear off Eden's back. The United States had to do this, if necessary, in its own interests.

To all the above, there is ample evidence, which even British historians have revealed. But there was one trouble—Eden and Dulles were not in communication, in the UN or anywhere else. Neither Eden nor the Foreign Office understood the basic casuistry that often dominated Dulles' mind. Dulles, a genuinely moral man and a man without moral doubts as to the rightness of his and America's cause, was also a man who could let the ends not be sullied by the means, if necessary. But Anthony Eden only understood this too late—if ever.

Condemned by the United States, threatened by the USSR, and faced by a rising howl from every Latin American and Asian and African nation, Eden simply lost his nerve. He delayed the landings at Suez, made Britain an object of scorn, and gave his own Labor party time to organize some of the most

257

massive demonstrations in history. He destroyed his political career at its zenith; Eden's, not Nasser's, nose was rubbed in the Canal.

Meanwhile, in the UN, the Western powers let all leadership slip out of their hands. The United States was self-paralyzed; Britain and France had abjured leadership through their actions. The USSR was emerging as the champion of the Arab world, and, by indirection, of all the colonial and ex-colonial world.

This was the breach and the vacuum Dag Hammerskjöld stepped into.

Hammarskjöld was deeply angry at the British and French secretiveness and the arbitrary nature of their actions, which ill became two democratic powers. But before the Council on October 30 and 31, he argued only for compliance with UN agreements already signed by those powers, passing no words of judgment.

While an Anglo-French convoy stood off Suez, and French and British jets bombed Cairo and Egyptian military installations, and Nasser ordered ships scuttled in the Canal to block it, Hammarskjöld stated that he wanted to resolve the crisis, and that under Article 99 he had certain initiatives. He stated also that if he did not have the confidence of the powers he would forthwith resign. With swiftness, the entire Security Council, including the French and British delegates, expressed complete confidence in him.

And now, in the face of great-power paralysis, Hammarskjöld began to explore a way out. The entire membership gladly sent the entire crisis up, as someone said, "to the 38th floor—Hammarskjöld's office." Moving swiftly, and without any real precedents, Hammarskjöld's Secretariat began to create a United Nations Emergency Force, or UNEF, made up from contingents of the armed forces of the smaller powers.

This would proceed to the Middle East and stop the fighting between the Egyptians and Israelis, and at the same time make the threatened Anglo-French intervention unnecessary. There was an immediate agreement among the Secretariat, backed by the Assembly, that the superpowers, the United States and the

USSR, would be bypassed on the call for troops. With keen good sense, Hammarskjöld tried to keep Suez removed from the Cold War as much as possible. Working with clarity and reason, Hammarskjöld showed himself utterly dedicated to the ideal of peace.

While Hammarskjöld united the small and neutral nations in one great moment of fusion, Eden was hesitating his way to disaster. The Labor party, logically, refused to back his move, both for ideological and political reasons. At least one half of Britain was either morally scandalized at the return to gunboat law or else desperately afraid of a war, and Eden did nothing whatever to unite the nation. Israeli forces reached Suez, and even pushed patrols to the east bank of the Nile, deep inside Egypt proper. And still Eden could not act, either to withdraw or proceed.

The landings at Suez, right or wrong, were the kind of act that "if it were done when 'tis done, then 'twere well it were done quickly." The world had proved a thousand times that it would accept a bitter, if irretrievable, fact. Dulles, still deeply annoyed, was prepared to accept one. On November 2, while Mollet of France, whose people were much more united on the logic of doing Nasser in, grew concerned at the delay, Eden quibbled. He went before Parliament, and as a concession to domestic outrage said he would welcome UN control of the Canal.

Finally, on November 5, after days of delay, Anglo-French forces landed in Egypt. The professed motives of the landing were made ridiculous by the fact that the Israelis had already won their war, and the Canal was in no danger. The Egyptians resisted, and there was heavy fighting, with atrocities on both sides.

The long delay allowed Hammarskjöld to form UNEF, which was voted by the Assembly and dispatched to the Middle East November 7. Now Eden's nerve collapsed completely, and he gave in. Colonel Nasser, losing every battle fought, won the war. The Israelis and Europeans would have to withdraw. The United Nations eventually paid for the clearing of the Canal, and the French and British did it for him.

With UNEF on the ground, the independent action of the powers was ended. It still required long and tricky negotiations to get the British out of Suez, the Israelis out of Sinai and Gaza, and the Canal back in operation on a basis acceptable to all. Hammarskjöld, now carrying the burden with everyone's agreement, eventually accomplished it all.

The basic tension of the Middle East, given a good nosebleed, continued to build up again. It would erupt in 1958, with the Iraqi revolution. But this time Dulles and Eisenhower were ready; the United States landed troops in Lebanon, took over the British subsidy in Jordan, and stabilized the situation.

The Russians, although the Arab world gave them most of the credit for stopping Eden and Mollet, never were quite able to exploit the foothold they gained in the area. Generally, all outside influence withered, compared to earlier times.

On balance, it would have been to the advantage of the West to have scragged Nasser. He came back stronger and cockier than ever. But, as Dulles saw, it could hardly be argued that removal under such circumstances would have improved the West's moral and political position. The U. S. policy now became one of trying to isolate Egypt within the Arab world, and this, under the newly proclaimed Eisenhower Doctrine of 1957, met with some success. Under this doctrine, the United States was unilaterally pledged to assist any Arab government or the Israeli regime if it were attacked, or asked for aid. The watchman took over another, and very messy, section of the wall.

At first, UNEF and Hammarskjöld's success seemed a brilliant victory for the UN and a splendid defense of the Charter. And so it was, if two things were overlooked:

First, Eden and Britain, the dominant power of the Anglo-French-Israeli coalition, with its own "Fifth Column" of sorts at home, were unusually susceptible to moral pressures. Both were basically incapable of defying world opinion, and one reason was that Britain no longer had the power to do so. Israel, likewise, was vulnerable to American pressure, since it was virtually living off a dole of private American citizens. It was these outside pressures, not the UN, that forced an end to the Suez action.

Secondly, the putting together of UNEF within a week seemed to assert a power of action within the UN. Ironically, this sowed certain seeds of UN destruction. There was no budget for expeditionary forces, and no way to finance them except through voluntary assessments—and the great powers paid almost all of the actual costs of the UN. France, logically, refused to pay its assessment for the Middle East UNEF. A dangerous precedent was set.

Although few saw it in 1956, it was again pointed up that the UN could not ignore the power realities, which included the power of money.

But above all, it was what happened in Hungary at the same time Suez broke that cut the Suez action down to size.

The Soviet block ceased to be monolithic almost from the day of Stalin's death. The divergence between China and Russia still lay in the future; but by June, 1953, there had been revolts in East Germany, put down with Russian tanks. These disorders had been an excuse for other Soviet leaders to liquidate deputy premier Beria.

The revolts, which began to break out in the Communist European Empire and which became accelerated after Khrushchev took his calculated risk of condemning Stalin in the Party Congress of early 1956, were based on a combination of both social and ideological resentments. Workers in Eastern Europe, horribly exploited and underpaid by a system that was supposed to favor them, rose in protest. Intellectuals, who were mainly Marxist intellectuals, were angered by stubborn and rigid thought control, often imposed by uneducated and stupid Party leaders. The whole populations of such ancient nations as Poland and Hungary, meanwhile, writhed under Russian political control. Eastern Europe had a long history of Russia-hating.

In October, 1956, an alliance of Polish workers and intellectuals succeeded in reinstating Wladyslaw Gomulka as Premier of Poland over Russian objections. After workers' riots in Poznan, the situation was very tight for a time, with Poles determined to

261

win relaxations of Soviet and Communist party rule and the USSR determined not to let the foundations of their empire be undermined. In Poland, because of basic good sense on both sides, an uneasy compromise was maintained. The Soviet hand was relaxed somewhat, but Poland did not try to kick over the traces.

Hungary, traditionally one of the most chauvinistic nations of Europe, was another story. Here, what started as an intellectual revolt by students and a protest by exploited workers turned into a nationalistic orgy that sparked an explosion.

Nikita Khrushchev's denunciation of Stalin at the 1956 Party Congress aroused the same kind of ferment in Hungary it had in Poland. Hungarian Communism had always taken a definitely Stalinist turn in the person of Matias Rakosi, the puppet Red Premier. By 1956 Rakosi was thoroughly despised by Hungarian Communist intellectual circles; the Rajk trial and its aftermath showed the stubborn Stalinist quality of the Hungarian party leadership.

Laszlo Rajk was a dedicated Communist who served in the Hungarian underground in World War II. With the Communist takeover he became Foreign Minister. But Rajk was not Moscow-trained or Moscow-oriented, and he was never trusted by the other satellite leaders who were. In 1949 he was arrested on trumped-up charges, made to confess in Communist fashion, and hanged for "anti-Soviet conspiracy" with Tito of Yugoslavia. But many Hungarians, particularly in the younger Communist circles, regarded Rajk as a patriot.

When Khrushchev attacked Stalin's memory and began a rapprochement with Tito, it was suddenly necessary to rehabilitate Rajk. With Tito again regarded as a "good Communist" it was embarrassing to have hanged a leader for "conspiring" with him. Rakosi, with very poor grace, announced that Rajk had been "posthumously" cleared of all his crimes. The utter cynicism of this about-face, as well as what it revealed about the leadership of Hungary, disgusted and inflamed thousands of Hungarians of all

262

political stripes. The Rajk trial became something of a Dreyfus case.

Angry over the Rajk revelations, and spurred on by the concessions Polish workers and intellectuals had won, five thousand students and workers' representatives met at the Building Industry Technological University in Budapest on October 22, 1956, in a stormy, eleven-hour session. Out of this meeting came sixteen demands, which included "immediate withdrawal of all Soviet troops," "election of new leaders by secret ballot," reorganization of the economy to suit conditions, revision of industrial norms and minimum wages, and "complete freedom of opinion and expression, freedom of the Press and a free Radio."

The students went with these requests to the State-controlled radio; quite naturally the radio refused to broadcast them. The students were not balked. They set up the University's duplicating machines and printed thousands of copies, which were distributed all over Budapest on October 23.

The result was a national explosion. After more than a decade of fear, exploitation, and rigid Stalinist control, at least one of the sixteen points struck home in the breast of every Hungarian citizen. Mobs began to throng the streets. The Hungarian national cockade came out of hiding and was pinned to hats and jackets. Men and women began to use the familiar form of address even to strangers, as a symbol of unity. Then the crowds began to rip out the Soviet-style emblems that had been added to the Hungarian national flag. As one British observer marching with them wrote, "We all wept from joy."

Erno Gero, the Stalinist who had been elevated to Party First Secretary in the smelly domestic power struggle that had hung Rajk and brushed aside the more moderate Imre Nagy, tried to talk to the crowds. But when he spoke of "the glorious Communist Party of the Soviet Union" shouts of "Down with Gero" went up.

The first shots were fired around ten P.M., when the hated AVH, the secret police, tried to arrest a body of students who had

263

again gone to the radio station with their petition. All of the AVH guarding the station were killed in a gun battle, and the rebels had control of the radio.

Now, Gero and the Hungarian party leaders made a fateful, and fatal, decision: they panicked and called Moscow. Gero painted a picture of rioting and disaster and begged for Soviet military aid. Someone in Moscow gave it to him—the Red Army in Hungary was ordered to help quell the uprising.

Until this moment, the Hungarian revolt was merely following a path already blazed in Poland, and it could probably have been damped in the same way: by restoration of the popular Nagy, and strategic concessions. Now, as Soviet tanks and troops entered Budapest on the morning of October 25, they came under heavy fire.

Not only the students and workers, but the small Hungarian army began to resist them. Mobs stormed armories, and the Hungarian soldiers refused to fire on them. Hungarian career soldiers joined the revolt. But the brunt of the fighting was always borne by the students, many of whom were very young. The Russians had introduced the book *Young Guard* by Fadeiev into Hungarian schools, and this book gave detailed instructions on how to fight a superior military force. Soviet tanks began to fall victim to Molotov cocktails and other guerrilla tactics.

While the fighting went on sporadically all over town, Imre Nagy was made Premier. Again, the AVH, now terrified of what was coming, opened fire on a crowd, killing nearly four hundred. The situation had got completely out of hand.

Mikhail Suslov and Anastas Mikoyan, two high Soviet officials, flew hurriedly into Budapest. Their meeting with Gero was later related by a Hungarian who was present. Mikoyan was utterly enraged because Gero had sucked Soviet armed forces into what was actually a struggle against Gero and the Hungarian Stalinists, turning it into a national revolution in which Soviet prestige was now at stake.

Mikoyan snarled that Gero had "stampeded" Moscow into an ill-advised act. Suslov told him to resign at once. Gero protested, saying he was required to hold the Hungarian party together. Mikoyan snapped that the Party had already fallen apart because of his "incredible" blunders. Mikoyan then suspended Gero, appointed Janos Kadar Secretary, and agreed to the appointment of Nagy as Premier. He told Nagy to announce a series of concessions, which included immediate withdrawal of Soviet forces. A cease-fire was set to go into effect October 28.

After heavy fighting between the "freedom fighters" and Russian regular forces, which did much damage to Budapest, the Soviet tanks and infantry withdrew. But what Mikoyan foresaw had already come about: the Hungarian crisis had passed from an internal revolt to a nationalistic uprising directed now against the USSR.

The Hungarian army and police were not controlling the citizenry; they (except for the AVH, which had crossed the line of no return and which was being hunted down) had joined in the fight against the USSR.

After six days of heavy firing, heavy casualties, and heroism on the part of Hungarians, it seemed they had won. Soviet tanks lumbered out of Budapest. But things had gone too far. Nagy told a wildly cheering crowd in Parliament Square that Hungary might now withdraw from the Warsaw Pact, the alliance the Soviets had drawn up with the Eastern satellites to offset NATO. A gaping crack was opening in the Iron Curtain. It shook official Moscow to the core.

Nikita Khrushchev was at this time on his long drive to supreme power. He had not yet gained it. Khrushchev's instinct told him that if he allowed Hungary to go the way it seemed headed, the Red Army and other realists in the USSR would send him the way of Beria. Khrushchev, like Eden at almost the same time, had to choose between bad image, bad propaganda, and good geopolitics, with his career in the balance. Khrushchev chose good geopolitics. He had no intention of presiding over the liquidation of the Soviet empire.

Soviet troops began a move to surround Hungary. They gathered in the countryside, until approximately 4,000 T-54 tanks and 200,000 regular troops were in striking distance of Budapest. On November 3, Budapest was sealed off by the Red Army; it had no communications with the provinces. Later that night, General Pal Maleter, Nagy's military commander, was treacherously arrested during a negotiation with three Soviet generals, despite the fact that at least one of the Russian soldiers vehemently protested the act. Maleter was executed, and the Hungarian freedom forces were leaderless. On Sunday, November 4, Russian tanks began to move into Budapest some time before three A.M.

Nagy went on the radio before dawn. "This is Imre Nagy speaking. This morning . . . Soviet troops began an attack on our capital, with the obvious intention of overthrowing the lawful and democratic government of Hungary. Our troops are now engaged in battle. I am informing . . . the whole world of this."

The battle could have only one outcome.

Free Radio Rakoczi, as the captured Hungarian radio had been dubbed, sent out a message at 1:55 P.M. Sunday. "This is Hungary calling! This is Hungary calling! The last free station. Forward to the United Nations . . . We are requesting you to send us immediate aid in the form of parachute troops over the Transdanubian provinces . . . for the sake of God and freedom, help Hungary!"

For the record, the message was forwarded.

The record also shows that it was soon all over. The Soviet empire in East Europe was restored, in an orgy of blood and destruction.

The sympathies of the West were wholly with the Hungarian people. Every resolution supporting them in the UN from late October through the next year carried. Then why was nothing done, except caring for the 190,000 Hungarian refugees who crossed the bridge at Andau into neutral Austria? Nothing was done because nothing could be done, short of World War III.

Russian representatives, suffering psychological damage from what their nation felt itself forced to do in Hungary, made this very clear to the United States people on the ground. The Security

Council first discussed the Hungarian situation on October 27, 1956. There was confused debate, and a brush between Cabot Lodge and Sobolev, the Russian representative. Three things were evident by the time this debate closed:

(1) The USSR was extremely sensitive over Hungary, and hideously embarrassed, to the point of irrationality. They were caught without a rationale for their actions that could be aired. This did not give the West an advantage. It pointed up deep danger.

(2) The USSR made it quite clear that Hungary was nonnegotiable as far as it was concerned. The Secretary General was not going to be allowed to visit the scene. UN expeditionary troops or any other outside army that tried to interfere was going to be met with force.

(3) The Secretary General understood the Russian attitude, and decided to pursue a hands-off course of action. Dag Hammarskjöld said not one word during the first bitter five-hour debate. Hammarskjöld sympathized with the Hungarians—but he was aware that the UN, which was barely able to raise a few thousand troops for UNEF and not even able to finance these, had no power to halt Russian aggression. By attacking the USSR he would destroy only himself, and gain nothing for the Hungarians or anyone else.

Hammarskjöld already understood as millions did not that the UN Secretary General might work effectively to damp outbreaks between smaller powers, but he could at best only serve as a go-between between the two superpowers; and he had to keep the good will, or at least the confidence, of both.

The United States did nothing beyond trying to rally the world propaganda-wise against the USSR. It did nothing because both Eisenhower and Dulles were not prepared to go to war with the USSR over Hungary. The issue of Soviet control over Hungary had been decided at Yalta and confirmed at Potsdam. The brutal nature of that control again put heavy pressures on U. S. opinion; and Dulles, for different reasons, felt much as Mikoyan had felt when he tongue-lashed Gero.

267

Outside of the United States, all the rest of the world's powers lacked the force to interfere in any way. "Superpower," applied to the USSR, meant exactly what it said.

Lodge said once in the UN, "We can truly say to the Hungarian people, 'By your heroic sacrifice you have given the United Nations a brief moment in which to mobilize the conscience of the world on your behalf. We are seizing that moment, and we will not fail you.'" He was crying into the wind.

By and large, not a single member of the Afro-Asian or Middle Eastern community took an active part in the Hungarian debates. Some were indifferent; they did not care what Europeans were doing to white Europeans anymore than many Europeans cared what Africans might do to Africans in most cases. They were also completely preoccupied with Suez, which touched much more sensitive nerves where they were concerned. Lodge's pitch for Afro-Asian support fell on deaf ears.

On most UN resolutions proposed by the United States condemning Soviet actions in Hungary from November 4 onward, the uncommitted bloc abstained repeatedly. Some, such as Ceylon, Indonesia, and India, worked to try to moderate the language and tone of Western proposals in the Assembly. When the General Assembly finally took up the crisis, November 19-21, the whole issue had become academic.

Hungary had been completely crushed by November 8. The only Hungarian government—through which the UN had to deal, and with which it had to negotiate—was Janos Kadar's, backed by the USSR. As one observer remarked candidly, the situation did not lend itself to new approaches.

Hungary never even allowed UN observers to enter.

Hammarskjöld again refused to take active leadership, though he did try to get inside Hungary, without results. Hammarskjöld never wavered from his position that Hungary was a big-power struggle in which Soviet vital interests were at stake and that the UN here could not take action. Hammarskjöld had read the Charter. Probably he also recalled what had happened to Trygve Lie. He continued to give the Suez crisis his major attention, on the quite sensible basis that with Suez he and the UN could do something.

During Hungary and Suez, Hammarskjöld may have remembered the words of an Arab diplomat in San Francisco in 1945, who said: "If two small powers fight, the organization steps in and that is the end of the fight; if a small power and a big power fight, that is the end of the small power, unless, of course, another big power steps in—and *that* is the end of the organization!"

Britain and France, after all, were not the Soviet Union.

The Soviet suppression of Hungary became a sort of annual agenda item for each following session of the General Assembly, for five more years, until gradually it was forgotten. In one sense, the Hungarian people's sacrifices had not been entirely in vain. After initial repressions, the Kadar regime showed it understood the factors that had caused the storm in the first place. Conditions in Hungary were eased, as they had been in Poland; and life for Hungarian citizens was never again quite so unbearable as it had been prior to 1956.

Some good came from the revolt in another fashion. The American public had to face the fact that it was not prepared to force the Soviet Union out of Eastern Europe, and this was all to the good. In certain ways U. S. actions had been irrational; the Soviet conquests were tacitly accepted by a realistic government, while at the same time Congress had appropriated $100 million in 1951 to foster rebellion and unrest in the Soviet empire. The so-called "Kersten Act" made sense only if the United States was prepared logically to follow up its consequences. After this, Dulles saw to it that efforts to foment unrest and rebellion behind the Iron Curtain—which the government certainly had no intention of supporting with American power—were strictly private in nature. Unlike the USSR, the United States could not in conscience use the dead bodies of Eastern European citizens to further its own propaganda or political ends.

The UN suffered deep and serious damage from some of its most ardent supporters over Hungary, because of its apparent failure. Cardinal Mindzenty, released from prison in late October, then sealed in the U. S. embassy later, said: "A man who is drowning needs no messages. What we need is that the Secretary General of the United Nations come to Budapest. . . . There has been too much voting and oratory."

Salvador de Madariaga, the world-respected writer, cried: "Why doesn't the UN send an ultimatum to the Soviet Union . . . ? Why doesn't the UN send a police force to Hungary?"

These men, and millions of others, unfortunately, never understood that while the world may have a conscience, conscience, like principle, is less than worthless without material power behind it.

Hammarskjöld wore the dusty mantle of the United Nations well, but even he could not walk on water.

16.

Hammarskjöld's Heresy

FAILING IN ANY ATTEMPT to bring an impossible world order between East and West, and assisting to hold a dubious status quo on the frontiers of Korea, Israel, and Egypt, the UN in the fifties found that its most important task was to aid the dissolution of the European colonial world order.

The United Nations Organization could not be instrumental in securing colonial independence. The reading of the trusteeship clauses, and the principle of national sovereignty prevented that. What took place between the people of Cyprus and the British Foreign Office and the Colonial Secretary was their affair, and not the UN's, and the transfer of power from London to Accra on the granting of Ghanaian freedom was based on local decisions, not the world's. But the great powers, after 1955, had agreed on the principle of universal membership in the UN. East and West stopped vetoing memberships in the attempt to maintain old voting strengths, and with very few exceptions virtually any new nation that applied was taken in.

The UN Economic and Social Council and organizations like the World Bank and the World Health Organization were immediately helpful to excolonial areas. In fact, to millions, this, not the debates at Turtle Bay, *was* the UN. And membership in the UN gave new nations an immediate legal and social status they could have had in no other way. UN membership served as an excellent ratification of national sovereignty.

The Congo crisis, beginning in July, 1960, brought a decade of such successful UN activity to a close. In the Congo the UN simply bit off more than the world organization could chew.

There had been a varying pattern to the abandonment of Eu-

271

ropean colonialism. The British, generally, had prepared for the day, and departed with good grace and even good will on both sides. The transfers of power between London and New Delhi, London and Rangoon, London and Accra, and London and Lagos in Nigeria were consummated with order. In almost every case, the British left behind a sense of national cohesion—which had never existed in most former colonies—and a corps of native senior civil servants. There was very little disruption of the economic order. The same thing occurred in the French Union, except for Algeria, where the large-scale presence of European settlers and their painful but politically necessary dispossession prolonged a bitter colonial war. The Portuguese showed no signs of ever relinquishing their overseas possessions gracefully, and the Belgians were among the last to go. Logically, the smaller the European power, generally the harder it held on to territories and possessions, which gave it economic power and some standing in the world.

The Belgian Congo was a vast, sprawling equatorial area in the center of Africa. It was one third the size of the United States, but with only thirteen million people. It had immense resources of copper, cobalt, and industrial diamonds, and it was an important source of uranium. These minerals were largely concentrated in a southern province, Katanga.

The Congolese population was a conglomeration of more than 125 separate tribes, with separate languages and customs. No tribe was dominant. The borders of the Congo, like most African borders, had been drawn arbitrarily by the European colonial power structure, without regard to ethnic or any other kind of consideration except European rivalries. Naturally, there had never existed any sense of nationhood or any loyalties extending beyond the tribe. The Belgian administration, unlike British colonial regimes in other areas, did nothing to instill a sense of higher loyalty.

The Belgian Congo had become a "Free State" in 1885, organized not as a Belgain colony but as a private commercial enterprise by Leopold II, King of the Belgians. The record of Leopold's administration and oppression of the African natives was one of the most brutal chapters in human history. Some Congolese tribes were virtually exterminated; others were enslaved. In fact, Leopold engaged in the slave trade, which took thousands of Congolese eastward to the Arab slave markets. Other thousands fled into neighboring colonies. Leopold II was the constitutional monarch of a democratic Belgium, but his rule of the Congo was that of a personal possession, and outside the Belgian Constitution.

The stench from the Congo's running human sores became so great that in 1908 diplomatic pressure from Britain and France forced the Belgian parliament to take the Congo away from the King. The province was made into a regular Belgian colony.

The Belgian administration immediately corrected the worst abuses—but did not change certain other deep-seated practices that had been designed to keep the Congolese under colonial control.

The Belgians taught a high percentage of Africans to read and write, but stopped all education at the elementary level. No Africans were taken back to Belgium for further training, or indoctrination in Belgian culture or democracy as it was practiced in Europe. The 10,000 colonial administrators were pure Belgian, and the 25,000-man Force Publique, or Congolese constabulary or army, was officered by 1,000 Europeans. The only centralizing influence was this Belgian administration, and no Africans were ever taken into it. None were ever allowed political experience.

The Force Publique was in some ways a holdover from the days of Leopold II. It was poorly paid, and it was raised by conscription on the tribes. It was never professional, nor did it offer a career in which men could find dignity. White officers were rigidly segregated from the African rankers; no close relationships developed. Worse, it was Belgian policy to let the Force Publique live off the land in the areas where it happened to be stationed: a certain amount of robbery, extortion, rape, and con-

273

fiscation of chickens and more valuable property was the order of the day. None of this affected the European Congo community, and it was winked at by Belgian officers.

Thousands of Belgians, and the world, were to pay a heavy price for this disastrous colonial policy. The Belgians, unlike the British or French, never built a cohesive military force that could enforce public order. No black African ever rose above sergeant.

In 1960, in the Congo there were not only no native military officers, but only sixteen college graduates and some fifty men who held the equivalent of a bachelor's degree in theology. There was not one doctor, lawyer, or diploma engineer among the Africans.

The Belgians seem never to have seriously considered giving the Congo independence before the late 1950's. By then, the winds of change were very strong, and certain African leaders were increasingly restive. In 1957 a plan of gradual—very gradual—transfer was begun. But the fact that in 1959 the French gave independence to the French Congo, just across the four-mile-wide Congo River from the capital of Leopoldville, touched off rioting. Congolese leaders began to demand independence and the withdrawal of all Belgians.

In January, 1960, a conference of Belgians and Africans surprised the world by agreeing to independence on June 30, 1960. The Belgians believed that they could transfer power, or the semblance of power, to a new African Congo regime and still continue to control Belgium's immense economic interests in the region. This was all the Belgian government was concerned with; Leopoldville, Elizabethville, and other cities were modern, European-style communities with all the conveniences—for Europeans —but there was no Belgian settlement as such. The 50,000 or more Belgians in the Congo were either businessmen or government administrators, with no real attachment to the soil. It was planned that this whole Belgian structure would remain intact after independence, just as Belgian officers would continue to control the Congolese army. A worse miscalculation was never made.

274

There were no African leaders who had anything like an all-Congo following; tribal loyalties were paramount. The lack of an African elite, the lack of any level of education beyond literacy, the lack of any governing experience, and the lack of roads and communications throughout the Congo, plus the tribal divisions, made any hope of an effective African administration very faint. A strong army might have enforced order on this sort of chaos, as so frequently happened in the developing world from Pakistan to the Sudan. But the Force Publique was to be the bitterest thorn in the new republic's flesh.

And with all the emerging politicos starting from scratch, there was an atmosphere in which the men who stepped forward, shot first, and claimed everything that fell, assumed unnatural importance. Such a man was Patrice Lumumba, who became first Premier of the Congo. Lumumba was completely unpredictable, erratic, unstable, prideful, and ambitious. He was also brilliantly voluble and charismatic. He could not lead the Congolese anywhere—but he could make an indelible impression on emerging African minds.

The plans for independence went forward smoothly, although understandably Lumumba, Kasavubu, Gizenga, and other politicians raised African expectations too much as to what independence would bring. It could not change the lot or basic way of life for the average tribesman for generations, but hopes were inflamed.

June 30 passed quietly, at first. Lumumba assumed the reigns of power, Joseph Kasavubu became Chief of State. Then Lumumba, speaking to the new Parliament, threw a reddish, bloody light over the new dawn.

He went into a tirade against colonialism; he brandished the bloody shirt. The representatives of all the major nations had made the usual platitudinous speeches in Leopoldville, and the U. S. representative had done the same. Lumumba reminded the Africans of "the ironies, the insults, the blows that we had to submit to morning, noon, and night because we were Negroes." Nothing Lumumba said was untrue. Nothing he said could serve any useful purpose except perhaps to establish Patrice Lumumba as a savior of black Africa.

The memory of past cruelty and, worse, subtle insult, was deeply imbedded in all African minds. The mere fact of European dominance had deeply alienated most Africans, which few Europeans as yet understood.

Lumumba was always a spark dancing around a powder keg —which even he at times recognized—sometimes frightening him, more often delighting him. It is almost impossible for an outsider to follow, let alone understand, the gyrations, thinking, and acts of Congo politicians. They lived in a different world from Europeans, and the natives are endowed with completely different minds and emotions.

Aroused by Lumumba's orations and Lumumba's promises, the Force Publique in Leopoldville and other cities demanded increases in pay and privileges. These Lumumba turned down. Both actions were not untypical; they were to occur in Kenya and other British possessions soon after independence. However, later army rebellions in other colonies were handled differently. Other leaders were more responsible than Patrice Lumumba.

The Force Publique rank and file, in retaliation, refused to obey the commands of its white officers, who were now theoretically at least responsible to Lumumba's government. The African soldiers sensed that the real authority behind those orders was gone. Then, drunk on the heady wine of independence and swept onward by memories of harsh discipline by members of what had become a hated caste, army units rebelled. Officers were disarmed. Some were merely locked up. Others were stripped naked, humiliated, and publicly beaten by their former charges. Once authority began to break down there was no end to it. Now began the series of outrages that horrified the world, and especially the Western community.

Congolese mutineers seized their officers' wives and engaged in mass rape. In many areas no European of any age or cloth was safe. Nuns as well as children were subject to raping, and the property of all Europeans was systematically looted. Many Afri-

276

can soldiers actually believed that independence had given them such privileges.

There was a thirteen-hour period of hysteria in Leopoldville, while the rampaging army was out of hand, and thousands of Europeans tried to cross the Congo River to Brazzaville, in the former French Congo. The anarchy, abominations, and terror ended only when Lumumba acceded to the mutineers' demands that all European officers were to be dismissed from the Force Publique.

Meanwhile, in answer to the frantic pleas of the European community, the Belgian government sent in twenty-three companies of paratroops. These seized vital centers and areas in an attempt to protect Belgian lives and property. Listening to the hysterics of European women, seeing the drunken Force Publique celebrating independence, the Belgian troopers gave any African caught out of bounds short shrift. Now, blood flowed, as murder was added to raping and looting. The murder was not restricted to either side.

The situation still might have been saved, in any other place in the world, and with any other leadership. But Lumumba was completely erratic. Terrified of his own soldiery, he still demanded that the Belgians withdraw. The Belgians refused. Thousands of civilian Europeans streamed out of the country, leaving chaos as the economy collapsed.

Then, on July 11, 1960, Moise Tshombe of Katanga Province declared Katanga independent of the Congo. Tshombe, and other Katangan leaders, were pro-Belgian in spirit. They had nothing in common with the Leopoldville leaders; they belonged to different races and tribes. They were aware that Katanga held almost all the real wealth of the Congo region and humanly saw no reason for sharing it with people who were even more foreign to them than the Belgians.

Tshombe himself was a genuine tribal chief, and the son of a Westernized African millionaire. He wanted to come to a working agreement with the Belgians, especially over the huge and wealthy Union Minière mining company, a European corporation that controlled most of Katanga's mineral interests. He asked Belgian troops to protect Katanga from the central government. The Belgians were interested. They may even have planned it that way.

Lumumba flew to Elizabethville, the capital of Katanga Province. Tshombe refused to see him, and Tshombe's gendarmerie kept him from leaving the airport. In a black rage, Lumumba returned to Leopoldville. Here, he began to behave almost as hysterically as the European women and children still trying to flee the Congo. He requested the United States government to intervene on his side against Tshombe and the Belgians. This was refused. Lumumba then appealed to Dr. Ralph Bunche of the UN Secretariat. Bunche was an American of African descent. Bunche replied to Lumumba, and also to President Kasavubu, that the UN would offer the Congo as much assistance as possible under the Charter.

The next day, July 12, Lumumba fired off another note to Dag Hammarskjöld, begging the Secretary General to provide him with "military assistance." Hammarskjöld scheduled an "informal" meeting of the members of the Security Council to meet over lunch on July 13 to discuss the problem.

But then, this same day, the situation chilled and began to become an international crisis. The USSR stepped in. The Soviet representative on the Security Council issued a note accusing the Belgian government of armed aggression in the Congo and demanded that Belgian paratroops withdraw. The Belgian government stated that its troops would remain in control of key points of the Congo as long as necessary, which meant until Lumumba restored order.

Now, Hammarskjöld sensed a real wind blowing up. Under Article 99, he called an emergency session of the Security Council for the night of July 13. And during the day of July 13 he received another cable signed by Lumumba and Kasavubu requesting the "urgent" dispatch of UN troops. The cable also stated that the sending of troops from metropolitan Belgium to assist the few

Belgian soldiers who had been on the ground violated the treaties between Belgium and the Congo, and that the "unsolicited" action was "an act of aggression." The Congo request was for aid to "protect the national territory of the Congo against the present external aggression which is a threat to international peace."

Here yawned an enormous trap for the UN. Hammarskjöld was not eager to rush into it. But he never recognized the immensity of the Congo problem, or its difficulties; and in stepping into the trap, he had help.

Taking the microphone, Hammarskjöld stated that Belgian troops had entered the Congo for "protection of life and for the maintenance of order." But he also said the "international tension"—meaning the determination of Russia to make an issue of it, as well as the hysterical reaction and hatred of the Congo government—resulting from the Belgian move made the presence of Belgian troops unacceptable as a stopgap pending the reestablishment of order. He concluded that the UN should honor Lumumba's and Kasavubu's request, and asked for authority to raise a UN police force—with the understanding that if such a force were sent to the Congo, Belgium would withdraw.

Henry Cabot Lodge stepped in quickly, drawing attention to the appalling famine and disease that had resulted from the breakdown of public order and services in the Congo. Placatingly, not to irritate America's NATO ally Belgium or the other African states, Lodge pointed out that it was not only futile but harmful to try to place blame for the situation. He argued that since there was a legitimate request for UN aid and the need was urgent, the UN must act with speed. Lodge, representing U. S. thinking, was eagerly rushing in where angels feared to tread. But again, no one in Washington was familiar with the Congo or the true situation there. There was a belief that a viable government for the Congo was just around the corner, if only the Belgians could be reextracted peaceably.

Arkady Sobolev of the USSR immediately accused the United States of direct conspiracy with Belgium against the Republic of the Congo. He also stated that Ralph Bunche was working hand in glove with Ambassador Timberlake for an American takeover of the region.

Lodge took a couple of dozen words to call the Soviet allegation nonsense, in the usual UN fashion.

Finally, a Tunisian resolution was passed by the Council that

(1) called upon Belgium to withdraw;

(2) authorized Hammarskjöld to secure military forces to assist the Congo;

(3) requested the Secretary General to report back, in time-honored fashion.

On this resolution, France, Nationalist China, and Great Britain abstained, but did not veto. There was some fear, for a time, that France might veto it. The French government clearly thought that the Belgians had acted with perfect propriety and with a perfect right, considering the fate of their nationals and their property. The British felt the same way, and in later situations acted in the same way, as when the armed forces of Kenya and other newly independent regimes rebelled four years later. And ironically, the United States in 1965 was to behave in Santo Domingo much as the Belgians had behaved, and with far less provocation.

But at three in the morning of July 14, 1960, few in the U. S. delegation saw things with the same clarity they saw them later. A Soviet resolution condemning Belgium was duly voted down, and at 3:25 A.M. the meeting broke up. Hammarskjöld said the decision to act in the Congo would mark an important step, and that he would move at once.

The die was cast. It would strongly influence later U. S. policy, cost Hammarskjöld first his usefulness and then his life, and deal the UN its most dangerous blow of all—possibly its death blow.

Within hours, Hammarskjöld was putting together ONUC (from *Force de l'Organisation des Nations Unis en Congo*). Ghana was the first to offer troops. Tunisia, Ireland, Sweden, and other nations would follow. The anticolonialist, "neutral" world, the United States, and the USSR were all, for one reason or another, in agreement on its dispatch.

Ironically, both the United States and the USSR were more worried about world opinion than concerned with cleaning up the Congo mess. Both were striving to hold leadership and influence in the Afro-Asian community, which was now strongly behind any move that would force the Belgians out.

Meanwhile, in Leopoldville, Belgian paratroops and Congolese soldiery fought a battle for control of the airport. The Belgians won. But on July 14, as the first Ghanaian forces under British General Henry Alexander, who was the Ghanaian Chief of Staff, arrived, smoke rose in the air, and burnt-out vehicles still littered the airfield area. The city was closing down; Belgians were still fleeing on special Belgian airlifts, and selling their cars and other property for pin money, or abandoning their possessions outright.

General Alexander himself was surprised at the effect of the ONUC troops, especially the blue-helmeted Ghanaians. The Belgian-Congolese fighting was on the verge of total war, but the UN forces quickly damped it—without bloodshed.

Within four days 770 Ghanaians, 460 Ethiopians, 1,250 Moroccans, and 1,020 Tunisian soldiers were in the Congo. Seven hundred men from Guinea arrived soon after. Each of the new African nations, as well as the old, was eager to assist ONUC. Most Africans leaders saw the UN effort mainly in the light of getting the Belgians out of Africa. Eventually, in addition to the African states, three European, one Asian, and one Hispanic-American nation sent troops. Sweden received permission to transfer 635 men who were then on what had become permanent duty with UNEF in Palestine. In all, at its peak, ONUC had 18,000 troops.

And ONUC quickly restored order, or at least stopped the fighting between Belgians and Congolese. The Belgian commander agreed to accept ONUC directives and to act only in situations where the safety of Belgian nationals was threatened. The Belgian government agreed to withdraw once ONUC had control.

On July 20 there was an emotional debate in the UN between Kanza, the Congo representative, and Premier Wigny of Belgium. Kanza stated that Belgium had violated its treaties with the Congo by sending in troops uninvited. Wigny admitted as much. But he argued that Belgium had acted to honor an obligation higher than international law: the protection of its own citizens. He went into great detail about the rape of Belgian and European women, as described by Belgian sources. Kanza, angry, told of Belgian atrocities in return. But in the debate both sides showed themselves amenable to reason; the Belgians were ready to withdraw, and the Congolese eased their incessant pressure for the move.

Now, the whole problem might have been settled except for two things: the Katanga secession, and the fact that in reality the Congo Republic did not have a government. Lumumba, Kasavubu, and Lumumba's Vice Premier, Antoine Gizenga, were noisily presiding over tribal chaos.

Tshombe of Katanga maintained his independence and insisted that Belgian paratroops stay in Katanga to prevent "anarchy and chaos happening in the Congo Republic itself." He protested Hammarskjöld's decision that all Belgians should leave the Congo and Hammarskjöld's further decision that Katanga was part of the Congo. He refused to let ONUC set foot inside Katanga.

Here the UN leaped into its first great Congo trap. Because there was no effective government in Leopoldville, ONUC ceased to be purely a peace-keeping and conflict-damping force, and it went considerably into left field. It accepted a considerable responsibility for the whole Congo, and it immediately put three questions to a severe test.

One was whether the UN was able to take over the entire fate of an emerging nation wholly unfitted as yet for nationhood. Another was whether the UN itself had the political stability to step into a political power vacuum and administrate a region with immense problems. The third was whether the UN could keep international rivalries and above all the Cold War out of such an operation and at the same time guarantee the borders of the old Belgian Congo.

The final answer was that the UN had taken on more than even the skillful and able Hammarskjöld could handle. The financial burden alone bankrupted the UN. In the next months and years the UN found itself meddling in a civil war, first on one side then another, and Hammarskjöld had to wage a losing battle to keep the UN from being used as an instrument of policy by one Congo faction or another, the new African nations, and even the United States. In the Congo, everyone soon had an axe to grind, and the net result was that Hammarskjöld was ground up badly.

The events in the Congo over the next five years were exceedingly bewildering. It was difficult for outsiders to understand the chaos a completely primitive society, which had been ruled by an iron hand, could fall into when the hand was removed suddenly. The Congo had modern cities, and these showed in news photographs. But the Belgian occupation had not really changed the vast hinterland's village and tribal economy, which soon returned to the anarchy of a century before.

It is necessary only to follow the broad outline of what happened. A day-by-day inspection of events is not only confusing, but sickening.

The nine African UN members of the UN played an immensely important and influential role in what happened in the Congo. Hammarskjöld at first worked closely with these nations, since he, as well as the United States government at the time, believed that any solution in the Congo made without approval of the other African states stood small chance of either permanence or success.

The leadership of these nations, especially the influential Nkrumah of Ghana, insisted vehemently that the Congo be maintained as one nation, and that the Katanga secession be suppressed. There was a logical economic argument: Katanga had most of the wealth, and the other provinces would be hamstrung without it. Moise Tshombe's administration could also be attacked in many ways; it was far from perfect. But personal prejudices and fears were mostly behind the African hostility of Tshombe. Tshombe's actions triggered a deep-seated fear in every African government.

All of the boundaries of Africa had been drawn arbitrarily by the European colonial power structure of the nineteenth century; few of them made any tribal, economic, or historic sense. Similar peoples were divided; dissimilar ones joined. Under colonial rule this made little real difference. When these peoples, in states like Ghana, the Congo, and Nigeria, had to make their own government, language, racial, and religious difficulties became just as important as they had always been in Europe.

Men like Nkrumah had inherited European-drawn nations, which they were determined to hold intact whether they made sense or not. Most Westerners never quite understood the fact that African boundaries were sacred primarily in African leaders' minds. If Tshombe succeeded, the precedent might shatter the emerging national patterns of Africa, based on European colonial boundaries.

Further, Tshombe, unlike most African new leaders, was not only a tribal chieftain, but a rich man. He had never suffered under the Belgian order, and had no hatred for it. He was not burning with resentment like the ex-beer-salesman, Lumumba. Tshombe considered it excellent business, since the Union Minière, his chief revenue-producing industry, was Belgian, to continue to work hand-in-hand with the Belgians. Each needed the other. This aroused an emotional outrage in European-hating African breasts, and also the fear that the Congo, under Tshombe, would continue as a Belgian colony in disguise.

Worse yet, Tshombe recognized his dependence on European skills. He had no scruples about hiring European mercenaries for his gendarmerie and basing his rule upon the stiffness such white mercenary commandos gave his native forces. Emotionally, this produced great African outrage, even though other leaders, in different ways, were doing the same. For both irrational and political reasons, then, Tshombe had to go.

At the same time, the Katanga leader picked up heavy support in the United States and Europe, again for both emotional and political reasons. Tshombe was obviously pro-Western; he was not even neutralist, as Lumumba professed to be. He was understanding of, and amenable to, the European economic interests and position in Africa. And he, white mercenaries and all, seemed to be a veritable island of stability in the roiled and unstable Congo sea.

France and Britain gave Tshombe immense diplomatic support, while the Belgians for obvious reasons helped him in any way they could. The United States tended to honor African opinion, at least on government levels. The USSR, wanting to make trouble and gain a foothold in Africa, opposed Tshombe bitterly; this furthered also the Russian aim of emerging as the leader of the excolonial states. All these conflicting policies, in the UN and out of it, tore Dag Hammarskjöld apart.

Hammarskjöld was in a situation for which there was no precedent. One of the first things recommended by the ONUC commander, Major General Alexander, was that the mutinous Congolese Force Publique be disarmed. He said the force could only continue to cause trouble. He also demanded specific objectives for ONUC, the right to intervene in certain troubles, and the authority to impose restrictions upon the Congolese soldiery and regime as needed. Dr. Bunche, representing Hammarskjöld, objected strenuously to these demands, stating that the ONUC was a "peace force" and that it had not come to the Congo to fight anyone, and that its policy was to cooperate with the government of the Congo.

Bunche and Hammarskjöld, legally, were absolutely correct. But in practicality, Alexander was perfectly right. Disarming the Congo army would have prevented much later bloodshed, since the army went on frequent rampages against its own people. What made the initial views of Bunche, Hammarskjöld, and the U. S. government nonsense was the fact that Lumumba was incapable

285

of governing—yet no one dared state the fact. It is impossible to cooperate with a government that does not exist, except in the persons of a few erratic leaders.

Lumumba, meanwhile, flew to the United States, where both in New York at the UN and at Washington he was given the full red-carpet treatment, much to the disgust of European powers.

In late July, Hammarskjöld went to Leopoldville, where he had a stormy session with the Congolese cabinet, which demanded that ONUC immediately suppress Tshombe, by force if necessary. Gizenga the next day made a very strong speech, accusing Hammarskjöld of collusion with the Belgians and of letting the Congolese down. Hammarskjöld quietly replied that the responsibility for putting Katanga and Tshombe down did not rest with the UN.

Meanwhile, Tshombe kept hurling sand into all the backstage diplomacy Hammarskjöld tried to arrange to bring the two factions together, calling Lumumba "an extremist, a Communist, a jumped-up little man." And he ordered mobilization of Katanga —a rather empty move, considering Katanga's resources as a state—to resist ONUC if it entered. By early August, Hammarskjöld gave up any plans of entering Katanga with ONUC, and further told the Congo regime that ONUC was not under its orders, and "under no circumstances would it become a party to an internal conflict."

Back in New York, the Secretary General stated that ONUC would not fight its way into Katanga to restore the Congo unless it was ordered to by the Security Council. This the USSR immediately demanded. But the Council passed, 9-0, France and Italy abstaining, a Tunisian resolution that called upon the Belgians to withdraw from Katanga, stated that United Nations forces were necessary in Katanga, but they would in no way become a party to or influence the outcome of the internal conflict between Leopoldville and Moise Tshombe. This resolution was a mishmash of compromise that satsified no one and accomplished nothing. The UN was now in the Congo crisis up to its neck, but as a neutral.

Hammarskjöld returned to Leopoldville. Here he assembled the force Tshombe called his "Swedish bodyguard." Hammarskjöld never hesitated to use his personal prestige upon the Swedish government or to call upon his own countrymen for help in UN business if he felt the need. On August 12 he flew from Leopoldville to Elizabethville in his famous white UN Convair. His "official retinue" included Swedish ONUC soldiers.

When Hammarskjöld stepped down from his plane he received a friendly greeting from Tshombe himself. But the Secretary General, obeying the Council resolution that called for a UN presence in Katanga, was not above playing a form of dirty pool. He ordered his Swedish retinue—on whom he knew the Belgian paratroops holding Elizabethville airport would not fire—to take control of the airfield in the name of the United Nations. This they did, while the Belgians stood by. Immediately, more ONUC troops, including a battalion of Swedes and Moroccans, were flown into the airport, putting the area completely under UN control.

At this point Hammarskjöld could have taken control of all Katanga, too. But he scrupulously obeyed the Council's instructions not to interefere in the Lumumba-Tshombe quarrel. Lumumba demanded that Hammarskjöld end Tshombe's secession. When Hammarskjöld refused to do this, Lumumba launched an incredible personal attack on the Secretary General, screaming that "affinity" between the Royal families of Sweden and Belgium had dictated the use of Swedish rather than African troops at Elizabethville. He demanded that all airports, which were being held by ONUC, be turned back to the Congolese army, that black African troops be sent at once to Elizabethville and all non-Africans withdrawn, that all UN aircraft be made available to him to transport Congo forces wherever they wanted to go, and that the issue of arms to Katangan partisans by Tshombe's regime be halted.

Lumumba did have one utterly legitimate concern. The UN build-up was on the brink of turning the Congo into an unofficial UN trust territory, if the UN chose to use its power. Ham-

287

marskjöld rejected all Lumumba's charges and demands, and in the Security Council meetings of August 21, icily threatened that he would recommend the complete withdrawal of ONUC if Lumumba kept on "spreading deep distrust and hostility fomented for political ends."

Hammarskjöld was following what was to him the only logical course; but in a way he could hardly see, he was arousing the hostility of the USSR toward him, through his frustration of Patrice Lumumba. The USSR had now seized on the unstable premier as its best political means of penetrating the Congo.

Thwarted in his desire to use the ONUC as a means of getting rid of his major problem, Tshombe, Lumumba appealed directly to the United States for military aid. The U. S. government was still responsive to Lumumba and still backed him. But the United States informed the Premier that it could not extend the kind of bilateral assistance he demanded without bypassing the UN, which was already handling the situation.

Lumumba, who had never possessed any understanding of governmental administration and who had come to office through his inspired oratory, now proved himself increasingly irrational. He was always unstable and unpredictable, but he revealed a neurotic hatred of anyone or anything that balked him. He had turned against the UN. Now, he turned against the United States. He radioed the USSR for military aid.

There was an immediate response. The USSR sent seventeen transport planes, 100 trucks, thousands of tons of food, and about 400 Soviet "technicians." The USSR was very eager at this time to establish a foothold in the center of Africa.

The U. S. Government tried to get Lumumba to change his mind. He refused. The United States then sought support from the nine African nations in condemning Lumumba and his opening the door to the Soviets. They refused. There was now left only the time-honored gambit of scraping up a "more moderate" regime closer to the U. S. viewpoint. Kasavubu, Lumumba's chief rival in Congo politics, seemed to be the man.

On September 5, Kasavubu dismissed Lumumba from office.

288

Lumumba refused to go, and ordered the ouster of Kasavubu. The Leopoldville regime fell into complete chaos. The Chamber of Deputies voted to invalidate both ousters. Then, the Senate backed Lumumba. While the Congo government went through a series of tragi-comic gyrations, the United States, from behind the scenes, supported Kasavubu, the USSR egged on Lumumba, and the Belgians told Tshombe to hold fast. Hammarskjöld and his ONUC desperately tried to remain neutral—but could not.

Rioting broke out in Leopoldville between the Lumumba-Kasavubu tribal factions. ONUC seized the radio station and the airfields and denied them to both parties. Both ONUC moves were logical. The first prevented inflammatory oratory or panics from being spread over the air; the second prevented unilateral meddling by any outside military force—such as the Soviet Union's—in the Congo's affairs.

Ostensibly neutral, ONUC's moves actually hurt Lumumba, who depended on inflaming the crowds for his power and who had turned to the Soviet Union for arms and technical assistance. Lumumba, cut off from the air, desperately made a round of Leopoldville bars, trying to gather mob support. But he had already made the moves that were to kill him.

Colonel Joseph Mobutu, once a sergeant in and now commander of the Force Publique, had been frightened by the large numbers of Czech and Soviet "technicians" arriving in the Congo. Now, with the government, such as it was, paralyzed between Lumumba and Kasavubu, Mobutu seized power. Kasavubu agreed to remain as figurehead, but on Mobutu's command he ordered all Soviet and Czech diplomats and nationals out of the Congo. It was one of the most stunning reversals Soviet policy ever received. Lumumba was placed under house arrest. Many of his followers were jailed.

The USSR took its frustration out on the Secretary General. On September 14 Valerian Zorin, who resembled no one so much as Vyshinsky, made a seventy-five-minute personal attack on Hammarskjöld. The Swede was called a lackey of Belgium, of the imperialist powers, a servant of NATO, and the deliberate

289

destroyer of Lumumba. It was quite true that both Hammarskjöld and the UN staff had had more than they could stomach of the unstable premier, but the attack was unjustified. U. S. representative Wadsworth sprang to Hammarskjöld's defense. But the damage was done.

The USSR also used its ninetieth veto to stop a new resolution on the Congo, assuring that the Afro-Asian nations would take the matter before the Assembly under the Acheson Plan. This also assured that the USSR would consider any further moves in the Congo illegal under the same protest it had used against the moves in Korea. The USSR never recognized the legality of the Acheson Plan, or recognized any obligation to honor or pay for any resolutions of the Assembly after a bypass of the Security Council.

The attack on Hammarskjöld, though few realized it, greatly damaged his usefulness. The attack was deliberate, and the Lumumba affair was only one excuse. Two things about Hammarskjöld had increasingly disturbed the leaders of the Soviet Union. The Swede had become a man of real world stature through his UN leadership of the small nations, and he had come to wield too much power. He was also proving himself on the side of a genuine world order, and not bound by any concepts of either the USSR or the United States of America.

A genuine peaceful order of the kind Hammarskjöld worked for was the last thing Russian leaders wanted. To spread Soviet influence in Africa and Asia they needed a further breakdown of order, social and economic as well as colonial. Lumumba, even as an unconscious agent, was their kind of man. Hammarskjöld was not.

Under a man like Hammarskjöld the post of UN Secretary General had grown too powerful in Soviet eyes. Hammarskjöld had twice brilliantly created United Nations Emergency Forces. If these set a trend, a certain viable order just might be possible in the world's unstable areas. In the Congo, ONUC was not just trying to keep the peace; it was actually feeding and administering the country. And Hammarskjöld, acknowledging the authority of the UN itself, recognized no great-power strings.

Zorin's speech, which shocked many observers, revealed a new Soviet policy: cut the man and the office back to size. Nikita Khrushchev came to the Fifteenth Session of the UN in New York in September, 1960, to do just that. On the floor, Khrushchev, the leader of the world's second greatest power, said: "Conditions have reached the point where the post of Secretary General, who alone directs the staff and alone interprets and executes the decisions of the Security Council and the sessions of the General Assembly, should be abolished."

He advanced what came to be called the Troika Concept, after the old Russian three-horse sleds. The Secretary General was to be replaced by a three-member front office. One member should represent the Atlantic military alliance, one member the Communist world, and the third the uncommitted nations. Later, Khrushchev made it clear each member was to have an effective veto over the others. Of course, such a system would completely paralyze the UN, which every member immediately recognized.

There was a great deal of Western oratory in Hammarskjöld's defense, plus illustrations of the new Soviet-style colonialism. Hammarskjöld chose to defend his office rather than himself. He said, "I would rather see the office break on strict adherence to the principle of independence . . . than drift on the basis of compromise."

In this session, attended by most of the world's chiefs of state or prime ministers from Cuba's Castro to Tito, Eisenhower, and Britain's Macmillan, and marked by Khrushchev's famous shoe-pounding—which delighted the Russian home audience and the representatives of many nations that had other than Western standards of parliamentary conduct—the Soviet Union's proposals were resoundingly defeated. Hammarskjöld refused to resign, as Khrushchev again demanded. He also said firmly that the USSR's proposal of a three-member executive for the UN would "make it impossible to maintain an effective executive."

291

He added that he had no right to resign. "It is very easy to resign; it is not so easy to stay on. It is very easy to bow to a big Power. It is another matter to resist."

The entire Assembly gave him a standing ovation, while Khrushchev beat futilely on his desk in protest.

But while Hammarskjöld was winning a battle he was losing the greater war. The Congo, meanwhile, was turning into a running sore that was draining the very substance of the United Nations, and souring its sense of purpose as well as bankrupting it financially.

Lumumba, placed under house arrest by Mobutu, escaped. A power struggle developed in the Congo provinces between Mobutu and Lumumba followers. Meanwhile, mutinous units of the Force Publique, renamed the National Army by Mobutu, roamed the countryside, raping and robbing, and killing supporters of Mobutu, Lumumba, and Kasavubu almost at whim. ONUC kept order in the towns, but only a very fragile order, which did not prevent Africans from killing Africans. The Belgians remained in Katanga, officering Tshombe's private army, paid by revenues from Union Minière. Thousands of private Belgian citizens, who had fled in terror in July, returned. They assumed much of their old importance in commerce in industry, both in the Congo in general and in Katanga in particular.

Lumumba made his way to Kasai Province, where Antoine Gizenga had set up another Katanga-like secessionist regime supported by some African states. But he was captured by Mobutu forces and returned to Leopoldville. Hammarskjöld tried to insure his good treatment, and was assured by the figurehead President, Kasavubu, that Lumumba would get a trial "according to the law of our country."

It was a fair statement. In front of Mobutu, Lumumba, tightly bound, was beaten and abused by the soldiery, while the Congolese colonel made no attempt to restrain the brutality. Then, in January, 1961, the Kasavubu-Mobutu coalition turned Lumumba over to his arch-enemy, Tshombe of Katanga—"for safekeeping."

292

UN troops watched him being taken from a plane at Elizabethville. He showed signs of a brutal beating. A Katangan detachment, commanded by a Belgian (at this time all Tshombe's officers were European) marched him away. The UN had no authority one way or the other to interfere, nor, probably, any real desire to.

On February 13, 1961, it was announced that Lumumba had been killed trying to escape. A Katanga reward was paid to the village where he died, a village known to be bitterly hostile to him for tribal reasons. A Belgian doctor signed his death certificate with the notation: "died in the woods."

Hammarskjöld ordered an investigation, in which Kasavubu and Tshombe refused to take part. No real investigation could be made.

The news produced an angry reaction throughout most of black Africa, where Tshombe was hated, and Lumumba immediately assumed the proportions of a martyr.

During 1961 the chaos continued. The UN recognized Kasavubu as the legitimate head of state; and Cyrille Adoula, a fairly able politician, became premier. Mobutu became increasingly enmeshed with Belgian interests, and gradually stepped out of politics, which he had never understood, anyway. Tshombe, offered the Vice Premiership, continued to play cat and mouse with Leopoldville, now seeming to cooperate, now closing the door.

Hammarskjöld could only hold on during 1961, cajoling increasingly restive nations to support ONUC, and try to muddle through. The United States was now equally trapped in the Congo, and in a UN straitjacket again. U. S. money, foreign policy, and prestige were at stake, both in keeping Soviet Communism out of Africa and in securing a Congo government. The decision to channel all U. S. actions in the Congo through the UN, where the United States was now bound by UN opinions and UN Assembly votes, was a mistake.

Few Americans ever realized that Hammarskjöld himself was deeply annoyed by the fact that the U. S. government kept refusing to act unilaterally. Hammarskjöld made this very clear to his aides. He felt his own position had to be squarely in the middle, and at the head of the little nations. He was as determinedly against letting himself be used by the United States in its own interest as he was against letting himself be used by the Soviets. Hammarskjöld's own views coincided with those of the United States: he wanted order in the Congo, and the Russians kept out. But by forcing Hammarskjöld to take over and run the order-keeping operation personally, the United States compelled him to use the office of Secretary General to oppose the Russian interest. This inevitably pulled the Cold War right into Hammarskjöld's lap, aroused the Soviet hatred, and destroyed his effective middle position of respect and trust by both superpowers.

To some people in the U. S. government it may have seemed that getting Hammarskjöld to come out against the Russians was a smart move, but any gain had to be measured against the loss of Hammarskjöld's future effectiveness in the UN.

Again, to the Secretary General's irritation, the United States spent a great deal of time defending him against Soviet attacks in UN debates, while it did nothing for the Congo or the ONUC cause behind the scenes, as Hammarskjöld wanted it to do. Power behind the scenes, Hammarskjöld believed, was required to solve the Congo muddle, and in retrospect he was entirely right.

Hammarskjöld was also hurt in the area of his greatest strength, among the little nations. These powers had expected a Congo solution to be easier, and were angry and frustrated when it was not. Khrushchev's public attacks cut away some of the Swede's prestige, also. They reminded Africans that he was, after all, both Caucasian and European. His strict neutrality, finally—the refusal to do away with Tshombe's Katanga, which most Afro-Asians now considered the cause of the whole trouble—destroyed his support among the third world.

A vote of confidence in Hammarskjöld's leadership of the Congo operation failed by one vote in December, 1960. This was, however, an expression of irritation rather than a demand that the Secretary General step down. During 1961 support for

Hammarskjöld and ONUC continued to decline, although no nation or leader had any practical solution to the mess.

The cost of the operation was also frightening. The small nations most eager to send troops to the Congo and most eager to use them in pursuit of their own national policies and prejudices, had no intention of paying any of the bills. The UN budget for 1961 rose by $200 million, to over $500 million. The UN was $200 million short. This was to prove an enormous and aggravating problem. In the end, as always, the United States, through UN bond sales or other means, picked up most of the tab. But the continuing cost was to present the UN with its most serious crisis in later years.

During 1961 the Congo National Army continued to terrorize the countryside, and even fell to fighting itself, as it split into quarreling tribal factions. Kasavubu and Mobutu had no real control, though for reasons of pride they adamantly refused to have the army disarmed. In scattered places, ONUC forces and Mobutu's riotous soldiery clashed. In other areas, hundreds of thousands of Congo tribesmen were starving; the most horrible conditions prevailed. There was even, in places, a return to cannibalism.

The Union Minière-financed, Belgian officered Katanga gendarmerie was little better. The Congo was that kind of place. This army also lived off the countryside, and when the Baluba tribe revolted against Tshombe, scenes of horror were repeated in Katanga. There was widespread anarchy near Elizabethville.

Tshombe's image as the "man who could take control" was damaged by the fact that he could not maintain discipline among his constabulary, let alone the rampaging tribesmen. Of course, it was often overlooked by outsiders that no one could any longer control the Congo scene, at least not without mass bloodshed. Katanga's African gendarmerie was no better than Leopoldville's National Army; only Tshombe's European mercenaries kept him in office.

Tshombe's always touchy relations with ONUC troops in Ka-

295

tanga deteriorated steadily. The Belgians, who had flocked back and who were not above trying to play off one side against the other, complicated his situation. African ONUC soldiers, generally proud and disciplined troops, and the Katangan gendarmerie hated each other. The rising tension was aggravated when a group of Italian airmen on transport duty as part of the UN operation were hacked to pieces by a group of tribesmen in Katangan territory where Tshombe's men had lost control.

In September, Katangan gendarmerie and ONUC forces began firing on each other in Elizabethville. The situation seemed serious. Hammarskjöld, still wanting to keep the UN neutral but hoping to halt the bloodshed, asked for a meeting with Tshombe in nearby Rhodesia, just across the Congolese border.

In the past, Tshombe had proven slippery in his dealings. His favorite tactic had always been to seem to agree when things looked bad for him, then to renege whenever circumstances permitted. Some of Hammarskjöld's Secretariat staff felt it was a mistake for Hammarskjöld to fly to Rhodesia now.

But on September 17, 1961, Hammarskjöld's plane left Leopoldville for Ndola, Rhodesia. He was killed when the plane crashed in the Congolese jungle.

Hammarskjöld's mistake was not in going to see Tshombe. He had made his real error long before, when he took the UN so confidently into the Congo.

17.

A Cigar for Uncle Thant

HAMMARSKJÖLD'S DEATH stunned the world.

It also stunned numerous chancellories that had great confidence in the Swede, but whose people also were aware that most of Hammarskjöld's Congo policy was in his head. Every political solution had crumbled to dust, because of the Congo's inability to achieve a viable government and the refusal of certain African nations to accept a Conciliation Commission to bring about a coalition government such as had been used elsewhere. The various UN special agencies were working night and day to feed the Congo population, with no end in sight. The thousands of ONUC troops were also eating the UN out of house and home, literally, when they were not skirmishing with either Mobutu or Tshombe irregulars.

The plane crash had a sobering effect, especially on the Afro-Asian countries. ONUC was continued in spite of growing disillusionment; at any rate, the United States was still picking up the bills. It would have been, perhaps, a good time for the USSR to insist upon its three-headed Troika scheme, yet the Soviets let the opportunity pass. They had, however, had enough of Scandinavians in the Secretary Generalship. The Soviets and the United States, both knowing one of their partisans was out of the question, settled on the selection of a neutral, but this time an Afro-Asian neutral.

The Russians tended to be happy with almost anyone; they felt none could be worse than the two preceeding. They had ceased to believe that any European could be "neutral" in this continuing power struggle for the world. The United States was ready to go along with a neutral, also, with an eye on the growing importance of the new-nation block. By 1961, membership in the UN had doubled since 1945, and the large majority of new nations were largely unconcerned with the Cold War.

The eventual choice, U Thant of Burma, had wide respect in all three areas of the world. He was no Lie or Hammarskjöld but a small, bespectacled, gentle Asian not likely to take the firm, incisive action the two Europeans had demanded. His very choice presaged a decline in European respect for the UN, a decline already pronounced since 1956 and accelerated since the Congo.

Lie had not been able to be neutral in politics. Hammarskjöld, finally, had not been able to remain morally uncommitted. But Thant, out of his nature and his background, was perfectly fitted to be both politically and morally neutral toward both the USSR and the United States. This seemed, in 1961, a great strength and asset. It was to prove otherwise and to damage the UN even more.

Hammarskjöld had never been wrong when he continually emphasized the moral nature of the Charter and the organization. Hammarskjöld had always tried to treat all powers with fairness, but he had never equated white with black, or tan with grey. Thant, however, was never to be able to distinguish between the moral values of East or West. Like the neutral nation from which he sprang, he tended to put a pox on both sides; trust they would not fight, but would keep the aid coming.

Thant inherited the Congo mess. For nearly a year, he and his staff worked on what they called the Plan, a scheme to join Katanga and the Congo Republic. With the approval of the Council—most of whose members now wanted out—Thant laid the Plan before Premier Adoula of the Congo, and had it accepted.

The Plan called for a Congolese federal state with widely decentralized administration between Leopoldville and the provinces. Katanga was to be virtually independent, but without a separate army, and subject to the central government in the question of foreign relations, finance, and amnesties. Tshombe was to stay as head of the provincial government, but his troops would be merged with Mobutu's and take an oath of allegiance to

298

Kasavubu. White mercenary officers, of course, were to be dismissed.

Tshombe acted with his usual slipperiness. He accepted the Plan at first, then quibbled on certain details. The heavy tax return from the Union Minière and other European corporations was to be shared fifty-fifty between him and Adoula, but Tshombe said a fairer plan would be to have Katanga collect all the taxes and turn over to Leopoldville any monies it did not need. He stalled on one pretext or another for months. By the end of 1962 Thant had become as discouraged with Congo politics as Hammarskjöld had ever been, and said so. Bad blood between ONUC soldiers and Katangan troops festered. There was continual sniping, and continual harassment of ONUC in Katanga, which Tshombe did not seem able to control. Meanwhile the entire Baluba area of Katanga rose against Tshombe, a tribal enemy whom the Balubas hated. ONUC tried to feed or otherwise protect the Balubas from Tshombe's ravaging gendarmerie. This action complicated things even more.

For the first time, some of Tshombe's Belgian supporters began to waver. They were businessmen, and above all they wanted peace and order so that they could continue their operations. This Tshombe seemed unable to provide in 1962. But a real and very significant defection behind the scenes occurred when Tshombe threatened to blow up Union Minière and other Katangan industries in the event the UN moved against him. Tshombe meant this as a war-of-nerves threat, but he frightened the Belgian owners and managers of Union Minière. Many influential Belgians now tried to make an accommodation with the Adoula regime in Leopoldville.

The day before Christmas, 1962, some of Tshombe's troops got out of hand. They opened fire on ONUC positions; they shot down a UN helicopter. In one case ONUC men remained impassive for five hours under Katangan fire. They had orders not to reply in kind. But Tshombe was cutting his own throat by his inability to control his men. U Thant and the UN staff, as well as a firm majority of UN nations, now saw Tshombe as the prin-

299

cipal barrier to peace in the Congo. The U. S. government held the same view; it was firmly backing the Kasavubu-Adoula government as the best means to this end. Hammarskjöld had insisted to the end on UN neutrality, and that the Congolese be allowed, even bloodily, to solve their own problems. But on December 28, 1962, under Tshombe's provocations, this dam broke.

ONUC received orders from Thant to return fire to protect itself. The order was actually an authorization to disarm Tshombe, and it was so interpreted. On December 29 a bitter battle was joined, but the Asian and African regulars of ONUC soon mopped up Tshombe's hired hands. By the first week of January, 1963, the white mercenaries had fled to Rhodesia; Tshombe's native gendarmerie capitulated, and Moise Tshombe, wily to the end, asked for terms.

Thant immediately offered him terms of a sort: safe conduct outside the Congo, over Adoula's angry protests. Tshombe had fled Elizabethville, retreating toward Rhodesia with his army. On January 9, 1963, he drove back to the Katangan capital in his long black limousine. Under Thant's orders, he was allowed to leave with his personal possessions and money—which, rumor had it, included the remnants of the Katangan provinial treasury. He flew to exile in Spain, but his first European stop was at a Swiss bank in Geneva.

Nothing, however, was really settled in the Congo. The National Army was still mutinous, still roaming the land killing and raping. No one could control it. There were more provincial secessions; Gizenga held on in Kasai. Each tribe went its own way, in an area as large as the United States east of the Mississippi. ONUC stayed on, doing what it could. A few thousand men in such a vast region could do very little, and even these few thousands were stretching the UN to its breaking point.

The Congo operation had started out as an exciting adventure in assisting a new country to nationhood. It turned into a disillusioning nightmare. ONUC stayed in place until June 30, 1964, but because the Soviet Union and France refused to pay special assessments, it was bankrupting the UN. Only special U. S. injections of cash or loans kept not only ONUC but the UN going. France and the USSR disagreed with the Congo policy, and they based their refusal to pay special assessments on the fact that the continued Congo operation was voted by the Assembly, not the Security Council. The USSR had never accepted as legal the Acheson Plan to bypass the Council.

By 1964, ONUC was forced to depart. Premier Adoula faced disaster. Rebel "Simbas," assisted by Red China, overran large parts of the Congo. Katanga Province and the Balubas were again out of hand. Missionaries continued to be speared and Belgian nuns raped, costing Adoula what European support he had.

Panicking, Premier Adoula sent word to Tshombe in Spain, asking him to return. Tshombe, with his support in Katanga, the wealthiest province and principal power basin of the Congo, appeared to be the only man who had a chance to hold the new republic together. Just as the last contingent of United Nations troops flew out of Leopoldville on July 1, 1964, Tshombe stepped off an incoming plane.

He replaced Adoula, becoming the country's fourth premier. And he did again exactly what he had done before. Realizing that to rely upon undisciplined Congolese troops would bring disaster, he got word to his old mercenary crew, many of whom were in Rhodesia or Portuguese Angola. These European fighters came back; others were recruited, and these white "commandos" became the spearhead of Tshombe's new central government forces. They, and they alone, in the opinion of every military man on the scene, prevented Gizenga's Red Chinese-armed and -influenced Simbas from taking over the region. The rebels were defeated and Gizenga driven into exile, in a campaign lasting into 1965. It was not a war, but a hideous welter of blood that at some stages became pure massacre. By the spring of 1965 Tshombe had as much control over the Congo as any man or government was likely to have during the century.

But black Africa howled, and everyone who had supported the former UN Congo policies gagged. The crushing irony was too much. One of the most ironic things of all was that now the United

States government was quietly supporting Tshombe all the way. U. S. Air Force transports even flew his white commandos from point to point, and these aircraft did not depart until August 1965.

Then, when Tshombe had brought the Congo to heel, President Kasavubu dismissed him as Premier. It appeared a new power struggle would develop.

In all this there must have been a lesson, if anyone could see it.

On January 20, 1953, John Foster Dulles, number two man at San Francisco and a principal architect of the UN, became U. S. Secretary of State. He was to be probably the strongest Secretary the nation ever had. The relationship between Dulles and President Eisenhower was that the President tried to see the world through Dulles' spectacles, but Dulles himself never tried to encroach on Eisenhower's office.

But with all his strengths, Dulles' half-dozen years in office can only be summed up in two words: *too late.* Dulles' principal ideas were forged in the 1940's. He came to power only after the world had changed. He inherited a world Truman and Acheson had made. He was not only unable to change it, but he was hard put merely to defend it and keep it intact.

Seven months after he took office the USSR exploded its thermonuclear bomb and approached nuclear parity with the United States. In the 1940's and early 1950's Dulles had argued for "massive retaliation"—the answering of Communist aggression or Communist challenge by the threat of nuclear retaliation on the Soviet homeland. This had been unacceptable to the gamesmen guiding U. S. policy, though it had a definite logic. When the Russian hydrogen bomb went off, however, the logic of massive retaliation was gone. The USSR now had ample power to reply in kind.

This nuclear parity made a forced rollback of the Soviet empire in East Europe, which had been another Dulles policy, largely academic. In the face of Russian bombs, the United States could not muster this kind of threatening power. The stand-off became more and more complete.

Again, another striking Dulles thought had been for an "agonizing reappraisal" of NATO. Dulles felt that France might have to be replaced as America's major continental European ally by Western Germany. Taken up in time, this diplomatic revolution might very well have prevented the fiasco at Suez. But after France's and Britain's actions in Egypt, Dulles was forced to rebuild the present alliance as it stood. Any further weakening of it after Suez or the Hungarian crisis could only have played into the Soviet leaders' hands.

What Dulles was forced to do, then, was not to change anything according to his original ideas, but to continue the policy of containment that Acheson, Kennan, and Truman had begun. He was never to solve anything, but was forced to run about jamming corks into bottles whose caps had already blown; he could not get ahead of the game. In the end he could only hand a defensive position on the world chessboard on to Rusk. In all this he had to battle not only the stone faces of Soviet and Chinese Communism, but also the harassments and hinderings of a home-front opinion that increasingly demanded an end to the Cold War.

Dulles never had the slightest power or opportunity to end the Cold War; he was not even able to do much about his principles, by which he continued to be haunted. Dulles never ceased wanting the kind of just world he had dreamed of at Versailles as a young man, and tried to bring about at San Francisco.

He made, perhaps, two significant mistakes. The first was that he never really tried to defy American public opinion on an issue even when he felt such opinion was wrong. The second was that, in possession of the facts, he never effectively tried to educate American opinion to reality.

These errors were understandable. He had worked closely with Dean Acheson in the Truman Administration, even though he disagreed with many of Acheson's ideas of containment; he

303

had been the principal architect of the Japanese peace treaty of 1952 from which the Soviets were frozen out. Acheson had paid no attention to public opinion. And while Truman had made it abundantly clear that Acheson's foreign policy was his foreign policy, Truman eventually reached the rank of near-great Presidents, while Dean Acheson, who normally advised Truman what to do, was crucified by both the American right and left as no Secretary of State in history had been. Acheson developed such an unfavorable image that even future Democratic administrations were afraid to use him again.

The reasons were partly political, partly personal. Acheson personally was not a good salesman; unlike Rusk he was a thorny witness in front of Congress. And the policy of containment was never popular with any large segment of the public. Anti-Communists and conservatives felt it did not go far enough; liberals felt it went much too far. Acheson warned Truman that his Korea decision would be unpopular, then ended up taking the blame for it. Ironically, Acheson was even tarred with the Communist brush: he refused to "turn his back" on convicted Communist agent Alger Hiss; the reasons were personal, not political, but were misinterpreted. Acheson was even blamed for the decision by the Joint Chiefs of Staff to abandon Korea in 1947, because he was the public enunciator of it. It must have amused Soviet statesmen immensely that Acheson, the principal architect of NATO, ended up in much of the American public mind as soft on Communism.

Dulles unquestionably took the nails in Acheson's feet and palms too much to heart. He decided not to fly in the face of American public opinion, even when he knew it was wrong. For example, Dulles realized the Summit Conference of 1955 was a snare and a delusion, and said so; but he made no real effort to stop Eisenhower from going. The public wanted a summit, with all its false hopes of détente and relaxation, so the public got one.

Just as Acheson had drawn Republican fire, Dulles faced constant running criticism from Democrats. Dulles' hardheaded views on Communism and dealing with the USSR alienated the liberal wing, which still hoped for some kind of accommodation. But some of Dulles' worst troubles came not from Democrats or the liberal left, but from the conservative wing of his own party, which refused to get off the massive retaliation or immaculate victory kick, or to recognize the true, protracted, and costly nature of the world power struggle, to which there was no "immaculate" or sudden solution.

Dulles, who admittedly helped light fires under Democrats over Korea, never forgot how deeply they burned when he faced his own Koreas. He was always reluctant to commit American boys, even if the Republican politico-military machine behind him would have permitted it.

Dulles was never as rigid as he was pictured. He would have been overjoyed to end the Cold War on favorable terms. In the attempt he spent endless hours flying all over the globe on missions he knew were useless. More than once he said privately: "There is no illusion greater or more dangerous than that Soviet intentions can be deflected by persuasion." But for political reasons, in the face of an American mass brain that was determined to negotiate with the other side, he failed to beat this refrain into the public mind.

Most of the public never realized that during Dulles' years the U. S. power position vis-à-vis the USSR was worsening from causes beyond Dulles' control. The United States did not deteriorate. But the USSR recovered from the war and made almost quantum leaps forward in science, rocketry, and nuclear power. Each advance made the Soviet star shine brighter, and gave Russian leaders greater influence and prestige. A Sputnik had much more effect on most world opinion than Hungary.

It was not until after the shock of Sputnik that the United States was driven into devoting more energy and capital into the vital areas of the world prestige race. The Russian rate of advance slowed in the late fifties, and the United States again spurted far ahead. But Dulles was forced to play his poker at the worst possible time.

He disappointed millions because he did not win. He disappointed others because he could not end the game. His worst critics did not seem to understand that the United States could not defy or destroy the USSR except at prohibitive cost, or that it takes two to détente as well as to tango. The Russian price for détente from 1953 till Dulles died was American withdrawal from Europe and the end of NATO. It was a price that could not be met.

There were never any "lost opportunities" like those some wishful thinkers continually dreamed up. In fact, some Americans were perfectly willing to accept the price of withdrawal—without thinking through consequences—if a face-saving procedure could have been found.

Dulles saw plainly that Khrushchev's toothy grin was just as dangerous to the long-term aspirations of the West as Stalin's frown. Dulles knew that "peaceful coexistence," Russian style, meant only the avoidance of nuclear conflict, never the end of the power struggle. The coming disorders, revolts, and wars of national liberation around the world were as deadly to the Western world order as a Russian military advance. Stalin had only tried for European hegemony in the 1940's. Khrushchev, with new power and prestige, was suddenly able to dream of "peacefully" burying the West.

The day had to come when Foster Dulles would be rehabilitated by public opinion in the West, just as some day Stalin would be rehabilitated as a Russian hero in the USSR. Because, overall, Dulles did not fail. *He held on to every inch of territory entrusted to him at the start.*

In his fight, he could never understand how millions of Americans who accepted the fact that the *sources* of American policy did not change from Roosevelt to Truman to Eisenhower, willfully convinced themselves that the sources of Soviet policy would change if only the Soviet government changed. Dulles knew that Soviet ambitions were not apt to change suddenly no matter who was at the helm, said so, and one reason he was long in being forgiven was that during the Kennedy and Johnson years he was proved right.

Dulles knew even before he took high office that the other side was cold-nerved. Quite reasonably, he figured it would take equally cold and steady nerves to face them down. The whole story of Dulles' diplomacy was this: he took cold-nerved courage into each confrontation with Communist power, from Vietnam in 1953 to Taiwan in 1955 and Lebanon in 1958. He played containment the only way it could possibly have been played in the 1950's, by "brinkmanship."

But he only went to the brink of war because the other side pushed him there. He was not aggressive. He accepted the status quo, and all he wanted from the Soviets or Chinese was that they do the same. He was willing to use threats to contain Communist expansion, even though he realized the implicit risk. The risk of not doing so seemed infinitely worse. He played the great game much as Acheson had, but with one difference: the stone face of Foster Dulles unquestionably frightened the stone face of Soviet Communism more.

In Korea in 1953, Dulles' threats of unleashing Chiang Kai-shek for a U. S.-supported mainland invasion and of using nuclear weapons against the Chinese positions helped speed the end of that war. His threats to intervene in Vietnam in 1953 and 1954 achieved a better settlement at the time for the West than anyone at Geneva really hoped to get. His threats over Taiwan and the offshore islands of Quemoy and Matsu (Dulles once said privately that he never really made up his mind to defend these small isles) made China think twice and back off. His threats over the Lebanon and Iraq situation of 1958, when it seemed Soviet influence again might penetrate the Middle East, dissipated that problem.

In each case, Red leadership was forced to ask its own military forces how things stood vis-à-vis the United States, and in each case the answer was sobering. There is a story, probably apocryphal, that when the Lebanon crisis was at its height, Nikita

Khrushchev queried his marshals whether Russia was prepared to stop the U. S. Strategic Air Command. The chief air marshal replied, "You must be kidding, Nikita Sergeyevitch."

But the effect of these threats must not be carried too far. Dulles could not have threatened the USSR out of Hungary or East Europe. This was vital, and therefore killing, ground. The gambits Communists tried in the 1950's were not vital to them; they could afford to back off. Dulles had better sense than to try a real game of "chicken," as some of his most rabid right wing supporters demanded.

In each case, Dulles had never made up his mind to act in any certain way, either to use nuclear weapons, unleash Chiang, or to defend certain islands. But he understood the important tactic of keeping the other side guessing, and thus off balance. Each time he won his point in this kind of peace, and each time he bought more of the same kind of peace.

But—and this should be understood—Dulles bought world peace sometimes at the price of the souls of the pacifists of the world.

His boss, Eisenhower, was recognized even by the Russians as a genuine man of peace. Eisenhower did want accommodation —with honor—with the Soviets. But in the face of the continued Soviet hostility and ambition, Eisenhower's pronouncements like "open skies" were just so much rhetoric. Dulles, in daily contact with Communist diplomacy, knew that the public dreams of accommodation were moonshine. But gloomily, and to his sorrow, again and again he let himself be talked into summits, Camp Davids, and the like. But it is very likely that had he lived—he died of cancer in 1959—he would never have let Eisenhower make the disastrous journey to the Paris summit conference in 1960. In the Congo the USSR and Khrushchev had shown they wanted no accommodation with the United States. At Paris, even without the U-2 incident, there was nothing to talk about.

An original backer of the UN, Dulles found himself increasingly disturbed by the organization. He understood the Cold War impasse. But he never understood the nature of the neutral nations now thronging in. He could never influence these nations, even with his most moral pronouncements. One reason was that Dulles, who had made himself the highest-paid corporation lawyer and one of the most successful men in the United States, simply could not understand the concept of the "underdog." He had small sympathy for or interest in anyone or any nation unable to lift itself out of the normal mire of human existence. He was remote, as a British historian wrote, from the messy way men and nations ran their lives. He could not suffer fools, even in Congress —a dangerous trait for an American statesman.

He was without moral doubts as to the rightness of his cause, and willing to use a corporation lawyer's casuistry and bluff in that cause. This, as much as anything else, drove Anthony Eden and the British Foreign Office out of their minds, because they could not understand a man who combined both brilliant intellectuality and unquestioning moral dogmatism into one policy. Dulles recognized the sovereignty of his God, but chose, when necessary, to do God's work at the bar of the world with whatever means he thought best. He was unfathomable to the post-Christian men who made a religion of intellectualism, and equally so to those who kept religious faith but never learned how to think.

Dulles sincerely thought there was a moral purpose to the world; he opposed colonialism in all its forms. This conviction of moral purpose was his strong armor. It made him impervious to fear, even nuclear danger. It frightened others into incoherency, for nothing is so intolerable to modern tolerant men as a genuinely righteous man.

As the UN, influenced by African sentiments and neutralist fears, began to move in strange ways between East and West, Dulles lost his regard for it. He could admire the skills of a man like Hammarskjöld but never accept his world of grays. He took U. S. policy out of the UN after 1956, and it was only after his death that the United States again became mired in it, in the Congo in 1960. Dulles would have worked in ways outside the UN God's miracles to perform.

He had one other failure: he was the worst administrator the

U. S. State Department ever had. He carried his ideas and diplomacy in his head; he had no real interest in the workings of the Department or even the people who manned it. He asked to be relieved of running the Department, but this was never done. Under Dulles the Department became something of a headless chicken, and he damaged it. He did not even bother to defend his employees—who he knew were innocent—from Senator McCarthy's most ridiculous charges. He once advised Eisenhower, who got hot under the collar about McCarthy, that the Senator would eventually hang himself. So he did, but not until much damage was done.

The United States was continually on the defensive, by choice, during the first two decades following the war. Even had Dulles felt he had the power to take the initiative against the USSR, Western public opinion would not have supported this. As it was, opinion barely supported a firm defensive stand when such a stand seemed to increase the chance of war.

The defensive stance also created an illusion in some quarters that the United States was losing the Cold War. But this was not so. Dulles from 1953 to 1958 lost no territory, and after 1957 the trend toward Soviet power parity slowed. The United States again spurted ahead. But Dulles did not succeed in changing the shape of the world or of the peace for three basic reasons:

(1) After Stalin's death in March, 1953, the Kremlin went into a power struggle that Khrushchev did not win until 1958. There was no one in the USSR with the power to negotiate for real.

(2) The tide in the 1950's seemed to be running the Russian way, economically, scientifically, militarily. Dulles was not in a position to negotiate from overwhelming strength—the only possible position from which to deal with the Communist mentality.

(3) By the time Khrushchev was Number One he saw no reason to negotiate on anything.

Dulles kept the faith as he saw it and held the Western world, but increasingly at the price of the Western soul. In the end, it

310

was not his but John F. Kennedy's destiny to play the greatest game of brinksmanship of them all.

On January 1, 1959, after a long, complicated revolutionary struggle, a charismatic, Marxist young man somewhat in the Lumumba pattern (but not yet allied with Moscow) came to power in Cuba, ninety miles from U. S. shores. Fidel Castro's revolution was not at first Communist-inspired. His fighters were a mixture of genuinely democratic groups, economic reformers, confused leftists, and a large middle-class element allied against dictator Fulgencio Batista's corrupt and increasingly intolerable strongman rule. The hard-core, or Moscow-run, Cuban Communists joined his revolution only in its last successful stages. But the Castro movement was definitely a protest seeking an ethic. The situation, and protest, in Cuba had become increasingly common in the developing (the new euphemism for "have-not") world. And given a choice, the logic of the times allowed the Cuban revolution to turn to Communist solutions rather than Western representative democracy.

Marxism provided three things to the underdeveloped or "third world" that Western democracy could not supply: an instant rationale that explained most of its past failures; an apparent means by which industrialization and centralization could be forced on economies that would not accept such reforms and changes voluntarily; and, finally, a rationale under which a small, educated, power-hungry elite could seize and exercise power in the name of the people. Marxism in the poorer tier of the world had nothing to do with starving peasants and city poor people—except that these provided a base of misery and unrest upon which revolutions could feed.

For five years, there was never a single *working* man in Fidel Castro's Communist Cuban cabinet. In the developing world, the true revolutionaries tended to be medical doctors, lawyers, and men with doctorates, like Castro. These groups, in Latin America and most of the third world, had never been part of the

311

real power elite and their disaffection was understandable, though seemingly it could not be understood by Washington. Woodrow Wilson had generally tried to judge all people living anywhere by Anglo-Saxon standards, and the practice long survived him.

The Cuban problem vis-à-vis the United States, if it had to be boiled down to a few words, was this: Cuba was simply not able to be self-sufficient. It was a strictly agricultural nation, producing money crops like sugar and tobacco, and not enough food to feed itself. It had to be an economic dependency of *some* industrial power, and for fifty years Cuba had been an economic dependency of the United States. The United States was never happy with the Cuban political situation; but over the years men like Batista, who did seem to keep order, had received support. This U. S. support of Batista had built up a Cuban reservoir of hatred.

If Castro and the men around him could have taken a Titoist course—made a Marxist state while maintaining strict neutrality in the Cold War—Castro probably would have had no real trouble with the United States. When he came to power the faults and miseries of Cuba had been well publicized; Castro was something of a hero in North America. He could have done almost anything at all to Cuba—and got away with it—if he had kept his hands off American interests on the island, and had had nothing to do with the United States' enemies. The first Castro could not do because of his background, instincts, and temperament. The second became necessary when Castro had estranged the United States.

Castro did not bring freedom or "national liberation" to Cuba. He changed a corrupt tyranny of the right for a tawdry dictatorship of the left, and switched from a dependency on the United States to a dependency on the USSR. And in doing it, he felt constrained to attack the United States with propaganda, confiscation of American assets on the island, and by mounting an agitation against American influence all over the Caribbean. The attacks were initiated by Castro; they took Washington by surprise, and Washington never quite knew what to do about the noisy fellow with the beard.

Some men in Washington learned a lesson they were to remember: that revolutions of Castro's sort, even when they contained democratic elements and were pressed against genuine grievances, seemed to be as conditioned as Pavlov's dogs. They could not refrain from hostility to the United States and all it stood for. The mere power and wealth and feeling for the status quo that pervaded the United States seemed an irresistible target, and produced an emotional hatred such movements went to great length to try to explain in political or economic terms.

Somewhat like Nagy's Hungarians, Castro was carried away. He took Cuba entirely out of the American sphere of influence, although Cuba was in America's backyard. This might have been acceptable, if unpalatable, but Castro tempted fate. He sought, and got, aid and alliance with the Soviet Union. This was the first penetration by a hostile power into the Western Hemisphere for more than a century.

The odd thing about this penetration was that Khrushchev never planned it. Castro threw himself into the Russian lap, and for long months the Russian leadership did not know quite what to do with him. In September, 1960, at the UN's fifteenth regular session in New York, Khrushchev apparently advised Castro to go slow, and to seek economic accommodation with the United States. Khrushchev did not think the United States would put up with Castro's style forever. Meanwhile, Khrushchev volunteered to make threatening noises in Castro's behalf, and to ship him conventional arms, including aircraft and tanks.

Khrushchev, however, reckoned without the peculiar and temporarily dominant kind of moral doubt about the nature of geopolitics that pervaded Washington at the beginning of the 1960's. In 1960 the Eisenhower Administration planned to do away with Castro; he had become intolerable. He had confiscated one billion dollars in American property without compensation, and he was trying to foment anti-United States feeling all over Hispanic America. The groundwork was laid for an invasion by a brigade of exiled Cubans—a quarter of a million had fled the Marxist revolution—supported secretly by American power.

313

The CIA was in charge of the operation. The whole project was handled with incredible ineptness, not so much because the CIA was inept but because the fact that the United States was determined to remain openly uninvolved hamstrung the operation from the start. U. S. concern for its image among the small nations—all of which opposed on principle any great-power interference with a small power for any reason—was paramount. If the American armed forces had been allowed to take part in the planning, and above all in the execution, the result of the Bay of Pigs fiasco in 1961 would have been vastly different. But the United States, true to its own confused ideas of principle, and true to its own idealism while at the same time realizing the world was going sour, chose good propaganda over good geopolitics, an error no Russian ever made in the Cold War.

As it was, a group of heroic Cubans were set ashore at the Bay of Pigs in April 1961. They met greater resistance than expected, and after much running around in panic Washington abandoned them—though it eventually ransomed the survivors from Castro's prisons. The failure was a horrible shock to the Kennedy Administration. But it was also an effective lesson. Some men never forgot the damage that could be done by moral doubts in the rightness of their cause at the wrong moment.

The United States achieved at the Bay of Pigs the rarest of all world phenomena: a complete diplomatic and political failure. By being involved the United States was tarred with the interventionist and "imperialist" brush; by failing ignominiously, the United States lost power and prestige—always interconnected in world politics—everywhere.

Here a dangerous thing occurred. Khrushchev simply could not comprehend how the men running a great power could come to believe they had no right to intervene in a case like Cuba. Soon afterward, Khrushchev remarked publicly that the United States was "too liberal" to fight. From the Bay of Pigs stemmed one of the worst years in U. S. diplomatic history.

Khrushchev did not even bother to be polite at Kennedy's abortive summit at Vienna in June, 1961. He had nothing to discuss, only ultimatums to deliver. He chose to blow the simmering Berlin situation up to crisis proportions, both by demands that the West withdraw and by the erection of the infamous Wall in August. There was increased Communist pressure in Laos, a fringe area in Asia. Finally, there was the Cuban crisis of 1962. The Communist world had become more aggressive than it had been for a decade. Khrushchev apparently felt he could get away with anything while the West was seeking new solutions to the Cold War and trying to resolve its own moral contradictions.

The strategic reasons the Russian government decided to ship nuclear warheads, intermediate range missiles, and jet bombers— all offensive weapons that could only be aimed at the United States—into Cuba is still unclear. There were several possibilities: one was that Russia was not so strong as the United States in long-range intercontinental missiles, though it had great quantities of intermediate-range rockets originally built to terrorize Western Europe. The implacement of these rockets in Cuba could have materially affected the United States-USSR balance of nuclear power. Second, such strengthening could only improve Khrushchev's hand in the war of nerves over Berlin.

But it was obviously a desperate risk, liable to provoke American reaction for both strategic and emotional reasons. The United States had still not decided whether a hostile Cuba—a small power—was off limits, but it had no such moral confusion as to the Soviet Union. Khrushchev and Soviet Intelligance believed that missiles could be slipped into Cuba secretly and, secondly, that since the United States had already accepted tacitly the Cuban entry into the Soviet bloc and the arrival of conventional arms and thousands of Soviet and Czech "technicians," the sky was the limit.

But the presence of Soviet missiles—a real threat to North American security—freed President Kennedy's hands as nothing else would have done. When American Intelligence from overflights revealed hard proof of burgeoning missile sites, Kennedy reacted with all the tough nerve of a Dulles.

On October 21, 1962, he challenged Khrushchev on the issue,

diplomatically called him a liar (Khrushchev had denied the missiles), and ordered a blockade—called a "quarantine" since a blockade was an act of war under international law—on further arms shipments to Cuba. The U. S. Navy stood to sea. The doors of U. S. missile bases swung open. American ground divisions and aircraft were concentrated in the state of Florida, ready to intervene in Cuba.

Then Kennedy informed the Russians that any use of Cuban missiles or any attack on Berlin by the puppet East Germans would be regarded as an attack by the USSR on the United States, requiring a "full retaliatory response." Any further hostile move anywhere would be met "with whatever action is needed."

This was brinkmanship as it had never been played before.

Kennedy still left room for the Russians to back away; both Cuba and Berlin were Russian initiatives. Cuba was of no importance to the USSR; in fact, it had already become an economic liability, costing one hundred million dollars a year. But for the first time Khrushchev was made to understand there would be no backdown in Berlin, and that Cuba had the same psychological and strategic importance in the American mind that Hungary had had in the Russian mind. Khrushchev was faced with the continuing U. S. nuclear superiority; and, *for the first time, he was faced with American conventional superiority in the area of operations.* Kennedy could take Cuba by ordering an invasion, and Khrushchev knew it.

Khrushchev lost face by backing away, but nothing else of any real value. But he backed away, showing visible signs of worry and fright. Kennedy followed the ground rules of previous confrontations: he tried for a stand-off, not a Russian humiliation. The Soviets were not asked to abandon Cuba, only to get their missiles out of the island. Thus Kennedy went too far for some people, and for others not nearly far enough.

Khrushchev played his cards coolly enough in the withdrawal. Castro gave trouble; Castro was not only shown up as a Russian puppet, but he was humiliated in the process, when Khrushchev demanded, and finally got back, the Ilyushin jet bombers transferred to the Cuban air force. Anastas Mikoyan, the old Hungarian trouble-shooter, went to Cuba to straighten Castro out.

Castro, however, balked at the U. S. demand for an inspection of Cuban soil to assure that the missiles were gone. This Castro claimed was a violation of Cuban sovereignty, and here Mikoyan backed him up.

And here, for the first time in what was to be a watershed crisis of the Cold War, the United Nations entered the picture.

The time of the Congo crisis and immediately afterward had seen the entry of a great number of new nations into the UN. Membership increased to more than a hundred, and one third of the membership now consisted of new African states, all but two of which (Liberia and Ethiopia) were ex-protectorates or colonies. Immediately after this influx, opinion among this third world enjoyed a period of great importance as far as U. S. policy was concerned. The paying of so much attention to non-Western or neutral opinion in Afro-Asia was perhaps illogical, but natural. They were obviously going to dominate the Assembly numerically. The United States was eager to convince them all to join the Western club and abide by Western rules of order, as well as to keep them from joining the rival club.

Dulles, with his moral distrust of neutralism in general and his distaste for failed men or failed societies, had not taken the United States very far down this road. But Dulles' successors in the Kennedy Administration, and men like Adlai Stevenson, the new U. S.. Ambassador to the UN, went down it gladly.

Kennedy's circle had writhed at the stagnation in East-West relations, and many of these men, including Kennedy himself, were at first convinced that the Cold War could be ended. When and if this happened, the emerging nations were going to be the most important political factor in the world, or so many in Washington thought. Whichever of the superpowers lined up the majority of them was most likely to influence the world its way once the reliance on military divisions and nuclear rocketry ended.

There was, under Kennedy, a return to a kind of idealism that Washington had last seen in the early 1940's. Dean Rusk, who

317

had worked in the second tier of statesmen under Truman, was not of this school. He was a much tougher-minded man than his soft Georgia drawl indicated. He became Secretary of State in 1961, but there were two facts about his stewardship that were at first obscured. Rusk, unlike Dulles, suffered fools gladly, and no Secretary since Hull was so popular with both Congress and the public generally. He kept his patience well and worked slowly. More importantly, Kennedy did not use a rigid command-line management system; Rusk was not necessarily running U. S. foreign policy at any given moment. Kennedy had a habit of paying attention to kibitzers without either responsibility or authority, and sometimes even without office. Rusk was just one orbiting satellite among many until he came into his own under Lyndon Johnson.

But the attempts to reach a sincere agreement with the USSR during 1961 and 1962 only resulted in American frustration and greater Soviet pressures. Khrushchev, sure he was winning, wasn't having any. Meanwhile, some of the tangles the United States got into around the world were due to the fact that American policy-makers were trying to please third-world opinion. The Congo situation was not attacked unilaterally by the United States but channeled through the UN for this reason. The wonderfully weird days during which the United States, through the UN, supported Patrice Lumumba and assisted in the downfall of Moise Tshombe—which a very large body of American opinion never understood—could only have happened in this way. There was a great confusion of popularity with power, and U. S. interest with the conflicting interests of other powers.

Because of this, and also because he was not typically American, John Kennedy projected an immensely favorable image around the world, Kennedy—it is painful for most Americans to realize this—may actually have been misleading to the world, as Johnson began to make apparent after Kennedy was tragically murdered. Johnson, Rusk, McNamara, Bundy, and Thomas Mann of Texas were all more inclined to count votes at home rather than overseas and also to look at things from a more typical

318

and hard-minded American light. With these men principles were splendid, but they were not power as they had come to recognize and use it. With them, right or wrong, the U. S. interest came first.

But from 1960 through 1962 there was a brief and haunting Indian summer of UN glory, and the illusion that somehow the Great Design was at last falling into place. The UN seemed responsive at times to Stevenson's measured idealism and defense of decency. To many, it seemed that the United States might actually forge an order based on firm acceptance of the Charter. These people never saw that the Charter often commanded even less respect among the new nations than it had among the old. Justice remained, among the nations, what it always had been to them: the fulfillment of what they ardently desired.

The reaction to U. S. involvement in the Bay of Pigs was a warning of the newly diluted UN's true responsiveness to the Western power position, which was actually the only hope of an orderly world. When Castro announced that American-built B-26 bombers (they were piloted by Cuban refugees) had flown over Havana, the third world sent up an ungodly screech. Stevenson took a bad beating in the UN. This noise unnerved the Adminstration, and may have been instrumental in the decision to abandon the project after it began to fail. The United States was accused of perpetrating another Suez, but the United States had prepared no counterpropaganda, nor did it make any attempt to explain the geopolitical realities of big-power life and the Cold War.

President Kennedy had to learn the hard way that the idea of power and the actual exercise of it are two different things. One can be ideal, the other is usually far from perfect, and messy.

When Kennedy finally moved to eject Soviet missiles and Soviet power from Cuba in October, 1962, there was again a terrible tension around the world. What many people overlooked then was that the third world screeched just as loudly as it had in 1961, and again demanded peace.

No one heard them. Kennedy's attention this time was not dis-

319

tracted. In a showdown between the superpowers, U Thant was definitely the dispensable man. The third world, and the UN's Thant, were thus placed in their real perspective.

Neither was interested in the preservation of Western values, or Western society, except as both benefitted them. Nor should they have been. It was stupid for anyone to believe peoples should join up or choose sides in a power struggle that was meaningless to them, unless they were caught up in it, or one side or the other impinged on them.

With American and Russian leaders eyeball to eyeball, the neutral world did not count. What did count was that the U. S. treaty allies lined up behind Washington in every case. Many of these allies did not approve of Kennedy's stand; it frightened most of them. But even De Gaulle understood there could be no middle ground *in extremis.*

During the worse hours of the crisis there was no time for traditional diplomacy or the handing of notes. Messages between Kennedy and Khrushchev were sent in the clear for rapid delivery. There was also no time for UN debate.

The UN, as neutral ground, came into prominence again only after the main outlines of the United States-Russian stand-off had been hammered out. There is much evidence to suggest that Khrushchev would have thrown Castro to the dogs if Kennedy had insisted; but he was able to preserve the Russian domination of the island, and even, finally, to get Washington to agree to substitute International Red Cross or United Nations on-site inspection of the arms removal.

Secretary General U Thant, who was suspicious of if not actually hostile to the idea of U. S. predominance in the Caribbean, enplaned for Havana in November, 1962. Thant's major worry, as with most of the members of the third world, was that peace, *at any price,* be preserved.

Arriving in Havana, Thant was told by Castro that Cuban sovereignty was inviolable unless Castro chose otherwise. Fronting for the United States in this case, Thant was not an effective spokesman for the idea that some nations had to be more, and others less, sovereign than others. Thant also considered it bad form to advise Castro that the USSR had already compromised Cuban sovereignty beyond recall. By agreeing to let the United Nations carry the ball in Cuba, Washington and Kennedy hoped to win world approval. But by allowing Thant, with different aims and philosophies from those of the United States, to decide the matter, the United States allowed its painfully-gained momentum to dribble away. Castro was able to seize the initiative.

Thant argued with Castro, but ineffectively. He could not disagree that small power's rights, even with their fingers caught in the cookie jar, were still inviolate. Both Mikoyan and Thant eventually returned to the United States and reported to Kennedy that there was no way to get U. S. observers on the ground short of invasion—which neither one was prepared to accept. Meanwhile, the momentum for invasion had inevitably passed away. Such things are best done quickly, or not at all, as Eden painfully learned.

Castro had won a life. The USSR had salvaged a position. The United States had again practiced containment at the brink, in the pattern since 1948. The UN again had been left outside the flow of events, except as a mirror and a sounding board.

U Thant (the word "U" in Burmese is a title of respect somewhat similar to "uncle") salvaged only a box of Havana cigars, which Castro gave him when he left.

Somewhere, the shade of Foster Dulles must have smiled a grim, gray smile.

18.

The Two Faces of Uncle Sam

IF MOST American citizens felt a basic confusion toward the UN it was because there was always a basic confusion after 1945 in the American world outlook. Because the actual makeup and trends of the world were not clearly seen, there was both moral and intellectual confusion.

The postwar world was divided into an ambitious Communist empire, itself united primarily in hostility to the West, a status-quo-minded Western, or Atlantic, civilization, and a Western-dominated colonial and economic order holding sway everywhere else. The colonial order, particularly that part in Asia and Africa that was under European flags, quickly became the "third world" of the neutrals or uncommitted. But the end of flag-hegemony did not mean the end of Western influence.

In Hispanic America, which was economically and geographically part of the colonial world, foreign-flag hegemony had not existed since 1821. Yet for decades the major decisions affecting Hispanic-American nations were made in North America or European board rooms, not local presidential palaces. The price of coffee was usually more relevant to a nation's well-being than who was chief of state, and over this no Hispanic-American country had any control.

The same kind of condition continued in Africa after independence. It was inevitable. The industrial North Atlantic community could live without coffee or bananas; the tropical south could not get along without medicines, automobiles, engineering, and tools. It was relatively easy to transfer political power from London or Paris to African capitals. It was impossible to change economic and geographic realities.

322

Thus the basic unhappiness of the third world did not stop with independence or the hauling down of the Union Jack or Tricolour. Most of the third world, including Hispanic America, wanted a kind of independence and status that simply wasn't in the cards. And by the 1960's this was leading to a new kind of revolution.

It was not possible for most of the new nations to industrialize. But they saw that in the modern world steel mills and potash plants and airlines, as well as large bureaucracies, were essential for national prestige and power. With the ultra-rational goal of prestige and power tempting them all the more strongly because of the sullen inferiority complex most colonial nations had acquired from their immediate, dominated past, the new nations found the status quo intolerable.

The urge to confiscate Western holdings was irresistible, and the dream of industrialization tended to wreck sensible efforts toward improving an agriculture that already was failing to feed growing populations. New nations built roads to nowhere, ran expensive airlines, and imported steel mills or cement plants they hardly needed, all in the name of prestige. Meanwhile, their peoples went hungry.

All of this meant accelerating trouble, because with the vision of the wealthy and technically successful Atlantic nations shining always before them, what Adlai Stevenson called the "revolution of rising expectations" had arrived. But those rising expectations were not, in most cases, going to be met. There was no way on earth they could be. A nation like Indonesia because of its tropical geography could never be another United States. A Cuba did not have the essential ingredients of ethic, climate, and location to become another Switzerland, even though it contained more minerals and richer soil.

The best the colonial-economy world could hope for was to improve its agriculture so that burgeoning populations—ironically rising because of Western medicines and sanitation—could be fed, and to industrialize judiciously where feasible. But this meant continued power inferiority vis-à-vis the West, and was unacceptable to most third-world leaders, even those who knew they did not have the social organization to change their status.

A desire for this kind of social organization was one of the principal attractions Marxism had for the emerging world. Marxism not only gave a rationale for forcing a population to limit consumption, but a rationale for power for those leaders and intellectual groups who felt the Western superiority most keenly.

World War II had destroyed the old myth of white, or European, racial superiority as a moral justification for continued European or North American domination. But at the same time a purely European, or American—since Woodrow Wilson was its greatest propagator—virus had spread southward. This was called national or ethnic self-determination; and most Americans, out of their history, could not see that it was one of the most disruptive and pernicious doctrines to sweep the earth.

Ethnic self-determination originally meant that each human racial or language group should have the right to choose its own form of government and control its own destiny, as Frenchmen and Englishmen had done for centuries. No one could argue with this. But self-determination soon meant that each grouping tried to run its own economy along national lines just at the time when world industrialization was demanding bigger and bigger economic units and marketing areas.

The multiplication of small states in Eastern Europe after World War I, following this doctrine, produced economic chaos. As Metternich had said, if a Danubian empire had not existed, men would have had to invent one. In this sense, when the Soviet empire filled this vacuum in 1945, it was a relief. The great worldwide depression in the thirties was caused in large part by a multiplicity of tiny economic units from France to Yugoslavia all trying to practice a new form of mercantilism, or control "their economic destinies."

Ethnic economic determinism crashed into the teeth of new technology, which was rapidly making the earth more interdependent. It produced intellectual idiocies such as the French

324

Canadians' desire to seize control of the economy of Quebec, a move that could endanger Canada's existence as a nation. A European Common Market and a Soviet Comicon were necessary regional groupings, yet on the one hand France and on the other Rumania disrupted them out of purely nationalistic urgings. France wanted to dominate her grouping; Rumania wanted steel mills and industries Comicon had ordained to go elsewhere.

And finally, ethnic determinism was the most destructive force that opposed the American ideas of a peaceful world order, because it was not humanly possible that every national or ethnic group enjoy equality or have equal control of all of its destiny. As Professor Edward Hallett Carr of England wrote in 1939, with a great war looming: "Any international moral order must rest on some hegemony of power." In all human history, no way has been found around this harsh fact.

Alexander the Great's grand vision of world Hellenism and the blending of peoples under one culture rested on his Macedonian phalanx. Without that phalanx Alexander would have never left the shores of Greece. Rome's imposition of law and order—the Pax Romana—and its great stabilization of civilization, which has haunted European minds ever since, was based upon the Roman legion. Rome was not a superior culture when it went out into the world. Like Alexander's Macedon, Rome was considered half barbarian by the older and more cultured regions. But both Rome and Macedon were infinitely better organized and disciplined and armed.

The Anglo-American-Western European hegemony of the nineteenth century came about purely because over most of the world the Atlantic nations enjoyed a monopoly of both economic and military power.

The German challenge was not the act of two generations of madmen, but a humanly logical if ultra-rational determination to destroy a hegemony in which Germany did not share. Japan and Italy joined in the drive for revision for the same reason.

The new Soviet and Chinese challenges followed the same

human pattern. The mere fact of American and European power had to be a challenge to Soviet Russia, and above all, to China, suffering from a hundred years of Western humiliations.

The Western world position rested on American moral, military, and economic power after 1945. American policy-makers, even when they were making mistakes, generally tried to live by the rule of give and take; men like Acheson and Rusk often got into trouble at home because they realized that policy to be effective and prevent out-right conflict had to oscillate between force and appeasement.

Neither force nor appeasement in itself was bad. There were times when each was necessary. Giving women the right to vote was a form of appeasement; opposing Hitlerian ambitions was a necessary use of force. The trouble was that men tended to confuse the two, and use one where the other was needed.

Some demands, like the Soviet Union's on Europe or China's for Asian hegemony, had to be resisted in the simple self-interest of the West. Other demands, such as Nasser's for Suez, and the Panamanians' for adjustment of the United States-owned canal, needed adjudication. Recognizing the need for appeasement, the Western powers generally abandoned their outright colonial position between the years 1945 and 1960. But beyond that, as John Locke wrote in the seventeenth century, men have a right to defend what they cannot legitimately give away.

There were general limits to the Western surrender. There had to be, if the West was to survive under challenge.

The kind of surrender Castro demanded of the United States in Cuba—a complete loss of moral hegemony as well as political influence and economic domination—was not acceptable when considered in the context of the Cold War and the massive Communist challenge to the entire West. Castro got away with it so long only because of the moral and intellectual confusion toward the real world situation that persisted into the 1960's in North America. But Castro's actions were unacceptable long before he actually permitted the USSR to implant its missiles.

326

Africa and most of Asia were European problems, but Hispanic America was America's own. Americans, who had not planted their flag in the region, often failed to understand the resentment to the other forms of hegemony they wielded to the south.

When a prominent Latin American once said: "You Yanquis have always been dominant socially, economically, militarily, and politically on this continent and you want to keep it that way," he was stating an absolute truth. All American policy of the nineteenth century had been aimed at making the United States dominant—and thus secure—in the Western Hemisphere. Yet in the twentieth century, out of moral and intellectual doubts as to the workings of international politics, many Americans wanted to argue the point.

What millions of Americans failed to understand after 1945 was that the matter of a moral world order and a moral hegemony over the world was not in question. Only the nature of that hegemony—a Western moral order or a Communist one—was. If the fact was so badly obscured at San Francisco in 1945 it was because at that time the Western moral supremacy was so immense that it hardly even occurred to men like Vandenberg or American liberals to think about it. They naturally assumed new nations freed from colonialism would follow the general trend of Holland freed from Spain, or a United States released from British rule.

Nothing could have been more wrong. In the third world, as well as the Communist one, the whole fabric of Western civilization, its mores, economics, and politics, was soon in question and soon in dubious battle, while many Westerners argued among themselves as to whether they had any right to engage in such a battle at all.

It was hard for Americans to understand that in the workings of world affairs if they did not remain predominant over the power vacuum that was Hispanic America, some other power soon would be. The United States never, except for a brief

327

fling in 1898, wanted flag hegemony over any other part of the world. But Americans had always felt they had a right to both reasonable order and reasonable trade anywhere in the world and above all in Hispanic America, close to home.

American idealism had fought for a United Nations order in 1945, while at the same time Nelson Rockefeller had worked very hard behind the scenes to have the special Western Hemisphere arrangements such as the Organization of American States and the Chapultepec powers recognized and accepted as co-equal with the UN. Over much little-power opposition, the United States had got its way. Even Vandenberg and Dulles realized what men like Australia's Evatt and the Philippine's Rómulo did not: great powers had no monopoly of brains or morality, but they did have a monopoly of power, and because of the power realities some nations would always be more sovereign than others.

The question was how that sovereignty would be employed. Russia, in Hungary, and China, in Tibet, showed plainly what the Communist employment of power would be. Cuba, America's Hungary, showed that the United States took its own morality seriously, even in the face of extreme provocation.

After the UN was founded, there was a great deal of writing and saying that the purpose of the UN was to "put humanity under the rule of law." Such writings usually recognized that the abolition of great-power status was a *sine qua non* of such a truly legal world. The only trouble was, how did one go about abolishing the fact of power, or abolishing superpowers like the United States or the USSR?

Foster Dulles, the great moralist, skirted this trap when he tried to make the UN a purely political, not a legal, entity. But the UN, and the whole idea of world order, was tinged with wishful thinking. Law, any kind of law, in the end is based on force. A court that cannot enforce its writ soon goes out of business. Western civilization was subject to the same law.

Each age has a natural aggressor: usually a younger culture

with a violent urge to seize the laurels held by its predecessors. One of the causes of the failure of the Nazi-Fascist-Japanese aggression was that none of these powers really tried to confuse things by injecting either ideology or the concept of a moral order into their attempts at aggrandizement. They could win no outside allies; the kind of world they pushed for could have no outside appeal. The Russian and Chinese revisionists, like the French revolutionaries of 1793, did not make this mistake.

Sorel wrote of the French revolutionaries, as they carried their doctrines with Napoleon's armies over Europe: "They confuse . . . the propagation of the new doctrine with the extension of French power, the emancipation of mankind with the greatness of the Republic, the rule of reason with that of France, the liberation of peoples with the conquest of states, the European revolution with the domination of the French Revolution over Europe."

The Russian and most modern revolutions followed the pattern of the French, not the American, Revolution. Substitue the word "Soviet" or the word "Chinese" for "French" in Sorel's terrible indictment, and the meaning of the modern world revolution becomes suddenly and horribly clear.

Yet it is taking millions of Americans a long time to understand it.

The UN they created to solve the modern problem had at first a single, Western ethic. But even in 1945 it had the seeds of multiplicity, through both Communist and emerging third-world membership. When the emerging nations achieved numerical superiority in 1960, the UN was no longer subject to a single moral force or a single set of values but a bewildering multitiplicity of moral values and views of justice.

What did international justice mean?

Arthur Vandenberg, speaking for perhaps a majority of Americans in 1945, considered justice to be self-determination plus the abolition of naked force in the settlement of disputes. Thus, justice to the United States meant the end of Soviet or Chinese

329

domination beyond Communist borders, and the end of Communist attempts to expand influence by arms, subversion, or revolution.

But to Western Europe generally, justice meant the abatement of Soviet pressure—not self-determination anywhere else.

To the Arab world, emerging, justice was the extinction of Israel—which that world saw as its principal threat.

For Africans of all stripes, justice meant the removal, by any means, of all European presence from their continent, including South Africa.

For Indonesians, justice became whatever Sukarno wanted.

For Latin America, justice remained a vague concept, but it was always on the Latins' side in any dispute with the American Colossus—because they were small and the United States was large.

For the USSR, justice was a useful tactical concept to be used like any other weapon. Inside the USSR it meant anything that furthered Soviet interests.

The Chinese contemptuously—and perhaps most honestly—refused to define it.

As Western civilization was challenged, the UN reflected not a single, shining concept of world order or justice, but each and all of these values.

The political framework of the UN was built to keep the status quo, both the Communist and the Western status quo. But the economic nexus of the UN, almost from the start, had a built-in bias for change. And when the Security Council, the political apparatus, became paralyzed by the Cold War, the Assembly and the Economic and Social Council carried the UN into new ground.

The West did not always oppose that shift. Colonies were freed, and billions in economic aid were given outside the UN. But when the shift began to be reflected in UN Assembly or World Health Organization demands for the expulsion of South Africa, and for the redistribution of world wealth generally, and for the immediate end of all vestiges of colonialism—these were

330

changes that affected the West's power position at the very time when it was meeting its hour of maximum danger from the East.

There was sympathy and even agreement with the third world's demands for revision in the West. The historian Toynbee wrote: "You must have some regular method for the perpetual redistribution of power, of wealth, of population, and of the goods of this world as well." But there was no precedent for any of this, and men always tended to fight before surrendering anything they felt they had no right to bargain away. And the demands could not be regarded sympathetically when they coincided with and even assisted the Communist surge for power.

After 1945 the United States of America, trying to stand for its own kind of moral order and principle, had to face two ways.

It had to be liberal with its goods and conservative with its policies on human government. The United States recognized that liberalism was good when it acceded to the satisfaction of human needs. But conservatism was good when it preserved human values that free Western man considered as important as bread. Change was not always progress. Sometimes it was disaster.

And sometimes the United States had to split things down the middle and be neither liberal with its goods nor conservative with its ideas of freedom, but simply defend its own interests. Any policy that does not admit self-interest must be hypocritical, for no government on earth ever adopted a policy without considering its own interests. Self-interest led the United States to support its Batistas and Ubicos in the Caribbean and its Diems and Tshombes in Asia and Africa. These men were not democrats, nor did they uphold the kind of moral or temporal order in which the United States believed. But they were no threat to Western interests. Their interests and Western interests often fused, just as British and Soviet interests fused in 1941 in the war against Hitler.

It was almost impossible for the United States to defend the Western world against attack everywhere and at the same time reform or revitalize that world. It was increasingly impossible while fighting a multifront war to take clear-cut moral stands on everything. No American government could state, as Radio Moscow once stated: "Morals or ethics is the body of norms and rules on the conduct of Soviet peoples . . . only those acts are moral which contribute to the building up of a new Communist society."

But the United States had eventually to view anything that weakened the United States or the West as morally dubious at best, even when it represented the legitimate aspirations of African, Asian, or Latin American peoples.

In Latin America, where any weakening of U. S. predominance always tended to play into the hands of Communist, pro-Communist, or neutralist forces, the United States soon discovered it could not tolerate social revolution. Castro's Cuba was the great watershed of U. S. policy, and the great watershed of moral doubts in official Washington about the right of the United States to act. No American President after Kennedy was likely to permit another Cuba, for any reason.

The United States in its own world interest had to be the great stabilizer in Hispanic America as it had been in Europe and parts of Asia. It had to stabilize even when this damping trampled legitimate local aspirations for change. Peaceful change—and this should be noted—was always acceptable, even when unpalatable. But change caused by revolution, subversion, or war was not peaceful, and not tolerable.

Washington even had to be against legitimate leftist reform groups if these groups tended to neutralism. There was some immorality to all this in terms of the Charter. But in this kind of peace decent nations sometimes had to act as if they were at war. International politics at times resembled domestic; the haves cannot always understand the drives of the have-nots, especially their hate not only of the haves but their whole system.

Ironically, America most likely would have taken up an explosive stand against colonialism everywhere except for the Communist challenge. The United States traditionally stood for the independence of all peoples and self-determination as far as practicable. But the Cold War, by its frustrating nature and its devolvement into Communist support of disorders and the so-

332

called wars of national liberation—all aimed at Western influence—torpedoed this. The operational problem in politics for the United States became that of not only defending the West but of trying to hold it together while the colonial order was being changed. This made it impossible for the United States to take rigid moral positions vis-à-vis colonialism or self-determination.

In each colonial world-European dispute nations such as France, Britain, or Belgium—all allied with the United States by treaty, blood, culture, and common purpose—continually invoked the anti-Soviet alliance and the Communist danger and placed their good will and future cooperation on the table. The United States could not simply take a black-white view, or back one side or the other completely.

For example, the United States could not back African aspirations in South Africa or the Congo without weakening its only real allies, nor could it trample on or be deaf to such aspirations without sacrificing potential Assembly majorities on Cold War questions. The issue was actually *timing,* not principle. The demands for "freedom now" generally seemed to coincide with Soviet pressure. With bases, raw materials, treaties, and world order itself at stake, anyone who said the United States could take one blanket position and not deviate from it was ignorant of the real situation.

The U. S. government from Truman to Kennedy tried to be honest. The questions were complex. Algeria, South Africa, the Congo were not amenable to black and white answers. Rigidity either way only showed rigid or fixed minds.

By 1961 colonialism as a world position was finished; Stevenson's stands in the UN revealed that Kennedy's administration knew this. But the United States could go too far, by pressuring the Netherlands to accede to unreasonable Indonesian demands for West New Guinea. As Pierre Ryckmans wrote with considerable irony: "If the foreign authority happens to be a colored people, nobody dreams of condemning this form of colonialism."

Some of the same people who failed to condemn also considered China had legitimate interests in dominating East Asia, at the same time they were adamant that American influence get out of Vietnam.

The U. S. government changed very little in its policies from Truman through Kennedy; partisan claims only made it seem so. In this mulitfront war the Congo or New Guinea or Cuba or Vietnam was only one front. And while overall goals were finite and coherent—peace and world order and protection of Western society—they often became seemingly conflicting when pursued in different places.

At home, the United States pushed armament in defense of the status quo of Western civilization. It pushed armament among its allies abroad and shipped weapons everywhere.

It accepted changes in the world political order provided such changes were peaceful and did not aid the Communist side. If they did not aid the Communists, often even violent changes, like Nasser's adventures in trying to conquer Yemen, were tolerated.

The United States wanted to alter the Soviet territorial arrangements in Europe, and thus it was also revolutionary, though half-heartedly. Meanwhile, the refusal to acquiesce to Soviet or Chinese regional domination of Eurasia blocked any real détente.

The United States tried to block any changes that weakened its own diplomatic, economic, or military position in the Western Hemisphere.

All was part of the whole.

It was a policy that was continually blasted as hypocrisy and imperialism by Arabian slave-traders, Middle Eastern persecutors of Jews and Christians, caste-segregated Hindus, and Indonesian colonialists putting down headhunters in New Guinea, as well as Communists. It was a policy that brought the United States into confrontation not only with China and the USSR but with the forces of revolutionary change everywhere.

The Cold War horribly complicated the American viewpoint toward revolution. Americans had long considered themselves a revolutionary society; they were the first colonial rebels. They had, in this tradition, supported the Hungarian and other Euro-

334

pean revolts of 1848, the Irish rebellion, and the idea of independence for India. They applauded the Hungarian rising of 1956, and the failure to aid it produced real trauma.

Gradually, however, it was dawning on Americans that revolution did not bring freedom in every case. The Soviet revolution of 1917 unleashed a new and terrible tyranny, not only on Russians but on the world. Each succeeding social upheaval cast genuine doubt upon the concept of the goodness of revolution itself. The Castro revolution in Cuba was disastrous not only for the U. S. position but for Cuba.

The Iraqi, Algerian, and Santo Domingan revolts from 1957 through 1965 each played into the hands of world Communism, and caused anger and confusion in American minds. Many of these revolts Americans felt were justified, but each one only did further damage to the Western power position without doing any lasting good to anyone.

This anger, and desire for order, turned America from one of the most revolutionary nations on earth to probably the most status-quo-minded by 1965. The logic of the age seemed to have gone beyond peaceful change—which was still a cardinal principle of American policy.

The Communist forces seemed to have understood that the risks inherent in nuclear warfare were unacceptable; even the Chinese in practical terms avoided direct confrontation. But while still shuddering from the effects of the last great war and haunted by visions of another one, the postwar era quickly embarked on a new age of limited conflict. Peaceful coexistence merely meant the recognition of Western nuclear superiority, not traditional peace. Each time Soviet pressure backed off from Europe after a confrontation, like the ones in 1948 and 1962, Communist pressures intensified elsewhere. From 1948 to 1950 men talked of Soviet power receding in Europe and some felt the USSR was settling down at last. After 1962, when Khrushchev blinked first over Cuba, men talked of Soviet power draining out of Europe, never seeming to realize that a new Korea-style war—the one in Vietnam—had already begun.

General Giap, the canny Vietnamese who beat the French at Dienbienphu, stated candidly that, if the West did not discover how to fight the new subversion and wars of national liberation, it was through. And gradually, Washington policy-makers believed it; in no other way could the American policies of 1965 be understood.

The United States, standing for peace, was fighting a series of limited wars. The prospect of abolishing all war broke against one bitter fact. Limited war was deplorable, but it was the most useful instrument man had ever found for his rational pursuit of his ultra-rational goals. Limited war, which included revolution, subversion, and insurgency not only in Vietnam or Laos but wherever it could be started in Asia, Africa, or Hispanic America—or wherever, as in Cuba, it started itself without an initial push by Communism—was the Communist powers' last, best hope of forcing major political change and of destroying the Western world position.

Both the USSR and Red China, even while at odds with each other and engaged in their own power struggle for Eurasia, supported any revolt against the Western status quo as far as possible without coming into nuclear confrontation. They openly called such wars "good."

And such wars were becoming endemic and threatened to change the balance of the world while millions of Americans were still paralyzed by something no longer relevant: the nuclear mushroom cloud.

The United States began to face a situation in which it was the only effective watchman on the walls of Western freedom, a job no American ever wanted. The job posed difficult choices: to submit to continuous erosion, to blow the whistle on the game and force nuclear showdown, or to raise the ante in limited fashion by entering the morally ambiguous contest of crushing small wars where it seemed feasible. All of these policies were dangerous. But as Machiavelli had dryly written some four hundred years before, no nation could always follow a safe policy or avoid one difficulty without running head-on into another.

336

After 1962 things seemed peaceful. But the U. S. government was being forced to make continuous estimates of the situation, understand and probe dangers, sense tides, and act according to its interests. It had to face two ways; it had to stand for stated principle and sometimes it had to trample what some men considered justice. But perhaps Thucydides had summed it all up long before, in reporting the Athenians' reply to a Corinthian petition during Athens' great power struggle with despotic Sparta:

"It has ever been the law that the weaker should be subject to the stronger. . . . Calculations of interest have made you take up the cry of justice—a consideration which no one ever brought forward to hinder his ambition if he had an opportunity of gaining anything by might."

19.

Cash, Cyprus, and the Lamps of China

A HISTORIAN once remarked while visiting a graveyard of the French Foreign Legion, "It would be hard to convince the men buried here that the period between 1815 and 1914 was a time of peace." The nineteenth century was merely devoid of big wars between big powers or coalitions of big powers. It was a time of incessant conflict on the periphery of Western civilization and of limited campaigns—from the French conquest of Algeria in the 1830's to the Anglo-French-Turkish attack on the Crimea in the 1850's to the final emergence of a new Europe in the series of swift, decisive military operations Prussia waged against Denmark, Austria, and France.

It was a time when power flowed in one direction or the other, nations rose and others declined. It was a time when the United States, beginning from almost nothing, grew to great-power status, not wholly peacefully. Corpses of American Indians, the bones of the Mexican empire of Santa Ana, and countless Confederates strewed the way. Recognition of American power status throughout the world came only after another brief but decisive war against the crumbling power of Spain.

In the imposition and maintenance of their kind of order France and Great Britain maintained huge standing armies—the British had a Colonial army of 500,000 in the 1800's—and fought without respite somewhere in the world, one year in China, the next in India or the Sudan. Some French fort was always besieged somewhere; if not in black Africa or Madagascar, certainly in Indo-China or Morocco.

Peace was relative: men in London or Paris considered they were at peace. The Plains Indians of North America, the Kabyles

338

of Algeria, and the tribes of the Northwest Frontier in India would have put an entirely different name on it if anyone had consulted them.

In the same way, the peace that followed 1945 was purely relative. Again, as following Waterloo in 1815, the logic of the times gravitated against another general war, and the technology of the atom bomb and missile-delivery systems added a potent argument to an already universal feeling. But the same historians who agreed and wrote that all recorded human history from about 4,000 B.C. through 1945 was primarily the story of successive human social units—tribes, city states, empires—trying to extend their power or influence over others, continually wrote that experience was not decisive. In fact, in the West, and not only among liberal elements, a great contempt for experience had developed. But any examination of history after 1945 would show that the pattern had not changed. Only the techniques were different.

Between 1945 and 1965 there were more than a score of wars or armed conflicts. Some were mere skirmishes, even though they decided territorial or social issues. Others were very respectable wars by any standard. Korea was one of these.

Any list of these peacetime wars would include the following:

1. The Chinese Communist Revolution, 1945–1949.
2. Vietnam, 1946–1954.
3. Greece, 1947–1949.
4. India–Pakistan–Kashmir, 1947.
5. Malaya, 1948–1958.
6. Israel–Arab States, 1948–1949.
7. Indonesia–Netherlands, 1949.
8. Taiwan–Red China, 1949–1965.
9. Korea, 1950–1953.
10. Indonesia (Moluccas), 1950.
11. Vietnam, 1954–1965.
12. Algeria, 1954–1963.
13. Suez, 1956.

339

14. Hungary, 1956.
15. Cyprus, 1956–1960.
16. Laos, 1960–1965.
17. Cuba, 1961 and 1962.
18. Goa, 1962.
19. India–China, 1962.
20. Congo, 1960–1965.
21. Yemen, 1962.
22. Sarawak, Irian, 1963.
23. Malaysia–Indonesia, 1963–1965.
24. Cyprus, 1964.
25. Santo Domingo, 1965.
26. India–Pakistan, 1965.

All of these conflicts were brought about by political conditions and were an extension of politics by armed force in the classic pattern. Each, one way or another, decided something that would not or could not be determined by diplomacy. Each of these wars altered the borders of peoples, determined the fate of governments and nations, and changed the balance of power in many areas of the world. Some of them did not seem decisive, particularly those still being waged in 1965 and 1966. This was only because the final outcome still lay in the balance.

None of these wars was accidental, not even the one between India and Pakistan in September, 1965. All of them grew out of definite political or geographic conditions, and all of them were fought for a finite purpose.

The seizure of Portuguese Goa by India in December 1961 was a typical, classic case of territorial revision through armed aggression by a larger power against a smaller. Goa was a tiny colonial enclave on the Indian coast; it had been ruled by Portugal for 451 years. Its 700,000 people showed no signs of wishing to join the mainstream of Hinduism; in fact, many were Catholic Christians. But Nehru, particularly after France ceded its similar enclaves in 1954, found the Portuguese colonial presence on the Indian subcontinent "intolerable." He tried to force the

Portuguese out by every diplomatic means. When all else failed, he ordered the Indian Army to invade. The weak Portuguese defenses quickly crumbled, and Goa was incorporated into India.

Both the UN's U Thant and the U. S. Ambassador to India protested. Both were ignored. What was revealed was not only Nehru's hypocrisy on "nonviolence," but the fact that even basically peaceful nations would use force to obtain, or hold, something they really wanted.

India's aggression was successful because of several factors. First, the military action resulted in a complete Portuguese defeat. Second, the USSR vetoed a UN Security Council call for a cease-fire; anything that damaged a NATO nation in any way was supported by the Soviet Union. Third, European colonialism was in very bad odor everywhere, although Asian or African colonialism, such as practiced by Mao of Red China, Sukarno of Indonesia, or Nasser of Egypt, was willfully not recognized by most of the world.

For example, any European power holding the Vale of Kashmir under the terms by which India took possession would have aroused a terrible storm of protest. India's claim was based on the cession of Kashmir by its ruling rajah, a Hindu, to India in 1947, although eighty percent of the Kashmir population was Moslem and preferred Pakistan. India occupied the area, fought a sharp, bitter war with Pakistan in the 1940's to keep possession, kept the Kashmiri premier in prison, and crushed all local independence movements with police action. Twice the UN Security Council passed resolutions calling for a plebiscite to decide Kashmir's disposition, because the Kashmir question was always an ominous source of war between India and Pakistan. India contemptuously refused UN advice, stating that Kashmir was an "integral" part of India and beyond the UN's jurisdiction—precisely the same argument used by the worst of the European colonial regimes.

Likewise, Nasser's adventures in Yemen, beginning in 1962, were part of an Egyptian plan to expand Egyptian influence and control within the Arab world. If a European power had sent occupation troops in to fight a legitimate government as did Nasser, the uproar would have been overwhelming.

Indonesia's territorial demands followed much the same pattern. The threat of armed force gained Sukarno the control of Western New Guinea from the Dutch; the United States put certain pressures on Holland to keep the war from breaking out. These pressures resulted in turning over vast areas and several hundred thousand inhabitants of non-Indonesian stock to Sukarno. Again, the threat of force was decisive.

Sukarno's pressures against the newly formed Federation of Malaysia, beginning in 1964, however, were less successful. Malaysia was the creation of, and was backed by, Britain—and Britain was not quite a Portugal or Holland. Indonesia, claiming (with some historic but no modern logic) that the Malayan areas were part of an ancient Indonesian empire, could not invade or fight British power, but a long, intermittent, and troublesome campaign of infiltration and subversion was begun against the Federation.

In one sense Sukarno's argument against Malaysia was correct: the Federation *was* jerry-built out of several ethnically hostile groups, primarily Malays and overseas Chinese in Singapore, and it *was* formed primarily to block both Indonesian and Red Chinese expansion in Southeast Asia. Economically, the areas included in Malaysia were important to the West. But the fact that Britain wanted to keep its economic interests intact in no way affected Indonesia—except as this blunted Sukarno's visions of empire and absorption of Malaya.

"Colonialism" was far from dead around the world. It had simply changed its aspect and image. Sukarno's hopes to bring down Malaysia were also far from dead, even in the face of British power. Indonesia could not fight British naval and air strength, but Malaysia, in its hostile groups, carried the seeds of its own dissolution, and in the summer of 1965 Singapore seceded from the Federation, the first step in that direction.

342

The United Nations played different roles in all these limited wars. In a few it was not involved at all, except for observing. In others it vainly tried to forge some kind of settlement short of bloodshed. It is significant that the most fervent supporters of the idea of a UN rarely wanted to discuss Goa, Kashmir, or Indonesia, cases in which the UN had been proved helpless. Indonesia, in fact, was so contemptuous of the UN that it withdrew in 1965, the first power to do so.

In no case, between 1945 and 1965, did the United Nations Organization prevent or even drastically alter the outcome of any small war. The often-advanced claims that it did do not bear inspection. UN observers merely established a cease-fire line in Kashmir in 1949 where the fighting had stopped. UNEF only formalized the end of combat in Palestine in 1949 exactly where the flow of battle had left off, due to Arab exhaustion. Four years of UN intervention in the Congo merely came full circle, and delayed, did not prevent, the final outcome: chaos in the provinces, Belgians in economic control, a strong Tshombe. As in Kashmir, the UN in 1956 accepted a tacit status quo in Hungary, and again at Suez UN forces only took over a line from national forces that had already decided to withdraw.

The Korean War was the most successful UN operation. But it was successful only because the United States used the UN as its instrument of policy, doing ninety percent of the fighting and providing ninety percent of the material resources. The UN influence itself, finally, strove only to restore the status quo of 1950; the UN drive was never to work for justice but to accept anything that prevented or seemed to prevent a major war between the great powers. And the United States would have intervened in Korea in 1950 with or without UN approval, as Washington made abundantly clear.

The UN Court of International Justice solved only *one* territorial dispute during its first twenty years of life, the case of the Channel Islands. France and Britain disputed sovereignty of certain Channel islands, including Minquiers. The matter was put to arbitration, and on November 17, 1953, the Court found for Britain. The decision stood, because neither of the disputants really gave a damn.

That was the problem. The UN, having no force of its own, could not solve any dispute where either side cared enough to use force, either in pressing a claim or defending one. The UN was a tool of the powers, but year after year men refused to regard it as such, trying to give it a mythical life of its own.

The UN did involve itself deeply in colonial matters, but again all it could do in this area was to ratify the decisions made elsewhere, either over negotiation tables or on the battlefield. Algeria was a case in point.

Algerian rebels opened up a colonial war against French rule in 1954. In the Tenth General Assembly Session, beginning in September, 1955, the Arab states sympathetic to the Algerians forced the issue of bringing up the Algerian question. France called this unjustified interference, which under the Charter it was, and announced that it would withdraw its delegation from the UN. This produced so much consternation, even among the Arab states, that the matter was dropped. Later, France protested Egyptian and other Arab interventions, mostly arms smuggling, on the side of the rebels. Again, the matter was tacitly dropped.

The UN never effectively influenced the Algerian settlement. The matter was fought out for years, and finally negotiated by France, giving Algeria independence in 1963. The UN immediately ratified the decision by giving Algeria membership.

Possibly the most promising peace-making action between 1945 and 1965 was the tentative nuclear test ban of July 25, 1963, signed by the United States and USSR and other nuclear powers. But this agreement again was reached completely outside the UN, and the UN was not allowed into the negotiations.

For after 1960, with the Council hamstrung by the veto and the Assembly showing more and more of an anti-big-power bias, the UN actually lost all ability to act. The Acheson Plan, pushed through by the United States in October, 1950, had

344

been designed to bypass the veto, by allowing the Assembly to take up security and peace-keeping matters when and if the Council failed to act. But Acheson did not anticipate the increasing third-world majority that swamped the UN. When a majority of the Assembly consisted of new, ex-colonial nations, the Assembly treated its new responsibility with ever-increasing irresponsibility, continually ignoring the power realities of the world.

Dag Hammarskjöld's action to save the Congo's borders had been both the Indian summer and the death blow of the organization; Hammarskjöld's own death was symbolic. The little powers, particularly the African states, demanded the Congo operation. But they could not support it, let alone agree on the precise course it should take. Understandably, after U Thant assumed direction and did away with Tshombe—the one point of agreement—the operation dribbled away. Symbolically again, Moise Tshombe returned to the Congo the same day the last UN troops left.

The Congo bankrupted the UN primarily because it was so utterly futile. There was too great a gap between expectations and the final reality. The European nations had never believed in it. The United States had allowed itself to get entangled in UN politics instead of taking action on the side that might have solved things more quickly and less expensively, as Hammarskjöld hoped. The Soviet Union got itself frozen out and suffered a defeat. The Red Chinese replaced the Soviets as the main supporters of African nationalism, though their success in exploiting this, like the Soviet success in the Islamic world, was strictly limited. The African neighbors of the Congo were utterly disgusted with the end result. The money, the extra $200 million per year, could have been raised easily if the UN had been accomplishing something, or had it been furthering a common big-power purpose. For example, the United States and the USSR alone were spending approximately $120 *billion* per year on armaments, which they did not consider futile at all. Armaments guaranteed that neither side would break the balance of terror.

345

What happened to the UN in the Congo operation was that the small powers could not or would not pay for UN actions—even those that pleased them. The big powers, once effective control of such operations had slipped from the Security Council, were not interested. France and the USSR refused, on reasonable legal grounds, to pay voluntarily for an operation they had not voted for. This hole in the UN special assessment fund left the UN at the brink of disaster, for lack of money.

A special UN bond sale in the United States plugged the gap one year. But by 1964 American opinion had revolted at paying virtually all of these costs, as well it might. The United States was asked to pay the piper, while the Assembly insisted upon its right to call the tune—simply because of an African plurality, which all told did not have the population or one-twentieth the wealth of the American Republic.

The United States, when it pushed the Security Council bypass in October, 1950, thought it was finding a way around the Soviet veto. It was, however, putting the UN into the same unrealistic limbo that idealism had carried the League of Nations into in the 1920's. *There could be no dichotomy between voting power and actual national power in the UN.* The men at Dumbarton Oaks knew and accepted this.

All the idealistic and legal arguments to the contrary broke on the simple fact that great powers had not surrendered, and never would, that kind of sovereignty. All notions of world order that began on the idea of a voluntary surrender of sovereignty were worse than useless; they were time-consuming and dangerous. Yet an amazing number of otherwise intelligent people called for this.

Sumner Welles and his staff never expected any such theoretical nonsense, although they understandably did not anticipate the deepness of the cleavage between East and West, or the extent of Soviet ambitions.

When the Cold War began, President Truman might have given the UN another chance for viable life, by remaking it into

346

an anti-Communist alliance. This was not nearly so radical a notion as some people thought. The UN had come into being as an anti-Axis alliance, and only gradually turned into a world forum. During the war the United States had had no hesitancy over dominating the various united nations, or using its immense moral and material strength to get its way on strategy or pronouncements. FDR usually got what he wanted, because he saw to it that he did.

But the curious idea that in *Weltpolitik* peace was different from war and the notion of universality torpedoed this. By 1955 it had been agreed on all sides that all nations should be taken into the UN, without regard for the most salient fact of international life—the East-West power struggle. Thus the UN, instead of becoming more significant, actually became more and more irrelevant to the real issues of the era. Neutralism had a place in the world, but only an insignificant one. No major power was a neutral.

Truman took his policies outside the UN, and other administrations did the same, while maintaining a façade of sincere support of the organization. The UN was only used when, as in Korea, it seemed to offer reasonable opportunities for success. But because the *idea* of the UN was strong, all U. S. governments tried to face two ways on the issue. None really used American power to the fullest extent inside the organization.

Significantly, Khrushchev once told a British confrere that he despised Eisenhower and de Gaulle for different reasons: one failed to use the power he had, and the other tried to wield power he did not enjoy.

Kennedy, in turn, faced a UN in which the balance of power had slipped over to the horde of underdeveloped neutrals. Where Dulles had tried to argue this group into seeing the rightness of the American cause, Kennedy tried a different tack. He catered to this third world in speech and tone, in the hope that since the third world needed the United States more than the United States needed it, American leadership would be accepted. This did not happen. Until Kennedy showed the real face of American power in the Cuban confrontation of 1962, all the United States got from neutrals in the Assembly was abuse.

The third world did need the United States; it desperately required American material aid. But most of these nations valued a psychological independence and an inferiority-born urge to insult American power even more. There was almost a neurotic compulsion to insult the United States—the symbol of what was most successful in the hated Western civilization—and to hamstring it in its fight for survival.

These nations were the real beneficiaries of the UN; they got almost all the good from its appendage organizations. Yet they did more than anyone else in the 1960's to destroy it.

When the UN tried to become truly neutral ground, its very ground narrowed almost to the vanishing point. There was no reason why either East or West should support a quarreling, neurotic, bitter Assembly that benefitted neither side.

In a truly peaceful world, the United States could have behaved with the "quiet dignity" and even the good humor that men like George Kennan, the first architect of containment, argued it should. But in this kind of peace, which was not peace at all but an era of protracted limited conflict, restricted on one side by a balance of terror but illuminated by clashes all over the globe, Americans could hardly accept such ground rules. The stoning of an American embassy became more and more a significant political act, detracting from American power and prestige. Power and prestige are not really separable, although some Americans tried to argue the fact.

By the time Rusk came into his own in the Johnson Administration, the United States was no longer willing to continue cajolery of the third world in the face of calumny. Rusk was perfectly content to close an American embassy, or withdraw American wheat. He did both, closing U. S. offices in Africa and stopping aid to Indonesia, though he was forced, for reasons of the federal Executive prerogative, to oppose certain Congressional measures in the same vein he did not really dispute.

348

Rusk's dissatisfactions with the UN were several: (1) the organization could no longer aid the United States in its battle against encroaching Communist power; (2) the UN seemed determined to create disorder and weaken the Western position by attacks on the vestiges of colonialism and even the Western economic position. Reasonable strategy required that the United States keep predominance in the fringes of Asia and over all Hispanic America. When the Assembly majority began, after 1960, to regard this predominance as co-equal with colonialism, both Mr. Johnson and Mr. Rusk had had enough. They could not say this for public consumption, however, because the *idea* of the UN, as opposed to its reality, was still politically strong.

It was this image, or idea, of a UN that defeated the United States in its battle to force delinquent nations to pay their arrears during the funding crisis of 1964 and 1965.

When France and the USSR refused to pay for the Congo operation, a considerable body of thought in the State Department privately agreed with them, both in terms of legality and practicality. There were always elements of illegality surrounding the Acheson Plan, since it violated the agreements at Dumbarton Oaks. It also opened up some dangerous paths, since no big power could or should be expected to obey the wishes or dictates of a group of smaller powers to its own detriment.

These career men argued behind the scenes that by supporting the unlimited right of the Assembly to engage in "peace-keeping" missions, the United States could find itself someday paying for a UN operation to free Portuguese Angola, or a drive to force Europeans out of South Africa or Rhodesia. The United States supported neither of these actions, but there was already majority support for them in the Assembly. It was completely within the realm of possibility than the Assembly might vote them in the future, and under the Acheson Plan the United States could not veto them.

But the majority sentiment in Washington prevailed, and this sentiment wanted to apply Article 19 of the Charter to the Soviet refusal to pay its assessments. Article 19 provided that any nation refusing to pay assessments lost its Assembly vote after two years in arrears.

The Russians, French, and eleven other nations in arrears fought back on the grounds that assessments by the Assembly were illegal; only the Security Council could engage in peace-keeping as outlined in the original Charter. The issue was taken to the World Court. The Court upheld the position that Article 19 did apply to both the Congo and the Middle Eastern operations. But the USSR and France refused to acquiesce in the decision. They refused also to pay, and it was the more than sixty million dollars owed by them that threw the UN into bankruptcy.

Unwilling to keep paying the Soviet share by "loans" or bond sales, the United States informed the regular UN session convened in December, 1964, that the United States would invoke Article 19, and demand its enforcement. Adlai Stevenson, who did not agree with the U. S. position, announced it reluctantly. Then, in order to give teeth to the stand and convince the members it meant business, the United States withheld its financial pledges to the UN Economic and Social Council operations until the question was settled.

The gambit did not work. The USSR agreed to pay the money it owed, but only with a string attached. It would make a "voluntary" payment of the arrears provided the United States dropped its insistence that Article 19 applied to assessments for the Congo. The USSR was going to force the issue of the Assembly's power to vote order-keeping assessments, and it showed itself completely willing to destroy the UN in the process if necessary.

De Gaulle's France took the same position. De Gaulle saw no further use to the UN, anyway.

As these positions hardened, all Assembly business ground to a halt. With the question of whether the USSR and other powers could vote unresolved, no votes could be taken, except on minor procedural matters. Finally, in early 1965 the session was adjourned, since nothing could be accomplished.

The U. S. stand had widespread American domestic support. The American public was increasingly tired of paying for up to two-thirds of the entire costs of the UN. Budgets had swelled immensely since 1945, but the United States was one of the few powers that had been willing to increase its assessment. Some of the most vocal and most consistently anti-Western nations among the "neutrals" were also among those who paid the least to support the UN, and fought all efforts to get them to pay more. All of this added up to much American sentiment for the U. S. position on Article 19, especially in Congress. A group of Republican Senators issued a resolution calling for the United States to stand firm, and the resolution had much quiet Democrat support. But the idea of the UN was too strong, and the United States had got itself in a trap.

Withdrawal of American money from the humanitarian and social works of the UN meant the collapse of those works. Very shortly after the money was withheld, it was again released. The United States did not want that kind of image.

The U. S. stand got no support in the General Assembly. Quiet soundings showed that a full majority of nations would refuse to back the imposition of Article 19 against the USSR. This should have been anticipated, but was not. In fact, some nations considered that it was the United States, not the USSR, that was trying to wreck the UN.

By February, 1965, as the UN adjourned, it was already clear that the United States would have to seek a face-saving device for backing down. The idea of the UN was still so powerful that neither President Johnson nor any other responsible American official dared risk being a party to its dissolution.

The enormous problem for the United States in 1965 became how to extricate itself from the payments-issue stand. The UN was still useful as a sounding board and a symbol, and it still provided many humanitarian functions. Washington decided to try to keep it in business.

If the voting issue were pressed, only two things could happen: the UN Assembly would defy the United States, or, if the United States won, the USSR would withdraw. Either step appeared a mortal blow. But if the issue were compromised with

351

face-saving language, it was obvious that there would be no further peace-keeping missions for the UN, because no one would ever be required again to pay for them. Either course seemed likely to deal the UN, its *coup de grâce,* even in the eyes of its fervent supporters.

Many men had seen this kind of impasse coming. The financial arrangements for the UN had always been poorly planned. Thomas K. Finletter in 1946 wrote, "A carefully restricted taxing power, for revenue only, will be necessary. The UN could be paralyzed if it had to rely on the good will of the nation-states to provide the necessary funds." The problem was that, not being a "government," the UN had no power to tax, and never would have. It had been considered that the potential loss of voting power would keep the nations in line.

The final compromise, in August, 1965, solved nothing and satisfied no one. Arthur Goldberg, whom President Johnson appointed as Ambassador to the UN shortly after Adlai Stevenson's death, announced that (1) the United States had abandoned all efforts to take away the delinquent nations' votes under Article 19, but (2) it still adhered to its position that they should be stripped of their rights. The rule, after all, was clear, whether the Assembly chose to enforce it or not. But, both to save face and to mollify the immediate anger in Congress, Goldberg asserted that the United States hereafter would reserve the right to refuse to pay for any future UN activity "if, in our view, strong and compelling reasons exist for doing so."

Goldberg made this announcement only after considerable controversy within the government. Britain and other European nations had urged the United States to give in on the issue, but to make no public pronouncement of the fact. Giving in with any kind of fanfare, the British advised, would only encourage other nations not to pay their dues. This seemed very likely, but Rusk, for one, insisted on a public pronouncement.

Rusk, and many of his associates, felt that the damage done would be not to the United States but to the Assembly itself. Rusk personally was disgusted at the Assembly attitude on the payments issue. Other State Department men wanted to open the door for an American refusal to obey future Assembly votes. After some of the irresponsible voting in the Assembly—where South Africa had been expelled from some organizations, and powers representing less than five percent of the shipping tonnage of the world had voted down maritime measures wanted by all the great sea-going nations—the U. S. State Department no longer put much faith in that body.

Goldberg himself was startled by some of the attitudes toward the UN he encountered in the State Department and Congress. The feeling that the United States should get all the advantage it could out of the Article 19 hassle, including the right to disassociate itself from any future UN move of which it disapproved, was strong. This attitude bothered Goldberg, who still liked to think of the UN in terms of international law, and continually fell into that trap when discussing it.

Arthur Goldberg, on taking office, resolved to counterbalance the denigration of the UN in the Cabinet more effectively than Adlai Stevenson had been able to do. He was a strong personality, and an effective advocate and mediator. His replacement of Stevenson, however, did no more to change the lasting courses of American policy than the replacement of Vyshinsky by Gromyko had affected Soviet policy. National policies were not made in New York, and never by UN ambassadors.

The immediate execution of the UN was thus postponed, but only at the cost of a further weakening of its prestige and a loss of support from some of its most sincere backers in Washington. Nor was the problem of ready cash resolved; even if the Russians paid back assessments and no other nations took advantage of the new loophole, the UN was still almost crippled by lack of finances. *Peace-keeping projects, as far as the UN was concerned, were a thing of the past.*

Actually, new policy forces like UNEF, still on guard in the Middle East, or ONUC in the Congo, had already been ruled out even before the Article 19 issue arose. The Cyprus crisis of 1964 proved this case in point.

353

Cyprus, an Eastern Mediterranean island forty-five miles south of Turkey and some six hundred miles east of Greece, had come under British influence in the 1870's, and Britain annexed it during World War I. It remained a rather lovely and reasonably prosperous—compared to Greece or Turkey—British possession until the rising tide of ethnic consciousness provoked a Greek Cypriot rebellion in 1956.

Greek Cypriots comprised eighty percent of the population, Turkish Cypriots some eighteen percent. The bad blood between these ethnic and religious groups went back to the time of the Crusades, though under British rule any conflict was irrelevant.

In 1956 Greek Cypriots felt the call of blood, and demanded *enosis,* union with the Greek mainland. It was purely emotional, not an economic, desire; the Greek economy was bogged down in its normal chaos.

And Cypriots, under British law, had more rights than Greek citizens had in Athens, which some Americans of Greek descent tried to point out to them. For one thing, they could enter the United States under British passports and under Commonwealth quotas. The Greeks, however, under their Ethnarch, Archbishop Makarios, began a long war of subversion and terror against the British. It was a classic guerrilla conflict, in which at one point Greek strategy called for the deliberate murder of British soldiers and subjects on the streets or in their homes whenever it could be done with impunity. The tactics worked. The British rulers had no stomach to reply in kind, although Cyprus was the strategic base of their Middle Eastern armed forces.

In 1960 the British agreed to leave. This 1960 Cyprus decision marked a final turning point in British colonial policy. After Cyprus, the British adopted a policy of granting independence to any colony that seemed prepared to fight on the issue, whether such independence weakened Western order or not. Many people in Washington were rather horrified at this decision. But, as the British point out, it was their soldiers and civilians being killed, and their government taking all the third-world and Soviet propaganda blasts by trying to hang on. The complete evacuation of British Africa came soon after, raising UN membership to more than one hundred.

But the Cyprus affair was not a purely Cypriot-British imbroglio. The Turkish people of Cyprus had supported British rule because they had no desire to become a part of Greece. During the long rebellion, in which many Turkish Cypriots served in the British law forces, Turkish-Greek relations soured. The Greek government was understandably interested in getting control of Cyprus. The Turkish government was even more understandably concerned that the rights of the Turkish minority be completely protected.

The British, by 1960, only wanted out, though they retained the right to maintain military bases. When the decision was reached, the *London Chronicle* thundered: "Thank God!" But Turkey put a veto on Cyprus' *enosis* with Greece, even to the point of threatening war.

With a flareup between the NATO partners at stake, Britain finally was able to hammer out an agreement in neutral Zürich between all parties. Cyprus would become independent inside the Commonwealth, and Greece, Turkey, and Britain would all guarantee its constitution. But that constitution reflected the ethnic and national problems flaring with increasing bitterness everywhere.

The President of Cyprus was to be Greek, and Makarios took office. The Vice President was to be a Turk, and Fazil Kutchuk filled the post. Kutchuk had veto power over any of Makarios' actions in the field of defense, foreign affairs, or internal security; furthermore, ethnic quotas of 60–40 were set for police and army. In effect, the Turkish minority of eighteen percent held complete veto power over the ethnic Greek state, and the power to block *enosis* forever. Britain, Turkey, and Greece each reluctantly accepted the arrangement as the best that could be had.

Makarios and the Greek Cypriot community did not. Makarios and Kutchuk were like two scorpions in one bottle. Finally, Makarios, with the support of almost every Greek on the island, set out to break the constitution. His actions in time showed he did not care if such breaking destroyed NATO, involved Greece and Turkey in war, or even caused World War III. Ethnic and religious passions are like that.

Bad blood, and Makarios' maneuverings by December 21, 1963, caused fighting to flare between the two communities. Immediately, the fighting turned into full civil war, with hideous atrocities on both sides. To Greeks the only good Turk was a dead one, and vice versa, regardless of sex or age. Both communities devolved into separate, armed camps, with the Turks getting the worst of it.

Under the Zürich agreement, both Greece and Turkey kept small garrisons on the island, and these soldiers soon were involved in the fighting, though not against each other—yet. The British government, alarmed, flew a sizable contingent of British troops back to Cyprus. But the British had already had their fill of trying to put the island down by force, and with an army of only 182,000 men Britain did not have the power. Britain merely tried to referee, as it had in Palestine, and with about equal results. The Turks demanded partition of the island. The Greeks demanded control of all of it. The fighting went on.

London called NATO into session, since this was a NATO matter. Greece and Turkey were becoming inflamed on the issue, each supporting the demands of its own ethnic group all the way. London asked that a NATO force be sent to Cyprus; and the United States, with exteme reluctance, approved. The United States was always quick, even now, to criticize British handling of crises in the colonial world, though extremely reluctant to assume any responsibility. But Makarios, as Cyprus President, vetoed the use of any NATO force to stop the fighting; legally, it was his right.

Makarios demanded that the UN send troops, and adjudicate the whole matter. London and Washington were horrified at the notion. UN intervention would open up a channel for the USSR into a serious NATO imbroglio, and involve the passions of the neutral or third world. Makarios was playing a dangerous but definite game. He understood that the UN, from its history in the Congo, would tend to back a formal or recognized regime. He knew UN intervention would also tend to keep Turkey—which was immensely more powerful than Greece, much closer to the island, and much more inclined to invade—at bay.

From January until March, 1964, America, England, Turkey, and Greece quibbled and dribbled the ball, trying to keep the UN out, trying to keep the war damped. But the killing on Cyprus continued; the British did not have the power or the will to open fire and halt the fighting.

However, this was a European matter, and most of the third world was not interested. Since justice involved only the fight against colonialism, it could not be involved here; Afro-Asia passed. The USSR, for several reasons, wisely decided not to interfere. Intervention seemed likely to produce direct confrontation with NATO, and Khrushchev was still quivering from Cuba.

Finally, the warfare on Cyprus reached such proportions, with hundreds killed and wounded, that it seemed Turkey would invade to prevent the Greeks from seizing the whole island and destroying the Turkish armed enclaves, already suffering from Greek blockades. The Security Council, with Stevenson now calling the action, moved. It voted unanimously in March, 1964, to (1) raise a UN peace-keeping force responsible to U Thant, (2) appoint a three-man committee for Cyprus, (3) appoint a UN mediator for the mess.

Now Thant, like Hammarskjöld in 1956 and 1960, got on the phone. But things were vastly different after the Congo fiasco. The first six nations Thant asked to send troops—and this time they would pay for these troops themselves, since the UN was already bankrupt from the Congo—were Canada, Sweden, Finland, Ireland, Brazil, and Austria. All except Sweden refused, and Sweden demanded at least one other neutral be in the force before it offered a single battalion.

Later, Canada and Ireland changed their minds. The United States offered no troops but $2 million. Britain offered $1 million. Indian General Thimayya, who had helped with the Korean

POW question, was appointed UN commander. In all, 6,100 men were raised and sent to Cyprus, never enough to enforce the UN will, if it had had a will.

Markarios was right; the UN showed itself unable to do anything he vetoed. The UN troops made a practice of trying to interpose their bodies between Greek-Turkish gunfire, and this had some effect. But the UN could reach no solution to this kind of ethnic stew, for there was none other than disarming both sides. But Makarios could not be disarmed without violating Cypriot "sovereignty."

The matter calmed considerably when Makarios forces began an attack on a Turkish beachhead at Kokkim, and Turkish Air Force jets bombed and strafed several Greek villages.

This Turkish air action in the summer of 1964 convinced Markarios as nothing else could have that Turkey held real veto power over his desires to crush the Turkish Cypriot community. Makarios was not too enthusiastic over *enosis*; with Cyprus "redeemed" into the Greek nation he would have become just another Greek politician. But he had a very understandable determination to rule his own house without Turkish interference. After the bombings, however, the threat of Turkish jets— Cyprus was beyond the range of Greek air power—brought the bitter civil war to an uneasy stand-off. The Greeks held back; the Turkish minority was too weak to do anything.

The Turkish community economy was ruined, however; and the Turkish enclaves were under blockade and boycott. Partition was the only logical answer, as it had been in Palestine, but it was anathema to the Greeks, while at the same time Turkey was prepared to invade to stop any change in the status quo. It was doubtful that the Turks would be able to get partition, for the Greeks continued to ship in arms and train a large militia. For the short run, anyway, Cyprus had turned into another Israeli-Arab situation, with no clear-cut right or wrong, burning hates on both sides, and no solution in sight.

Thimayya's peace-keeping force was hamstrung because it could not infringe on Makarios' sovereignty. The U. S. government, working behind the scenes with the Greek and Turkish regimes, did more to control the crisis where it was really dangerous. It did not matter too much what the Cypriots wanted, or even did, as long as Greece and Turkey could be kept from each other's throats in a war neither wanted. The UN-force mandate was renewed regularly at three-month intervals, rather to the disgust of the small powers supporting it.

Natty in their neat blue helmets, the men of this force became a seemingly permanent body of observers, not actors, on the Cyprus stage. Unable to end the crisis, they had become a symbol of UN weakness rather than UN strength.

While the leaders of the USSR—Khrushchev was deposed from power in October, 1964, without a change in Soviet policy —showed they had no interest in meddling in current European problems after 1962, the stage of world action had again shifted to the Far East. The pattern of 1948–1950 was being repeated; and, though few in the United States seemed to realize it, a new Korea-type situation was blowing up rapidly.

The case of Vietnam followed the Korean parallel closely. The country had been split between Communist and non-Communist halves at the Geneva peace conferences in 1953–1954. Partition was forced after the defeat of the French, who had dominated Indo-China (the modern Vietnam, Laos, and Cambodia) since the middle of the nineteenth century.

The war against the French had been primarily an anticolonialist struggle, which early in the game had come under control of Vietnamese Marxists such as Ho Chi Minh and Vo Nguyen Giap. The Marxists had a definite advantage in rising to the leadership of such struggles, since they alone in Asia, or even Latin America, had discipline, a rationale, and a coherent program of action. Other forces, whether military, democratic, or rightist, were fragmented.

As in North Korea, a Communist state under the broad influence and hegemony of China was erected. This state had social and economic problems, but it possessed the one vital ingredient

359

for viable government in Asia: iron control. South of the 17th parallel, a non-Communist state was erected from the remaining half of Vietnam. Here, out of a local power struggle, a mandarin named Ngo Dinh Diem assumed control. For a number of years he maintained a strong government, and the United States began to back him as the man best able to keep Communist influence from spreading.

The parallels between Diem and Rhee were again very strong. Both were autocratic. Both were Christians, in non-Christian nations. Both were Western-oriented, and thus in tune with U. S. notions of world, if not local, order. Both waged war effectively against Communist subversion for a time, then both fell as a result of their own policies at home. In each case, the military took over. In Korea and Vietnam, which were not nations in the sense of European nation-states, the military was the only cohesive force available.

Vietnam, containing both Westernized Saigon intellectuals and hill tribes that hated the Vietnamese themselves, had no citizenry in the Western pattern. Without such a citizenry, any kind of government on the American or Western level was impossible, which Washington, if not all U. S. citizens, accepted. The problem for the United States was to keep expansionist Chinese Communism contained, while trying to support a local regime that did not give the United States a propaganda black eye—a problem not always easy to solve.

The Geneva conferences, which ended the first phase of the Vietnamese war, had envisioned a neutralized Southeast Asia. Cambodia did become neutral, though highly susceptible to Chinese influence. Laos, with a large built-in Communist faction, soon became split between rightists supporting the West, neutrals, and Communists. Each side made mistakes in Laos. Rightwing putsches sparked Communist offensives, with neutralists fighting in the middle. Gradually the country became split, with Communists dominating the north of Laos, while non-Communists held the capital, Vientiane, and the south. And in Vietnam itself, on the coast, the Communists from the north continued

360

the war for dominance through a campaign of terrorism and subversion that gradually, between 1956 and 1960, became a full scale internal war.

It was a local, civil war in the same sense as the Korean War had been: that is, the area was caught between two outside forces as part of the vaster power struggle between Communism and Western world order. The South Vietnamese insurgents were completely supported, armed, and aided by their compatroits in the north. Without such support the local South Vietnamese Viet Cong, or Communist movement, would have easily been defeated. Without U. S. support, the various non-Communist South Vietnamese regimes would have been overrun.

The major American error in going into Vietnam in the middle fifties and beginning the support of President Diem was that the magnitude of the problem was not seen. As one American military officer said in 1963, "We figured with a few advisers and a few shekels the problem would take care of itself."

But after ten years, more than a billion dollars, and with some 225,000 U. S. military personnel committed to Vietnam, the United States was in a full-fledged limited war. The various American Administrations from Eisenhower to Kennedy to Johnson had each tried to minimize the problem, and by doing this confused the American public greatly, for the war continued to expand.

The Asian Communists had learned the hard way that armies crossing frontiers openly, as in Korea in 1950, produced immediate Western reaction. Supporting a bitter, bloody, almost clandestine war in South Vietnam was another matter. They had a good chance of winning, considering the moral confusion in the West toward such wars. Many men in the United States worried more about America's right to intervene than about the 10,000 South Vietnamese civilian officials or government supporters murdered in 1964 by the Viet Cong.

Washington, more than the American public, was becoming aware that there was no longer such a thing as a "local civil" war without international repercussions. In each local war, power

361

swung one way or the other in a divided world. The outcome of each such internal conflict aided either East or West. It was that simple, and the Communist world was never confused.

The United States, supporting South Vietnam, never had any intention of doing away with the status quo in the North. It did not care to provoke a bigger war. But it did not dare let South Vietnam fall into Communist control, and there was nothing to negotiate about until the Communists ceased their drive to control it.

It would not have mattered greatly—except to some "moralists"—whether the Viet Cong was aided by the North or not. A Viet Cong victory would have moved all of Vietnam inside the Communist orbit, a fact no one argued, and a fact the United States in its own interests could not permit, any more than they could have permitted South Korea to become a Communist dagger pointed at Japan.

The older notions of geopolitics in Washington had changed. During most of the century it had been believed that Mackinder's old idea of the world island, a Eurasian "heartland" under one power center, and its eventual ability to dominate the world was correct. Such notions had strongly influenced American entry into two world wars, to prevent Germany from gaining control of such a "heartland." The same fears had provoked early opposition to, and containment of, Soviet Communism.

But by 1947, it was seen that control of the Eurasian heartland was not necessarily fatal to the "island" and sea-oriented economies or the power position of the West. But it was essential that the "island" powers—the United States, Western Europe, Japan—keep control of or, at the worst, neutralize the European and Asian "rimlands."

If the coastlines of both Europe and Asia fell into hostile hands, the island United States was in serious geopolitical trouble. Professor Spykman of Yale first advanced this theory in 1947; and by 1949 in Europe, and by 1950 in Asia, the United States was living according to its dictates. If the powerful rimland of Europe remained outside Communist control, the power

362

balance was not apt to be upset; and if the strategic rimlands— Korea, Southeast Asia, parts of Africa—remained outside the Communist sphere, the trading economies of the Western powers would remain strong.

The trouble was, few people in the United States generally understood the relationship of the Asian rimlands to Japan. Japan, a true if anesthetized power center, was a trading nation like Britain. It had to have markets to live. Its markets were in East Asia.

In fighting World War II primarily to gain markets in Asia, which the old European colonial exclusion policies had denied it, Japan actually succeeded. Japanese victories and conquests in the early months of the war destroyed the old myth of Western invulnerability and superiority and doomed the Western colonial structure in its prewar form. By 1950 a revitalized Japan was trading freely with an Asia that had been denied to it in 1940.

But a Communist hegemony—there was no need for Red Chinese flags to cover the region; subtle control would do—that barred the Japanese from the Asian rimlands would soon put Japan in desperate straits. The United States and Europe were hardly prepared to share their internal markets with industrialized Japan. If Red China, reversing the roles of two decades earlier, dominated Asia, the odds were that it could not soon fail to control or dominate Japan.

Thus Southeast Asia, its raw materials and markets, were vital not to the United States, but to the U. S. concept of world society and world order, which included a peaceful and prosperous Japan.

The United States had once stopped Japan, by fighting, from achieving its East Asia Co-Prosperity Sphere. Ironically, by 1950 the United States was fighting for it for the Japanese. Japan, like Germany, had entered the Western sphere strategically and commercially, if not wholly spiritually.

The Communists, one way or another, were determined to break both connections and alter the world power balance forever in their favor. It had become too dangerous to try further moves in Berlin. But the fringe areas of Asia still provided great opportunity.

By 1963 Red China had become America's greatest diplomatic problem. The problem was complicated almost ridiculously by the fact that, diplomatically, the United States did not admit China existed.

Over British warnings, Roosevelt had insisted upon including Chiang Kai-shek's China among the great powers of the UN, more in recognition of China's traditional friendship with the United States and its potential than from any sound reading of the current situation. Both the American understanding of geopolitics and the crystal ball of the future were cloudy.

For one thing, any truly powerful Chinese state was bound to come into confrontation with Western interests in Asia; it could no more accept Western domination of its own rimlands than the United States was apt to sit by for French, Russian, or German domination of Mexico. Chiang Kai-shek would hardly have stood for FDR's patronizing during the war or the sellout of Chinese interests at Yalta if he had had even the power of a Churchill at his command.

But the situation became crucial only when China had the revolution Anthony Eden predicted in 1943; and China came under the control of a government not only logically, but ideologically, hostile to the United States. The result in Asia was quite untidy. When Mao's Communists took over Peking in January, 1949, any real hope of peaceful order on the borders of Asia went out the window.

One resultant mess was the confusion on the Security Council. Chiang's regime fled to the island of Taiwan, where it remained as an American protectorate and from where it continued to sit in China's great-power seat. The real power center of China (which admittedly would not have signed the Charter) was not only not represented in the UN, but its entrance was subject to veto by the regime in Taiwan.

For a number of reasons, which included China's immediate

364

hostility, Chiang's recalcitrance on the matter, the way the Reds had come to power, and an influential Taiwanese lobby in Washington, the United States did not recognize the Peking government in 1949. After the undeclared war between Americans and Chinese in Korea from 1950 to 1953, recognition of an unrepentant China became emotionally and politically impossible.

This problem occupied legalists, lawyers, moralists, and political rationalists for years. Meanwhile, China stayed outside the UN, Taiwan remained on the Security Council, and the United States was unable to come up with a coherent China policy—which was nothing new.

The Chinese reaction to the world after 1949 was understandable, if hardly palatable. China was an ancient country. The empire of Han China had been contemporary with that of Rome; the two had traded silk and spices for gold; they had not fought because each had reached natural geographical limits that did not overlap. If China had not risen quite so far as the Hellenic West, it had also never fallen quite so far. Until the beginning of modern times, Chinese emperors could quite logically and factually regard the Western ambassadors begging to trade as barbarians.

The Industrial Revolution changed all that. When iron warships stood off the China coast, landing disciplined men armed with mass-produced rifles against Chinese soldiery wielding broadswords and matchlocks, it was the Europeans who laughed at the Chinese.

At the beginning of the twentieth century the one ferment that ran through all educated China was that some changes had to be made: in modern terms China was a failed society. Men like Mao Tse-tung and Chou En-lai, Communist leaders, were born into a decaying Confucianism. In their youth they experimented with the republican institutions of the West, or saw them experimented with in China. They came gradually and cohesively to Marxism in their twenties, for the most part, seeing it not so much as a philosophy but as a power technique and a form of organiza-

365

tion that fitted a land like China. It provided the rationale both to kill the dead past and to seize power and even create a new empire.

This same ferment, arising out of the humiliating Western power predominance, went on all over the highly civilized non-Western world. Japan became schizophrenic trying to adopt all the techniques of Western industrialism while holding on to all the customs and forms of East Asian culture. Japan ended up sending out soldiers who carried German-style machine guns and wrote charming haiku when they were not shooting. Seven decades of too-rapid change eventually left Japan etherized, physically in the Western world but not yet spiritually part of it.

India had its own schizophrenia: the adoption of British socialism as a means of trying to create something India had never had, the secular state, while at the same time rejecting all spiritual alliance with the sources from which that socialism sprang. India was less homogenous than Japan, therefore less disciplined, and therefore less ambitious. India tried a path of British popular democracy blended with economic socialism laid over deep cultural plurality—a real stew if there ever was one.

Egypt stirred its own mess: a militant national socialism overlaid upon all the dreams, traditions, and prejudices of Islam. Some German scientists of Nasser's felt at home, because there were certain resemblances between the Egyptian and the former German National Socialism.

All of these adoptions had one aim: to break an old pattern of life that could not oppose the Western power dominance, while at the same time emotionally holding on to all the things non-Westerners thought gave them identity.

Of all these societies China had the oldest traditions and nursed the most ineradicable dreams of worldly grandeur. China called itself the Middle Kingdom, implying ownership of everything suspended between Heaven and Hell.

Marxism did not create the Chinese revolution any more than Marxism created Castro or what happened in Moscow in 1917. But it provided a ready tool for what men thought needed to be

366

done. Marxism gave Mao's cohorts instant justification for the seizure, retention, and exercise of power. It provided the rationale and the discipline for rapid industrialism, which no form of genuine democracy could have done. Nehru in India chose to depend on votes; he had to go slowly. Mao went as fast as the backs of his people could stand.

Even Marxists knew that capital cannot be voted; it must be made out of sweat and tears. They also knew that any nation, to be heard, had to speak not only with eloquence but with steel mills, potash plants, nuclear reactors, aircraft, and a hydrogen bomb or two, all meshed into coherence by a vast bureaucracy. The United States and the USSR were not dominant powers because of moral suasion or cultural influences. Britain had more of both.

Marxism alone probably had the things needed if one's aim is enormous power in a country like China: ruthless discipline, relentless momentum, and a towering vision of tomorrow that keeps people's mind occupied.

For all Mao's and Chou's crimes against humanity, they would be forgiven in China if China emerged as a transcendant power. Russia forgave Peter the Great, and by 1965 was on the way to forgiving Stalin.

Starting at the bottom of the Asian Chinese-Japanese-Indian triangle in 1950, China in ten years reached the top.

Nehru's government inherited the British mantle in India. He had problems and complexities, but he also inherited a nation with a history of strong central government, British made; considerable wealth; a superb civil service; and a budding industrial plant that outstripped anything in Asia. India was not homogeneous. But neither was China; more people spoke Russian or English than any one dialect of Chinese. In India, despite the Hindu-Moslem riots, there was an orderly changing from British to Indian rule. China had not had a real central government for generations. There were thirty years of war lords and revolutions, invasion, and war. Mao took over wreckage in 1949.

The crimes, failures, and enormities of the Chinese Communists were watched with rapt attention in the West. Nehru's crashing errors were glossed over. But while India stewed in its own juices, the Chinese ferment seemed to take hold. The Chinese did not split themselves between East and West, like the Indians. They bent the ideas of Karl Marx to the purposes of historical China. Nothing, by 1960, was so apparent as the existence of ancient imperial China under the bureaucratic puritanism and Marxist gloss of Mao's revolution.

When Pandit Nehru died in 1963, it was apparent that India's foreign policy had been a failure. Nehru misjudged the kind of world he lived in—the kind of world in which Chinese armies attacked Indian troops in the Himalayas in the fall of 1962, and defeated them disastrously.

China did not invade deeply; China wanted to rule no part of India. China was merely showing the rest of Asia who had won the race for Asian leadership. Refusing to recognize the power struggle in Asia, Nehru was the first to lose it. Nations that had looked to India for guidance in 1950 avoided India sadly in 1963. It was Mao's dragon that overshadowed Asia, worried Russia, scared Pakistan into accommodation, drove Cambodia into neutrality, and even made Charles de Gaulle of France consider the Western presence in Asia doomed.

It was Chinese influences, seeping down into Southeast Asia, that kept the Vietnamese war going. If Red China had not existed, North Vietnam would not have dreamed of continuing in the face of American opposition.

China had power deficiencies, the worst of which was the terrible handicap of excessive population. China had more than six hundred million people. If it had had only two hundred million, with the same territory and resources, China would have approached Russia and the United States in total power very soon. China was temperate, with an intelligent, hard-working population and with vast natural resources. But while China exploded its nuclear device in 1964, it was still a nation that could send only thirty or forty army divisions abroad and support them with equipment and munitions for any extended length of time.

Six hundred million people on China's soil subsisted on less than half an acre of cropland per person, and spread China's resources much too thin. In this sense, population was not power, though at the same time it created terrible pressures drawing the Chinese toward the surplus rice-producing areas of Southeast Asia such as Vietnam. The very effort required to feed this population reduced the effort that could be devoted to industrialization.

But Chinese exportable divisions, as well as its prestigious if not very useful atom bomb, gave China great status in Asia. Ever since 1950 the various American administrations had suffered from the "Korea syndrome"—a fear of ground involvement in Asia based partly on the difficulties involved and partly on fear of domestic political reaction.

Truman had sent troops in; the voters had sent Truman's party out. The lesson had been taken too much to heart; and it tended to make U. S. policy, and threats, ineffective along the rimlands of Asia. For this reason, China's thirty divisions overshadowed every strategic conference on Vietnam that was held in Hawaii. They haunted every Washington decision to get tough with North Vietnam. The United States could handle North Vietnam with standing forces. But an entanglement with China meant partial mobilization, easy enough to accomplish, but unpleasant politically to order.

The Korea syndrome lingered on in spite of the fact that through 1964 China gave every indication that without the aid and even with the opposition of Soviet Russia it was bent on power predominance in East Asia. The Chinese were determined to replace the Pax Americana with a Pax Sinica in the very rimlands American strategists had determined they could not lose. China was on top in Asia, and stirring.

When the Communists took over Peking in 1949, some American propagandists tried to show that the lights had been put out in Asia. It seemed more likely that unless the United States stood fast, the lamps of China were coming on again.

20.

The Faith and the Future

IT IS HARD to tell exactly where a watershed of national policy begins. The move may be gradual, and like Truman's, it may be obscured from the public for a time. By early 1965, the similarity between Truman's and Johnson's policy-making in foreign affairs was clear. With the exit of Kennedy's people during 1964, there had been something very like the turnover in Washington after FDR's death. The policy-makers who stayed on—Bundy, McNamara, Rusk were the big three—enjoyed new prominence. Johnson, like Truman, tended to leave affairs to the men he considered pros.

Dean Rusk, who was more of a hardhead than a man blinded by notions of a Great Design in world politics, began to dominate his own department. The only great design Rusk could see clearly in 1965 was the design of Communist disorder and subversion around the world. The Viet Cong pressure in Vietnam had stepped up enormously; the Communists had varying control over two thirds of South Vietnam. The South Vietnamese army, brought to battle in battlion-sized engagements, was being bled white almost without any mention in American newspapers, which dutifully recorded the handful of American advisers being killed or wounded.

Some time in early 1965 the Korea syndrome broke. The Administration decided it had to salvage the situation even if it sank itself at home. American aircraft began bombing raids on military targets in North Vietnam, in a move to induce the Communists to ease their pressures in the South. Thousands of U. S. ground troops were sent into South Vietnam. Quietly, they began preparations to enter the shooting war in earnest. Whatever was

370

required to hold Vietnam, or at least keep it neutralized—from bombing the North to accepting ground combat in the South—would be done. An indication of the determination involved was illustrated by the private feeling in many Washington quarters that the bombing would not suffice. But it was felt that six or seven American divisions would.

The United States had begun to grapple in this kind of war without paying too much attention to the niceties of diplomacy and international law. It was involved in another Korea-action almost without the public becoming aware of what was happening. But after twenty years of this kind of peace, the public was getting inured, and the government seemed to be getting smart.

There was an abrupt end to Kennedy's attention to and solicitude for the United Nations and all its quarreling, schizophrenic, multiple values. There was a strong feeling in Washington that the UN could be of no use whatever in a situation like Vietnam or in stabilization operations in Latin America or Africa. Worse, the UN, now unresponsive to American or Atlantic aims and values, could be a positive hindrance to the United States. Not world opinion, but somebody's use of power, was going to decide the outcome of each operation.

President Johnson, however, was far too astute a politician to denigrate the role of the UN openly in front of the millions still emotionally attached to it. Furthermore, he realized that the UN could still be of immense value in certain situations to U. S. policy; it was his considered aim to try to keep it alive and even, where possible, enhance its image if not its substance. As he said to Ambassador Goldberg on one occasion: "If I wanted to liquidate the UN, I could do it." But Johnson, like his close advisers, saw the UN as a tool, not a mystical force in world affairs, though he did not have to advertise the fact.

Both Truman and Johnson acted with vigor when it was required to protect American interests. But Johnson was a far better salesman of policy than Truman; he was not only capable of putting up a better smoke screen and getting public opinion on his side, he was much more concerned with doing so than Truman or Acheson had ever been—to their sorrow.

The Johnson Administration did not advertise its changes of policy; in fact, it often obscured them, if possible. The hundreds of thousands of ground troops ordered to Vietnam were sent with as little fanfare as possible, and all the while the United States continued to call for negotiations. They began to engage in heavy ground combat, which was vital if the course of the war was to be turned, almost without the public realizing the fact. Meanwhile, public reaction to the newer, tough policy showed a growing realization of the stark necessities of international politics in a great-power world.

Adlai Stevenson's speech in Toronto, Canada, in late May showed the enormous changes in official American thinking that had come about. Stevenson, whom no one could accuse of illiberality or lack of affection for the UN, told an unresponsive audience of young Canadians that under present conditions national power was the only means of dealing with the challenge posed by Communist support for the so-called wars of national liberation. He said that when any nation was beset by Communist influences, the nation most likely to reply to any appeal for aid was the United States. He said, finally, "The framers of the Charter of the United Nations could not foresee the threats to peace inherent in the doctrine of 'just wars of national liberation.' Nor is the international peacekeeping machinery—or the procedures for using it—which have been developed at the United Nations adapted to these new techniques of intervention."

Adlai Stevenson, who from the first had been one of the staunchest supporters the UN ever had, whose image in the third world needed no burnishing, whose humanity had never been in question, was saying that the UN as a peace-keeping body was dead.

The same week President Lyndon Johnson, in an address at Baylor University in Waco, Texas, called for regional solutions, outside the United Nations, to problems of revolution and subversion in the Western Hemisphere. The United States government was already trying to organize a permanent peace-keeping force from the Organization of American States. Its commander would not be a North American, for political reasons. But no one doubted that the force would serve as an instrument of North American policy, which called for the stabilization of Hispanic America.

Secretary of State Dean Rusk, meanwhile, was working behind the scenes to reorganize SEATO, the Southeast Asia Treaty Organization, organized under Dulles, which had never become a viable force. This organization, with military participation by such nations as the Philippines, Australia, New Zealand, and even South Korea, would seek regional military solutions to the problem of wars of national liberation, meaning national Communization, of Asia.

The United States had finally come around to Churchill's original vision of world organization: regional bodies, regional solutions. The world was too broad and alien, despite jets and instant communications, and too multivalued for one all-embracing world organization to forge world order. What order there was was being kept not by the UN but by the regional alliances American power had strung around the globe.

NATO, by 1965, was in apparent disarray. The appearance was misleading. NATO had served its purpose; Europe was viable, and no longer in danger of Russian subversion or invasion. Even if every European nation renounced NATO in 1969 when the treaty expired—an event not likely to happen—every European nation, and the USSR, knew that the United States would move at once if any Russian threat were made in Berlin or in Europe anywhere.

The United States had not suddenly gone over to military response alone. A whole tier of economic assistance programs, from the Alliance for Progress in Hispanic America to a proposed Asian Development Bank, were in existence or in birth. The attack on world disorder had to be many-pronged. It could not rest on guns alone, although guns were still a necessary ingredient.

The United States was also aware that Germany and Japan were slowly coming out of their World War II anesthesia; they were powerful and viable nations and would sooner or later demand and take a place in world affairs. The United States needed to cement stronger relations with both, particularly as far as future aims and policies went. No sane or sensible course for Europe or Asia could be established without them.

In the meantime, no one had found any better solution to expansionist Communism than containment. Policy had to oscillate between appeasement and force to be practical, but it had been amply proved in the 1930's that appeasement in a power struggle seldom brought a desired response.

Rusk himself was deeply disturbed by criticism inside the United States of American policy. Some quarters were calling for negotiations with China and North Vietnam over the rimlands when there was nothing to negotiate, and for appeasement of Communist drives that were not apt to be appeased. Rusk said: "I sometimes wonder at the gullibility of educated men and the stubborn disregard of plain fact by men who are supposed to be helping our young to learn—especially to learn how to think."

To Rusk, Vietnam, the Dominican Republic, and the Congo had become test cases to determine whether the free world could make the Communist techniques of subversion, infiltration, confusing the issue with civil wars, and insurgency in supposed national causes as sterile as the older, overt forms of aggression.

Only a series of Communist bloody noses might change the Communist logic of the age. Nothing else had. After the crisis of 1962 and the nuclear confrontation, many writers and diplomats had referred wisely to a new "détente." Even Rusk, for a time, thought one was in the offing. But it was obvious through the new quiet in Europe that none of the issues of the Cold War had been settled. Germany, Korea, and Vietnam were still divided by frontiers of hate. The power struggle had not ended.

There was one immense difference between the views many people had and the view in Washington. Johnson's policy-makers had facts, and the facts told them that no relaxation was in sight.

When Russia quietened, China arose. When China had been pacified, if such a time came, a new power would arise on the horizon, surly and demanding change, probably unreasonable change that would strike at the foundations of the Atlantic world.

As long as the United States remained a great power and as long as it remained in the greater world, some part of the American people would have to watch the walls. The world was like that. New frontiers replaced the old.

It was the distressing realization of this situation that seemed to be producing what the State Department called the "neo-isolationism." The old isolationism had been based on the idea "America First" with a strong if never quite admitted dose of pacificism and peace at any price. It had been Republican-oriented.

The new isolationism came primarily from the men who had been most internationally minded in the 1940's. For the most part, they were Democrats. They included a sizable group of Senators: Morse, Fulbright, Gruening, Mansfield. They had been most eager for the United States to enter the greater world, but these were the very men who had badly misjudged the shape of the world and had equated an independent colonial order with the values and restraint of an independent Europe. They had seen their ideals break under the actions of men like Nasser and Sukarno, whom only a lack of real power kept from being new Napoleons or Hitlers.

Big nations had no monopoly of brains, but they also had no monopoly of arrogance, aggressiveness, and ultra-rational dreams of importance or status. Some of the new isolationists were haunted by something no longer relevant: the nuclear war. More of them were haunted by any kind of war at all, not realizing that they lived in an age of limited conflict. Some of them feared honestly for American society and American freedom and social advances such as Johnson had promised in the Great Society, if the United States were to throw its military and economic strength too heavily on the walls.

The Congo, more than anything else, had been the breaking point. It showed what a dirty, bloody, and heartbreaking job stabilization could be. The only way the Congo had been pacified, and then only temporarily in 1964, was by slaughter. If the United States was going to guarantee borders, it was going to have to kill people to do it.

Ironically, one of the President's staunchest supporters was Senator Everett Dirksen, the old isolationist warhorse from Illinois. The new isolationism of America seemed to center on the old interventionist areas, the two sea coasts. The heartland of America, which had never been very sanguine about world order in terms of the United Nations to begin with, was much more inclined to support the President's policies.

Again, it was mostly on college campuses and in intellectual centers that men seemed most intent on pursuing the chimera of peace where there was no peace or adjusting reality to a set of conditions that had never existed. There were even some supposedly intelligent men who lacked the moral courage to fight but at the same time lacked the moral courage to be crucified. But in this world you could not have it two ways at once.

The historian Toynbee wrote: "When a frontier between a more highly and a less highly civilized society ceases to advance, the balance does not settle down to a stable equilibrium but inclines, with the passage of time, in the more backward society's favor."

Many of the intellectuals who most feared American involvement in world stabilization or the advancement of Atlantic civilization were historians who agreed with Toynbee—*where Rome was concerned*. They saw nothing in history, especially if the lesson was unpleasant, that applied to the present. One of the tragic weaknesses of Western intellectual thought in Western society's time of troubles between 1870 and 1965 was its refusal to accept the unchangeability of man and the nature of his politics.

They continued to build, as Francis Bacon had pointed out centuries before, imaginary laws for imaginary commonwealths, which like the stars shed little light because they were so high and remote from the crushing reality of earth's mud.

376

A new kind of barbarism, by Western standards, had settled along an uneasy frontier with Western civilization. Marxism itself was frozen; it was not a true movement but a vehicle for nationalist power drives. But it pretended to see the shape of the future. It was aided by the terrible world malaise that cried with the Communist playwright Bertolt Brecht: "Sink into the mud; embrace the butcher—but change the world. It needs it!" No one in the West argued that the world did not need change. But it hardly needed the kind of change Brecht and others had in mind. Anyone who thought the United States would not fight for its own world vision against that kind of change was making as great a miscalculation as Hitler.

Americans and Russians and Chinese—the three prime movers in the world of the late twentieth century—were in many ways alike. They inhabited continental land masses; they thought big. They each used the term "American," "Russian," or "Chinese" synonymously with "good." They all had a lust for size. They all believed deeply in a poorly defined but infinitely improved future.

But there the similarity ended.

No one, not even the most frustrated and aggrieved nation in Hispanic America, believed that the United States posed a danger to world order, or a genuine imperialist threat. The United States was a shining symbol of frustration to certain countries and peoples—yes. A danger to law, order, and peace—no.

The same forces of nationalism and ethnic consciousness that did so much to spur the Russians and Chinese also held the seeds of frustration for their contemplated empires. Even Marxists who, like Marx, had ignored nationalism were beginning to see as much.

In the meantime, when the music of Glinka's "Glory, Glory to the Russian People" crashed and a Titov or other astronaut mounted the Stairs of Honor in the Kremlin, it was well to remember that the masses of the Roman Republic were ragged and ill fed, that Rome was far from the wealthiest power in the Mediterranean world, and that as Roman power, based on steel

377

will and discipline, reached out to engulf the more highly civilized Greek world, Italian agriculture was in the process of hideous dissolution, the Roman populace was dispossessed, and countless Romans themselves were purged on crosses.

By 1965, the men in the operating areas of American foreign affairs had made up their minds about one thing: if there was any way to change the Russian and Chinese drives, it was to subject them to multiple, repeated, foreign failure. This firm policy was dangerous. It always put the souls of Western pacifists and men of good will on the chopping block. It might even drive either the Russians or the Chinese over the line of sanity.

A possible, and fearful, flaw of the policy of containment was that it had to be based on the ultimate rationality of powerful men, and powerful men are not always rational.

But all historical evidence, as men like Rusk, Johnson, and McNamara believed, showed that continued success for the forces of Communist expansion would finally force the war no one wanted. There were some things men cannot bargain away. The kind of world the United States still believed in was one of them.

This was the faith and this was the future twenty years after the conference at San Francisco, where some men thought the world might be changed. Where did the United Nations fit into this brave, grim, new world? A speech that was written but never made is significant.

U Thant planned to speak at Queen's college, Kingston, Ontario, May 22, 1965. Thant was at this time deeply disturbed over what was happening in Asia, Latin America, and by the funding crisis in the UN. He was aware, painfully, that the United States was not only not making the UN the cornerstone of its policy but it was actually doing its best to keep its policy unhampered by the UN.

Thant would have said: "For various reasons, the role of the United Nations has been ignored or avoided in the settlement of some recent disputes, thus causing profound uneasiness in the minds of those who maintain that the United Nations represent the world's best hopes for peace.

"A further drift in this direction, if not arrested in time, will mark the close of a chapter of great expectations and the heralding of a new chapter in which the world organization will provide merely a debating forum, and nothing else."

Thant cancelled this address, because on April 28, 1965, the United States sent troops into the Republic of Santo Domingo in the Caribbean, to halt what gave every indication of being a Castro-like, leftist revolution in that country. The UN was not only not consulted; the observer Thant sent to the area was ignored. The United States had been down the painful road of debating its policy in Turtle Bay once too often. The United States was going to finish what Truman had begun in Greece: a policy of intervention and stabilization outside the UN.

There was more than one way to defend the Charter and the spirit of the Charter, if anyone stopped to think about it. The United States had defended the Charter before it had been written and before there was a UN.

The United Nations, however, could still be useful in areas of problems where the United States had no immediate, direct, vital interest. President Johnson's top advisers had made him clearly aware of this, and a perfect illustration was the Kashmir crisis of September, 1965. Washington much preferred to have the UN, rather than the U. S. government, play the predominant role in bringing a cease-fire to the Indian-Pakistani war.

Right or wrong, U. S. policy-makers had substantial reasons, none of which was a real concern for the importance or future of the UN. The Kashmir-Jammu problem that brought India and Pakistan to limited war had enormous religious, ethnic, and emotional overtones. A direct political solution was almost impossible; the UN had arranged a cease-fire in the 1940's fighting but had never been able to make the slightest headway toward a permanent solution. The fact was that a negotiated solution was out of the question; neither the Indian nor Pakistani governments could give any ground, after years of taking hardening positions, and still hope to survive. Any real solution would have to be enforced, rammed down the throat of one or both of the dispu-

379

tants. The UN had had no power to do this, despite two resolutions calling for a plebiscite in Kashmir, and the U. S. government was not about to accept the responsibility.

The India-Pakistan problem had enormous ramifications. Pakistan was a CENTO ally of the United States, and had received large amounts of military aid. But India, which had got lesser amounts of armaments from the United States after the Chinese-Indian clash of 1962, was the kingpin of American hopes of eventual stability in Asia. Even while India remained vociferously neutral between East and West, U. S. planners pinned much of their hopes for the offsetting of Chinese designs for Asia on the ability of the huge subcontinental nation to survive and prosper.

India, and not ally Pakistan, ironically was the only Asian power with any potentiality for balancing Red Chinese influence. If India dissolved—which, given its immense ethnic differences and separatist tendencies, was highly possible—the American problem in the rimlands would become that much more acute. Even a neutral India, already overshadowed by China, lent some check to Chinese power, and therefore assisted U. S. aims.

By 1965 only huge shipments of American wheat enabled India to avoid famine. These shipments were made not only for humanitarian reasons but because Washington regarded them as being in the American interest.

Because of this food assistance, and U. S. arms aid to Pakistan, the United States held immense influence over each nation. Both tacitly recognized the United States as the world's leading power. But Washington did not want to wield its influence over the subcontinent where Kashmir was concerned. Kashmir provided the United States with Hobson's choice: in a quarrel so fundamental the United States could hardly fail to alienate one or both disputants if it tried to solve the matter. Forced to choose, the United States would choose India, not because of India's rightness but because of India's greater strategic importance. But Washington determined to avoid any such overt choice, even

380

while policy-makers realized that, in American interests, the fighting needed to be halted.

The American decision to throw the problem into the UN was a direct, though not very subtle attempt to take the monkey off the American back and to try to obscure American intervention by operating through the Security Council. The move seemed to enhance the prestige and importance of the UN, but only to those whose main knowledge of international politics came from reading the newspapers. The move in no way committed the United States to bring the UN into other, more personal American interests.

Ironically, neither India nor Pakistan desired the Kashmir war. In both countries there was a clear understanding in ruling circles that only Red China, looming to the north, could gain from Indian-Pakistani conflict, if the war turned serious. This fear haunted the strongly anti-Communist Pakistani army, the power behind President Ayub Khan, and it damped any fighting enthusiasm the Indian Cabinet, in response to popular Indian demand, might have had.

Both governments privately asked the United States to intervene unilaterally. The British government offered to join Washington in such action. At the same time the Soviet regime openly submitted a proposal to both belligerent leaders to settle the dispute on Russian soil, through Russian good offices. But Washington, worried over the fighting, saw the proposals for American intervention as a trap.

Neither the Pakistani nor Indian governments were prepared to give any ground; neither could end the fighting on disadvantageous terms and hope to survive popular wrath. Emotions in both countries had been inflamed for years over Kashmir.

When the fighting began, the Security Council passed two resolutions, each calling for a cease-fire. Neither resolution had any teeth, since there was no mention of reprisal or enforcement. Both were ignored. U Thant flew to the scene; he was equally ignored. Thant represented no real power.

The third resolution, a U. S.-sponsored order for cease-fire coupled with the threat of sanctions, had more influence. Since only American aid was significant, this was merely a round-about way of doing what the United States could have done at once, unilaterally. The decision to make the move through the UN was political, based both on the desire to cloak American actions so as to arouse no direct hostility in either belligerent, and on the belief that without such action the UN might be dealt a completely fatal blow. After all, the UN was supposed to handle this kind of thing.

The USSR did not obstruct (only Moslem Jordan abstained) because in this case American and Russian aims converged. Russia wanted a strong, neutral India for the same reason the United States did: to offset Chinese ambitions in Asia. The Russians were Communists, but they were better geopoliticians.

The shaky cease-fire that was obtained did nothing to resolve the basic dispute. Significantly, Pakistan's acceptance of the UN demand was conditional on the UN's ability to end the crisis. Otherwise, Pakistan threatened to leave the UN. And India's acceptance showed an equal lack of respect: India denied its territory to any UN peace-keeping force in the unlikely event one was raised.

UN observers in Kashmir could still only question, beg, and dodge bullets as hostilities continued. They could not order or demand. In this way the Kashmir trouble resembled the Palestine crisis. With no Cold War questions dividing the United States and the USSR, the UN still could not enforce Council decisions because of the immense reluctance of the United States to become involved or to use force to push Security Council decisions through. Many American planners privately wanted a plebiscite in Kashmir to determine the matter once and for all, but the U. S. government did not quite dare to alienate India. On the other hand, for similar reasons they could not quite order Pakistan to forget Kashmir.

Problems like Palestine or Kashmir were not solvable by rational negotiation; historically they had never been solved by any

382

means but power. Short of bloodshed and letting the fighting take its course, Kashmir could only be ended by an outside power strong enough to enforce decisions without becoming involved on either side. The UN lacked intrinsic power; the United States, the only nation that in this case could give force to the UN orders, lacked any real feeling of responsibility. While both belligerents seized on the Council order as an excuse to try to end fighting neither wanted, there was always grave doubt that the United States would do what it had threatened through the UN: cut off food to India, in order to enforce a plebiscite—the only action that would permanently allay Pakistan.

American neutrality could hardly be faulted; American planners had correctly evaluated Red China's threats against India's frontiers during the Kashmir fighting for what they were: pure bluff. This was not an American war. But the American determination to avoid responsibility in the long run might prove indefensible.

It was probably politic to channel American action through the UN, if only to keep the UN alive at this time. But to strike for a temporary cease-fire, and not a solution, was to permit a dangerous situation to smolder on. The Kashmir crisis could only aid China as long as it was allowed to continue, because it would keep India and Pakistan eternally at each other's throats. As in the American Civil War, it was better for one side or the other to lose, decide the question forever, and then try to bind up the wounds.

The U. S. channeling of the crisis through the UN rather than working unilaterally (in either case, only American power, however employed, stood any chance of settling things) was faintly dangerous on other grounds. It gave immediate rise to illusions of a change in American policy toward the UN and of a substance to the UN that did not exist. The United States was interested in keeping the UN alive, because in Washington's eyes the UN could still be useful in situations of this kind.

It still had no intention whatever of turning Western Hemispheric matters, or the war in Vietnam, over to any international body. The UN was still incapable of handling any of the real issues of the day, which centered on the Russian-American-Chinese struggle for the world, and the fomenting or stabilization of world revolution against the power position of the West. Here the UN was still moribund, able only to argue over sideline crises.

The UN was not dead; it would not close its doors. But for that matter, the League of Nations did not close its doors the year the Western powers refused to impose sanctions on Mussolini, or even the year they gave ground to Hitler at Munich.

Twenty years after its birth, it was useless to write tracts about what the UN should do or what the United States should do in, or to, the UN. Too many tracts had already been written, most of them from ivory towers too far from the slush of reality.

The UN was no longer really relevant, and that was its one overriding, crushing problem. Men were learning more by watching history unfold on the ground than by debating it in glass towers in New York. The UN was irrelevant at last, but the idea was far from dead. As the Swiss historian Burckhart had written: "The spirit is always building a new house." Something would take its place. In the bitter spring of 1965, as in the bitter spring of 1945, man might still prevail.

During the first twenty years of its life, the United Nations was never a single entity. There were really three different UN's, each operating on different planes.

The first UN was the order-keeping apparatus designed at Dumbarton Oaks. This was the Security Council and General Assembly, one to provide a form of collective security for free nations, the other a forum against injustice.

It had its teeth drawn almost at once by the Cold War.

The greatest handicap this UN suffered from was the determination of many UN supporters to saddle it with goals utterly beyond the reach of its vital machinery. It could not mediate the

Cold War, nor could it prevent American-Soviet conflict if either power were bent upon it. There was no apparatus known or designable by man that could. Nations and peoples and powers exist; they go their own ways; they can sometimes be tempered by reason; but they can be exorcised only by fire and blood. Recognition of that fact to start with would have been all to the good.

Those who questioned the value of the UN as a whole because it could not prevent a major war never understood Dumbarton Oaks or the facts of life. The UN could not force the retreat of Communist power a single inch. But then it had never been intended as a Communist-control organization. The UN never found a means of coping with the modern strategem of the satellite state—but neither did international jurisprudence or standard diplomacy.

The UN did not assure collective security. As the British government suggested during the war, and as Churchill pointed out in his great speech at Fulton, security for nations rested upon regional groupings and alliances, NATO, Rio, the Warsaw Pact, and others. The UN started as such a grouping, and could have remained one.

When the concept of a United Nations was extended to include most of the nations of the world, collective security within the body became impossible. When, by 1945, the UN had ceased to be an alliance, the real alliances that delineated and tried to stabilize the world had to move outside it.

There is no such thing as a true balance in nature, and such balances as exist are always changing. The so-called "balance of nature" is always in flux. So is the balance of national power. The balance of power is an inherently unstable system, but over the past three hundred years of unbridled territoriality and leviathan states, the mind of man has been able to devise nothing better. If Richelieu, Pitt, Metternich, and Talleyrand sought a balance of power, so did Harry Truman and John Kennedy.

In the light of all the above, the UN was a failure. But it was

385

still not a total loss. The UN could not enforce its will, because it had a schizophrenic will built into it. But it could focus attention on dangerous matters. It could, and perhaps at times did, provide a sounding board to prevent a blind stumbling into war. It furnished, as in the first Berlin crisis, the faceless, antiseptic rooms in which coldly sensible if ultra-rational men could sit together and accomplish face-saving stratagems.

The first UN was worth the dough. It was dangerous only if men put too much faith in it or expected it to bring a millennium or the jubilee.

The second UN was the diffuse apparatus of the Economic and Social Council. The appendages of this Council began during the Second World War, as wartime measures. They continued into the peace and Cold War as international humanitarian programs.

UNESCO, the World Health Organization, the Farm and Agricultural Administration, these were general wars against poverty, disease, and ignorance. This UN carried far more of the seeds of international cooperation than all the lawyers' words in the Charter. It was the only UN that could stand proudly and entirely upon its own rationale.

This UN was hampered and restricted by the Cold War, but had nothing to do with it. It was and is important mainly to the non-European world. It has saved the lives of millions of men, women, and children who would never hear of Berlin.

Noticeably, as the first UN seemed to fail its function, the attention of more and more decent men centered on the second. Some came to think and say that this was the real United Nations. It was the one most likely to survive in one form or another.

Yet it was overrated. It could not make decisive change. It could not alter the circumstances, domestic, geographical, cultural, or climactic that created and continued world poverty or suffering. It could not alleviate basic problems; it would never have enough money, men, or, for that matter, the know-how. It

386

treated symptoms. It was a relief program, and it suffered from all the ugly defects a relief program always has. It was almost wholly one-way in direction, from the North Atlantic nations to the others.

The preamble of this UN stated, "Wars begin in the minds of men," but its supporters seemed ignorant of the fact that serious wars always have been and always will be beyond the reach of the desperately poor. The poor cannot afford guns. They cannot even afford butter. They are a fester on civilization, but they rarely threaten it. The Germans were rich people. The Soviets, when they began to build rockets, were rich people. The Chinese will be very dangerous only when they have riches, too.

The second UN was of enormous humanitarian value; but it could not attack the real sources from which the malaise of mankind sprang.

The third UN, which Vandenberg and certain others saw, was less spectacular than the other two. Yet this last UN was the one that over the years would prove most valuable, and that justified the American faith. It was a UN that provided a mechanism for settling disputes in the non-Communist world. The East-West argument was not negotiable. Most other conflicts were.

This was the UN that guaranteed against a stale and sterile static world, or the status quo that haunted Foster Dulles after Dumbarton Oaks. This UN gave the stamp of approval to the changing colonial order.

Before the twentieth century, all nations were born in blood and iron. The existence of the third UN could give new and emerging nations certain legal status and approval; membership, not victory in war, was their birth certificate.

The decisions, of course, were not made in New York. They were made in London, Paris, or in the government houses of Africa. But the UN helped. In a new and peculiarly effective way, so effective it went almost unnoticed, the apparatus in New York could ratify the outside decisions, by the admission of new states to membership.

This third UN, also, was the one that provided expeditionary forces for inflamed areas, to stop small wars before the great powers were sucked in.

The ratification and the damping were not always easy. Both always needed the support of at least one of the great powers. When there were emotional factors and indecision, as in Palestine, this third UN failed. The one prerequisite for effectiveness of this third UN was that in its functions the great powers never come into confrontation. When they did, as in the first UN, the mechanism soon broke down.

This was still a UN that, even when it worked, could not bring the millennium. It could ratify the orderly removal of power from London to Accra, but it could not make the British go.

Nor could it cure emotional disorders like Egypt's dream of an Arab empire, or Indonesian insistence upon a place in the shade, or the chaos in the Congo.

But without this UN, the enormous amount of peaceful change that altered the postwar world would have been more difficult. War, for the first time, was no longer the only ratification of the international revolution.

If Arthur Vandenberg had been alive two decades after San Francisco, he would have considered all the time, effort, and money the United States put into this UN well spent.

It is futile to blame mechanisms for human failures. It is what goes into machines that makes them run. It has always been desperately hard for men to be both realistic and keep the faith. Power is not principle, nor does principle take the place of power. One reason man has not solved his crisis of existence upon this earth is that he cannot, at the same time, keep both ideals and institutions in mind.

The answer has never been God or Caesar, but God and Caesar. Although the two will never blend, each is an indispensable part of human existence. The minds of all men look for both moral and temporal order. A Khrushchev will seek one path, a Vandenberg another. But the search is much the same.

Too many of the higher purposes that erect cathedrals just as easily dig torture pits. The truly exalted man is always a man with a closed mind, whether Christian or Communist. Almost every real attempt by men to create heaven on earth, from Calvin to Karl Marx, has created new maps of hell. That is something to bear in mind. The twentieth century, nuclear-armed, is no time for slogans or soaring solutions.

This is the day of the national state; and, as Laski wrote, all national states have been built both on the "conscience of men" and by the "agency of war."

The United States was built upon a Bill of Rights *and* erected over the dead bodies of countless Americans. Without *both* policies there would have been no America as we know it. An America without the moral certainty to dominate its own continent would still be cowering behind the Appalachians, complaining to the world of Indian raids.

In their great day the British, as Thomas Mann said, knew how to guard the unity of conscience and action, of spirit and power, at least subjectively. They pursued politics as an art, and they knew that power could never be entirely freed from a vitally useful strain of evil; but they never quite lost sight of the higher purpose of human decency and morality. To Thomas Mann, the German tragedy was that the German mind regards this as hypocrisy; it simply cannot understand a unity of conscience and action. It was a German statesmen who snapped: "We do not consult Jesus when we are discussing . . . the construction of the State."

If you separate God and Caesar far enough, you can justify Nazism with hardly any trouble at all. But there must be a unity of conscience and action, as Hitler proved. All other Reichs are built on shifting sand.

But if the German mind tends to see all human order as essentially evil and to pursue its ambitions and politics in such a light, the North American mind goes too far in the other direction.

Politics cannot be divorced from power. All human order, national and international, is based on a shimmering quicksand of conscience and coercion, hatred and love, domination and sub-ordination, war and peace. Even democracy is based on force. Anyone in a democratic society who acts in a thoroughly un-democratic way will soon find that out.

There has never been a time when no power element has been present in world affairs. No weak or unarmed people ever influ-enced international politics, as Pandit Nehru sorrowfully dis-covered. Christianity had been an idea for three hundred years; only when it gathered an organized and highly disciplined fol-lowing did the Emperor Constantine make an alliance with it.

No civilization ever rose without a day of supreme temporal power. Without the superiority of its ships and heavy hoplites, there would have been no Periclean Athens. Without the disci-pline of the Roman legions there would have been no Roman law, no universal Christian church. France illuminated Eu-rope, and French replaced Latin as the diplomatic tongue, only when it was the power *par excellence,* and Louis XIV battered at all France's frontiers. British parliaments, and British business methods, overspread the earth only when Her Majesty's Navy ruled the waves. The United States of America was first taken seriously when its armies entered Europe. The American way of life—mass production—took hold and flourished only be-hind mass armies and an awesome umbrella of American atomic power. In the twentieth century, if only Castro propagated Com-munism, the world could laugh.

There is such a thing as a world community. But it is a com-munity without coherence or stability. It is a community only because all men are forced to live together on this earth.

All concepts of world order, the order that men have always sought, from Rome to Dumbarton Oaks, have always implied rec-ognition of the strongest to assume hegemony. Change has been sometimes based on justice, but most often on shifts of people and power. Policy, from Darius to Dulles, has oscillated between the seemingly incompatible opposites of force and ap-peasement.

390

There has always been a struggle for equality; but, as historians have shown and the minds of some men reject, the struggle for equality can rarely be distinguished from the struggle for predominance.

The twentieth-century world is in a great watershed of history. It may be an age as decisive as that when the Persian hordes entered Hellas or when Rome determined *Carthago delenda est*.

In this watershed of history the policy of containment had one enormous flaw: its aim, whether avowed or not, was stalemate. To keep the game going—the dangerous game that seemingly had to be kept going—required that no one, on either side, win big. The other side could be subjected to frustration but never extinction. But history proved that stalemates, unlike diamonds, do not last forever.

If the regional power blocs insisted on competing, sooner or later one would get the other by the heels. Or they could repeat the fatal error of the Sassanian and Byzantine Empires in the seventh century who fought it out to their mutual exhaustion and destruction. In the end, a brand-new power—Mohammedan Arab hordes out of the desert—swallowed them both. If the United States and Russia fought any kind of titanic war, China would be the victor. Or if all three engaged in a three-sided mutual destruction, the eventual dominator of the world might be Brazil. The possibilities were not infinite, but many.

Hopefully, the spirit of Yalta—in many ways as gray and unpalatable as the spirit of Vienna in 1815—might last another twenty years, or even the fifty FDR mentioned. The spirit of Yalta had made a world in which the new great empires could continue to exist by observing one principle: freedom of each empire to act as it pleased within its own zone.

In essence, the principle was well-observed. The West surrendered its former principle, the Atlantic Charter, over Poland and East Europe. It confirmed the decision again in Hungary in 1956. The United States acquiesced to China's actions in North

Korea, and in Tibet, both on China's frontiers. If Red China conquered Tibet, and exterminated the lamas, this was tacitly agreed to be Chinese business.

Conversely, the Russians could afford to sell Castro and Cuba down the river in 1962. They could, and did, permit Communists to be crushed in Greece. In fact, the confrontation over Cuba cleared the air. It would not prevent the Soviets from dabbling in the Western Hemisphere any more than the West would quit trying to split Poland diplomatically from Russia. But neither side would ever go to nuclear war over that kind of issue. *In extremis,* the outside power would back off, as long as both sides obeyed the rules. West Europe, East Europe, in each case, was off limits.

The trouble came where the new great empires overlapped. Both the United States and the USSR felt they had a vital security stake in divided Berlin. To defend Western civilization, all U. S. geopoliticians and strategists agreed that America had to hold the vital rimlands of Eurasia. Certain compromises could be made, but it was always dangerous to give an inch. On shifting sands, the other side might grab a yard.

But rising China believed its manifest destiny included control of Southeast Asia, and certainly the coastline of all Vietnam.

The result was a quarter of a million American troops on permanent stand in Europe, and a continual, smoldering, limited brushfire war in Asia. In Washington, in 1965, no planner saw a way out of either stand.

With the collapse of the European state system and the failure of the projected United Nations, the world was really ruled by three new regional Romes. The spirit of Yalta could not prevent each Rome from wanting to be first. Khrushchev dreamed of the Third Rome, and called it Moscow. Mao Tse-tung and Chou En-lai, brooding with the sullen weight of centuries, believed it eventually must be Peking. America's empire was the glittering spread of Western civilization, not ruled, but defended, from the capital on the marches of the Potomac. America's destiny,

392

which Kennedy said, and Johnson saw, was to mount the Western guard.

In this new world of empires, no United Nations could take the place of walls and legions, or rockets on alert.

The three new Romes could not plant their eagles everywhere; there could be no single flag, even within the empires. There was no imperium in which all citizens could appeal to a single Caesar. The reins of apparent power were too diffuse. There was too much ethnic conciousness, and the world was too broad and alien for all of that.

These power centers had one serious problem, besides each other. Somehow, before nuclear weapons proliferated and potential nuclear destruction spread, they had to agree on some way to control the forces of disruption and ambition. They had to be able to influence, moderate, direct—or in extremity, to destroy. Someday, the USSR might have to put down Poland, or the United States destroy Egypt—and in the interests of world peace. The problem of how to do this, without two empires becoming involved, remained unsolved.

In 1939, after twenty years of international anarchy, Edward Hallett Carr wrote: "The new international order can be built only on a unit of power sufficiently coherent and sufficiently strong to maintain its ascendancy without being compelled to take sides in the rivalries of lesser units."

In 1965, no single power unit of sufficient strength had emerged. The world went back to empires, and regional solutions, whatever they were called. The UN never had a chance to order the world; the UN was made incoherent at the start.

Nothing like the United Nations will ever forge the kind of world order Americans desire. No human order is logical. They simply come about. In George Washington's time it was absurd to imagine that the prime ministers and chiefs of state of dozens of nations would march in the funeral cortege of our thirty-fifth President. It happened. Today it is absurd to dream that Nigeria or Brazil may some day rule the world. But it could happen.

393

Order never stems from logic, but from a combination of principle and power. Western civilization will need both, in tremendous quantity, to survive.

Woodrow Wilson, on July 14, 1914, said:

"My dream is that as the years go by and the world knows more and more of America it will turn to America for those moral inspirations which lie at the basis of all freedom . . . and that America will come into the full light of day when all shall know that she puts human rights above all other rights, and that her flag is the flag not only of America, but of humanity."

That could happen, too.

Index

398

400

DISCARDED